Japanese American Millennials

In the series *Asian American History and Culture*, edited by Cathy Schlund-Vials, Shelley Sang-Hee Lee, and Rick Bonus. Founding editor, Sucheng Chan; editors emeriti, David Palumbo-Liu, Michael Omi, K. Scott Wong, and Linda Trinh Võ.

A list of additional titles in this series appears at the back of this book

Edited by
MICHAEL OMI, DANA Y. NAKANO,
AND JEFFREY T. YAMASHITA

JAPANESE AMERICAN MILLENNIALS

Rethinking Generation, Community, and Diversity

TEMPLE UNIVERSITY PRESS
Philadelphia • *Rome* • *Tokyo*

TEMPLE UNIVERSITY PRESS
Philadelphia, Pennsylvania 19122
tupress.temple.edu

Library of Congress Cataloging-in-Publication Data

Names: Omi, Michael, editor. | Nakano, Dana Y., editor. | Yamashita, Jeffrey,
  editor.
Title: Japanese American millennials : rethinking generation, community, and
  diversity / edited by Michael Omi, Dana Y. Nakano, and Jeffrey Yamashita.
Description: Philadelphia : Temple University Press, 2019. | Series: Asian
  american history and culture | Includes bibliographical references and
  index. |
Identifiers: LCCN 2018057935 (print) | LCCN 2018059503 (ebook) | ISBN
  9781439918265 (E-book) | ISBN 9781439918241 (cloth : alk. paper) | ISBN
  9781439918258 (pbk. : alk. paper)
Subjects: LCSH: Japanese Americans. | Generation Y—United States.
Classification: LCC E184.J3 (ebook) | LCC E184.J3 J3385 2019 (print) | DDC
  305.8956/073—dc23
LC record available at https://lccn.loc.gov/2018057935

9 8 7 6 5 4 3 2 1

Contents

Figures and Tables

Figures

Tables

Acknowledgments

This volume attempts to revitalize Japanese American studies and situate it within the broader scholarship on race, ethnicity, and generational change. We hope it inspires a rethinking of the field—its dominant narratives, prevailing conceptual frames, and the established subjects and sites of inquiry. We are deeply indebted to the contributors to this volume who shared our passion and enthusiasm for the project. In dialogue with them, we engaged in an iterative process to shape and deepen the themes presented here. Special thanks goes to Sara Cohen, our editor at Temple University Press, who provided guidance, advice, and unwavering support. Rick Bonus, the coeditor of the series on Asian American History and Culture, provided insightful comments and suggestions that strengthened the volume as a whole. We also wish to acknowledge and thank the two anonymous reviewers of the manuscript. Their comments, rooted in their deep knowledge and understanding of Japanese American studies, helped us clarify our overall project. Support is also given in material ways and we thank Dean James Tuedio, College of Arts, Humanities, and Social Sciences at California State University, Stanislaus, and the Asian American and Asian Diaspora Studies program at the University of California, Berkeley for providing resources to help make this anthology a reality. Our thanks go to Eryn Kimura for the wonderful artwork that graces the cover of this volume. Finally, we'd like to acknowledge and thank each other for the seemingly endless conversations we have had in defining and imagining this anthology, and for the work each of us has done in soliciting chapters and working with authors. We could not have completed this volume without relying on each other.

Japanese American Millennials

Introduction

Michael Omi,
Dana Y. Nakano, and
Jeffrey T. Yamashita

In 2015, Ryan Kenji Kuramitsu, a youth columnist for the *Pacific Citizen*, the ninety-year-old national newspaper of the Japanese American Citizens League, warned of the "danger" of maintaining and advancing a singular, grand narrative of the Japanese American historical and contemporary experience. Disrupting such a narrative requires the inclusion of a broader range of stories and viewpoints, particularly from individuals and groups who have been marginalized or rendered invisible in prevailing accounts: "We must hold space for each of our unique perspectives rather than anxiously demanding that a single story of 'the Japanese American legacy' be snapshotted, mummified and delicately retold in a crisp, acceptable way to each succeeding generation. We must insist upon greater airtime for our counter narratives—the hidden perspectives from which we often learn far more than from those stories we already know" (Kuramitsu 2015). This volume seeks to take up this challenge by presenting multiple perspectives of who Japanese Americans are, how they think about notions of community and culture, and how they engage and negotiate multiple social identities. We do so by focusing on the experiences, perspectives, and aspirations of Japanese American millennials.

Why millennials? We argue that focus on this historical generation allows us to problematize, deconstruct, and perhaps subvert the normative generational framework within Japanese American studies. While much has been written about Japanese Americans as a unique and distinctive racial and ethnic group, the existing literature overwhelmingly relies on a singular historical narrative and generational framework (Azuma 2016; Nakano

2017). Sociohistorical accounts center on the early settlement of Japanese immigrants, the tragic episode of mass incarceration during World War II, and the presumed rapid assimilation of Japanese Americans in the postwar period. Shifts in Japanese American social identities and experiences are referenced and understood in relationship to differences between generational cohorts (e.g., issei, nisei, sansei, yonsei, gosei). These cohorts are presumed to be reflective of both genealogical distance from immigration and characteristic of specific historical periods. It is generally taken for granted in the existing literature that the experiences, identities, attitudes, and behaviors of Japanese Americans can be largely understood and explained by a generational analysis.

The generational "labeling" of Japanese Americans continues to be a profound and persistent practice in the current scholarship and in the popular imagination. Both the uniqueness and institutional embeddedness of Japanese American generational categories are evident in the race and ethnic statistics compiled by the U.S. Census Bureau. The Ancestry Code List for the Census Bureau's American Community Survey lists 999 ancestry categories (e.g., Alsatian, Sicilian, Nicaraguan, Cayman Islander, Somali). Remarkably, the only ethnic group on the entire list that has generational labels designated for coding are Japanese: Issei (Code 741), Nisei (742), Sansei (743), Yonsei (744), and Gosei (745) (U.S. Census Bureau 2017, 19).

The continued investment in the prevailing generational paradigm, and the meanings assigned to these generational categories, is problematic. By uncritically adhering to this framework, the existing literature on Japanese Americans tends to overlook other historical periods, other subsequent waves of Japanese immigrants in the postwar era, and other ways of narrating and conceptually framing the Japanese American experience. This volume, through a focus on the experiences, perspectives, and aspirations of Japanese American millennials, addresses some of these absences in the current literature and suggests how we might alternatively study Japanese Americans as a whole.

It is not without a sense of irony that we examine and leverage a generational cohort (i.e., millennials) in order to dislodge the dominant generational framework that has come to so profoundly structure research in Japanese American studies. While our intent is to problematize this framework, we do acknowledge the persistence and analytic power of the paradigm in shaping popular conceptions of Japanese American identity and community formation. Our goal is to disrupt prevailing notions of fixed generational cohorts, stable social identities, and shared understandings of community by highlighting the contemporary diversity of the Japanese American millennial population. Examining this generation requires us to take seriously the daily negotiations undertaken by Japanese American millennials to situate themselves among multiple axes of stratification and difference—according to generation as well as gender, sexual orientation, class, nativity, and religion—and the exponential diversity such intersections create. Such an intersectional perspective must consider the impact of different social sites, geographic spaces, and institutional contexts as they deeply affect, shape, and structure how Japanese American millennials understand themselves. Drawing upon their experiences forces us to pay attention to the ways in which Japanese American community institutions are not simply fading away—following the predictions of classical assimilation theory—but are being changed and reimagined to fit the needs of an emergent, digitally connected generation.

Our intent is not only to capture and present the heterogeneity of the Japanese American millennial cohort but also to illuminate and address broad questions that continue to be central to the study of race, ethnicity, and social transformation in the United States. How might we understand the persistence or the twilight of ethnic identity over time and across generations and in relationship to other identities and social statuses? How are ethnic community institutions and practices maintained, transformed, and reimagined by generational change and group affiliation? How do mixed-race individuals and groups complicate our understanding of racial and ethnic categories, social boundaries, and identities? How are racial and ethnic consciousness, identities, and institutions shaped in transnational space? In this volume, we address these broader questions utilizing Japanese American millennials as a case study to highlight the different manifestations and expressions of Japanese American ethnicity. Acknowledging and mapping this diversity allows us to notice, comprehend, and appreciate the multiple and complex meanings of what it means to be Japanese American in the twenty-first century.

Who Are Millennials?

Time magazine loudly proclaims in its May 20, 2013, cover story that millennials are "The Me Me Me Generation." Joel Stein, the author of the cover article, admits that while old people have always bitterly complained that the younger generation is lazy, selfish, self-indulgent, and entitled, he claims, "Unlike my parents, my grandparents and my great-grandparents, I have proof" (Stein 2013). According to Stein, millennials, defined as those born from 1980 to 2000, have a dramatically higher incidence of narcissistic personality disorder; they are fame obsessed; they are convinced of their own greatness; and they are lazy. Such a critique of this generation resonated in other quarters. Most notably, motivational speaker Simon Sinek's 2016 interview about entitled millennials in the workplace went viral on social media (Gosse 2017). In a 2017 interview, Australian millionaire Tim Gurner blames millennials' inability to invest in property on their trendy consumption of pricey avocado toast (Calfas 2017).

Although these popular depictions of the millennial generation are, of course, one-sided and unfair, millennials are not without distinction. Neil Howe and William Strauss (2000) tout millennials as a technologically savvy generation that is more numerous, more affluent, better educated, and more ethnically and racially diverse than any previous cohort. Coming of age alongside the internet and the rise of social media, millennials are "digital natives" (Pew Research Center 2014). Engaged with each other on the growing number of social media platforms and mobile apps, they are the most connected generation (Pew Research Center 2014). The very name "millennial" references their embrace of and aptitude for technology, while maintaining a sense of promise and change (Howe and Strauss 2000). Millennials are often critiqued as nonjoiners, but they are also self-critical and poised to bring insight and change to the institutions they choose to engage with (Pew Research Center 2014).

In 2016, millennials became the largest living generation in the United States—surpassing the baby boomers—with a growing population of over seventy-five million individuals (Frey 2016). Howe and Strauss (2000) estimate that, inclusive of migration, the millennial generation could surpass one hundred million at its zenith, almost a third more than the height of the baby boomer generation. Millennials are the most racially and ethnically diverse generation in U.S. history with a nonwhite segment of the population comprising 43 percent of the total, the highest share of any existing generation (Pew Research Center 2014). While a relatively small percentage of millennials are immigrants, one in five has at least one immigrant parent and one in ten has a noncitizen parent (Howe and Strauss 2003). With regard to sexual orientation, 20 percent of millennials identify as lesbian, gay, bisexual, transgender, or queer (LGBTQ), a two-thirds increase from the previous generation (GLAAD 2017).

Despite its noteworthy size and diversity, relatively few studies have explicitly examined the millennial generation as an empirical grouping, much less within ethnic studies. Millennials are said to be a protected generation, both by their baby boomer parents and by society at large. They have been sheltered from many hardships, disappointments, and loss. Sinek asserts that millennials "were told they were special—all the time, they were told they can have anything they want in life, just because they want it" (Gosse 2017). Perhaps it may be better to understand millennials as the "most watched over generation in memory" (Howe and Strauss 2000, 18). Citing a University of Michigan study, Howe and Strauss state that from 1981 to 1997 "free" time among adolescents dropped by 37 percent. Instead, the childhood "free" time of previous generations became heavily supervised with enrollment in various and numerous extracurricular activities. Such a high level of extracurricular participation tempers the conventional portrait of millennial disenchantment and individualism and raises questions regarding whether millennials reject or engage with existing social, cultural, political, and religious institutions.

In this volume, we draw upon the Japanese American millennial experience as a unique lens by which to understand the simultaneous participation in and seeming rejection of social institutions in a period of profound community transformation. Although Japanese American millennials share many experiences and characteristics with other millennials, the chapters presented in this volume examine how the racial and ethnic identities of Japanese American millennials find expression within the Japanese American community (and beyond it) and what that says about our notion of community itself. While previous studies have found a lack of affiliation with any political, cultural, or religious institutions among millennials, chapters in this anthology demonstrate that community institutions often serve as important mechanisms for the maintenance of ethnicity. Rather than turn their back on existing institutions, Japanese American millennials appear to be reimagining them to suit the contemporary needs and realities of the multiple social networks they affiliate with. Their experiences demonstrate fluid racial and ethnic boundary formations in local, national, and transnational contexts.

Rethinking the Dominant Narrative in Japanese American Studies

Taken as a whole, the articles in this volume describe the heterogeneity and diversity of who Japanese American millennials are. They are not only yonsei (fourth generation) or gosei (fifth generation) in terms of the prevailing generational paradigm with its emphasis on the trajectory established by pre-1924 Japanese immigrants but also immigrants arriving in the postwar era and their children, called *shin-issei* and *shin-nisei*, respectively. They are also *zainichi*, ethnic Koreans with roots in Japan, as well as mixed-race individuals who claim multiple racial and ethnic identities. They are individuals who view their Japanese American ethnicity as their primary social identity, as well as those for whom it is a more minor source of affiliation in contrast to other categories of identity such as gender and sexuality.

The significance of noting and mapping this diversity cannot be overstated. It constitutes an important response and challenge to much of the existing literature on Japanese Americans. Historian Eiichiro Azuma (2016) states that "racial formation in Japanese America is highly slanted in terms of generation, citizenship status, and geography" (Azuma 2016, 257) and argues that the existing literature highlights and privileges some experiences to the exclusion of others: "Nikkei [Japanese American] history is unarguably one of the most deeply probed in Asian American studies. Despite the impressive volume of scholarship, it has created—and cemented—only a particular understanding of the ethnic group and its history" (258–259). Similarly, Dana Nakano (2017) argues the oversimplified definition of generation and the narrow historical narrative continues to be deeply embedded in the scholarly and popular understandings of the Japanese American experience.

Certain historical moments are foregrounded in the dominant historical narrative with particular attention given to the experiences and struggles of nisei, second-generation Japanese Americans born to Japanese parents who immigrated to the United States before 1924. Most nisei were children or young adults at the outset of World War II. While enjoying expanded political rights in sharp contrast to their immigrant parents who were legally defined as aliens ineligible for citizenship, nisei faced both social and economic discrimination that were manifested in patterns of residential segregation and limited occupational mobility. In the aftermath of the attack on Pearl Harbor, nisei constituted two-thirds of Japanese Americans on the West Coast who were forcibly removed and incarcerated during the war years. Much of the literature on Japanese Americans describes this traumatic period, chronicles the varied response among the nisei generation to the tragic circumstances they encountered, and the effects of the camps on subsequent generations. Attention has also been given to the immediate postwar period (1945–1965) when Japanese Americans were "reintegrated" into American life and achieved a modicum of social and economic mobility. Far less attention has been given to sansei (third generation) though accounts have examined the rise of ethnic consciousness and political mobilization among sansei in the wake of the civil rights and black power movements (Pulido 2006; Maeda 2009).

In the 1980s, attention was focused on the movement for Japanese American redress and reparations that culminated in the Civil Liberties Act of 1988 being signed into law by President Ronald Reagan. Yasuko Takezawa (1995), in her ethnographic study of the redress movement in Seattle, argues that the historical memory of wartime incarceration and the later groundswell of activism in support of redress and reparations were central to Japanese American ethnic identity formation during the 1970s and 1980s. But what happens when an important chapter in Japanese American history comes to a close? What comes to serve as a rallying point for ethnic consciousness and solidarity when a defining issue that has mobilized the Japanese American community for generations is finally resolved? Japanese American millennials may offer us some clues. They constitute the first post-redress generation within the Japanese American community. Thus the ways they narrate and negotiate ethnic identity provide a revealing window into how Japanese American ethnicity is now thought about, maintained, and transformed.

Diversity within Generations

The dominant narrative in Japanese American studies has either ignored or tended to flatten diversity *within* generational cohorts. But exceptions do exist that provide generative examples of how to study Japanese American millennials. Azuma's *Between Two Empires* (2005) utilizes a transnational framework that allows for a more nuanced reading of different issei outlooks, desires, and goals. For the nisei generation, scholars, such as Tamotsu Shibutani in *The Derelicts of Company K* (1978), have illuminated forgotten and often suppressed stories to provide an alternative understanding of the nisei generation beyond the prevailing trope of the patriotic "model minority." The eclectic experiences of sansei student activists and their roles in different social movements are illustrated both in Jere Takahashi's *Nisei/Sansei* (1997) and Daryl Maeda's *Chains of Babylon* (2009). Takahashi's account also disrupts the discrete construction of generational identities by emphasizing the impact of historical context on "intragenerational tensions and diversity" and "intergenerational continuities" in terms of nisei and sansei politics (Takahashi 1997, 11–12).

In many ways, the articles in this volume draw upon and extend the insights of defining generations, exploring their historical significance and discerning their overall coherence in the face of internal diversity. Looking at the heterogeneity and corresponding diverse experiences of Japanese American millennials also prompts us to reconsider and challenge key social science paradigms of race, ethnicity, and generational change.

Cultural Compatibility, Assimilation, and Symbolic Ethnicity

From 1947 to 1950, an interdisciplinary research team from the University of Chicago studied the social adjustment of some twenty thousand Japanese Americans who had arrived in Chicago from the wartime incarceration camps. The researchers were struck by the rapid social mobility and popular acceptance of this group as they settled and adapted to their lives in the city. William Caudill and George De Vos (1956) argued that such quick integration was attributable to overlaps between Japanese and American middle-class culture: "The Japanese Americans provide us, then, with the case of a group who, despite racial visibility and a culture traditionally thought of as alien, achieved a remarkable adjustment to middle-class American life because certain compatibilities in the value systems of the immigrant and host cultures operated strongly enough to override the obvious difficulties" (1117).

In his influential essay and subsequent book, demographer William Petersen (1966, 1971) extended this cultural compatibility argument, observing how Japanese Americans "could climb over the highest barriers our racists were able to fashion in part because of their meaningful attachment with an alien culture" (43). Representing Japanese Americans as a "model minority" did have a dark side. In the midst of the tumultuous race relations of the 1960s, the model minority image was strategically evoked to suggest that institutional racism was not the cause of persistent inequalities, the problem was that certain groups simply lacked the right "cultural stuff" to assimilate.

In contrast to these allegedly culturally deficient groups, Japanese Americans became the poster child for the dominant social science framework of assimilation. The assimilationist paradigm sees each succeeding generation of an immigrant-origin group shedding their ethnic distinctiveness through socioeconomic upward mobility and integration into the mainstream of American social and cultural life (Gordon 1964). In their recent revival of straight-line assimilation theory, Richard D. Alba and Victor Nee (2003) utilize later-generation Japanese Americans' ability to cross, indeed transcend, the color line as proof of assimilation's continued theoretical validity. Through a detailed analysis of aggregate, quantitative data, Alba and Nee demonstrate that Japanese Americans have achieved high scores on all the traditional markers of assimilation success (i.e., English as a primary language, acculturation, nativity, education, income, residential integration, interracial marriage), often times surpassing that of native-born whites. Becoming assimilated also entails the declining salience of ethnic consciousness and identity and their impact on shaping one's social location and daily life. Herbert J. Gans's (1979) concept of *symbolic ethnicity* has described the nominal and symbolic way ethnic identification persists among later-generation white ethnics. Symbolic ethnicity is a private and voluntary practice—nostalgic, intermittent, and optional (Gans 1979; Alba 1985, 1990; Waters 1990; Tuan 1999)—with little impact on life chances and everyday behaviors.

Assimilation theory not only predicts the eventual diminishment of ethnic salience but also suggests the gradual blurring of racial boundaries. As Gans (2005) also asserts, assimilation is a process of social whitening. In its most extreme formulation, the concept has been employed to suggest that Japanese Americans might become "white" under a broader definition of "whiteness." Michael Omi (2016) argues that just as previous "outsiders" (e.g., the Irish, Jews) have been historically incorporated into our notions of who is white, speculation now increasingly centers on whether Asian Americans are following a trajectory of inclusion under a more expansive understanding of "whiteness." Political scientist Andrew Hacker (1992), for example, argues that the racial category of white is an elastic one. The question is not "who is white," Hacker asserts, but "who can be considered white." With this in mind, he believes that Asian Americans are "merging" into the white category.

Assimilation theory also predicts the blurring of racial boundaries through intermarriage. The theory presumes that intermarriage rates serve as an important indicator of reduced social distance between racial groups. Thus, a crucial indicator of a group's assimilation is the rate of outmarriage, particularly with whites. As a group, Japanese Americans have high rates of outmarriage, 53 percent among native-born Japanese Americans (U.S. Census Bureau 2012). The high rates of outmarriage have led to a dramatic rise in the number of multiracial Japanese Americans, with 40 percent of Japanese Americans identifying with more than one race or ethnicity (U.S. Census Bureau 2012). Assimilation scholars posit that multiracial individuals complicate racial boundaries and structures. In particular, Jennifer Lee and Frank D. Bean (2007) argue, "Based on patterns of multiracial identification, Asians and Latinos may be the next in line to be white, with multiracial Asian-whites and Latino-whites at the head of the queue" (579). As multiracial Asian Americans are more likely to identify as "white" in comparison to multiracial blacks (Lee and Bean 2007), they demonstrate the blurring of racial boundaries and the prospect of impending whiteness.

While acknowledging the blurring or malleability of racial boundaries, it is equally important to recognize that an ever-expanding white category is not inevitable nor is it the only potential outcome. Lee and Bean's (2007) assertion hinges upon the visual recognition and "passing" of mixed-race Japanese Americans as white. But multiracials may not have the necessary physical characteristics or be otherwise reluctant to pass. Rebecca Chiyoko King-O'Riain (2006, 21), in her study of Japanese American beauty pageants, demonstrates that both monoracial and multiracial individuals undertake "race work" that problematizes the alignment between phenotypically based notions of race and ideas about cultural authenticity. Multiracial pageant contestants, for example, put significant effort into maintaining their connection with other Japanese Americans and legitimizing such connections in cultural and racial terms. Furthermore, as visually cued racial distinctions are bestowed importance through complex processes of social construction, it is also possible that blurred boundaries can be reorganized into new hierarchies that continue to disadvantage darker-skinned individuals and communities (Bonilla-Silva 2018; Glenn 2009).

In our assessment, we deem the core tenets of assimilation theory to be flawed, misleading, or at the very least, insufficient in its ability capture and narrate the full breadth of the historical and contemporary experiences of Japanese Americans. Behind assimilation theory is a deep teleological assumption—one that assumes a natural progression for select "outsiders" to eventually achieve integration through the shedding of racial and ethnic difference. Rather than undergo a process of ethnic attenuation, the articles in this anthology demonstrate the continued persistence of ethnic identity and engagement with ethnic institutions among Japanese American millennials. But the specific ways that identity, history, and community are thought about, expressed, organized, and lived by this generation are varied, diverse, and intersectional.

Intersectionality and the Japanese American Millennial Generation

Ethnic identity and community continue to play significant roles in shaping the everyday behaviors, social networks, and practices of Japanese American millennials. Surveying this generation serves as an opportunity to not only highlight the limitations of the prevailing narratives of Japanese American assimilation but also to advance a counternarrative that better captures the diversity of their experiences. An explicit focus on millennials as an historical generation serves to disrupt the conventional organizing and separation of Japanese Americans by immigrant generation—issei, nisei, sansei, yonsei, shin-issei, shin-nisei. As we shall see, millennial experiences are not neatly divided and categorized by such generational terms. While the focus remains on ethnic identity, Japanese American millennials are more readily conversant in asserting and explaining their experiences in the language of intersectionality—"the critical insight that race, class, gender, sexuality, ethnicity, nation, ability, and age operate not as unitary, mutually exclusive entities, but as reciprocally constructing phenomena that in turn shape complex social inequalities" (Collins 2015, 2).

Intersectionality has, of course, always constituted a lived reality for all Japanese Americans. But the millennial generation possesses a consciousness and vocabulary that is more apt to acknowledge and reflect on how the cohort's internal diversity is illuminated and shaped by multiple axes of social stratification and difference. Their identities as Japanese Americans are clearly acknowledged to be complexly interwoven with other identities and social cleavages organized along the lines of gender, sexual orientation, class, geography, religiosity, and indeed, race. The chapters gathered in this collection capture and reflect on the ways the intersectional—and persistently racialized—identities of millennials confront, challenge, and refashion existing ethnic institutions and identities.

Such a reading stands in sharp contrast to an analysis of generational change that subscribes to a linear trajectory of assimilation and the presumption of increasing ethnic attenuation. The Japanese American millennials profiled within this book pursue different and varied paths, define their identities in constant negotiation with multiple systems of stratification, and find distinct social spaces by which to assert and live out their identities.

Themes and Chapter Descriptions

The chapters in this volume present and critically reflect on the varied experiences and identities of Japanese American millennials in different social spaces, geographic locales, and institutional contexts. We have clustered the essays under five broad rubrics while being fully cognizant that aggregating the essays in this manner is somewhat arbitrary. Many of the essays could have been grouped differently and situated under more than one of the five rubrics. What this reflects are the ways that the individual essays presented in this volume directly engage each other and address the multiple and overlapping dimensions of what it means to be a Japanese American millennial.

Part I, "Sustaining Community," focuses on how Japanese American millennials experience long-standing ethnic institutions and how they work to maintain and, in many instances, to transform active ethnic community ties. In the face of profound demographic change in the Japanese American community, what are the social spaces and institutional contexts in which ethnic identity finds expression? And, how does ethnicity continue to shape the social interactions and institutional affiliations of millennial Japanese Americans? In "'We've Got Team Spirit!': Ethnic Community Building and Japanese American Youth Basketball Leagues," Christina B. Chin looks at the role of co-ethnic basketball leagues in shaping the ethnic identities of Japanese American youth. She argues that even among highly assimilated Japanese Americans, the leagues serve as an active space for constructing and preserving a sense of connection to ethnic community. Lisa Hirai Tsuchitani, in "Millennial Understandings of *Nikkei Seishin* in San Jose Japantown," illustrates the impact of a Japanese American summer cultural program on its millennial-age student graduates. She highlights how student understandings of Japanese American identity and community have been profoundly shaped by participation in these heritage school programs. Dana Y. Nakano, in "To Be Yonsei in Southern California: Persistent Community as Postsuburban Minority Culture of Mobility," provides a critique of spatial assimilation theory by focusing on community-building practices among dispersed, suburban Japanese Americans. The millennial youth in Nakano's sample not only travel to ethnic institutions in urban and postsuburban locales to build and sustain social relations, but also actively seek out other Japanese Americans in traditionally non-ethnic spaces.

Part II, "Spiritualities," examines the role of religion and spirituality in the lives and identities of Japanese American millennials. Among other questions, how does religious affiliation shape and structure understandings of ethnicity and ethnic community? Dean Ryuta Adachi, in "Redefining 'Camp' in Japanese America," presents the long history of Japanese American Christian youth camps to situate the contemporary experiences of millennial summer camp participants. Adachi argues that the camps provide a unique version of Protestant Christianity that serves to provide a common identity among an increasingly heterogeneous Japanese American millennial population. Drawing upon survey data, Brett J. Esaki, in "Religious Nones? Increasing Unaffiliated and Christian Religiosity among Japanese American Millennials," examines whether Japanese Americans are following the broader sociological trend of millennial nonreligious affiliation. While affirming this trend, Esaki gestures to the notion that a nonspecific spirituality has enabled Japanese Americans to cultivate multiple religious traditions. Chenxing Han highlights how religious and cultural identity are intertwined for many Japanese American Shin Buddhists in "'I Am Trailblazing': Young Adult Japanese American Shin Buddhists Negotiating Complex Identities." The respondents in her study adopt an open and flexible approach to their spiritual lives that help them negotiate the multiplicity of cultural and religious identities they embrace.

Part III, "Redefining Ethnicity," examines how new immigrants complicate our existing notions of Japanese American identity and community. How does the influx and settlement of new Japanese immigrants revise our collective understanding of who Japanese American are? Are these new groups absorbed into the broader existing Japanese American community or do they remain a distinct and separate community? Kyung Hee Ha, in "Of Transgression: Zainichi Korean Immigrants' Search for Home(s) and Belonging," examines the ways ethnic Korean immigrants from Japan articulate and confront their sense of displacement in the United States. Ha finds that her respondents negotiate and maneuver between different nationality and immigration laws in order preserve their legal status in multiple nation-states. Aki Yamada explores three major shin-issei groups in her essay "Millennial Shin-Issei Identity Politics in Los Angeles." Among other findings, Yamada argues that shin-issei imagine their homes and community as Japanese spaces within the United States and resist social and cultural assimilation into the mainstream of American life.

Part IV, "Intersecting Identities," explores the multiple and overlapping nature of race, ethnicity, gender, sexuality, and generation in the Japanese American millennial experience. How are identities shaped in reference to important axes of stratification and difference and how might they reflect generational change? In "Mixed-Race Japanese American Millennials: Millennials or Japanese Americans?" Rebecca Chiyoko King-O'Riain situates mixed-race individuals with reference to millennials as a whole, to other Asian Americans, and to previous generations of Japanese Americans. Arguing against prevailing assumptions regarding the dissolution of the ethnic community, King-O'Riain illustrates how the Japanese American mixed-race population is transforming our understanding of Japanese American culture, identity, and community. Takeyuki Tsuda's chapter, "The New Second Generation: Biculturalism and Transnational Identities among Japanese American Shin-Nisei," disrupts the predominate focus on pre–World War II nisei by looking at the children of Japanese who immigrated to the United States after 1965. In studying this group, Tsuda argues that the experiences of the shin-nisei are best understood through the concept of biculturalism rather than the assimilationist concepts that were applied to prewar nisei. Amy Sueyoshi presents a compelling interview with a Japanese American millennial individual in "Techie, Gender Queer, and Lesbian: Interview with

Shin-Nisei Mioi Hanaoka." In this conversation, the intersectionality of identities is made clearly evident and gives us a sense of how an individual negotiates the demands of being in very different social spaces—including the immigrant family, the church, and the Japanese American community more broadly.

While many of the essays in this volume touch upon the theme of transnationalism, the chapters in Part V, "Crossing and Bridging Boundaries," centrally focus on the transnational dimension of millennial Japanese American experiences and identities. In "Japanese American Millennials in Contemporary Japan," Jane H. Yamashiro draws upon the experience of millennials who have migrated to Japan and find themselves falling between the established social categories of "Japanese" and "foreign" in Japanese society. Yamashiro finds that millennial experiences with the social and cultural structures and practices in Japan highlight the ways in which ethnic, racial, and regional identities—Japaneseness, Okinawanness, and Hawai'i Japaneseness—are negotiated and renegotiated across various regional and national contexts of Japan, Hawai'i, and the U.S. mainland. Wesley Iwao Ueunten, in "Questioning the 'World': Millennial Generation Okinawan American Identity *Matters*," explores "Uchinanchu" identity formation among millennium Okinawan Americans within the context of the World Youth Uchinanchu Association (WYUA) formed in 2011. Ueunten reveals how the discourse of identity for Okinawan American youth has been shaped in dramatic engagement with youth from Okinawa and the broader Okinawan diaspora. Lori Kido Lopez, in "United Hapas: The Global Communities of Mixed-Race Nikkei on YouTube," presents a textual analysis of YouTube videos that focus on the mixed-race Japanese American millennial experience and identity in globally dispersed, but virtually connected, spaces. Lopez argues that these millennials operate within a diasporic universe rather than relying on the nation or locality as a site for ethnic belonging, identification, and community.

Noting the Limitations

Though this anthology presents and examines the understudied voices and experiences of Japanese American millennials, we recognize several limitations of the volume as a whole—geographical considerations, political engagement, and socioeconomic class. With respect to the geographical contours of millennial Japanese America, the chapters in the anthology largely focus on the diversity within an Asia-Pacific realm—Japan, Hawai'i, and California. Japanese American millennials do exist outside of this zone, such as locales in Chicago and New York City. In the larger field of Asian American studies, Asian American scholars have pushed the analytic to examine Asian American experiences located beyond the West Coast and into spaces "East of California" (Sumida 1998). While we acknowledge this important turn in the scholarly field, we hope that the current chapters illuminate the fact that thinking through the spaces of Japan, Hawai'i, and California is a large undertaking in itself. However, we remain hopeful and excited to see future scholars address the issues and perspectives that Japanese American millennials face and experience in spaces and contexts residing "East of California."

While chapters in this volume explore the ways Japanese American millennials engage social institutions, explicit discussions of political engagement are absent. Millennials as a whole are a difficult generation to pin down with respect to politics. In 2012, eighteen- to twenty-nine-year olds constituted over 21 percent of the eligible voting population, but only 50 percent of them voted (Gilman and Stokes 2014, 57). Many millennials eschew traditional party labels and party affiliation. Roughly 44 percent of millennial registered voters describe themselves as independent compared with 32 percent of boomers (Pew Research Center 2018, 8). While their electoral participation is mixed, millennials do tend to volunteer at higher rates than other generations, and 44 percent of them use social networking sites to promote political issues, post thoughts on these issues, and encourage others to act and organize (Gilman and Stokes 2014, 58).

Race is highly correlated with political attitudes and social identities, and the millennial generation is no exception. A 2017 survey of a nationally representative sample of over 1,750 millennials found that 82 percent of African Americans, 74 percent of Latino/as, 71 percent of Asian Americans, and 60 percent of whites think that racism remains a major problem in the United States (Cohen et al. 2017, 7). When asked what identities have had the most impact on their life in terms of defining their lived experience, 81 percent of African Americans, 80 percent of Asian Americans, 59 percent of Latino/as, and 40 percent of whites responded, "race/ethnicity" (30). A crucial aspect of millennial identity, race shapes, in profound ways, identity and consciousness.

We surmise that Japanese American millennials continue to "live" race and that it provides a continuing backdrop to their experiences, interactions, forms of affiliation, and political attitudes and civic engagement. Interestingly, when millennials were asked about their top-three strategies for making racial progress in our society, no racial/ethnic group listed voting in federal elections as a preferred strategy for change (Cohen et al., 38). Most millennials were drawn to local politics beginning with their immediate communities. Such a focus on communities is expressed throughout this volume and can be seen as a form of civic engagement by which Japanese American millennials are expressing their political beliefs, values, and concerns.

Lastly, this anthology often seems to leave the impact of socioeconomic class unexamined. While some chapters make references to the class diversity among Japanese American millennials (see Chapters 7 and 8, by Ha and Yamada, respectively), most contributions focus on seemingly (upper-) middle-class formations. One reason for this homogenous treatment is that the Japanese American population is fairly homogenous in terms of socio-economic class. Only 8.4 percent of Japanese Americans live below the poverty line, compared with 12.1 percent of Asian Americans and 15.1 percent of all Americans. Nearly 50 percent of all Japanese Americans have a bachelor's degree or higher, compared with 30 percent of all Americans (U.S. Census Bureau 2012). Nevertheless, class diversity does exist among Japanese Americans, millennials or otherwise. The lack of explicit examination of working-class Japanese Americans is certainly a shortcoming of this anthology. This absence, however, does not mean that the chapters in this anthology fail to take a class analysis seriously. To the contrary, many of the contributions consider the distinct impact of middle-class status on ethnic identity and community formation (in particular, see Chapter 3 by Nakano). Furthermore, this seemingly homogenous middle-class reality provides the context and launchpad for multiple diverse formations, evidenced throughout this anthology. Transnational movement, suburban settings, technological savvy, youth sports leagues, and summer camps are often accessed through and predicated upon middle-class status.

Conclusion

With a few recent notable exceptions (Tsuda 2016; Yamashiro 2017; Hirabayashi 2016), little has been written about the contemporary experiences of Japanese Americans. At least two factors account for this absence in the literature. First is the sustained scholarly and popular interest on the wartime relocation and incarceration of Japanese Americans. Such a focus is quite understandable given how historical experiences continue to shape—indeed haunt—the present. "Days of Remembrance" events that commemorate the signing of Executive Order 9066 over seventy-five years ago still draw large audiences and serve as forums to discuss the consequences of displacement and dispossession, the legacy of intergenerational trauma, and the fragility of civil liberties. If anything, the recent wave of anti-immigrant and anti-Muslim sentiment in the United States has heightened interest in the wartime experience of Japanese Americans, given the obvious and disturbing parallels that are easily evoked. Indeed, many Japanese Americans have drawn upon this experience to mobilize in defense of immigrant, refugee, and Muslim civil rights (Stop Repeating History! 2018).

The second factor that accounts for the dearth of materials on the contemporary experiences of Japanese Americans is the assimilationist paradigm itself. As noted in the beginning of our introduction, scholars have regarded the assimilation of Japanese Americans, both culturally and structurally, as complete. From this perspective, there is no longer much to be gleaned from a survey and analysis of how a once-despised racial and ethnic group became successfully integrated into the mainstream of American life. The trajectory of their incorporation has been sufficiently studied and mapped, and their very distinctiveness as a racial and ethnic group is now regarded as highly questionable.

But if we are not witnessing the "twilight of ethnicity," if assimilation is never a done deal, what questions can be asked about contemporary Japanese American ethnic identity, consciousness, and community? The essays in this volume pose these questions and offer some answers. They address them by considering varied and different social actors, by examining institutions in transition, and by engaging and critiquing prevailing narratives of incorporation and difference.

Several broad themes are apparent in this collection of essays. First, a great deal of diversity exists within the category of those whom we glibly refer to as "Japanese American millennials." They constitute a somewhat amorphous group who defy easy classification, given differences in social composition such as immigrant status and generation. Indeed, Japanese American millennial identity is itself forged and filtered through other social identities of difference including gender and sexuality, mixed-race identity, religious affiliation, and generation. Second, contrary to the prevailing literature, ethnicity is more than simply "symbolic" for many Japanese American millennials. Both continuity and change are evident in the multiple expressions of ethnic consciousness, identity, and affiliation. Japanese American millennials continue to retain a connection to the Japanese American community through both established ethnic institutions and new forms of social media that create and sustain virtual communities. Through their engagement, Japanese American millennials are dramatically transforming the very nature of Japanese American community institutions and practices. Lastly, Japanese American millennial identity is increasing shaped in a transnational context and space. New Japanese immigrants and short-term migrants to Japan learn to navigate and negotiate multiple identities in different national settings. Transnational social and cultural identities have emerged from diasporic convenings and networks that rearticulate the very meaning of ethnicity. These broad themes are by no means an exhaustive list of what is conveyed in this collection of essays, but they do serve to flag and highlight future areas of inquiry.

Consider this volume a call for the revitalization of Japanese American studies. Kuramitsu, in the *Pacific Citizen* youth column cited at the beginning of this introduction, asks us not to succumb to the ease, simplicity, and comfort of a single story, but to seek out and embrace multiple stories of Japanese Americans: "For Nikkei, not all members of the Japanese American community fit neatly into the concentration/loyalty/liberty model of history as we have grown used to telling it. We are the descendants of both draft resisters and go-for-brokers, Nisei and Japanese nationals. We are of multi-racial and monoracial ancestry, and we inhabit a vast spectrum of genders and sexual orientations, all of which should encourage us to push back against our flattening into a single story" (2015).

Agreed. What is required is a rethinking of the field—its dominant conceptual frames and narratives, its familiar sites and modes of inquiry, and its understanding of how Japanese Americans are situated within the broader scholarship on race and ethnicity. With an emphasis on generation and generational change, consider this volume a step in that direction.

REFERENCES

Alba, Richard D. 1985. *Italian Americans: Into the Twilight of Ethnicity*. New York: Prentice Hall.

———. 1990. *Ethnic Identity: The Transformation of White America*. New Haven, CT: Yale University Press.

Alba, Richard D., and Victor Nee. 2003. *Remaking the American Mainstream: Assimilation and Contemporary Immigration*. Cambridge, MA: Harvard University Press.

Azuma, Eiichiro. 2005. *Between Two Empires: Race, History, and Transnationalism in Japanese America*. New York: Oxford University Press.

———. 2016. "The Making of a Japanese American Race, and Why Are There No 'Immigrants' in Postwar Nikkei History and Community? The Problems of Generation, Region, and Citizenship in Japanese America." In *Trans-Pacific Japanese American Studies: Conversations on Race and Racializations*, edited by Yasuko Takezawa and Gary Y. Okihiro, 257–287. Honolulu: University of Hawai'i Press.

Bonilla-Silva, Eduardo. 2018. *Racism without Racists: Color-Blind Racism and the Persistence of Racial Inequality in America*. 5th ed. Lanham, MD: Rowman and Littlefield.

Calfas, Jennifer. 2017. "Millionaire to Millennials: Stop Buying Avocado Toast If You Want to Buy a Home." *Time*. Accessed July 27, 2018. http://time.com/money/4778942 /avocados-millennials-home-buying.

Caudill, William, and George De Vos. 1956. "Achievement, Culture and Personality: The Case of Japanese Americans." *American Anthropologist* 58(6): 1102–1126.

Cohen, Cathy J., Matthew Fowler, Vladimir E. Medenica, and Jon C. Rogowski. 2017. *The "Woke" Generation? Millennial Attitudes on Race in the US*. Genforward.com. Accessed July 27, 2018. https://genforwardsurvey.com/reports.

Collins, Patricia Hill. 2015. "Intersectionality's Definitional Dilemma." *Annual Review of Sociology* 41:1–20.

Frey, William H. 2016. *Diversity Defines the Millennial Generation*. Brookings Institute. June 28, 2016. https://www.brookings.edu/blog/the-avenue/2016/06/28/diversity -defines-the-millennial-generation/.

Gans, Herbert J. 1979. "Symbolic Ethnicity: The Future of Ethnic Groups and Cultures in America." *Ethnic and Racial Studies* 2:1–20.

———. 2005. "Race as Class." *Contexts* 4(4): 17–21

Gilman, Hollie Russon, and Elizabeth Stokes. 2014. "The Civic and Political Participation of Millennials." In *Millennials Rising: Next Generation Policies in the Wake of the Great Recession*, edited by Neil Howe and William Strauss, 57–60. Washington, DC: New America.

GLAAD (Gay and Lesbian Alliance against Defamation). 2017. *Accelerating Acceptance 2017.* Accessed July 27, 2018. https://www.glaad.org/publications/accelerating -acceptance-2017.

Glenn, Evelyn Nakano, ed. 2009. *Shades of Difference: Why Skin Color Matters.* Stanford, CA: Stanford University Press.

Gordon, Milton M. 1964. *Assimilation in American Life: The Role of Race, Religion, and National Origins.* New York: Oxford University Press.

Gosse, David. 2017. "Transcript of Simon Sinek Millennials in the Workplace Interview." Ochen.com. Accessed July 27, 2018. https://ochen.com/transcript-of-simon-sineks -millennials-in-the-workplace-interview.

Hacker, Andrew. 1992. *Two Nations: Black and White, Separate, Hostile, Unequal.* New York: Charles Scribner's Sons.

Hirabayashi, Lane R. 2016. "Conjecturing Communities: The Ebbs and Flows of Japanese America." Special issue, *Pan Japan* 12:1–2.

Howe, Neil, and William Strauss. 2000. *Millennials Rising: The Next Great Generation.* New York: Vintage Books.

———. 2003. *Millennials Go to College: Strategies of a New Generation on Campus.* Washington, DC: American Association of Collegiate Registrars.

King-O'Riain, Rebecca Chiyoko. 2006. *Pure Beauty: Judging Race in Japanese American Beauty Pageants.* Minneapolis: University of Minnesota Press.

Kuramitsu, Ryan Kenji. 2015. "Youth Perspective: The Danger of a Single Japanese American Story." *Pacific Citizen* (Los Angeles). Accessed July 27, 2018. https://www .pacificcitizen.org/youth-perspective-the-danger-of-a-single-japanese-american -story.

Lee, Jennifer, and Frank D. Bean. 2007. "Reinventing the Color Line: Immigration and America's New Racial/Ethnic Divide." *Social Forces* 86:561–586.

Maeda, Daryl. 2009. *Chains of Babylon: The Rise of Asian America.* Minneapolis: University of Minnesota Press.

Nakano, Dana Y. 2017. "Telling the Right Story: Narrative as a Mechanism of Japanese American Ethnic Boundary Maintenance." *Sociological Inquiry* (June 13): 1–29. https://doi.org/10.1111/soin.12188.

Omi, Michael. 2016. "The Unbearable Whiteness of Being: The Contemporary Racialization of Japanese/Asian American." In *Trans-Pacific Japanese American Studies: Conversations on Race and Racializations,* edited by Yasuko Takezawa and Gary Y. Okihiro, 39–59. Honolulu: University of Hawai'i Press.

Petersen, William. 1966. "Success Story: Japanese American Style." *New York Times Magazine,* January 9, 22–26.

———. 1971. *Japanese Americans: Oppression and Success.* New York: Random House.

Pew Research Center. 2014. *Millennials in Adulthood: Detached from Institutions, Networked with Friends.* Accessed January 23, 2018. https://www.pewsocialtrends.org /2014/03/07/millennials-in-adulthood/.

———. 2018. *The Generation Gap in American Politics.* Accessed March 3, 2018. https:// www.people-press.org/2018/03/01/the-generation-gap-in-american-politics/.

Pulido, Laura. 2006. *Black, Brown, Yellow and Left: Radical Activism in Los Angeles.* Berkeley: University of California Press.

Shibutani, Tamotsu. 1978. *The Derelicts of Company K: A Sociological Study of Demoralization.* Berkeley: University of California Press.

Stein, Joel. 2013. "Millennials: The Me Me Me Generation." Cover. *Time,* May 9. Accessed July 27, 2018. http://time.com/247/millennials-the-me-me-me-generation.

Stop Repeating History! Accessed July 27, 2018. https://stoprepeatinghistory.org.

Sumida, Stephen H. 1998. "East of California: Points of Origin in Asian American Studies." *Journal of Asian American Studies* 1(1): 83–100.

Takahashi, Jere. 1997. *Nisei/Sansei: Shifting Japanese American Identities and Politics.* Philadelphia, PA: Temple University Press.

Takezawa, Yasuko. 1995. *Breaking the Silence: Redress and Japanese American Ethnicity.* Ithaca, NY: Cornell University Press.

Takezawa, Yasuko, and Gary Y. Okihiro, eds. 2016. *Trans-Pacific Japanese American Studies: Conversations on Race and Racializations.* Honolulu: University of Hawai'i Press.

Tsuda, Takeyuki. 2016. *Japanese American Ethnicity: In Search of Heritage and Homeland across Generations.* New York: New York University Press.

Tuan, Mia. 1999. *Forever Foreigners or Honorary Whites? The Asian Ethnic Experience Today.* New Brunswick, NJ: Rutgers University Press.

U.S. Census Bureau. 2012. *2008–2012 American Community Survey 5-year Aggregate.* http://factfinder2.census.gov.

———. 2017. *American Community Survey and Puerto Rico Community Survey: 2067 Code List.* Accessed November 2, 2017. https://www.census.gov/programs-surveys /acs/technical-documentation/code-lists.2017.html.

Waters, Mary C. 1990. *Ethnic Options: Choosing Identities in America.* Berkeley: University of California Press.

Yamashiro, Jane. 2017. *Redefining Japaneseness: Japanese Americans in the Ancestral Homeland.* New Brunswick, NJ: Rutgers University Press.

PART I

SUSTAINING COMMUNITY

1

"We've Got Team Spirit!"

Ethnic Community Building and Japanese American
Youth Basketball Leagues

CHRISTINA B. CHIN

Sports play an important and often understated role in the fabric of Japanese American history, shaping the lives and experiences of players and their families, as well as the ethnic community as a whole. Instead of seeing sport as a whimsical activity with little to no social consequence, examination of Japanese American communities and their sporting practices in California offer a unique window into the Japanese American experience regarding ethnic identity, racialization, and community building. While the first generation of Japanese immigrants started a tradition of playing in co-ethnic sports leagues, the passion, practice, and legacy continues to thrive in later-generation Japanese Americans in the form of community-organized youth basketball leagues. As participation in these leagues continues to grow, this essay examines the role that Japanese American youth sports play in shaping ethnic community among third- and fourth-generation Japanese Americans.

Offering a critique to the assimilation literature predictions, I demonstrate how some later-generation Japanese Americans continue to seek social spaces with other co-ethnics, finding a sense of ethnic "connectedness" within Japanese American basketball leagues. My research demonstrates that with lower rates of Japanese immigration (Hoeffel et al. 2012), higher rates of outmarriage (Le 2012; Lee and Bean 2007), and lack of a traditional ethnic enclave (Li and Skop 2007), some Japanese Americans have turned to basketball leagues as a moving and evolving source for ethnic community that is both local and transnational. These basketball leagues and respective social interactions have become one way to manage identity; co-ethnic social interactions are sites for negotiating between mainstream U.S. society, various segments of the Japanese American community, and consumptive practices of the popular cultural realm of basketball.

Scholars such as Stephen Fugita and David O'Brien Jr. (1991) argue that in spite of the rate of assimilation and demographic changes to the community, "it is still likely there will continue to exist a Japanese American community which can rely on the contribution of its members to collective goals" (126). Yet they offer few examples to explain *how* ethnic community will continue to exist. As Japanese American youth, in particular, and Asian American youth, in general, are often relegated as inconsequential subjects in communal identity formation (Kwon 2013), I argue that league members build various co-ethnic networks using several social and structural strategies that bring together a diverse age demographic and offer suburban Japanese Americans an outlet for ethnic community building. Specifically, league members use the engagement and practice of sports to create an expansive co-ethnic local and transnational social network that was missing in their everyday interactions and social spaces. Secondly, the league also forged connections among co-ethnics by strengthening social and cultural capital to provide additional support along social and economic lines.

Examining how later-generation Japanese Americans use these creative strategies to sustain ethnic community provides new ways of understanding the messy, shifting, and always complicated intersections of ethnic identity, belonging, and citizenship. While both racial and ethnic categories can be defined by a combination of self-identification and social assignment, ethnic identity and community building are frequently adopted, asserted, and negotiated by group members themselves and can provide a counternarrative to combat negative racializations (Cornell and Hartmann 1998; Nagel 1994; Portes and Rumbaut 1996). Particularly within Japanese American sports leagues that give priority to Japanese ancestry, these spaces can be seen as a racial project (Omi and Winant 1994; Hartmann 2003; King-O'Riain 2006) where members connect meaning in discursive practices, social structures, and everyday experiences that are racially or ethnically organized. Contributing to the process of racial formation, members use these co-ethnic leagues to manage their racialized experiences (see Burdsey 2007, 2011; Carrington 2010, 2012; Chin 2015), shift the racial dynamics, and assert their own expressions of ethnic identity.

Japanese Americans, Sports, and Assimilation

Sports leagues, particularly basketball leagues, offer a unique perspective into Japanese American experiences and communities. The first immigrant arrivals set in motion the start of many roots into the sports community while negotiating their lived experiences in a space underscored with the racialization as the "yellow peril" and white-nativist resentment. Among this generation, traditional Japanese sports such as sumo and American baseball were the most popular and practiced sports among working-class and farming communities (Nakagawa 2001; Niiya 2000). Samuel O. Regalado (2012) emphasizes the transnational link between Japanese American consumption of baseball and the U.S. greats, such as Babe Ruth, spreading the gospel of baseball in Japan. By the second generation, Japanese Americans became more involved in other Americanized sports, such as wrestling, bowling, and basketball. This transition toward American sports activities signaled a shift in the Japanese American community, in particular, and the Asian American community, in general, regarding their acceptance and growing passion for American leisure culture; it was through baseball and basketball games where they could actively participate in Americanized culture while also maintaining a sense of ethnic identity and community (Yep 2009, 2012).

American sporting cultures continued to play an active role during World War II when the Japanese American community faced some of their most challenging times. Under President Roosevelt's Executive Order 9066, one hundred ten thousand Japanese American men, women, and children, two-thirds of whom were American citizens by birth, were systematically uprooted from their homes and transplanted to temporary "assembly centers" and "relocation centers" located in desolate and remote regions of the United States. This political and militarized action functioned as a racial project—one that defined, enforced, and legitimated boundaries to shape the collective membership of the Japanese community along racial lines and perceived threats (Omi and Winant 1994). During these years of internment, many Japanese American men and women were quick to set up sporting activities and teams within the confines of their barbed-wire communities, including baseball and basketball teams. Sports was a form of entertainment— an enjoyable way to pass the time, break up the boredom within the barren confines of the camp, and challenge the dominant representation of them as national traitors who were "forever foreign" (Lowe 1996; Pearce 2005).

After Japanese American internees were allowed to leave the internment camps for voluntary resettlement, sports in the post–World War II era continued to be instrumental in sustaining community. During this time, Japanese Americans struggled to plant new roots, often in cities and towns where anti-Japanese sentiments were still high. Japanese Americans turned again to the baseball fields and basketball courts to bring together a disbanded ethnic community. It was on these "American" playing grounds where Japanese Americans could both validate their identity as Americans and prove themselves loyal to the country (Sullivan 2000). By the 1980s and 1990s, the third- and fourth-generation Japanese Americans began moving away from their inner-city niches into suburban communities where they created new sports leagues and organizations to meet their athletic and social needs.

Participation in ethnic sporting spaces continues to play a central role in the lives of some Japanese Americans despite high levels of assimilation. Over several generations, scholars consider Japanese Americans one of the most acculturated and established ethnic groups, noting key factors including their socioeconomic success and residential patterns (Alba and Nee 2003; Zhou and Gatewood 2007). Japanese Americans also claim a higher rate of multiracial identification compared with other groups. In 2010, just over 40 percent of Japanese Americans reported being of more than one racial group or ethnic Asian group, making them the highest mixed-race group among other Asian groups (Hoeffel et al. 2012). This substantial growth in Japanese and Asian multiracial populations is likely due to the high rates of intermarriage between whites and nonwhites that have risen sharply within this community (Lee and Bean 2007; Zhou 2004). Moreover, unlike other Asian American groups, Japanese Americans have fewer new immigrants coming into the United States to replenish their shrinking population; while populations of other Asian groups have steadily grown over time, the Japanese American population has shown a slow decline, from 852,237 in 2000 to 841,824 in 2010 (Hoeffel et al. 2012). Finally, as one of the first and oldest Asian groups to immigrate to the United States, Japanese Americans are the only Asian-origin group whose U.S.-born population is larger than the number of foreign born. As such, Japanese Americans are one of the few Asian groups to have a fourth generation and many U.S.-born elderly in the same population.

As Japanese Americans continue to achieve high rates of integration, some scholars argue that these assimilation patterns will result in a loss of community and identity as ethnic boundaries continue to erode (Alba and Nee 2003). In this case, individuals' ethnic origins would become less relevant and desired; groups would mutually perceive themselves with less frequency in terms of their ethnic categories and increasingly under specific circumstances. Yet my research demonstrates that for some third- and fourth-generation Japanese Americans, the longing and desire to stay connected to other co-ethnics remains a salient part of their social lives. Drawing from ethnographic data, I argue that youth basketball leagues provide a social and cultural space to address shifting changes within this community by offering participants an opportunity to negotiate ethnic identity while they maintain an ethnic community.

Research Site

Japanese American basketball leagues are currently thriving cultural and athletic organizations involving over ten thousand youth and adults participating in year-round leagues and tournaments in Southern and Northern California (King 2002; Watanabe 2008).[1] The popularity and size of these leagues show no signs of slowing down; the Japanese American community and the larger Asian community as a whole seem to have a steady interest in creating more sporting opportunities. Given the legacy of sports activity and teams within the Japanese American community—one that has extended several generations, often surviving different social and political climates— these leagues offer a rich site to explore the role that sports organizations play in constructing and affirming ethnic identity and community, particularly among older and presumably more assimilated generations.

The Pacific Coast Youth (PCY) basketball league, which is one of the earliest Japanese American youth sports organizations in Southern California, was the center of my ethnographic fieldwork.[2] The PCY league is connected to the Southern California Sports Association (SCSA), an athletic youth organization that oversees the PCY along with eight other Japanese American and Asian American youth sports leagues. The PCY started in the 1960s as a volunteer-based organization run by a committee of elected members. Initially baseball comprised most of the league's sporting activities, but over time and as membership continued to grow, the league began forming basketball teams as well. The increasing popularity of basketball, especially in the 1980s and 1990s with National Basketball Association players Magic Johnson, Larry Bird, and Michael Jordan, made it commonplace in communities across the racial and gendered spectrum, both locally and globally (LaFeber 1999).

The PCY league sponsors thirty-two male and female basketball teams with players ranging between seven and eighteen years of age. During the summer, the league sponsors a basketball camp for children between the ages of five and seven to give youth an early introduction to the game and opportunities to develop their coordination and ball-handling skills while also learning the principals of good sportsmanship and teamwork. The organization also hosts an annual basketball tournament that draws up to four hundred youth and adult teams from Southern and Northern California.

Although the PCY league does not hold or enforce any formal rules that require specific racial or ethnic backgrounds for membership, the majority of players are overwhelmingly Asian American, with over half of the participants having full or mixed Japanese American heritage.[3] The subtlety of racial exclusion is part and parcel of the experience of racial exclusions in other sporting spaces and the guiding parameters of membership in the Japanese American leagues (see also Chin 2015; Thangaraj 2010, 2012).

Methodology

Participant Observation

To understand the role and significance that ethnic sporting spaces play in the lives of players, families, and other league participants, I conducted participant observation from December 2007 through June 2008 after Institutional Review Board (IRB) approval. During this time, I followed a total of eight different teams—a male and female team in the third, sixth, ninth, and twelfth grades—for one season. By observing teams at different ages, I was able to capture how the role of ethnic sports leagues can evolve over time and experience.

As an outsider to the community with little skill playing basketball myself, I was mindful to attend and observe several events to better understand the interactions and weekly activities as they naturally occurred. This included attending weekend practices, games, and tournaments for both the junior season (second through seventh grade) as well as the senior season (eight through twelfth grade). During these events, I was able to capture the everyday lived experiences and nuanced interactions among players, coaches, families, and fans as they played out both on and off the court in social settings. I also attended monthly PCY commissioner meetings, which gave me more insight to the internal and institutional decisions that were made regarding the organization of the league and its goals. These observations made it possible for me to map the social connections and networks that existed among members and the larger ethnic community. Moreover, this extended engagement with members' involvement with basketball illustrated to me the long histories and futures of Japanese American sports leagues that contest the normative understandings of them as never "American" enough.

Interviews

In addition to participation observation, I conducted sixty-four open-ended, in-depth interviews with league members to capture the memories, opinions, and lived experiences as they were told through the words and expressions of the participants themselves. Collection of interviews began in December 2008 and concluded in October 2009 after IRB approval. Interviewees were selected first from the eight teams I had followed and expanded through a snowball-sampling method to include other teams within the organization (Thangaraj 2010).

To document the origins of the league and its initial goals, I interviewed two league founders and several former players about the social and cultural circumstances that influenced and inspired the creation of ethnic sports leagues. Interviews with current players, coaches, and family members captured not only the motivations of joining an ethnic league but also provided insight to the social and cultural role that these spaces provided within participants' lives. I also interviewed league organizers regarding the bureaucratic, organizational, and political aspects of the league, including the league's guidelines and procedures for gaining membership into the organization and its involvement within the larger ethnic community, both locally and globally. Moreover, I interviewed participants who were also actively involved in nonethnic basketball leagues such as high school teams or city-sponsored leagues. These interviews offered a comparison between participation in the Japanese American league and mixed-race leagues.

Searching for an Ethnic Connection

Instead of an expected erosion of community or ethnic identity, many later-generation Japanese Americans within the PCY organization took an active approach to providing opportunities for members to socialize with other co-ethnics and maintain a connection to ethnic roots. While ethnic enclaves are often considered a source for ethnic livelihood, socialization, and community building, the legacy and the role and use of traditional Japanese American enclaves have changed over time. No longer residential hubs for Japanese Americans, the Japantown in San Francisco and Little Tokyo in Los Angeles are now mostly symbolic centers for commerce and cultural symbolism (Alba and Nee 2003; Zhou and Gatewood 2007). Especially as more Japanese Americans move into predominantly white suburban communities, locating a thriving ethnic community presents a particular challenge for this group. Participation in the PCY league became a likely solution to address challenges to foster an ethnic connection.

Particularly for families who lived in predominantly white and suburban neighborhoods, parents frequently expressed a pressing concern about their racial and ethnic isolation. As one parent observed living in Orange County, "You know, there's not a whole lot of Japanese Americans around these days." While these families had structurally assimilated into suburban Southern California neighborhoods, many felt racially marginalized in their day-to-day lives. Moreover, without a thriving number of Japanese Americans in social spaces like schools, church, or community organizations, members were concerned that their children would lose their ethnic identity. Betty, a third-generation Japanese American parent, conveyed this particular concern during her interview:

> Betty: I like the community involvement that [PCY] gives Thomas. I'm hoping it teaches [my son] something. I just like him being part of an Asian organization. That's important to me.
> Author: Why does it have to be Asian?
> Betty: Because he's Asian! [Laughs] No, seriously! For no other reason than he's Asian! At the school he goes to, he's probably the only Japanese [student]. . . . I don't want him to lose where he came from, or not know where he came from, or what he is. . . . The [PCY] league was our opportunity—seeing that we're not

real active in church—to get him to have other Japanese friends.
. . . I just think it's important that he knows who he is.

Betty and her husband, Mike, considered themselves an "old-fashion kind of Japanese couple"; they still wanted their son Thomas to be connected to an ethnic community and in doing so, he will have a greater understanding about his Japanese heritage. Thomas, who attended a private school in Orange County with mostly white students, had few opportunities to socialize with other Asian or Japanese youth. While the Buddhist church could be an active social space for some Japanese Americans to congregate, Betty's family did not regularly attend. I demonstrate later in this essay how the social and organizational structure within the PCY league became a popular and successful solution to alleviate racial marginalization.

In addition to feeling ethnically and racially isolated in predominantly white, suburban neighborhoods, some Japanese American parents were concerned that their children would not share a similar upbringing that included strong ties to their ethnic community. For example, Coach Gavin, a forty-eight-year old, second-generation Japanese American, expressed concern that his two daughters would not have the same opportunity he had growing up near Little Tokyo to be actively engaged with serving the Japanese American community. Growing up, Coach Gavin's father served on various boards for Japanese language schools and a Buddhist church while his mother organized health fairs in Little Tokyo. After moving to a predominantly white and affluent suburb in Orange County, Coach Gavin's personal motives to join an ethnic sports league were "a little bit selfish"; he wanted his daughters to have a similar social connection to their ethnic community and to foster a sense of civic responsibility. Through basketball, his daughters "were still part of the Japanese community."

Moreover, some members also expressed concern that the high outmarriage rate among later-generation Japanese Americans would create additional challenges for the maintenance of ethnic identity and community. Recognizing how difficult it can be for Japanese American youth to meet other co-ethnics, some parents embrace the leagues as a potential social site for their teenage children to find other Japanese Americans as dating partners. Regarding the PCY tournament dance, I overheard Annie prodding her teenage son, Brent, "So are you going to the dance tonight to meet a nice Japanese girl?" Brent, embarrassed by his mother's comment in front of his teammates, quickly shot back, "Yes, you'd like that, wouldn't you?" Laughing, Annie quickly responded, "Yes, your dad and I would love that!" While most Japanese American parents did not express any explicit expectation that their children would date or marry other Japanese Americans, parents like Annie did acknowledge the challenges for co-ethnic partnerships in their community. She quipped, "There aren't any Japanese girls at Brent's school—if he's going to meet one, it will be through basketball." The league, be it intentionally or unintentionally, created its own relational desires premised around race without having to explicitly state it.

Examples such as these reveal a strong desire among later-generation Japanese Americans to not only seek out but also maintain future ethnic community ties among their children's generation. Their integration into white suburban neighborhoods and an increasing outmarriage rate resulted not in a declining need for ethnic community, but rather in degrees of racial and ethnic isolation that left many families concerned that their children would not have the opportunity to be engaged with co-ethnics and the larger Asian American community as a whole. As Lacy (2004) notes in her study on black middle class living in predominantly white suburban neighborhoods, black families experienced something inherently pleasurable about being with others of their own racial group and maintaining a social and cultural connection. Similarly, PCY members actively sought out and deeply enjoyed the associations and networks with other Japanese and Asian Americans that the league provided. The types of co-ethnic intimacy within the PCY league were a source of pleasure not readily available in multiracial settings. Rather, multiracial leagues were often sources of anxiety, marginalization, and emasculation for Asian Americans, especially Asian American men (see Thangaraj 2012, 2015). Co-ethnic leagues provided a respite to some of the negative racialized and gendered assumptions that players experienced in mixed-raced leagues.

Strategies for Creating Co-Ethnic Connections

While other Asian ethnic groups have found similar co-ethnic spaces like churches (R. Kim 2006), ethnic language schools (Zhou and S. Kim 2006), or neighborhood enclaves (Zhou and R. Kim 2003), many later-generation Japanese Americans turned to youth basketball leagues as a popular and crucial outlet for securing a sense of ethnic connectedness. To foster this connection, league members first created expansive co-ethnic local and transnational social networks that were missing in their everyday interactions and social spaces. Second, the league also bridged gaps along social and economic lines by sharing social and cultural capital and creating opportunities to participate in civic engagement to support their community.

Building Co-Ethnic Local and Transnational Social Networks

Youth sports often foster close relationships among players and families (Fine 1987; Messner 2009), and Japanese American leagues were no different in that regard. With weekly practices and games, monthly meetings, annual tournaments, and other league commitments, PCY members were constantly connecting, reconnecting, and socializing with one another. Thus participation in PCY was a daily practice of identity and community formation. The outcome of these social interactions often produced close networks of friendship, extended family, and even romantic relationships with other Japanese Americans that were not possible in other sporting and nonsporting social milieus.

The success of these spaces in producing meaningful and lasting friendships along co-ethnic and racial lines was a common experience among current and former players. The majority of players reported that "hanging out with friends" was one of their favorite aspects of playing in these leagues. Coach Randy, a forty-year-old, third-generation Japanese American, grew up playing in the leagues as a child and remained active in the organization as the head coach for the sixth-grade boys' team. During our interview, he fondly shared with me how he was still good friends with former teammates he used play with when he was ten years old—"I've made friends for life. Right now I can tell you one person from high school that I still keep in touch with. But I can tell you dozens of names that I grew up with in [the leagues] that are my friends now." For Coach Randy and other former players, participation in these leagues had solidified lasting friendships that spanned several decades to create an extended network for companionship with other Japanese Americans. Moreover, many members participated in year-round tournaments that occurred in several major cities in California and Las Vegas. Interestingly, some parents found themselves reunited with former childhood teammates when their children faced one another on the court. These tournaments made it possible for teams to compete and connect with other Japanese Americans within the state.

The vast network of co-ethnic friendships helped to alleviate some of the ethnic and racial isolation members experienced in nonsporting spaces. As one parent highlighted, "My son can look around and see other players that look like him, and he can't do that in his high school. We came to PCY to be able to do that." Parents saw the league as an alternative community space for parents and children to find other Japanese friends. In these racially exclusive spaces that gave priority to Japanese descent, it was some parents' hope that their children would not be as "whitewashed" by attending predominately white schools. They reasoned that the continual exposure to other Japanese American youth would somehow infuse a connection to ethnic and racial identity and belonging.

In addition to creating opportunities for lifelong co-ethnic friendships, participation in these leagues strengthened family ties, particularly bridging generations of families together. In the absence of ethnic enclaves, which commonly feature multigenerational family continuity, later-generation, suburban Japanese Americans have found familial cohesion through basketball leagues. For example, Melissa, a third-generation Japanese American mother, proudly stated that her two daughters, Linda and Lori, were the third-generation of basketball players in her family to play in the leagues—Melissa and her mother used to be former Japanese American league players when they were younger. She exclaimed, "Basketball runs in our family! We give you a basketball as your first toy growing up." In these cases, membership in ethnic leagues created a family tradition that served to strengthen familial networks with grandparents, aunts, uncles, and cousins; all were welcomed to support other family members in the league—even if they played on opposite teams. Moreover, multigenerational participation in sports shaped how sporting performances and identities were passed down from men to boys and women to girls. These generation linkages further complicate the performances of Americanness that is not limited to the youngest, often thought as most assimilated, members of the family (see also Lowe 1996).

Leagues also provided opportunities for members to find potential dating partners within the Japanese American community. Bruce, one of the league founders, expressed his desire that these leagues could help facilitate possible matchmaking among co-ethnics: "The main reason why I started the league was to give [players] a social environment for meeting other Japanese and give them the opportunity to eventually someday marry if they want to. . . . And if they don't like other Japanese, that's their prerogative. We weren't trying to say you have to marry Japanese, like some parents. I just wanted to expose them—that's the best word—expose them to other Japanese." By providing a social environment for greater exposure to other Japanese youth, Bruce was hopeful that relationships built within this space might lead to marriage. Often PCY boys and girls teams would attend each other's games to support one another and would comingle afterward. Moreover, tournament dances also brought opportunities for teenagers to socialize and flirt. Similar to the pre–World War II dances in Valerie Matsumoto's (2004) study of second-generation Japanese Americans, basketball tournament dances brought opportunities for socializing, flirting, courtship, and romance for the next generation of Japanese Americans. In a sport where gender performance and sexuality are constantly scrutinized and on display, female basketball players are often subjected to stereotypes of being too "butch" or lesbian for lacking traditional displays of femininity (Rand 2012; Carrington 2002). Yet, Japanese American leagues allow female bodies to conform to heteronormative expectations. As possible outlets for heterosexual dating, leagues become a space not only for racialized and gendered understandings but also sexualized contours that include an emphasis on co-ethnic, heterosexual partnerships.

The league's efforts to create social ties went beyond the local ethnic community, even extending its boundaries on a global level to create transnational sporting connections. This transnational relationship was made

possible through the Yonsei Basketball Association (YBA)—a highly selective and competitive traveling basketball team that competed against other
youth teams in Japan. Established in 1993, YBA's objective was to provide
fourth-generation Japanese American youth the opportunity to experience
their Japanese heritage firsthand by providing homestays with local families
so players could experience an immersion of everyday Japanese culture. Selected male and female players between thirteen and fourteen years old participated in a goodwill exchange of ideas and cultures by traveling and living
with local Japanese families, competing in basketball games against their
Japanese counterparts, and visiting prominent cities in Japan for one week.[4]
Yonsei players were able to return the favor a few months later when they
hosted players from Japan for a tournament in the United States. This athletic exchange program successfully created a transnational network among
Japanese and Japanese American youth, many of whom still remained
friends with their homestay families through email or Facebook. One Yonsei
team went back after their first visit three years ago to have a "rematch" with
their Japanese counterparts. As Janet fondly reminisced, "It was like some
big, international family reunion." Basketball, in this case, was the medium
through which the gaps between Japanese American and Japanese communities were bridged. As one of the few Japanese American sports leagues to
participate in international travel and competition, this organization embodied the growing transnational and global influence within sports cultures. Moreover, in the absence of replenished ethnicity in the form of
continuous immigration (Jiménez 2010), transnational friendships created
through sports communities made it possible for members to pique their
interest in cultural heritage while also providing ways to distinguish the difference between being Japanese and being Japanese American.

Connections through Shared Cultural Capital and Civic Engagement

A sense of ethnic connectedness goes beyond social networks and the number of co-ethnic relationships that are forged through basketball. One must
also consider the outcome of these types of relationships and the purpose
they served in bridging together networks and the larger ethnic community
as a whole. Relationships that emerged from these leagues created a means
for members to share cultural capital that often stretch far beyond the logis-
tics, knowledge, and concerns of practices, games, and gyms; PCY families
frequently use this co-ethnic social network for support and advice in other
spheres of life beyond basketball. As Coach Randy explained, "so these are
not only friends, but connections that open up avenues for work or even my
auto mechanic. Everyone knows someone so that if you need someone, it's
like, 'Yeah, I have a friend who can help you out.' . . . It's nice to know that if
I ever had a problem or something happened to my family, I know there is a

support structure there that I wouldn't have to worry about anything. And that's all because of the people I have met through these leagues growing up."

By sharing information and referring trusted networks within the Japanese American community, it was possible for members to create an informal support system among co-ethnics. I frequently overheard conversations among parents trading stories and discussing tips regarding academic matters including which middle school had a stronger academic record, suggestions for SAT prep courses, or tips about college applications. These networks were also used to assist with other mundane matters such as finding a trusted mechanic, real estate agent, or a cheap place for catered desserts. This method of cultural vouching served to strengthen the bonds and trust among other Japanese Americans.

Occasionally, these leagues also served as an extended "family" offering support during times of crisis. This communal support system was especially evident when Jessica Kubo, a fifteen-year-old PCY player, was diagnosed with Hodgkin's lymphoma. The PCY league, along with the parent organization SCYA, organized a fund-raiser to help raise money for the Kubo family during the end-of-the-year holiday party. Each team crafted and sold red ribbons during game events and collected donations for the family to help with Jessica's medical costs. In an organization as large as PCY, most of the families did not personally know Jessica or the Kubo family. Yet their outpouring of support, both symbolically and financially, was far-reaching. Mr. Kubo expressed his sincerest gratitude with a tearful speech thanking PCY for their support and love. These acts of generosity were reflective of the fluid and inclusive definition of "family" within Japanese American leagues, allowing members to reach out to one another in moments of crisis or need. As one father from the sixth-grade boys' team expressed, "That could have been my daughter who was diagnosed—[Jessica] might not be my blood, but she's still part of the PCY family." Similar to immigrant networks in previous generations (Nee and Sanders 2001; Zhou and Bankston 1998), later-generation Japanese Americans continue to use the co-ethnic social networks with the league to share various forms of capital to help provide financial, educational, and emotional support to one another.

The PCY organization also had goals for youth to branch out beyond the basketball court and gyms to be actively engaged with their local ethnic community. As Andrew, the PCY league president emphasized, "It shouldn't be all just basketball—but kids should also give back to the [Japanese American] community." This was largely accomplished through the PCY's Youth Volunteers Group (YVG)—a volunteer group started in 2006 and comprising youth from the PCY basketball league and other Japanese American leagues in Southern California. In this capacity, the YVG frequently organized volunteer events that assisted Japanese and Asian American organizations and community events. Quoting Sabrina, the parent leader for the YVG, "I think it's good if we do [volunteer] projects in the Asian community. If we don't do it, then who will?" With that spirit in mind, youth volunteered their time to assist at local Japanese cultural festivals as well as organized outings to visit the Japanese American National Museum in the interest of giving back to their community.

The league also maintained a strong connection with a local Veterans of Foreign Wars post composed of Japanese American war veterans. Through volunteer and social events, some parents hoped that engagements with older-generation Japanese Americans could provide rich historical knowledge regarding social and political challenges experienced by the community. As another parent, Andrew, reflected, "With all the generations of [Japanese Americans] that are still involved in the league, these kids could learn a lot— about the internment, about the wars they fought in. . . . Those [veterans] aren't going to be around much longer." League organizers hosted an annual high school senior banquet that brought graduating PCY seniors and veterans together to honor the accomplishments of both groups. During that evening, veterans spoke informally with youth about growing up in internment camps, their military service, and their economic and political contributions after the war while high school seniors shared their postgraduate plans and dreams. These social connections that extended across generational lines could pique interest about their shared history, particularly during times of discrimination and internment. Rather than rely on history books or documentaries, later-generation Japanese Americans could turn to second-generation elders to learn about their lived experience as internees or veterans. Moreover, this epistemology also constituted one way to provide racially centered counternarratives to the model-minority tropes surrounding political passivity and inaction (Prashad 2000; Dhingra 2007; Thangaraj 2012, 2013).

Conclusion

Investigation of the various social networks within co-ethnic basketball leagues reveals how these sporting spaces were active sites in fostering ethnic community and a sense of connectedness among third- and fourth-generation Japanese Americans. Largely attributable to social isolation and anxiety over a loss of ethnic ties, later-generation Japanese Americans turned to co-ethnic youth sport leagues as a solution to alleviate racial and ethnic marginalization along social and spatial lines in their suburban neighborhoods. Youth who participated in these leagues learned the basic fundamentals of basketball, teamwork, perseverance, and hard work, but players and their families also experienced greater exposure to co-ethnics and rich opportunities to forge lasting social ties. As I have mapped out in this essay, members fostered closer ties to co-ethnics across different social networks, bridging a diversity of Japanese American communities together. Through weekly practices, games, and other league functions, players and their families were brought together on the court where members fostered closer social relationships around friendship, family, dating partners, and global teammates. Within these networks, players and families strengthen a shared social capital to provide additional social, economic, and emotional support to create extended families and transnational connections.

Significant in these findings are the active efforts of third- and fourth-generation Japanese Americans to create and utilize these spaces to bring youth of similar ethnic and racial backgrounds together. Subtly, without using the language of race, PCY league was one racial project through which Japanese Americans challenged the racial contours of Americanness and claimed their place, locally, nationally, and transnationally. Contrary to existing models that predict a continuous and irreversible "straight-line" path of assimilation resulting in the erasure of ethnic distinctiveness, the collective work among later-generation Japanese Americans to carve out ethnic social spaces through sports leagues suggests an alternative model that allows for the maintenance and promotion of ethnic community through sports culture. Especially within an ethnic group that has undergone rapid transformation with fewer new immigrants, and few institutionalized cultural hubs, these leagues were a strong indicator of the growing need and continued desire to actively use cultural and social spaces to build a stronger ethnic community within this generation. My research demonstrates the role and importance of sporting communities in providing a much-needed social space for ethnic bonding and cultural participation. Sport is a key site to understand the shifting and fluid terrain of ethnic communities and social networking within later-generation Asian Americans.

While the presence of ethnic culture is largely symbolic at best (Gans 1979; Waters 1990), the strategies that members of the PCY league adopt to maintain community present new ways of thinking about how cultural distinctiveness and livelihood can move beyond traditional ethnic cultural markers to take on an emergent culture of hybridity—one that blends ethnic communities with American practices. In this culture of hybridity, later-generation Japanese American youth share a Durkheimian collective consciousness and collective sense of belonging around sporting practices. As one youth reflected, "I don't know any Japanese kids that don't play ball or that doesn't have a sibling or a cousin that plays. . . . You're kind of an outsider to the [ethnic] community if you don't play." In spaces like Japanese American basketball, ethnic connectedness and identity become less centered around traditional ethnic cultural markers such as language, religion, or ancestry, and more focused on the embodied and social practice around the quotidian and spectacular engagement with sports. In other words, for some members, being part of the Japanese American community has become synonymous with playing in co-ethnic youth sports leagues. This shift in identity practice and community formation pushes us to consider the unique ways in which sporting cultures shape and complicate the way athletes embody ethnic and racial ways of being and the narrative of incorporation both on and off the court.

NOTES

This chapter was previously published under the same title in *Ethnic and Racial Studies* 39, no. 6 (2016): 1070–1088.

1. See Thangaraj's (2013, 2015) work and his examination of Asian American leagues' participation on the East Coast and U.S. South.

2. All names have been changed to protect the identity of participants and the organizations involved.

3. This percentage was determined through informal interviews with families and by examining the names and photographs of players in the 2007 and 2008 tournament handbook and team yearbook.

4. Players who apply to participate in the Yonsei Basketball Program are self-selected; these players and their families have an explicit desire to visit Japan and participate in a cultural exchange that is different from their own.

REFERENCES

Alba, Richard, and Victor Nee. 2003. *Remaking the American Mainstream: Assimilation and Contemporary Immigration.* Cambridge, MA: Harvard University Press.

Burdsey, Daniel. 2007. *British Asians and Football: Culture, Identity, Exclusion.* London: Routledge.

———, ed. 2011. *Race, Ethnicity, and Football: Persisting Debates and Emergent Issues.* New York: Routledge.

Carrington, Ben. 2002. "Fear of a Black Athlete: Masculinity, Politics and the Body." *New formations* (45): 91–110.

———. 2010. *Race, Sport and Politics: The Sporting Black Diaspora.* London: Sage.

———. 2012. "Introduction: Sports Matters." *Ethnic and Racial Studies* 35(6): 961–970.

Chin, Christina B. 2015. "'Aren't You a Little Short to Play Ball?': Japanese American Youth and Racial Microaggressions in Basketball Leagues." *Amerasia Journal* 41(2): 47–65.

Cornell, Stephen E., and Douglas Hartmann. 1998. *Ethnicity and Race: Making Identities in a Changing World.* Thousand Oaks, CA: Pine Forge Press.

Dhingra, Pawan. 2007. *Managing Multicultural Lives: Asian American Professionals and the Challenge of Multiple Identities.* Stanford, CA: Stanford University Press.

Fine, Gary Alan. 1987. *With the Boys: Little League Baseball and Preadolescent Culture.* Chicago: University of Chicago Press.

Fugita, Stephen, and O'Brien, David Jr. 1991. *Japanese American Ethnicity: The Persistence of Community.* Seattle: University of Washington Press.

Gans, Herbert J. 1979. "Symbolic Ethnicity: The Future of Ethnic Groups and Cultures in America." *Ethnic and Racial Studies* 2(1): 1–20.

Hartmann, Douglas. 2003. *Race, Culture and the Revolt of the Black Athlete: The 1968 Olympic Protests and Their Aftermath.* Chicago: University of Chicago Press.

Hoeffel, Elizabeth, Sonya Rastogi, Myoung Ouk Kim, and Hasan Shahid. 2012. *2010 Census Briefs—Asian Population: 2010.* U.S. Census Bureau. https://www.census .gov/prod/cen2010/briefs/c2010br-11.pdf.

Jiménez, Tomás R. 2010. *Replenished Ethnicity: Mexican Americans, Immigration, and Identity.* Berkeley: University of California Press.

Kim, Rebecca. 2006. *God's New Whiz Kids? Korean American Evangelicals on Campus.* New York: New York University Press.

King, Rebecca. 2002. "'Eligible' to Be Japanese American: Multiraciality in Basketball Leagues and Beauty Pageants." In *Contemporary Asian American Communities: Intersections and Divergences,* edited by L. T. Vo and R. Bonus, 120–133. Philadelphia: Temple University Press.

King-O'Riain, Rebecca Chiyoko. 2006. *Pure Beauty: Judging Race in Japanese American Beauty Pageants.* Minneapolis: University of Minnesota Press.

Kwon, Soo Ah. 2013. *Uncivil Youth: Race, Activism, and Affirmative Governmentality.* Durham, NC: Duke University Press.

Lacy, Karyn R. 2004. "Black SPACES, Black Places: Strategic Assimilation and Identity Construction in Middle-Class Suburbia." *Ethnic and Racial Studies* 27(6): 908–930.

LaFeber, Walter. 1999. *Michael Jordan and the New Global Capitalism.* New York: W. W. Norton.

Le, C. N. 2012. "Interracial Dating and Marriage: U.S.-Raised Asian Americans." Asian-Nation.org. Accessed August 1, 2012. http://www.asian-nation.org/interracial2.shtml.

Lee, Jennifer, and Frank D. Bean. 2007. "Intermarriage and Multiracial Identification: The Asian American Experience and Implications for Changing Color Lines." In *Contemporary Asian American: A Multidisciplinary Reader,* edited by M. Zhou and J. V. Gatewood, 381–392. New York: New York University Press.

Li, Wei, and Emily Skop. 2007. "Enclaves, Ethnoburbs, and New Patterns of Settlement among Asian Immigrants." In *Contemporary Asian American: A Multidisciplinary Reader,* edited by M. Zhou and J. V. Gatewood, 222–236. New York: New York University Press.

Lowe, Lisa. 1996. *Immigrant Acts: On Asian American Cultural Politics.* Durham, NC: Duke University Press.

Matsumoto, Valerie J. 2004. "Nisei Daughters' Courtship and Romance in Los Angeles before World War II." In *Asian American Youth: Culture, Identity, and Ethnicity,* edited by J. Lee and M. Zhou, 83–99. New York: Routledge.

Messner, Michael. 2009. *It's All for the Kids: Gender, Families, and Youth Sports.* Berkeley: University of California Press.

Nagel, Joane. 1994. "Constructing Ethnicity: Recreating Ethnic Identity and Culture." *Social Problems* 41(4): 152–176.

Nakagawa, Kerry. 2001. *Through a Diamond: 100 Years of Japanese American Baseball.* San Francisco: Rudi.

Nee, Victor, and Jimy Sanders. 2001. "Understanding the Diversity of Immigrant Incorporation: A Forms-of-Capital Model." *Ethnic and Racial Studies* 23(3): 386–411.

Niiya, Brian, ed. 2000. Introduction to *More than a Game: Sport in the Japanese American Community,* 14–67. Los Angeles: Japanese American National Museum.

Omi, Michael, and Howard Winant. 1994. *Racial Formation in the United States: From the 1960s to the 1990s.* New York: Routledge.

Pearce, Ralph. 2005. *From Asahi to Zebras: Japanese American Baseball in San Jose, California.* San Jose: Japanese American Museum of San Jose.

Portes, Alejandro, and Rubén G. Rumbaut. 1996. *Immigrant America: A Portrait.* 2nd ed. Berkeley: University of California Press.

Prashad, Vijay. 2000. *The Karma of Brown Folk.* Minneapolis: University of Minnesota Press.

Rand, Erica. 2012. *Red Nails, Black Skates: Gender, Cash, and Pleasure On and Off the Ice*. Durham, NC: Duke University Press.

Regalado, Samuel O. 2012. *Nikkei Baseball: Japanese American Players from Immigration and Internment to the Major Leagues*. Urbana: University of Illinois Press.

Sullivan, Cheryl Lynn. 2000. "All American." In *More than a Game: Sport in the Japanese American Community*, edited by B. Niiya, 194–201. Los Angeles: Japanese American National Museum.

Thangaraj, Stanley. 2010. "'Ballin' Indo-Pak Style: Pleasures, Desires, and Expressive Practices of 'South Asian American' Masculinity." *International Review for the Sociology of Sport* 45:372–389.

———. 2012. "Playing through Difference: The Black-White Racial Logic and Interrogating South Asian American Identity." *Ethnic and Racial Studies* 35(6): 988–1006.

———. 2013. "Competing Masculinities: South Asian American Identity Formation in Asian American Basketball Leagues." *South Asian Popular Culture* 11(3): 243–255.

———. 2015. *Desi Hoop Dreams: Pickup Basketball and the Making of Asian American Masculinity*. New York: New York University Press.

Watanabe, Teresa. 2008. "At Long Last, Little Tokyo to Get Its Gym." *Los Angeles Times*. https://www.latimes.com/archives/la-xpm-2008-sep-24-me-tokyogym24-story.html.

Waters, Mary C. 1990. *Ethnic Options: Choosing Identities in America*. Berkeley: University of California Press.

Yep, Kathleen S. 2009. *Outside of the Paint: When Basketball Ruled at the Chinese Playground*. Philadelphia: Temple University Press.

———. 2012. "Peddling Sport: Liberal Multiculturalism and the Racial Triangulation of Blackness, Chineseness and Native American-ness in Professional Basketball." *Ethnic and Racial Studies* 35(6): 971–987.

Zhou, Min. 2004. "Are Asian Americans Becoming White?" *Context* 3(1): 29–37.

Zhou, Min, and Carl Bankston III. 1998. *Growing Up American*. New York: Russell Sage Foundation.

Zhou, Min, and J. V. Gatewood. 2007. "Transforming Asian America: Globalization and Contemporary Immigration to the United States." In *Contemporary Asian American: A Multidisciplinary Reader*, edited by M. Zhou and J. V. Gatewood, 115–138. New York: New York University Press.

Zhou, Min, and Rebecca Kim. 2003. "'A Tale of Two Metropolises': Immigrant Chinese Communities in New York and Los Angeles." In *Los Angeles and New York in the New Millennium*, edited by David Halle, 124–149. Chicago: University of Chicago Press.

Zhou, Min, and Susan Kim. 2006. "Community Forces, Social Capital, and Educational Achievement: The Case of Supplementary Education of the Chinese and Korean Immigrant Communities." *Harvard Educational Review* 76:1–29.

2

Millennial Understandings of *Nikkei Seishin* in San Jose Japantown

Lisa Hirai Tsuchitani

I n *Between Two Empires: Race, History, and Transnationalism in Japanese America*, Eiichiro Azuma (2005) notes how many issei (first-generation Japanese immigrants) believed in the importance of cultivating *Nippon seishin*, or "Japanese spirit," in the second-generation nisei during the early 1900s. According to Azuma, this term referred to two core elements consisting of "a set of moral values that they regarded as authentically 'Japanese'" and "a strong sense of racial pride or racial consciousness" (122). More specifically, issei leaders, Japanese officials, and the Japanese social elite adopted a project of moral reform "to create an overseas community that would properly represent modern Japan" in an effort to curtail increasing anti-Japanese sentiment in the United States while also furthering the diplomatic and nation-building efforts of Japan (36). Through Nippon seishin, the issei hoped to inculcate in the nisei a strong sense of self-discipline and obligation to ensure economic, political, and social stability within the growing Japanese American community (122).

Toward this end, the Japanese immigrant community established Japanese schools and language institutes as early as 1902 (Ichioka 1988, 196). In 1914, these schools numbered thirty-one in California; by 1923, this number had grown to fifty-five (206). Initially, these schools were premised upon a *dekasegi* ideal of preparing the nisei to enter the public schools of Japan.[1] This ideal was formally abandoned, however, at a historic 1912 conference sponsored by the Japanese Association of America at which assembled immigrant educators throughout the state of California adopted several resolutions declaring that "the primary role of American public schools would be to provide the intellectual and physical aspects of their education while the language schools would handle the moral dimensions of Nisei education" (Takahashi 1997, 26). More specifically, these educators advocated that Japanese schools assume the responsibility of teaching nisei the importance of extending "benevolence to all" and other universal precepts as outlined in the Imperial Rescript on Education of Japan, learning the Japanese language, and maintaining "a positive Japanese identity" while in the United States (Ichioka 2006, 15–16).

Some hoped that these schools would play a critical role in improving communication and relationships between issei parents and their nisei children. Others hoped that these schools would help the nisei better understand and appreciate their cultural heritage (Azuma 2005, 123). Overall, the issei hoped that teaching the nisei an appreciation of their linguistic and cultural heritage while they were simultaneously being educated as permanent residents of the United States would lead to "greater amity between generations" (Takahashi 1997, 33).

With the onset of World War II and the forced removal and incarceration of an estimated one hundred twenty thousand persons of Japanese ancestry residing on the West Coast as a result of Executive Order 9066, the majority of these schools were forced to close.[2] During the sixties and early seventies, however, community-based heritage programs and schools would begin to reemerge as an outgrowth of the Asian American movement, a historic coming together of diverse Asian American youth who had established a common identity as "Asian Americans" despite their distinctive social, cultural, and political differences in "a collective undertaking to promote social change" (Takahashi 1997, 159–161). Today, at least eight Japanese American heritage programs and schools exist in the state of California alone in such cities as Sacramento, San Francisco, El Cerrito, Fresno, and Los Angeles.

Given the changing demographics of the Japanese American community over time, I am interested in understanding the objectives of these programs and schools today. More specifically, what role(s) do Japanese American heritage schools play in the Japanese American community? How do they shape our understandings of what constitutes Japanese Americanness, or *Nikkei seishin*? What possible insights do these schools provide for our understandings of contemporary Japanese American life? These are a few of the questions that I explore in my research.

Methodology

The focus of this ethnographic study is a forty-year old Japanese American heritage school located in San Jose, California. Based in San Jose Japantown, Suzume no Gakko (SNG) is a parent-participation summer program for children entering kindergarten through the sixth grade.[3] Using SNG as a lens for understanding how Nikkei seishin is conceptualized and taught, I analyze how processes of Japanese American identity formation are negotiated by millennial-age graduates of SNG in an effort to gain deeper insight into the complexities of contemporary Japanese American community life.

More specifically, through this study I examine how the site of the heritage school can serve as a critical lens for analyzing how the Japanese American community has evolved from the past. I also am interested in understanding how self-identified millennial graduates of SNG made sense of their experiences. Did their educational experiences at SNG shape their understandings of their identity and sense of place within the Japanese American community? If so, how?

My research findings presented in this essay are based on my personal experiences as a parent and member of the Board of Directors of SNG. Monthly attendance at board meetings over the course of four years provided consistent opportunities to engage with parents and staff members, all of whom were either alumni of the school or had children enrolled in the program, about how they understood the role of the school in their lives both personally and professionally. Classroom observations while the program was in session also offered invaluable insights into how students responded to the various curricular objectives upon which the school was founded. Informal conversations with over fifty current and former students, staff members, and board members of SNG further contextualized these discussions and observations about the program presented in this essay. Finally, my own experiences as a former SNG student during the seventies informed my analysis as well.

In addition to utilizing participant observation as a research methodology, I interviewed, over the course of one year, eight self-identified millennial graduates of SNG who were born between 1985 and 1995. The majority of my interviewees were living in San Jose with the exception of two, who currently are living on the East Coast. Two were married, and one was expecting a child at the time that these interviews were conducted.

I located the majority of my interviewees through referrals from my first three interviewees, as well as from local community leaders with whom I had been acquainted for years. All interviews were conducted over the phone and lasted between forty-five minutes to one-and-a-half hours in length. Two of my interviewees ultimately wished not to be cited directly in the study but offered insights that have been most helpful with its framing. All interviewee names and identifying information have been changed out of respect for their privacy.

Suzume no Gakko: A Brief History

During the spring of 1977, a young sansei mother had returned from an Air Force tour of Japan. During this trip, she began to wonder how she could pass on the cultural and historical legacies of her Japanese ancestors to her young children. Up until that time, Karen Akahoshi had not given much thought about these legacies of her extended family in Japan. But "discovering her roots" in Japan had awakened in her a fascination and admiration for a "centuries-old" culture with which she felt she could identify both racially and ethnically and which she "felt was really important to share with my kids."

Upon her return to the United States, Karen became acquainted with another young mother with children who were the same age as her own, Ann Saito, whose family had moved to California from India. Through Ann she later would meet Karlene Koketsu, a mother of six with an ardent interest in arts and crafts. One day these three newly acquainted women began to discuss a newspaper article about Jan Ken Po Gakko, a Japanese American summer cultural heritage program that recently had started in Sacramento. This article prompted them to consider starting a similar school in San Jose. Karen recalls,

> We got together one day, over a bowl of noodles, to talk about starting a program here in San Jose. Really close friends of mine from Cal [University of California, Berkeley] and the Alameda Buddhist Temple had started Jan Ken Po Gakko recently. So they were really generous about coming to San Jose and being really open about sharing with us everything they did to open their school. We ended up taking their framework and adapting it. Later I would get a call from another friend from UC Berkeley who was interested in starting a similar program in Berkeley. And another friend from Cal in Watsonville too asked us to help them start a program there. I gave them both our help and "paid it forward." And then these communities would help "spread the word" further. But it all began with Jan Ken Po Gakko in Sacramento.

These founders would call upon their relatives and friends to assist with the collection and development of lesson plans, as well as to help teach classes. Weeks later, Suzume no Gakko, or "The School of Sparrows," opened its doors for the first time.

The first summer session of SNG ran for two weeks, five days a week, at the San Jose Buddhist Church Betsuin. The program consisted of four combination classes at that time, ranging from kindergarten through the sixth grade, with a total of fifty-nine students enrolled. Incorporated in 1979, the school has continued to rely heavily on parent participation to support all aspects of its program. While modeled after the Jan Ken Po Gakko program in Sacramento, the SNG program would adopt a locally based curriculum to meet the cultural and social needs of the San Jose Japantown community.

Today SNG runs for three weeks, five days a week, at Wesley United Methodist Church located a block away from the San Jose Buddhist Church

Betsuin, with an enrollment of approximately 110 students annually. Despite its change in location, the program itself has not changed significantly in its forty-year history. The ringing of the original school bell, which has been used since the school was first founded, still heralds the start of each day that the school is in session. Students, teachers, student interns who are recent graduates of SNG, and staff members still line up in rows to do *taiso* (Japanese exercises) in the church parking lot every morning before both teachers and students are dismissed to their classrooms. Children from the nearby Lotus Preschool, a private nonprofit preschool operated and located at the San Jose Buddhist Church Betsuin, as well as parents and grandparents who dropped off their children that morning, also stay to participate in this multigenerational morning ritual.

The days are filled with lessons in subjects that staff members and Board members not only consider to be important aspects of Japanese American identity but which also address the following stated purposes of SNG:

1. To encourage an awareness of Japanese American culture and heritage
2. To promote and maintain a positive image of Japanese Americans
3. To maintain a positive identity within the American community[4]

Toward this end, students of all grade levels receive lessons in the Japanese language historically taught by a native speaker of Japanese, learning how to write and read *hiragana* (the more widely used and basic form of Japanese writing), as well as gaining speaking familiarity with commonly used nouns and phrases in Japanese (i.e., numbers, days of the week, etc.). All students have lessons in *odori* (Japanese dancing) on a weekly basis as well. Taught by community members classically trained and certified in *nihon buyo* (Japanese classical dance), students learn the movements and the history behind Japanese folk dances typically done at local Obon festivals.[5] Music lessons in Japanese children's songs reinforce these lessons in Japanese language and dance.

Arts and crafts projects also reinforce cultural and social aspects of Nikkei seishin as defined at SNG. Third-grade students, for example, paint papier mache Kabuki masks (masks typically worn during a form of classical Japanese dance-drama) that are molded from their own faces, while first graders make cherry blossom trees out of painted grains of rice. Such activities complement the lessons that take place in the kitchen using food as a medium for further understanding Japanese American culture; students learn how to make what is considered to be "culinary staples" in Japanese American cuisine such as spam *musubi* (rice balls with spam), *shoyu* hot dogs (hot dogs cooked in soy sauce), and *mochi* (sticky rice).

An additional sense of Nikkei seishin has been cultivated at SNG through regular excursions to businesses and organizations located in San Jose

Japantown. Founded in 1890, San Jose Japantown is nationally recognized as one of three remaining Japantowns in the United States. Drawn by the need for agricultural labor in the farming community of Santa Clara Valley at that time, issei migrant workers initially resided in San Jose's Chinatown, Heinlenville, located north of the downtown area. With the arrival of Japanese women, issei pioneers would establish their own community next to Heinlenville by the early twentieth century, that ultimately would grow to fifty-three businesses by 1941 (Domrose 2000). This steady growth of San Jose Japantown, however, would come to an abrupt halt in 1942 with the signing of Executive Order 9066 by President Franklin Delano Roosevelt and would not officially resume until December 1944.[6]

Today San Jose Japantown is the only Japantown in the nation that remains in its original location. By 1947, one hundred families and forty businesses had relocated back to this community and, by the 1950s, its population had doubled. The civil rights and antiwar movements of the 1960s further contributed to its growth, as third-generation sansei activists in particular strove to meet the cultural, social, economic, and political needs of their community: "Out of the counterculture and anti-war movements of the late 1960s, the political activism of the Sansei sparked a cultural awareness that bolstered efforts to renew Japantown" (Fukuda 2017). As a result, a series of redevelopment efforts has ensued in San Jose Japantown, including the construction of new housing complexes to complement and supplement the existing network of churches, businesses, and nonprofit organizations serving a variety of community needs.

The curriculum of SNG is greatly enriched by its proximity to this network of residents, business owners, and community leaders. Field trips to local businesses such as Shuei-Do Manju Shop, Minato Japanese Restaurant, Santo Market, and San Jose Tofu, for example, have allowed students to learn about and appreciate the challenges of running a family business, as well as the processes for making such Japanese delicacies as *manju* (sweet Japanese pastry) and tofu from scratch. SNG students also perform Japanese American songs and plays for the seniors of the Yu-Ai Kai Japanese American Community Senior Service of San Jose.[7] School assemblies featuring local Japanese American artists, writers, and leaders including San Jose Taiko[8] and the San Jose Chidori Band[9] expose students to a variety of role models and activities that they may not have been familiar with before attending SNG.

Despite changes in the development of San Jose Japantown over the years, the stated mission of the SNG program has remained unchanged since its founding. While this mission has not changed over time, however, what have students of SNG learned about what being Japanese American means today? How have they experienced and understood Nikkei seishin, not only as individuals but also as members of a larger Japanese American community?

The Generational Legacy of Incarceration

All who were interviewed for this study described the significant impact that learning about their Japanese American heritage at SNG had on them throughout their childhood. Mariko, for example, grew up in San Jose Japantown. In fact, a few members of her extended family were responsible for starting and managing several key businesses and organizations in the San Jose Japantown community, and they still play indispensable leadership roles in the community to this day. Although she had "easy access and exposure" to what she considered to be Japanese American values and customs through her family, she still appreciated greatly the importance of SNG in her life: "We learned about culture through performing arts, music, language, and writing. . . . Three weeks dedicated to learning about my culture amongst a community of friends was a significant experience for me. I enjoyed taking it all in. I liked being exposed to cultural things that I wouldn't normally get exposed to—playing the koto [a traditional Japanese stringed musical instrument], taiko [drum], Kabuki mask making. . . . SNG was the beginning of my journey to learn more about what it means to be Japanese American." For Mariko, SNG was an important institutional space that allowed her not only to learn more about her heritage but, even more importantly, to do so "surrounded by a cohort of peers and community members who also understand the deep and rich legacies of the community."

David also valued the important space that SNG offered for him to explore his cultural identity as a Japanese American. Growing up in a suburb in San Jose, he was one of only several Asian Americans at his elementary and middle schools. He recalled being teased for "eating rice" and "being too academically successful," but never questioned or challenged these stereotypes about himself until he started attending SNG: "At Suzume no Gakko I learned that there was more to me than what my peers thought of me. Up until then, I never realized the struggles of my family, because I did not learn about them until then." To David, his experiences at SNG helped him better understand his identity as a Japanese American in ways that his active participation in such community institutions like the San Jose Buddhist Church Betsuin and the San Jose Community Youth Service (CYS) did not.[10]

Brent also believed that SNG was an important place where he could take pride in being Japanese American among his peers. A self-identified "hapa with a Japanese American mom and a white dad who grew up around Japanese Americans," he fondly recalled doing "taiso, singing, making sushi, making clay projects, and taking trips to Santo Market and San Jose Tofu" while he was a student there.[11] Although he was active in a number of organizations in San Jose Japantown such as San Jose Taiko and the San Jose Buddhist Church Betsuin Young Buddhist Association, SNG helped him to gain a deeper appreciation for the importance of "life-long connections" within the Japanese American community: "I always say I am Japanese even though I'm hapa. I went to SNG because my family and friends went. We did everything together. . . . I learned about my family history there—the stories about my grandparents' origins and why they came to the United States. SNG was a fun and positive thing." Today Brent still maintains close ties to the community, actively assuming leadership roles in the very organizations in which he spent a great deal of time during his childhood.

Learning about the incarceration experiences of their parents and grandparents was particularly impactful for the majority of my interviewees. In fact, many had not even heard about this historical period until they attended SNG, despite their active participation in Japanese American community life in San Jose Japantown. According to Donna Nagata, this silence surrounding the subject of incarceration within the Japanese American community was not necessarily atypical. Her findings from the Sansei Research Project, the first large-scale research project ever about the impact of the incarceration on third-generation Japanese Americans, revealed that silence actually was a common strategy employed by nisei in response to the trauma they experienced during their wartime incarceration (Nagata 1993, vii–xi).

The main focus of study during the fifth grade at SNG, the subject of Japanese American incarceration during World War II, was taught using a variety of pedagogical methods that were designed to be culturally mindful of the difficulties of talking about this history. For example, students were asked to interview a family member or friend who had been incarcerated about their wartime memories. If students were unable to find someone willing to be interviewed, instructors helped them find local community members who were open to sharing their experiences with them. This interview would serve as the basis for a series of classroom activities and projects for the rest of the session, which were designed to help students better contextualize the lived experiences of their interviewees. Such activities and projects would include having students make a barrack out of construction paper and wooden coffee stirrers, pack a backpack of items that they would have brought with them had they been forcibly evacuated and write about the significance of each item they packed, and develop an oral presentation about the significance of the incarceration in their lives today.

Kelly, for example, spent a great deal of her childhood attending institutions considered to be "cultural pillars" in Japantown. As a former student of Lotus Preschool and an active member of the San Jose Buddhist Church Betsuin Girl Scout troop, she grew up with "a great appreciation for the culture and history of Japanese Americans." Her parents also served actively on the San Jose Buddhist Church Betsuin Board of Directors.

While she enjoyed "morning taiso, Japanese language classes, and plays in the upper grades when I had to speak all of my lines in Japanese," learning about the incarceration history of her family was most significant for her: "I just remember learning about the camps at SNG for the first time and paying attention to it since then." While she admitted to a "general awareness" about this historical period before attending SNG, she added that she did not truly understand the difficulties that her family and community members experienced during World War II until she was a student at SNG. For her, SNG became an important space, both physically and emotionally, from which to explore the impact of the incarceration of her relatives on her own cultural awareness and overall identity as a Japanese American.

A self-identified millennial of Japanese and Chinese ancestry, Kyle was profoundly affected by the learning experiences he had while he was a student at SNG as well. Like Kelly, he too had spent a great deal of his time as a child participating in numerous organizations centered in San Jose Japantown, including the San Jose Buddhist Church Betsuin Boy Scout Troop 611. His family never spoke to him about their experiences during World War II, as "it felt too raw or taboo [for them] to bring it up." Learning about this history at SNG, however, "honestly sparked a huge interest in me to learn more about Japanese American history." He remembered "a woman coming to speak to our class about a visit to the dentist. Her dentist criticized her for taking poor care of her daughter's teeth. What he did not realize was that because of camp, she was not able to provide her daughter with proper dental and dietary care. She told us how she spoke out against the dentist for his unwarranted criticism. This was powerful. I always will remember her speaking out. This wasn't anything anybody told us about in the community." Her story continues to haunt and inspire him to this day.

Like both Kelly and Kyle, Mariko spent a great deal of her childhood in San Jose Japantown. Despite her exposure to a variety of cultural and historical sources of information about the experiences of her relatives during World War II, she too did not learn about the wartime history of her family until she was asked to interview her grandparents while she was a student at SNG: "Camp was not covered in public school at all so attending Suzume no Gakko really exposed me to what my grandparents and great-grandparents went through during World War II. We interviewed family members for the first time because of an assignment for Suzume no Gakko. It was so interesting to learn about their experiences during this time. . . . I remember chalking out in the parking lot the space that would have been the size of the room that my great-grandparents and grandparents lived in. I didn't realize until then that [their living space] was so small." For her, learning about this family history was a lesson in how to be "prideful, humble, and respectful for what my ancestors have gone through to get me to where I am today."

For David, being assigned to interview his grandparents about their incarceration experiences was personally significant too. Before attending SNG, he "never knew about all of the hardships that my family went through during this difficult time." He attributes his feeling more grounded in his cultural heritage as a Japanese American, as well as his ability "to accept and respect the struggles of our ancestors and other minority groups," to his learning experiences about the incarceration at SNG.

A Place of Multigenerational and Transnational Learning

SNG helped its students come to terms with their unique generational relationship to the historical legacies of their parents and grandparents. As Kelly notes, "I feel that a lot of fourth- and fifth-generation Japanese Americans are not necessarily tied to Japan, but something that I noticed in general at SNG is a feeling of strong family orientation and a profound respect for our grandparents and great grandparents—the lives that they built and what they endured during World War II. And because of that, the parents and kids are very family-oriented and hard-working." Mariko too acknowledged the role that her family's wartime experiences had played in shaping her understandings about her identity and, more specifically, her role within the Japanese American community moving forward: "At SNG I learned that previous generations all faced adversity at some point in their lives. All other generations had to work hard to accomplish the goals they had. We haven't been faced with that adversity yet. I think that makes the older generation so strong, and we as millennials need to do the same thing—work hard to maintain our culture. We can play a stronger role in keeping our culture alive." By attending SNG and thus increasing their historical and cultural awareness as Japanese Americans, both Kelly and Mariko gained a deeper appreciation not only for their elders, but also for their own roles as agents in the preservation and perpetuation of Nikkei seishin.

As a parent-participation school, this form of "generational learning" always has been a critical component of the program from which both students and their parents have benefited. Whether working in the classrooms as aides, staff members, or members of the Board of Directors for the school, parents also have learned a great deal from being involved with SNG. Founding director Karen Akahoshi recalls, for example, how enthusiastic parents were to be engaged with the school: "When we first started SNG, back in those days we needed a lot of support from parents, so we decided that parents would have to be assigned to their child's classroom—this was a requirement. The thing was, however, that the parents were so excited to be involved because they too wanted to learn more [about Japanese American culture]. We actually had to turn parents away who wanted to come and help! They were so happy for their children and for themselves to be able to learn more about their Japanese American heritage." According to Karen, this excitement that the parents shared about the mission of the school was critical not only to its longevity but also its impact on those associated with the school and the San Jose Japantown community at large.

A strong advocate for her children "to be exposed to, learn about, and understand the different cultural aspects of their Japanese American heritage," Leslie Tsukimura was one of these early parents who played an active role in the classroom and also served on the SNG board while her daughter and son were students there. She recalled that enrolling her children into the program was so competitive that even getting in line an hour before the official registration start time was not a guarantee that they would be able to get in. For her, however, this long wait time was worth it: "The cultural aspects of the program were so important—the food, songs, arts and crafts, plays, etc. This was an education that our children would never get elsewhere—and an education that we as parents never formally received either. . . . We as parents got a lot out of that experience—seeing and being a part of what our kids were learning at SNG. We parents also got a sense of community from this too by meeting people on the same 'cultural wavelength.' SNG in this sense thus supported us in making sense of our Japanese American identity for ourselves too." Even today, she speaks with sentimental pride about the class projects that her children did over twenty years ago that she still has on display in her home. She also has remained active in the San Jose Japantown community, volunteering with a variety of its organizations to further the lessons of cultural and historical awareness that she attributes to her involvement at SNG.

These intergenerational relationships have been reinforced further by the physical location of the school itself. Situated within the heart of San Jose Japantown, SNG became a place to discover, explore, and celebrate cultural and historical aspects of Japanese American identity when other avenues to do so were not necessarily nor readily available. Volunteers and staff members were trusted parents and grandparents, extended family members, friends and neighbors, and community leaders. Thus, learning about historically difficult topics such as the incarceration occurred in ways that both students and parents alike may not have been able to pursue in other formal educational and personal settings. At SNG, students could learn about and further reflect upon "the camps" in personally meaningful ways while surrounded by a cohort of peers and community members who shared and understood the complex legacies of the wartime incarceration experience in their lives.

In addition to a place of learning about what Nikkei seishin meant historically, culturally, and generationally, SNG also served as an important space for students to explore what their identity as Japanese Americans meant transnationally as well. More specifically, for the majority of my interviewees, SNG was the first place that they learned about the distinction between "being Japanese" and "being Japanese American." Kelly, for example, noted how: "I feel more American than Japanese, but feel more Japanese because of SNG. I would not feel so culturally Japanese now if it weren't for SNG." While she described what she learned at SNG as "Japanese," she nonetheless still strongly identified herself as Japanese American, attributing cultural values such as a strong work ethic and respect for one's family as uniquely "Japanese American" in comparison to other racial and ethnic groups, but still understanding these values to be historically and inherently "Japanese."

Mariko made clear distinctions between what she considered to be "Japanese American" and "Japanese" as well, although she too used understandings of "Japaneseness" to define her sense of Nikkei seishin. This distinction became particularly clear when discussing the topic of food, which she considered to be critical in defining Japanese American culture: "I know that my great-grandparents and grandparents cooked a lot of Japanese food. I should know how to make these dishes; I need to learn something as simple as that to keep these important traditions alive. . . . Yet, I know that the sushi that we eat here is not the sushi eaten in Japan. I still think, though, that we still need to maintain our ethnic identity through these Japanese culinary traditions." For Mariko, being Japanese American meant being respectful of the cultural traditions and values of her grandparents and their predecessors, which for her originated in Japan.

David also attributed first learning about the difference between "being Japanese American" and "being Japanese" to his experiences at SNG. He admitted to continuing to struggle with this while in college, but appreciated the cultural and historical lenses that he had been provided with during his childhood within the spaces of SNG and San Jose Japantown in general: "While in college I struggled with what it means to be Japanese American vs. being Japanese. I thank SNG for sparking that cultural identity for me. I joined the Nikkei Student Union, where we always talked about that." To David, being "Nikkei" meant honoring the legacies of his Japanese and Japanese American ancestors.

While Kelly, Mariko, and David still made references to "Japanese values" and "Japanese traditions" when talking about what it means to be Japanese American, Yuri did not. Growing up, Yuri and her family had played very active roles in a variety of organizations located in San Jose Japantown, including the San Jose Buddhist Church Betsuin and CYS. She too felt that SNG had "fueled my curiosity to learn more about the history of Japanese Americans"; she was excited to learn how to write her name in hiragana, trace her lineage through family trees and maps, and learn how to sing folk songs in Japanese. Unlike the rest of the subjects of this study, however, she would spend time living in Japan upon graduating from college, an experience which she felt "began her journey to learn more about what it means to be Japanese American" in relationship to Japan.

In *Redefining Japaneseness: Japanese Americans in the Ancestral Homeland*, Jane Yamashiro (2017) analyzes the experiences of Japanese American migrants living in Japan. Through her study, she reframes the relationship between Japanese Americans and Japan, exploring how Japanese American understandings of Japaneseness transform while living in their ancestral homeland: "From a US-based perspective, Japanese Americans may go to Japan, learn about Japanese culture, then return 'more Japanese.' But the experiences in Japan that Japanese Americans have and their exposure to Japan-based categories and expectations make it a more complicated process than this . . . experiences in Japan help Japanese Americans to think more carefully about issues of cultural authenticity" (150). When her interviewees returned to the United States after having lived in Japan, they "reassessed what it meant for them to be Japanese American, what form of Japanese culture they identified with and where it was located" (150). For Yuri, this was true as well.

Having studied Japanese in both high school and college, Yuri sought to "find a balance between being ethnically Japanese but raised within an American cultural context." Toward this end, after graduating from college she traveled to Japan through the Japanese Exchange and Teaching (JET) Program.[12] Her experiences living and working there helped her to better contextualize her ancestral heritage as a Japanese American both in the United States and in Japan: "Understanding my parents and grandparents was about learning about what they went through during World War II and learning about why I as a Yonsei don't have the same relationship to the language and culture of Japan that they do. It has been about learning that after World War II, our community occupied a unique location that is different from other groups in the United States because we were incarcerated. And that I occupy a unique position culturally. . . . My family maintained Japanese cultural traditions and customs, but after living in Japan I realized that these were very blended—very Japanese American." As a result of her experiences in both countries, Yuri not only was able to understand the limitations of defining Nikkei seishin based on Japanese language ability and sociocultural knowledge of Japanese society alone. She also challenged commonly held assumptions that Japanese American identity can be reaffirmed by simply "replenishing cultural knowledge lost over generations" that originated in Japan (Yamashiro 2017, 150).

On Cultural Preservation and Transformation

While the Japanese American community has grown increasingly diverse over time, the common characterization of the millennial generation as culturally "less engaged" with their Japanese American heritage did not ring true for any of my interviewees. Mariko, for example, decided to major in Asian American studies and sociology while in college. Upon graduating from SNG, David served as a child-care coordinator for the program for several years. He would continue his interest in exploring what Nikkei seishin meant for him in college by becoming an active member of the Nikkei Student Union. Kyle served as a child-care coordinator for SNG upon graduating from the program as well. Inspired by what he had learned from the program, he would pursue his interest in Japanese American history in college, eventually serving as a docent for the Japanese American Museum of San Jose after graduation.

While they unanimously had favorable memories about their educational experiences at SNG, all of my interviewees did express disappointment that they had not been taught earlier about the incarceration experiences of their family and community members. In fact, some actually felt that the "legacy of silence" associated with the incarceration experiences of the issei, kibei (nisei who were sent to Japan during their adolescence for schooling), and nisei may have in fact compromised the future development of the Japanese American community. For example, because his family "never talked about the camps," Kyle felt even more compelled to learn about Japanese American history. Nonetheless, he was upset about not being exposed earlier to the "legacies of structural and personal exclusion during World War II." He added, "Because camps were not talked about a lot, our generational cohort does not want to talk about it anymore too. I have felt isolated in my interest about Japanese American history and the camps. And I get upset when my [Japanese American] friends seem apathetic about this." As a result, he has felt the absence of a "generational cohesiveness" amongst his peers that he believes has hurt their ability to collectively create and redefine what they believe to be "uniquely Japanese American."

Brent shared this frustration over "the loss of knowledge and history of our elders" expressed by Kyle. While he acknowledged the importance of embracing change as the future of the Japanese American community becomes "increasingly difficult to predict as it becomes increasingly diverse," he also expressed uneasiness about his generation losing a shared sense of understanding about what defines them: "I learned a lot being active in the community. I've learned about hard work from the elders there—communication and leadership skills. . . . Change is good, but if we don't talk to our elders now, we risk losing their experiences forever." To him, SNG as a space of cultural and historical affirmation of Nikkei seishin thus played a critical role in his personal and generational identity.

For some, increased educational, economic, political, and social opportunities have compromised their generational "cohesiveness" as Japanese Americans. As David noted, "It is up to us to take over community leadership that our parents and grandparents assumed. But because we are not moving back home after college, we are having difficulty keeping that 'community mindset.' . . . To me, a 'community mindset' means remembering that if we don't fulfill our responsibilities to the next generation—our children—then community will no longer exist." Yuri also expressed consternation about the inability of her generational cohort to "stay connected to each other." She said, "We are more inclined to live further from where we grew up, or are more focused on our careers, or have more opportunities to pursue interests we could not before. My sense is that we are more distant to each other and perhaps this affects our community at large." While both David and Yuri suggested that social media possibly could improve and increase both intra-generational and intergenerational communication, they still believed that this tool could never serve as a replacement for building relationships in person within the context of the San Jose Japantown community.

As a result of this lack of collective generational identity, several interviewees suggested that members of their generation have found it easier to embrace a pan-ethnic identity as "Asian Americans" instead. More specifically, they feel that being "Asian American" has taken precedence over embracing a "Japanese American–specific identity." While they acknowledged that these identities were not mutually exclusive from each other, they nonetheless expressed concern over giving priority to what they perceived to be a more "generic," albeit politically salient self-identification, at the expense of a more culturally and historically specific one.

Despite the increasing rates of demographic dispersal of Japanese Americans, as well as the perceived loss of a shared sense of Japanese American cultural and historical memory, all of my interviewees continued to think about San Jose Japantown as "home." Although Brent no longer lives in the area, for example, he still thinks about San Jose Japantown with great affection: "It's a place of shared experiences and memories. A meeting place. A place that we can come back to, where we always will have memories growing up and are guaranteed to feel a sense of comfort and belonging." And spaces like SNG were perceived as key to the perpetuation of a sense of Japanese American community that is not based on geography alone. They may not have agreed on what constituted Nikkei seishin for their generational cohort; nonetheless, they still respected and even craved a sense of belonging and community that they felt was nurtured at SNG.

While my interviewees affectionately considered SNG and San Jose Japantown to be important cultural and historical spaces, they did not necessarily feel fully accepted in these spaces. Despite increased and improved intergenerational relationships through the SNG program, for example, interviewees still felt criticized by elders in the community for not understanding or honoring their Japanese American heritage enough. Kelly, for example, shared how, despite her active volunteer work in the community, her contributions still went unrecognized by elders who held leadership positions in the community based on assumptions made about her generational cohort: "A lot of people present us as lazy, not hard-working, self-entitled, and addicted to technology. I get where that comes from but don't feel that way about myself."

David felt this criticism too as a result of what he felt to be perceived generational differences in communication style: "My grandparents' generation was the 'quiet' generation because they could not question anything postwar. My parents' generation did not ask too much either. Millennials, however, can speak more freely, ask questions, and connect with people more easily than the generations preceding them." While such critiques did not deter Kelly and David from continuing to care about the future of the Japantown community in San Jose, they nonetheless approached working with elders within the community with a certain degree of deference and hesitation for fear of "overstepping their generational place."

Others like Kyle felt that because his generation had not faced the same degree of adversity that prior generations had to face, he and his peers should be doing even more in the community. He did not feel that his peers were necessarily compelled to do so, however, which was a source of frustration for him: "The older generation bonded together and put programs in place that helped us be successful. We took this for granted. We need to start relying on ourselves to keep their legacies alive. . . . I want programs in the community that I grew up with for my own children. Yet, if I'm not doing my part, then how can I expect this?"

Brent too expressed concern and dismay about the lack of interest and action on the part of his peers to preserve the historical memories of community elders, despite their access to technological advances that could facilitate this archival process more easily than ever before: "Technology defines us. Yet, we still don't use it to benefit the community. And the 'old timer' knowledge is being lost in the community—the history of things that you should know [about Japantown] but won't ask about until it's gone." In spite of and perhaps because of their frustration, both were very active in gently encouraging and recruiting their peers to join them in their leadership efforts within the community.

Although the subjects of my study made proactive attempts to serve as "generational ambassadors" and role models for their peers, they still felt a degree of uncertainty and discomfort about how best to redefine their identities and roles within the Japanese American community—both in relationship to each other and to their predecessors. In response to this discomfort, interviewees unanimously asked for more opportunities for intergenerational dialogue and collaboration to increase and improve their participation levels and experiences within the community. Mariko most concisely captured this sentiment expressed by all: "I think it's important to be around multiple generations—to know their stories and how they can continue to grow a community and maintain a community. We as a generation also need to be more educated and informed. We need to be more aware of what is happening in the community. . . . We need to have 'give and take' on both sides of the generational divide. We need to be open to learning. And the older generation needs to be open to change." And all agreed that programs like SNG were a positive step toward resolving these issues, both individually and collectively, in personally satisfying and institutionally meaningful ways.

Nikkei Seishin and the Need for "Reinvention"

As a sansei who was incarcerated as a child with her family during World War II, SNG founder Karen Akahoshi recalled growing up feeling like "a second-class citizen." Not wanting her own children and grandchildren to grow up with "this sense of being less than," she served as the first director at SNG for over ten years. Forty years later, she still remains both proud and astonished that the program has continued to thrive in San Jose Japantown: "One of the most crucial things we felt as young parents is that we wanted kids to grow up with a strong sense of self-esteem. For those growing up in camp, we didn't have self-esteem. Once I had children of my own, I wanted them to have a strong sense of self and be proud that they are Japanese Americans. We didn't have a clue as to how long this program would last! I am amazed that people still wanted to keep this program going." In fact, her grandson, who is both Italian and Japanese American, will be attending the program soon.

SNG was a place to explore not only one's historical legacy but also one's contemporary position within the Japanese American community. As Karen noted, curricula for the program had to evolve continually since such materials were nonexistent at the time of its founding: "We didn't have Japanese American studies back then. I was a student at Cal and I took every Japanese class I could. But there were no Japanese American studies classes. And yet a lot of us had an affinity for our heritage. Our parents wouldn't talk about the camps. So there was a thirst at that point in time to learn more about our Japanese and Japanese American roots—and a subsequent coming together of people of like minds who had that interest and desire. And I think those were the people we spoke to." Parents and students, staff members and board members, and the community-at-large would play an active role in shaping how the program was developed over time.

This case study of one of the oldest Japanese American heritage schools in California explores the salience of Japanese American ethnicity and community life through the eyes of its more recent millennial-age graduates. While the experiences of my interviewees may prove to be unique in comparison with Japanese American heritage schools not located within the physical proximity of a Japantown, future research efforts in Japanese American studies should address the increasing racial, ethnic, generational, and regional diversity within the Japanese American community today. Will the objectives of such Japanese American heritage programs and schools continue to change over time given the increasing diversity of our community? Is there consensus amongst existing programs and schools about what being Japanese American even means today? How will such programs fare in the face of increased dispersal rates of Japanese Americans from Japanese American community spaces?

For the subjects of this study, the SNG program played a significant role in allowing them to explore their collective and individual identities in meaningful ways. Not only did such explorations occur within their generational cohort but also with the intergenerational support of their elders. As David notes, "At SNG, my grandparents taught me to carry on their legacy. I feel honored that they struggled for me to live a better life. Up until that point, I never appreciated the struggles of my family, because I never had to struggle. . . . And I thank SNG for sparking that cultural identity for me." Learning both from and with their elders about their cultural heritage, they developed and transformed their understandings of Nikkei seishin through the institutional and personal relationships that were encouraged by the program.

Interestingly, despite popular characterizations of millennial-age Japanese Americans as being too "Americanized" to care about their ancestry, my respondents strongly felt that their identity as Japanese Americans still remains rooted in the past. The incarceration experiences of their family and community elders continue to resonate strongly with them. Kelly, for example, spoke about being inspired by the courage of those who experienced World War II behind barbed wire: "Most people I met are still extremely positive people after that experience. It meant a lot to me that they could still be positive after all that they endured. And that they were able to transition to establish themselves and raise their children was very impressive. Their successes, professionally and otherwise, spoke a lot to the type of strength that people walked away from this experience with." In fact, all of my interviewees attributed their economic, political, and social successes today to the hard work, sacrifices, and dedication of their parents, grandparents, and community elders.

All participants in this study also still believed in the importance of programs like SNG despite the fact that only two of them lived in or near San Jose Japantown anymore. Although they were unable to assume community leadership positions because of geographical distance, they nonetheless were adamant about the need for their generation to "step up" and protect important community institutions like SNG that played such an invaluable role in their early lives. Mariko, for example, shared how she believed that her generation "should be doing more to help take over for people who have been working hard for so many years." She added, "Our successes have led us away from our community roots, so now I feel that we are not aware of the issues and needs of the community. What is it going to take for us to 'step up'?

What do we want to change about ourselves? What change do we want for the community?" For many, not "stepping up" would threaten the very existence of the San Jose Japantown community in the future.

Interviewees additionally expressed concern over a lack of a "generational cohesiveness" that could define their experiences like the incarceration did for their predecessors. Nonetheless, programs like SNG provided important opportunities for them to discover what they in fact did have in common, as well as to create and to redefine a sense of Nikkei seishin that was uniquely their own. As David expressed, "We need to advocate with our collective voice for our cultural identity and a stronger Nikkei community—to recreate something that is ours." In this sense, programs like SNG actually can serve as places of empowerment for the millennial generation—places where they can assume ownership over the ways in which they understand, define, and recreate cultural and historical meanings about Nikkei seishin for themselves. To do so, however, they have had to challenge perceptions and assumptions held by others and themselves about their generational identity, as well as their current and future roles in the further development of Japanese American community life.

These recent graduates of SNG additionally have found ways to challenge understandings about Nikkei seishin that use Japaneseness as the defining criteria for "Japanese Americanness." While all of them with the exception of Yuri made reference to cultural values and traditions based in Japan when defining what it means to be Japanese American, they also referred to the salience of the incarceration experiences of their family and community members in their own identity formation as millennials. Additionally, while most no longer lived near San Jose Japantown, they nonetheless regarded this space and its programs to be important to their ethnic and generational identity for cultural, social, and historical reasons.

For them, Nikkei seishin thus was not merely nor necessarily a measure of one's familiarity with the language and culture of Japan. Rather, being Japanese American for them was a relational identity, the result of a dialectical process by which relationships between Japan and America, the past and the present, and youth and their elders are forged, converge, and change within specific geographic, cultural, and social spaces such as SNG and San Jose Japantown in general. In this sense, contemporary and future understandings of Japanese American identity and community become difficult to conceptualize without considering the unique individuals and the unique contexts in which they are located and defined. By reframing our conceptualization of Nikkei seishin as relational as opposed to generationally specific, perhaps we can better understand and analyze the complexities of Japanese American identity formation and community development in ways that the constantly changing demographics of our community truly necessitate.

NOTES

1. According to Yuji Ichioka (1988), the term *dekasegi* "refers to "the practice of Japanese laborers leaving their native place temporarily to work elsewhere. . . . *Dekasegi* always includes the ideal of returning home [to Japan] eventually" (3).

2. Signed by President Franklin D. Roosevelt on February 19, 1942, Executive Order 9066 authorized the mass forced removal and incarceration of an estimated one hundred twenty thousand persons of Japanese ancestry residing on the West Coast, over two-thirds of whom were U.S. citizens (Commission on Wartime Relocation and Internment of Civilians 1982, foreword).

3. The passage of California State Senate Bill 307 in 2001 provided funding for the development of plans for "the historic and cultural preservation of the remaining Japantowns in Los Angeles, San Francisco, and San Jose. San Jose Japantown is considered to be one of the last three remaining historical Japantowns in the United States" (Fukuda 2017).

4. Suzume no Gakko (2014), Suzume no Gakko Bylaws, San Jose, CA.

5. An annual Japanese Buddhist festival held during the summer, Obon honors the spirits of one's ancestors. Festival participants "express their joy to be living happily and to honor loved ones who have passed away" through folk dances and the lighting of *chochin* (lanterns) at family shrines and gravesites. The first American Obon Festival was observed in Hawai'i in 1905 (Osa 2006).

6. Public Proclamation No. 21 by acting Commander of the Western Defense Command, Major General Henry C. Pratt, officially revoked Executive Order 9066 and restored the right of those incarcerated to return to their former homes (Embrey 1972, 12).

7. Yu-Ai Kai is a nonprofit senior center that offers a variety of services for seniors (fifty-five and up) and their families, including social services, senior day care, nutrition, and activities. Its mission statement is "to promote healthy aging and successful independent living, and to advocate for all seniors, while embracing Japanese-American tradition." Yuaikai.org, accessed August 10, 2017, http://yuaikai.org/about-us.

8. Since 1973, San Jose Taiko (SJT) has been dedicated to the advancement of the taiko art form (Japanese drumming) through the development of an internationally recognized performing ensemble and conservatory—the first of its kind in the United States. In 1987, SJT became one of the first American taiko ensembles invited to tour Japan. Since then, the company has been recognized for its artistic and managerial excellence by such organizations as the California Arts Council, the Rockefeller Foundation, the Knight Foundation, and the Chevron Award for Excellence. Taiko.org, accessed August 10, 2017, http://www.taiko.org/history-traditional-japanese-drumming-rhythm-world-beats.

9. Founded in 1953, the San Jose Chidori Band initially was formed to provide Japanese music for the first-generation Japanese American issei. Many of the founding members of the band had played in musical groups while incarcerated during World War II. Its development occurred during a critical period of transition for the community, which was in the process of rebuilding itself after the war. Chidoriband.com, accessed August 10, 2017, http://chidoriband.com/wp/?page_id=36.

10. Founded in 1961, CYS is a parent-participation nonprofit organization "active in the Nikkei community" that "provides children with the opportunity to learn and develop skills in dance and individual and team sports." Sanjosecys.org, accessed August 10, 2017, https://www.sanjosecys.org/about-cys.

11. The term "hapa" historically has been used in the United States to refer to both Japanese Americans and Asian Americans of mixed heritage. According to the 2010 U.S. Census, people of Japanese ancestry reported the highest proportion of multiple

heritages of all Asian groups, claiming two or more races or ethnic groups. Demographers predict that if this trend continues, the majority of Japanese Americans will identify as being of mixed heritage by 2020 (Hoeffel et al. 2012).

12. Founded in 1987, the Japan Exchange and Teaching Program is a teaching exchange program managed by the Japanese government. The program offers its participants from over forty countries internationally the opportunity to work in schools, boards of education, and government offices throughout Japan. Jetprogramusa.org, accessed August 10, 2017, https://jetprogramusa.org.

REFERENCES

Azuma, Eiichiro. 2005. *Between Two Empires: Race, History, and Transnationalism in Japanese America*. Oxford: Oxford University Press.

Commission on Wartime Relocation and Internment of Civilians. 1982. *Personal Justice Denied: Report of the Commission on Wartime Relocation and Internment of Civilians*. Washington, DC: U.S. Government Printing Office.

Domrose, Cathryn. 2000. "Japantown Thrives in Culturally Diverse San Jose." Sfgate .com. http://www.sfgate.com/bayarea/article/Japantown-Thrives-in-Culturally-Diverse -San-Jose-2754786.php.

Embrey, Sue Kunitomi. 1972. *The Lost Years: 1942–1946*. London: Moonlight.

Fukuda, Curt. 2017. "History: San Jose Japantown." Jtown.org. http://www.jtown.org/ cat/history-san-jose-japantown.

Hoeffel, Elizabeth M., Sonya Rastogi, Myoung Ouk Kim, and Hasan Shahid. 2012. "The Asian Population: 2010." *2010 Census Briefs*. Washington D.C.: U.S. Census Bureau.

Ichioka, Yuji. 1988. *The Issei: The World of the First Generation Japanese Immigrants, 1885–1924*. New York: Free Press.

———. 2006. *Before Internment: Essays in Prewar Japanese American History*, edited by G. Chang and E. Azuma. Stanford, CA: Stanford University Press.

Japan Exchange and Teaching Program. 2017. "About JET." JETprogramusa.org. Accessed August 10, 2017. https://jetprogramusa.org.

Nagata, Donna K. 1993. *Legacy of Injustice: Exploring the Cross-Generational Impact of the Japanese American Internment*. New York: Plenum Press.

Osa, Susan. 2006. "Gathering of Joy: A History of Japanese American Obon Festivals and Bon Odori." Discovernikkei.org. http://www.discovernikkei.org/en/journal/2006 /7/8/obon.

San Jose Chidori Band. 2017. "History." Chidoriband.com. Accessed August 10, 2017. http://chidoriband.com/wp/?page_id=36.

San Jose Community Youth Service. 2017. "About CYS." Sanjosecys.org. Accessed August 10, 2017. https://www.sanjosecys.org/about-cys.

San Jose Japantown Business Association. 2017. "History: San Jose Japantown." Jtown.org. Accessed August 10, 2017. http://www.jtown.org/cat/history-san-jose-japantown.

San Jose Taiko. 2017. "San Jose Taiko: Our History." Taiko.org. Accessed August 10, 2017. http://www.taiko.org/history-traditional-japanese-drumming-rhythm-world-beats.

Suzume no Gakko. 2014. Suzume no Gakko Bylaws. San Jose, CA.

Takahashi, Jere. 1997. *Nisei/Sansei: Shifting Japanese American Identities and Politics*. Philadelphia: Temple University Press.

Yamashiro, Jane H. 2017. *Redefining Japaneseness: Japanese Americans in the Ancestral Homeland*. New Brunswick: Rutgers University Press.

Yu-Ai Kai (Japanese American Community Senior Service of San Jose). 2017. "About Yu-Ai Kai." Yuaikai.org. Accessed August 10, 2017. http://yuaikai.org/about-us.

3

To Be Yonsei in Southern California

*Persistent Community as Postsuburban Minority
Culture of Mobility*

DANA Y. NAKANO

I n the foundational assimilation text, *Assimilation in American Life*, Milton
M. Gordon (1964) outlines seven types of assimilation but focuses on
structural assimilation as "the keystone in the arch of assimilation" (81).
For Gordon, structural assimilation includes "large-scale entrance into
cliques, clubs, and institutions . . . on the primary group level" (71). Contemporary studies of immigrant incorporation have come to focus on socioeconomic and residential integration as measures of structural assimilation
(Alba and Nee 2003; Brown 2007; Charles 2007). Douglas S. Massey and
Nancy A. Denton (1993) bring together socioeconomic mobility and residential integration under the framework of spatial assimilation theory. This
theory posits that individuals accrue socioeconomic capital and upward mobility into the middle class that they convert into better housing, most commonly associated with leaving ethnically concentrated urban neighborhoods
for suburban neighborhoods with predominantly white residents (Massey
and Denton 1993; Charles 2007). Spatial assimilation relies on the assumption of residential integration and physical proximity as proxy measures for
social distance. With residential integration should come increased social
interaction between various collocated ethnic and racial groups. Certainly,
spatial and structural assimilation studies often demonstrate the movement
of upwardly mobile minority populations into white-dominated neighborhoods. However, their quantitative analyses are unable to provide an understanding of community formation practices in the suburbs or how this
reduction of physical distance impacts community formation practices
among suburban minorities.

Given the postulates of spatial assimilation theory, suburban later-generation Japanese Americans present a puzzling case. While Japanese Americans have achieved upward socioeconomic mobility and certainly moved into the suburbs (Fugita and O'Brien 1994; Alba and Nee 2003; King-O'Riain 2006; Spickard 2009), Japanese American suburban community studies have not proliferated in the same way as studies of other ethnic communities. I argue the reasons for such stagnation in Japanese American community studies is multifold. First, Japanese Americans are seen as a shrinking population attributable to a lack of immigration and high rates of outmarriage. While historically Japanese Americans were a common subject of sociologists and Asian Americanists, scholars have moved their attentions to larger and newer ethnic populations. Second, Japanese Americans present an outward appearance of full assimilation based upon quantitative measures of incorporation. As an assimilation success story, Japanese Americans are an ethnic group whose story has already been told. Lastly and most importantly for the present study, Japanese Americans in suburbia do not live in residential clusters. They are a dispersed ethnic group, perceptually fulfilling the promise of spatial assimilation. Given their dispersion, Japanese Americans lie outside the purview of recent scholarship interested in the formation of "ethnoburbs": the development of suburban-ethnic residential and business clusters beginning in the 1960s (Li 2009).

Residing in Orange County and south Los Angeles County, my respondents consistently describe their neighborhoods as predominantly middle class and white, sometimes with substantial portions of Latino and Asian American neighbors. Save the few who grew up in Japanese American residential concentrations in Gardena and Torrance, none reported a notable number of Japanese Americans living in their vicinity. As hypothesized by spatial assimilation theory, Japanese American residential integration and movement to the suburbs is an outgrowth of their upward socioeconomic mobility. Although my respondents reported participation within "cliques, clubs, and institutions of the host society," they did not consistently report a strong sense of attachment with such institutions or the disappearance of co-ethnic community bonds with other Japanese Americans (Gordon 1964). Rather, my respondents consistently discussed a conscious seeking of ethnic community outside of their proximate neighborhoods. The persistent desire for ethnic community hardly describes the path lit by spatial assimilation's hypothesis. While I recognize the residential integration and solidly middle-class status of many Japanese Americans, and certainly for those represented in my study, I argue their experiences and effort to seek out ethnic community call into question the assumption of resulting social proximity and sense of local belonging. It would seem later-generation Japanese Americans have not achieved full structural assimilation as described by assimilation scholars. Furthermore, persistent racialized difference is a root cause of the limited structural assimilation and persistent ethnic identity and community formation for Japanese Americans across multiple generations.

In this chapter, I examine the strategies and practices employed by later-generation Japanese Americans in seeking and building community. The data for this chapter are drawn from a larger study on the feelings of belonging and substantive citizenship among third- and fourth-generation Japanese Americans (sansei and yonsei, respectively) in the suburbs of Southern California. Given this anthology's focus on the millennial generation, this chapter relies on the in-depth interviews conducted with 39 yonsei who fall within the millennial category. The yonsei included in this study are millennials born between 1980 and 2000. These suburban, middle-class, fourth-generation Japanese Americans implement creative strategies and are accustomed to traveling significant distances and utilizing decentralized community institutions to fulfill social necessities rather than rely on their immediate vicinity. These necessities continue to include social connections, often of the ethnic variety.

Minority Cultures of Mobility and the Failure of Spatial Assimilation

Ethnic-community scholars, with their focus on ethnic residential concentrations, challenge spatial assimilation theorists by asserting that residential integration is not always the desired end point. However, scholars have found that even in circumstances of decreased spatial distance between racial groups, social distance and perceived racial difference can persist (Bratter and Zuberi 2008; Lacy 2007). Jenifer Bratter and Tufuku Zuberi (2008) examine the impact of increased social contact with racial diversity on inter-racial marriage patterns and determine that increases in racial diversity decreases the likelihood of African American–white, Native American–white, and Latino-white interracial unions. Similar trends were found for Asian American–white unions, but with insignificant results. Bratter and Zuberi's study demonstrates that increased interaction between racial groups does not always lead to positive movement along other assimilation measures. Lacy (2007) demonstrates that middle-class African Americans seek out co-ethnic community from a desire for a safe place away from their daily interactions in predominantly white spaces but also because such communities are pleasurable in themselves. For Lacy and other scholars of the black middle class, the reduction in physical distance and movement into predominantly white spaces does not negate persistent forms of racism or create full social acceptance and belonging, but often augments feelings of racial marginalization and the seeking out of co-ethnic community. Similarly, middle-class Japanese American movement into suburban Southern California placed them increasingly within predominantly white spaces and certainly added to the racial diversity of south Los Angeles and Orange Counties in the postwar period. However, the increased interaction and reduced physical distance did not allow Japanese Americans to eliminate the social distance between themselves and their white neighbors.

Despite high socioeconomic attainment and spatial assimilation, this study unfolds the persistent ethnic-community-seeking practices of fourth-generation Japanese Americans. Simultaneously, it presents an opportunity to understand how a racialized minority navigates the middle class in a way that differs from the white racial norm. While assimilation theory tends to equate upward mobility and entry into the middle class with a process of social whitening (Gans 2005), Kathryn M. Neckerman, Prudence Carter, and Jennifer Lee (1999) examine the lived experiences and paths taken by the distinctly *nonwhite minority* middle class. They introduce the concept of minority cultures of mobility, defined as "draw[ing] upon available symbols, idioms, and practices to respond to distinctive problems of being middle class and minority," as a means to call attention to the shortcomings of spatial assimilation theory (949). Looking at the case of middle-class African Americans, Neckerman, Carter, and Lee find that being minority and middle class gives rise to experiences that are distinct from both middle-class whites and co-ethnics from other, particularly lower, class backgrounds.

Studies making explicit examination of race within the middle class have largely overlooked the Asian American experience. Despite the frequent assertion that Asian Americans, in general, are upwardly mobile, the minority culture of mobility thesis has yet to be explicitly applied to an Asian American case. Perhaps because of the ascribed model-minority label and their positioning as honorary white, it is assumed that the Asian American middle class is the same as the white middle class and therefore unworthy of further investigation. Through the life experiences of my respondents, I find that residentially integrated, suburban yonsei do not find a fulfilling sense of belonging within their local communities and neighborhoods, as spatial assimilation would predict. I find such lack of belonging and community-seeking behaviors result from persistent racialization and racial microaggressions. This is not to say that Japanese Americans are ultimately marginalized. Nonetheless, Japanese Americans actively seek out co-ethnic community as a place of comfort and refuge from their racialization in mainstream society.

In this chapter, I examine the community-building practices of millennial yonsei as an example of a minority culture of mobility. These practices are a direct result of their suburban upbringing and high levels of interaction with white middle-class peers. In understanding suburban Japanese America as a spatially dispersed and residentially integrated population within this region, I am interested in how Japanese Americans come together and form community in the absence of proximity. In the face of suburbanization and residential integration, fourth-generation Japanese Americans must employ creative strategies and cultures of mobility to form community given their

ethnic dispersion. As occurs in concentrated urban areas, local ethnic institutions continue to bring Japanese Americans together. However, in the
suburban context, Japanese Americans must travel further distances to participate in such institutions. Extended travel times highlights the conscious
effort made by later-generation Japanese Americans to find co-ethnics despite
the ready access to more local, nonethnic community and institutions. Even
as Japanese Americans participate in semilocal community institutions, they
also seek out and find each other and form relationships in nonethnic specific spaces (e.g., school, athletic organizations, and places of employment). Ultimately, the Southern California yonsei experience directly challenges the
conventional wisdom of structural and spatial assimilation as the lynchpin of
full integration. Persistent practices of ethnic-community formation demonstrate a need to further explore and critique the mechanisms of assimilation.

Southern California Postsuburbia

This study focuses on the Southern California region, particularly Orange
and south Los Angeles Counties. In the postwar period, this region transitioned from its agricultural roots into a suburban paradise for urban Los
Angeles white flight, reaching one million inhabitants in 1963. Today, driving north on the 405 (I-405) and 5 (I-5) freeways from the southern tip of
Orange County toward Los Angeles, it would be difficult to tell the exact
location of the county line separating these two politically distinct bodies.
The cityscapes of wide streets, low-rise concrete façades framed by trees and
grass-lined sidewalks throughout the Southland are slow transitions, and
the traversing of borders often goes unnoticed. Only minimal signage on the
side of the highway marks the legal boundary. Even locals often puzzle over
which cities lying along the counties' border (Cerritos, Los Alamitos, Whit-
tier, La Habra) belong to Orange or Los Angeles.

Such visions have made coastal Southern California the model of urban
sprawl, or what Rob Kling, Spencer C. Olin, and Mark Poster (1991) have described as the "postsuburb" (1). While traditional suburban developments are
characterized as "peripheral bedroom communities from which commuters
travel to workplaces in the urban core," postsuburbs have a distinct business,
cultural, and residential life distinct and autonomous from nearby urban centers (5). Hallmarks of Orange County as a postsuburb include "distinct and
separate centers: residential neighborhoods, shopping malls, and industrial
parks" often separated by drive times ranging from fifteen to thirty minutes
(ix). This decentralization and division of social spaces has important implications for the possibilities and forms of community created in Orange County
from the postwar to the present. Debra Gold Hansen and Mary P. Ryan (1991)
argue that "the paucity of sustained social connection between residents
handicaps [Orange County residents] in their attempt to create a local iden-

tity, common belief system, and homegrown values" (165). Postsuburban de-centralization and division of social spaces creates new contexts for the forma-tion of community and fosters new practices and forms of community.

Japanese Americans are, of course, not the only Asian Americans to seek ethnic-community maintenance or to be impacted by the postsuburb. How-ever, Japanese American suburban formations differ from those of Chinese Americans in the San Gabriel Valley or Vietnamese Americans in Orange County, who exist within ethnoburbs that draw residential, business, and community organization concentrations to a singular geographic location (Li 2009). Importantly, the concepts of postsuburb and ethnoburb describe two distinct phenomena in residential development, but are not mutually exclusive. Both exist at the periphery of the urban center, but the postsuburb is not fundamentally tied to a particular racial or ethnic formation. The postsuburb simply describes dispersed development that creates cultural, social, and political centers autonomous of the urban core. On the other hand, ethnoburbs are ethnic residential and business concentrations in a suburban setting (Li 2009). Hypothetically, an ethnoburb could exist within a postsuburban development. The Japanese American case in postsuburban Southern California, however, does not constitute an ethnoburb. The Japa-nese Americans in this study are not geographically concentrated in residence or business. Chinese American and Vietnamese American ethnoburbs help to temper the postsuburban effects on ethnic-community formation, miti-gating the need for extended travel times to suburban- and urban-ethnic institutions or the seeking of community by happenstance.[1]

The impacts of distance are more exaggerated for Japanese Americans in Orange County attempting to build ethnic community as the vast majority do not live in neighborhood clusters as they had before their World War II incarceration. However, as Hansen and Ryan (1991) rightly point out in their study of public celebrations in Orange County, the greater dispersion and "reduced" social interactions do not eliminate the possibility of public life and community building. Rather, the postsuburban reality urges Orange County residents to consider alternative forms of connections and concep-tions of community. In seeking and building community, middle-class Jap-anese Americans in south Los Angeles and Orange Counties must navigate ethnic dispersal compounded by the postsuburban realities of travel times and decentralized community institutions to fulfill social necessities. As such, the Southern California Japanese American population offers a unique perspective on the development of suburban minority cultures of mobility.

Building Japanese American Community in the Postsuburb

Following the mass 1950s migration of white flight, upwardly mobile Japa-nese Americans took advantage of the new residential developments on the urban periphery participating in the suburbanization of Southern California. Between 1950 and 1960, the Japanese American population in Orange County more than tripled from 1,186 to 3,890. The population continued to grow rapidly to 10,645 in 1970 and 21,841 in 1980 (Orange County [hereinafter OC] Almanac 2004–2006a). As immigration from Japan did not significantly increase following the end of the U.S. ban on Japanese immigration in 1952, most of this growth was attributable to domestic migration into the county's new suburban developments. Japanese Americans were the largest ethnic minority population in the county through 1970 (OC Almanac 2004–2006a).

Despite the growing size of the Japanese American population in Orange County throughout the postwar period, residential clusters of Japanese Americans did not develop. Movement into the suburbs of south Los Angeles and Orange Counties resulted in the dispersal of the Japanese American community into predominantly white neighborhoods. While such trends may be marked as successful spatial assimilation, such dispersion and residential integration did not negate concerted efforts on the part of Japanese Americans to maintain local ethnic-community ties. Japanese Americans in south Los Angeles County and Orange County react to their residential integration and the dispersed reality of their local ethnic community in at least two ways. First, similar to their urban counterparts, suburban Japanese Americans rely on local ethnic institutions to bring them together (Kurashige 2002; Matsumoto 2014). While they may not share neighborhoods, my respondents reported traveling rather significant distances to interact with other Japanese Americans through community institutions and organizations. Second, Japanese Americans were also able to find each other through nonethnic-specific means. Whether through "mainstream" community organizations, school, or places of employment, Japanese Americans gravitated toward each other based on perceived commonalities in experience and culture.

The Continuing Importance of Ethnicity

Before demonstrating the ethnic-community-seeking practices of millennial yonsei, I will briefly address some of the impetuses of such practices. In short, why do yonsei continue to seek out community with other Japanese Americans? While answers to this question may be highly personal and varied, I find two frequently recurring reasons among the yonsei participating in this study: racial microaggressions and a sense of comfort.

Yonsei continue to experience overt and covert forms of racism in their daily lives. Most frequently, respondents commented on racial microaggressions, which often positioned them as forever foreigners despite their advanced generation, high levels of acculturation, and middle-class socioeconomic position (Tuan 1999). Importantly, such frequent racial incidences are directly and indirectly tied to middle-class status and suburban location, both place middle-class minorities into higher rates of contact with white peers (Patillo-McCoy 1999). In separate interviews, both Jennifer and Andrew express how their racialized appearance continues to mediate how others view and treat them.

> Jennifer: They see someone who looks like a certain race. They don't see your ethnicity, your generation, your background, your family. All they see is your race. So they'll say things like, "We love the way she looks when you guys are ice-skating." Or "We love Panda Express." Or "Oh, have you ever had dim sum before?" And it's so funny, because I'll tell them that's not actually the right culture, but it's just, I think, that that's the first thing people see.
>
> Andrew: I guess I've always felt that, no matter what, no matter how I act, the job that I have, the clothes that I wear, I still always look Asian, you know, and I feel like that because you will always be treated like that. I feel like that for me, even if I became like a successful multimillionaire, right? I would be seen as like, "Oh, that one Asian guy, you know, who is a successful multimillionaire."

Andrew and Jennifer express how race continues to be a central part of their identities, in large part because of how they are perceived by others. Their racialization as Asian and other is inescapable within predominantly white and middle-class spaces. Such microaggressions lead Japanese Americans to seek out community with co-ethnics as a form of respite. Among other Japanese Americans, as Jennifer might say, "your ethnicity, your generation, your background, your family," are more readily recognized and validated, not a struggle.

While racism and racial microaggressions may lead some yonsei to seek out ethnic community as a retreat from the racial hang-ups of mainstream society, other yonsei were not actively looking for a social escape. Rather, they appreciated the heightened level of comfort experienced with Japanese American peers a priori. Lacy (2007) similarly demonstrates this phenomenon among middle-class African Americans who seek out black communities and institutions because they are pleasurable in their own right. Clara expressed an overwhelming sense of comfort she feels among her Japanese American friends.

> Clara: With my Japanese American friends . . . I can act more like I do at home. Kind of like, I'll say a word in Japanese and you know what I'm talking about or like, make some rice guys and I'm making some rice. How much you want me to make? Or

things like that. It was really like, comfortable, and then with my other friends I'm not as. With Japanese friends, it's like more family and then like other friends it's kind of like, you're my friends, you're really my good friends, but I'm not going to act like I act at home.

In comparison to her non-Japanese American friends, Clara feels an added layer of comfort, understanding, and closeness with her Japanese American friends. Clara does not directly express experiences with microaggressions or racial hostility, but nonetheless appreciates the company and community of other Japanese Americans. Whether as refuge or for a sense of comfort, yonsei have ample reason to seek out other Japanese Americans. In the following sections, yonsei express the tremendous lengths they undertake in order to find community among Japanese Americans; a sense of community that is not afforded to them within the suburban middle-class neighborhoods where they grew up.

Postsuburban Traveling to Ethnic Institutions

Reflecting their postsuburban context, middle-class Japanese Americans in south Los Angeles and Orange Counties have become accustomed to traveling significant distances and utilizing decentralized community institutions to fulfill social necessities rather than rely on their immediate vicinity. These necessities continue to include social connections, often of the ethnic variety. Many Japanese Americans traveled considerable distances across the postsuburb to join other Japanese Americans in ethnic organizations and institutions. Most prominent among respondent recollections were Japanese American religious institutions such as Anaheim Free Methodist Church, Wintersburg Presbyterian Church, and Orange County Buddhist Church, and community organizations such as the Southeast Youth Organization (SEYO) basketball league, the local Japanese American Citizens League chapter, Suburban Optimists Club, and Orange Coast Optimists. While ethnic institutions exist within the postsuburban development of Orange and southern Los Angeles Counties, their service areas are much wider than their urban counterparts because of their more geographically dispersed memberships.

Laura, a sansei, spoke extensively about her own exploration of her ethnic identity and community seeking as an adolescent coming of age in suburban Cerritos in the 1970s. However, now as a mother, she also expressed her eagerness to support her own millennial daughter's community pursuits. Now living in Redondo Beach, Laura shared her participation in various churches, finally settling into a Japanese American church some thirty miles away from their home.

Laura: The church we go to in Anaheim, Anaheim Free Methodist, is primarily Asian. Most of our friends there are Asian. We went to church [near our home]. Mostly those friends are a mix, Mexicans, and I'm still very close to those friends.[2]

Interviewer: And what made you interested in traveling to a church all the way in Anaheim?

Laura: My daughter made some friends there. She went to a church camp, it was predominantly Asian, and she met some friends from Anaheim. She visited the church, and we just kept visiting that church. So we ended up going there primarily, and it's because I think she felt a part of the community more. I think, growing up around here, she didn't think of herself as really being Asian as part of her identity so much, except for family things. And then she started to build that part of her identity. The next generation, they seek to discover, and then to further that goal of identity. They still want to feel close and feel comfortable than with those that have some other background.

Laura's Redondo Beach neighborhood is ethnically diverse, a hallmark of Japanese American residential integration. However, Laura and her daughter choose to travel the extensive distance to church because it enables community building with other Japanese Americans. Laura's desire to support her daughter's pursuit of ethnic community was common among sansei parents, who often wanted their millennial yonsei children to enjoy the same community support they experienced in their childhood. As Laura stated, she is willing to commute such distances so her daughter and the rest of her family could join ethnic institutions membered by Japanese Americans and other Asian Americans and feel more part of the community. Community has a continued importance for her own sense of identity as well as for the sense of identity and community for her millennial yonsei daughter.

Religious ethnic institutions serve as destinations in the seeking and building of community among many other yonsei respondents as well. Jonathan, a yonsei, and his family attended the same church as Laura and her daughter and traveled the same distance, but from the opposite direction. He stated, "My parents commuted to Anaheim from Lake Forest, which is about thirty miles, every Friday, Saturday, and Sunday, to participate in activities with Orange County Methodist Church." Crystal, a multiracial yonsei who grew up in La Habra, highlighted her childhood church as a site for building Japanese American community. However, this church was not located in her neighborhood. Rather, her family traveled over fifteen miles and over half an hour at least once per week to attend a church with a Japanese American congregation. According to Crystal, "I went to church in Montebello, and our church was a historic Japanese American church—and I also played basketball, so those were my two Japanese American outlets, although, granted, I didn't appreciate that or think about it."

Similar to Laura and Jonathan, Crystal's family's commitment to attend this particular church extended beyond just religion. The willingness to travel such distances is intimately attached to their desire for ethnic community housed within the religious institution. As previously discussed, ethnic community provided a sense of comfort and, at times, a refuge from being racialized in mainstream society. Such religious institutions also provided other activities and mechanisms for community building with other Japanese Americans. As Crystal alludes, basketball is a popular activity often attached to church affiliation. Japanese American basketball leagues have long been a site for community maintenance, with many stretching back to the years following World War II and the closure of the internment camps (King 2002 and Christina Chin's chapter in this volume). Yonsei Henry, who played in a Japanese American basketball league throughout his childhood, goes so far as to equate playing basketball with being yonsei and Japanese American: "I grew up playing SEYO basketball. I still have friends from there when I was a teenager. . . . If you're a yonsei, you play basketball. If you grew up in Orange County, that's pretty much it."

This is a sentiment shared by many of my yonsei respondents, speaking to the ubiquity of such leagues and ethnic community in the experience of fourth-generation Japanese Americans in the suburbs. For Henry, the decision to play in the Japanese American basketball league was not based on the lack of recreational leagues available to him closer to home. Rather, he continued to play with, and later coach, his Japanese American team because of the deep sense of community that developed, a community lacking in more local leagues. Similar to participation in various churches, Crystal and Henry's basketball participation require considerable travel time within the Orange County postsuburb. To attend games, practices, and tournaments, Crystal and Henry's travel time ranged from fifteen to forty-five minutes, well outside the immediate neighborhoods they grew up in.

Beyond basketball, Japanese American religious institutions also provide other community facilitating activities. Similar to basketball, these activities often reflect a hyper-Americanism, such as the Boy and Girl Scouts. Additionally, Japanese American religious institutions were not always Christian. Amber, a yonsei from Long Beach, grew up playing basketball and attending Girl Scouts at the Orange County Buddhist Church, some twenty-five miles away in Anaheim. "I never noticed that they [my parents] tried to when I was younger. I mean, I didn't realize it, but I was involved with the Japanese community just being involved in that Japanese league, the basketball league. That church was all Japanese. My Girl Scout troop was all Japanese. I thought that all Girl Scout troops did this. . . . They say 'Namu amida butsu' [a Buddhist chant meaning "I follow Amida Buddha"]. I thought that was, like, a standard thing for Girl Scout troops."

Amber did not realize while growing up that she was participating in any ethnic specific community. For her, these were simply mundane after-school and weekend activities. She thought they were the same for everyone else regardless of ethnic and racial background. In this way, Japanese American community and ethnicity were naturalized as part of Amber's upbringing. Such naturalized ethnic connections are a far cry from the full assimilation allegedly achieved by later-generation Japanese American. For Amber and other yonsei, their spatial assimilation, represented by their residence in sub-urban Southern California outside of ethnic concentrations, does not mark an end for the importance of ethnic identity and community. Their willing-ness to travel such distances to regularly participate in ethnic religious insti-tutions and affiliated activities is a testament to the realities of postsuburban life and the level of importance such community formations hold.

Institutions, such as those utilized by Laura, Crystal, Henry, and Amber, are noted throughout my sample of millennial yonsei who grew up in the Orange County suburbs, as well as their sansei parents. While these long-standing institutions have certainly undergone internal changes from the time they were membered by nisei and sansei, their remarkable longevity speaks to the continued interest and need for such organization by dispersed suburban Japanese Americans. The long-term existence and continued par-ticipation by yonsei in ethnic-specific organizations with the intended pur-pose of cultivating ethnic community and identity further reinforces the shortcomings of their structural assimilation. Some scholars have noted that some processes of assimilation may be delayed for some ethnic and racial minority groups, but will occur eventually (Bean and Stevens 2003; Brown 2007). While this statement may be utilized to allay fears of the unassimi-lable minority, it remains important to recognize the structural and institu-tional factors that lead such delays to occur along racial lines. Furthermore, as racial disparities are examined across multiple generations, it is equally important to question the notion of "delay" and the a priori assumption of assimilation as an end goal. Yonsei in this study make a strong case for the persistent value of ethnic community, against the assimilationist imperative of ethnic attenuation.

Traveling to the Urban Ethnic Enclave

While reliance upon postsuburban ethnic institutions are prevalent among millennial yonsei, respondents also noted the ethnically concentrated busi-ness and residential communities further north in Los Angeles County, such as Gardena, the Crenshaw district, and Little Tokyo, as sites of ethnic con-nection. In this way, the urban center continues to play a role in ethnic iden-tity and community formation for postsuburban youth. For other respondents who grew up in the greater Los Angeles postsuburban development, the ethnically concentrated communities only served as destinations for the occasional day trip to stock up on Japanese foodstuffs or participate in annual festivals or sporting events. These communities were too far to serve as consistent hubs for ethnic community interaction. For other postsuburban yonsei, the long commute times did not deter them from utilizing urban enclaves like Little Tokyo as sites for identity and community development. Returning to the words of Crystal, the mixed-race yonsei who grew up in La Habra and played basketball with her Japanese American church in Montebello, she did not feel that she really developed an ethnic consciousness until she began to work in Little Tokyo during college, despite her heavy involvement with Japanese American organizations as a child: "Growing up, I think that—well, through basketball, but it wasn't about identity, even though it really should be. I think the leagues should work on that. It was just about basketball and snacks after basketball and playing in tournaments. You don't really discuss identity . . . I didn't start doing Japanese American stuff until I did the Nikkei Community Internship Program [in Little Tokyo, Downtown Los Angeles]."

Crystal's childhood participation in numerous Japanese American institutions put her into direct contact with many co-ethnics. However, she did not perceive the experience as directly building her ethnic identity and consciousness. She did not feel such consciousness develop until much later in her life. Crystal's words, echoing Amber's earlier discussion of Girl Scout meetings at the Orange County Buddhist Church, demonstrates how ethnic associations are seen as mundane parts of everyday life. While the basketball league may have been seen as little more than sports and postgame snacks to a young Crystal, the league is nonetheless part of a rich local Japanese American history and fostered the continuation of ethnic community for contemporary Japanese Americans. For Crystal, a stronger meaning and attachment to her Japanese American identity and the building of ethnic community came during college as she explored the historic Little Tokyo as an intern. Crystal's college experience marked the beginning of her career working in Little Tokyo institutions and developing Japanese American youth programs throughout Southern California.

As yonsei seek out community in distant urban ethnic enclaves, often up to fifty miles away, it is not simply because they feel absolutely marginalized within their local, often predominantly white, communities. But, as Jason notes below, even with some semblance of belonging, yonsei often spoke of melancholy: feeling a part, yet apart (Cheng 2000): "I didn't feel marginal or on the outside [in my local neighborhood]. I had a good time hanging out with the high school folks, the white folks, but somehow there was a need also to connect with other Japanese Americans and Asian Americans. So that's why we went up to Gardena and Torrance or the beach at 22nd Street. Something probably was missing that I couldn't name." For Jason, his local belonging did not negate his need to connect with other Japanese Americans. Reflecting the simple pleasure and comfort of being around and forming community among other Japanese Americans, Jason continued to seek out co-ethnics despite some sense of belonging among his predominantly white neighborhood and school peers. Furthermore, to find other Japanese Americans, Jason traveled significant distances to areas with higher concentrations of Japanese American residents or locations known to be Japanese American youth hangouts, underscoring the importance of such relationships. As Crystal and Jason demonstrate, the ethnic urban center continues to hold a sacred place for the Japanese American community, even within the postsuburb. Whether through postsuburban sites or within the urban ethnic enclaves, the normalization of ethnic community in the lives of these millennial yonsei again points to the continuing importance of racialized ethnicity and the failed promise of structural assimilation.

Community by Happenstance: Non-Ethnic Paths to Ethnic Community

While the majority of my respondents participated in Japanese American organizations or institutions in some fashion as a way to connect with co-ethnics, these spaces were by no means the only locations for ethnic community building. Alongside participation in Japanese American organizations and institutions, many yonsei were simultaneously active in mainstream, or predominantly white, organizations both within their communities and through school. However, even within these predominantly white spaces, Japanese Americans found each other. My respondents note that they gravitated toward the other Japanese Americans they came into contact with by happenstance. Similar to the targeted travel to ethnic institutions, yonsei gravitated toward other Japanese Americans because of the sense of comfort and refuge from racial microaggressions they provided. Yonsei sisters Natalie and Elizabeth stated, "I think that that's kind of the theme for us, that everything kind of just happens by chance. We don't—we're never out seeking like to be part of the community." As an example of this, Elizabeth shared a story of how she was recruited to be part of a Japanese American basketball team at a birthday party for a non–Japanese American friend from school: "I was at a birthday party and the coach's daughter happened to be at this birthday party. I didn't know her at all. She said, 'Are you Japanese?' So, I said, 'Yes.' And so, yeah. I talked to my mom at the end of the birthday party and I started playing basketball." Kristina, a multiracial yonsei, also highlights this trend of happenstance: "I played soccer in junior college and this is where I met Tracy [another Japanese American] and played soccer with her, and I'd say we kind of hit it off right away. So just like okay you play soccer and we're like, two or three Asian girls on the team so, you know, you tend to bond right away. So she was probably one of the first Japanese American people that I stayed in touch with for most of my life, for a good amount of years. Almost eight years later, you know, she's one of the longer friends that I've had." Ethnic background, coupled with the common interest in soccer and personality, provides Kristina and Tracy an additional layer of commonality that leads to a lasting relationship originating in a nonethnic connection, a college soccer team. Kristina could relate to Tracy through their common interest in soccer and as teammates, but was able to create a stronger and more lasting relationship with Tracy in comparison to other, non–Japanese American, women on the team. Kristina's reflection on her friendship with Tracy demonstrates that even within participation in mainstream organizations and cliques, which is a hallmark of structural assimilation, race and ethnicity continue to matter for Japanese Americans.

Carrie, who also played soccer at the collegiate level, discussed whether the racial and ethnic background of her teammates impacted the type of bond she was able to build with them. "We played soccer, so we're friends. But I think it's easier to make friends when they're the same race as you, just because there's not a lot of Japanese people, so you tend to be like, 'Oh, there's another Japanese person!' You don't meet that many. It isn't like everybody's Chinese. It's like, 'Oh, it's just another Chinese person.' Here it's like, 'Oh, it's another Japanese person,' so you're actually like—and it's kind of racist or whatever you want to say, I was Lauren's host [another Japanese American player] when she came on her training trip, probably because I was Asian, they put the two Asian people together." The obvious bond between teammates transcended race for Carrie. However, she also noted that finding other Japanese American players enabled a stronger and more enduring bond, in part because it was so rare to come across other Japanese Americans. Carrie's experience also demonstrates the ways in which the importance of ethnic bonds is also ascribed by outsiders. The coaching staff of Carrie's team housed a Japanese American recruit with her. While such placement may have been unintentional, Carrie interpreted the move as somewhat racist, lumping the Asian Americans on the team together. Such an imposition highlights the ways in which Japanese Americans cannot simply fade into the American melting pot. They continued to be a racially marked other, far from completing the assimilation process of social whitening (Gans 2005).

While Carrie's collegiate friendships were diverse, it was also apparent that some of her relationships took on a heightened relevance because of ethnic similarities. She did not gravitate toward other Japanese American athletes simply because of practices of racial lumping by coaches. Aside from her continued friendship with Lauren, Carrie was able to name several other Japanese American friendships. Reflecting on her interracial interactions and friendships, Carrie stated: "I don't know that I would be in contact with anybody else that wasn't white. Jon's white, but also half Asian [Japanese]. Other than that, Dave, he's half Japanese, too. I think that's it. There's not that many Asian people in sports, so that's also a problem." As Carrie spoke about these friendships, she did not state that such relationships were based on shared ethnic background. They were formed more through happenstance, but certainly demonstrated a larger pattern of an underlying ethnic affinity. The fact that the Japanese American and Asian American student-athletes found each other is especially noteworthy given their relatively small number, as noted by both Carrie and Kristina.

As postsuburban and residentially integrated lives place considerable distance between co-ethnics, yonsei must often rely on happenstance and nonethnic-specific means to find other Japanese Americans. Again and again, yonsei in my sample commented on the excitement and sense of immediate connection felt with other Japanese Americans they would meet through school, local organizations, and sports teams. Such reaction to the rare find of other Japanese Americans does not point to a reduced salience of ethnicity for Japanese Americans, but rather to something that is constantly being sought out in the unlikeliest of places.

Conclusion

Despite yonsei residential integration and achievement of spatial assimilation in the postsuburb, Japanese American identity and community take on a sense of ubiquity and mundanity. While ethnicity is normalized, there remains an intentionality in community formation practices as millennial yonsei travel to ethnic institutions in the postsuburb and urban ethnic enclaves and seek out other Japanese Americans in traditionally nonethnic spaces. This ethnic normativity is a far cry from the symbolic and optional ethnicity that should be presented by later-generation ethnic Americans, according to assimilation theory (Alba 1985; Gans 2005). Importantly, later-generation Japanese Americans are not resisting assimilation, acculturation, or a more symbolic practice of ethnicity. As established in countless previous studies, Japanese Americans have on average achieved high levels of socioeconomic success and middle-class, if not upper-middle-class, status. The high level of postsuburban residential integration demonstrated by my respondents is another testament to this fact. However, the persistent racial othering of Japanese Americans prevents full assimilation. For later-generation Japanese Americans, their ethnicity coupled with their race continues to structure their lives and impact relationship and community building.

Returning to the work on minority cultures of mobility and the minority middle class (Neckerman, Carter, and Lee 1999; Pattillo-McCoy 1999; Lacy 2007; Aguis-Vallejo 2012), ethnic and cultural practices by middle-class minorities clearly impact and structure their daily lives in meaningful ways.

Minority cultures of mobility, then, are not simply an extension of assimilation theory but also offer a new way to understand how a consequential ethnicity persists among upwardly mobile minorities. Residential integration does not signal the "twilight of ethnicity" for later-generation Japanese Americans as they continue to make concerted efforts to maintain ethnic community outside of their immediate neighborhoods and often travel significant distances to do so (Alba 1985). By seeking community in these ways, Japanese Americans exemplify practices of minority cultures of mobility.

Japanese American community formations represent an ethnic practice and minority culture of mobility that move beyond the symbolic for the later generations. To be clear, the formation of ethnic-specific community spaces by Japanese Americans does not diminish the fact that they are often active participants in other, nonethnic specific communities. They hold multiple community memberships. Nonetheless, ethnic community continues to be one of these multiple communities of membership for later-generation Japanese Americans, one that has a significant impact on their lives. Members of my sample proved themselves to be upwardly mobile, and at the time of the interview nearly all my respondents were solidly middle class. Japanese American culture of mobility is evident in terms of reaction to increased interactions with whites in public settings and their community formation practices with co-ethnics. This culture is carried out in community formation practices that have Japanese Americans traveling significant, often inconvenient, distances to ethnic institutions or seeking out other Japanese Americans in nonethnic spaces and organizations. As demonstrated throughout this study, building community and relationships with other Japanese Americans remains important for my respondents' sense of self and place within U.S. society. Connections with other later-generation Japanese Americans allow respondents to understand their personal racialized experience with marginalization as part of a broader pattern of systemic racism rather than aberrations within a postracial, color-blind nation. In this way, ethnic community and relationships are cultural practices that pave the way for an increased sense of belonging to both broader local and national communities.

NOTES

1. The existence of Asian American ethnoburbs and other Asian American–ethnic groups certainly impacts the ethnic identity and community formation practices of Japanese Americans. Japanese Americans interact quite frequently with other Asian Americans in Southern California because of their overlapping geographic and class locations. Elsewhere, I argue that such proximity highlights comparisons and lumping with other Asian Americans, leading to a common racialization as forever foreign. In response to Asian racialization, Japanese Americans undertake explicit identity work to distinguish themselves from other Asian Americans and maintain their ethnic-specific communities (Nakano Forthcoming).

2. While Laura references the church membership as generically "Asian," Anaheim Free Methodist Church is historically Japanese American, and the majority of its members continue to be Japanese American.

REFERENCES

Aguis-Vallejo, Jody. 2012. *Barrio to Burbs: The Making of the Mexican American Middle Class.* Stanford, CA: Stanford University Press.

Alba, Richard D. 1985. *Italian Americans: Into the Twilight of Ethnicity.* New York: Prentice Hall.

Alba, Richard D., and Victor Nee. 2003. *Remaking the American Mainstream: Assimilation and Contemporary Immigration.* Cambridge, MA: Harvard University Press.

Bean, Frank D., and Gillian Stevens. 2003. *America's Newcomers and the Dynamics of Diversity.* New York: Russell Sage Foundation.

Bratter, Jenifer, and Tufuku Zuberi. 2008. "As Racial Boundaries 'Fade': Racial Stratification and Interracial Marriage." In *White Logic, White Methods: Racism and Methodology,* edited by Tufuku Zuberi and Eduardo Bonilla-Silva, 251–270. Lanham, MD: Rowman and Littlefield.

Brown, Susan K. 2007. "Delayed Spatial Assimilation: Multigenerational Incorporation of the Mexican-Origin Population in Los Angeles." *City and Community* 6:193–209.

Charles, Camille Zubrinsky. 2007. "Comfort Zones: Immigration, Acculturation, and the Neighborhood Racial-Composition Preferences of Latinos and Asians." *Du Bois Review: Social Science Research on Race* 4:41–77.

Cheng, Anne Anlin. 2000. *The Melancholy of Race: Psychoanalysis, Assimilation, and Hidden Grief.* New York: Oxford University Press.

Fugita, Stephen S., and David J. O'Brien. 1994. *Japanese American Ethnicity: The Persistence of Community.* Seattle: University of Washington Press.

Gans, Herbert J. 2005. "Race as Class." *Contexts* 4(4): 17–21

Gordon, Milton M. 1964. *Assimilation in American Life: The Role of Race, Religion and National Origins.* New York: Oxford University Press.

Hansen, Debra Gold, and Mary P. Ryan. 1991. "Public Ceremony in a Private Culture: Orange County Celebrates the Fourth of July." In *Postsuburban California: The Transformation of Orange County since World War II,* edited by Rob Kling, Spence C. Olin, and Mark Poster, 165–189. Berkeley: University of California Press.

King-O'Riain, Rebecca Chiyoko. 2006. *Pure Beauty: Judging Race in Japanese American Beauty Pageants.* Minneapolis: University of Minnesota Press.

Kling, Rob, Spencer C. Olin, and Mark Poster. 1991. *Postsuburban California: The Transformation of Orange County since World War II.* Berkeley: University of California Press.

Kurashige, Lon. 2002. *Japanese American Celebration and Conflict: A History of Ethnic Identity and Festival, 1934–1990.* Berkeley: University of California Press.

Lacy, Karyn R. 2007. *Blue-Chip Black: Race, Class, and Status in the New Black Middle Class.* Berkeley: University of California Press.

Li, Wei. 2009. *Ethnoburb: The New Ethnic Community in Urban America.* Honolulu: University of Hawai'i Press.

Massey, Douglas S., and Nancy A. Denton. 1993. *American Apartheid: Segregation and the Making of the Underclass.* Cambridge, MA: Harvard University Press.

Matsumoto, Valerie J. 2014. *City Girls: The Nisei Social World in Los Angeles, 1920–1950.* New York: Oxford University Press.

Nakano, Dana Y. Forthcoming. "The Racial Replenishment of Ethnicity: Asian Immigration and the Persistence of Japanese American Community."

Neckerman, Kathryn M., Prudence Carter, and Jennifer Lee. 1999. "Segmented Assimilation and Minority Cultures of Mobility." *Ethnic and Racial Studies* 22:945–965.

Olin, Spencer C. 1989. "Community in Orange County: Historians' Perspective: Reconceptualizing Community in the Information Age." In *Conference of Orange County History*, edited by L. Estes and R. Slayton, 138–140. Orange, CA: Chapman College.

Orange County Almanac. 2004–2006a. "Historical Census of Race/Ethnicity in Orange County 1890 to 1960." OCAlmanac.com. Accessed March 18, 2011. http://www.ocalmanac.com/Population/po20.htm.

Pattillo-McCoy, Mary. 1999. *Black Picket Fences: Privilege and Peril among the Black Middle Class.* Chicago: University of Chicago Press.

Spickard, Paul R. 2009. *Japanese Americans: The Formation and Transformations of an Ethnic Group.* Rev. ed. New Brunswick, NJ: Rutgers University Press.

PART II

SPIRITUALITIES

4

Redefining "Camp" in Protestant Japanese America

DEAN RYUTA ADACHI

On February 19, 1942, President Franklin D. Roosevelt signed Executive Order 9066 that led to the relocation of all one hundred twenty thousand Japanese Americans living in the western United States into concentration camps. Today, historians consider this blemish in American civil rights to be perhaps the defining moment of the Japanese American community. Despite an overwhelming national distrust in their loyalty, Japanese Americans used the concentration camps as a rallying point for unity and justice. This incarceration of Japanese Americans has led to the popular joke that states, "You know you're Japanese when you know that 'camp' doesn't refer to a cabin in the woods." However, for today's generation of Japanese American youths—who themselves are multiple generations removed from the internment experience—"camp" may in fact refer to the weeklong highlight of their summers, ironically, spent in a cabin in the woods.

Each July, over one hundred Japanese American youths spend a week together at the Northern California Japanese Christian Church Federation's (NCJCCF's) Junior High Camp. In August, another one-hundred-plus Japanese American youths attend the United Methodist Church's Asian American Summer Camp. These young Japanese Americans come from a network of historically Japanese American United Methodist churches located throughout the western United States. While the youths attend Junior High Camp and Asian American Summer Camp to grow and develop as young Christians, they also use the camps as a vehicle to connect with others youths within the greater Japanese American community. As today's Japanese American youth population is widely dispersed and primarily of the fourth, fifth, and even sixth generations, these youths have few opportunities in their daily lives to interact with other Japanese Americans and establish a group identity. These thriving youth camps present opportunities for young Japanese Americans to define their identity as individuals, as Christians, and as Japanese Americans.

This essay examines the long history of Japanese American Christian youth camps and studies two remaining contemporary examples within the United Methodist Church to illustrate their current role in fostering a physical space for the establishment and growth of today's increasingly heterogenous Japanese American youth communities. These camps provide a physical space to instill a common identity for Japanese American youths that are easily classified as Asian Americans, but perhaps facing difficulties in emotionally identifying as such. Despite the growing distance between yonsei (fourth-generation), gosei (fifth-generation), and rokusei (sixth-generation) youths and the language, culture, and traditions of their immigrant issei (first-generation) predecessors, I argue that today's young Japanese Americans are attracted to these camps to (1) build and maintain their own ever-expanding and increasingly diverse Japanese American networks, (2) identify the evolving definitions and markers for Japanese America, and (3) discover avenues of individual and group expression in an increasingly globalized society. Additionally, these camps provide a uniquely Japanese American version of Protestant Christianity for them to identify with.

The Role of Religion within Japanese America

As Japanese Americans dispersed from Japantowns, "the one place where the Japanese American community continued to evolve was within the churches" (Asakawa 2004, 94). According to Stephen Fugita and David O'Brien (1991), "The most important voluntary associations in Japanese American communities are the churches. Despite the high degree of structural assimilation in many areas of life, most Japanese Americans who attend a church belong to a congregation whose members are of the same ethnic background. What is perhaps most striking about this situation is the high degree of continuity across generations and across rural and urban areas even though there are substantial differences in affiliation with Buddhist versus Christian churches" (43–44).

Religion has a unique importance within Japanese America. Buddhism—specifically Jodo Shinshu, or Pure Land Buddhism—was the dominant religion for the immigrant issei due to the rituals concerning birth, marriage, and death (Yoo 2002, 121). Paul Spickard (1996) states that "religion was not a regular activity in the schedule of most people, but it was an important part of one's identity linking one to a web of relationships in one's family and community" (154). Throughout the history of Japanese in the United States, increasing numbers of Japanese Americans began to convert to Protestant Christianity, which has long been the dominant religion in the United States. David Yoo (2002) stresses the importance of the relationship between religion and race as a "persistent force in the lives of Japanese Americans that accentuated a lasting marker of difference" (122). In other words, despite the fundamental theological differences between Japanese American Buddhists and Japanese American Christians, both religious groups played similar and important roles in terms of promoting the social well-being of their members, who continued to be racialized by the mainstream American society.

Religion in general has been essential to the development of Japanese America. Historian Yuji Ichioka (1988) was one of the first to highlight the social services provided by Protestant missionaries that facilitated issei settlement in the United States (16–19). Following the Gentleman's Agreement of 1907 that limited the immigration of laborers, women became the primary immigrants. With this new immigrant demographic came the second generation, as well as several prominent markers of ethnic communities, such as Japanese language newspapers, schools, and religious institutions (Yoo 2002, 123). As a result of the discriminatory policies and other hardships that made life difficult for Japanese Americans, many of the issei and their nisei children were able to find refuge and hope collectively in their religious communities.

In the early twentieth century, the Japanese American Buddhist temples and Christian churches catered to the development of young Japanese American life, both "religious and otherwise" (Yoo 2002, 126). From language schools that served as "initial sites of contact with the faith" to social organization such as the Young Buddhist Association (YBA) and Young People's Christian Conference (YPCC), which were the primary social spaces for niseis, these institutions allowed young Japanese Americans "to craft ways of seeing their world and their place in it" and "cope with harsh realities of marginalization they encountered" (127).

Stereotypically, Japanese America is assumed to be primarily Buddhist. In the early 1930s, a Stanford University survey stated that 78 percent of Japanese Americans were Buddhist, while 18 percent identified as Christian (Strong 1934, 168–170). By 1942, 68 percent of issei and 49 percent of nisei claimed affiliation with Buddhism, while 22 percent of issei and 35 percent of nisei with Christianity (Kurashige 2002, 31). In 2001, 24 percent of Japanese Americans identified with Buddhism, as opposed to 43 percent claiming Christianity (Lien 2004, 50). Interestingly, according to a Pew Research Center study in 2012, Japanese American Christians have dropped to 38 percent, but still remain more prevalent than the 25 percent that identify as Buddhist (Pew 2012). These statistics attest to the changing dominant religious identity for Japanese Americans. This change raises the question as to how the Japanese American community has voluntarily embraced Christianity in such large numbers. According to Russell Jeung (2005),

> the Christian Church provided institutional space where they could practice their faith as both [Japanese] and Americans. The missions initially started with efforts to Americanize the immigrants, so their activities paralleled other American churches, with Sunday schools, temperance efforts, youth leagues, scout troops, and choirs. Because the immigrants instead took control of the congregations, especially to further nationalist efforts, their children grew up in churches that valued the members' primordial roots. Within this ethnic institution, the second generation received not only language instruction but also cultural training to maintain their sense of cultural loyalty. Watershed historical moments, especially Japanese American wartime internment . . . suppressed transnational political ties. Although the native-born generations became both culturally and structurally assimilated into American society, they still retained an ethnic identity organized around ethnic institutions and cultural hybridity. (25)

Rather than Japanese Americans discarding their cultural traditions by assimilating to American Christianity, a specific Japanese American Christianity emerged to fill the needs of their racially isolated community.

The United Methodist Church in particular has a long history within the Japanese American community. Kanichi Miyama was the first Japanese immigrant to the United States to be baptized a Christian in a San Francisco Methodist church in 1877. In addition to becoming the first Japanese American ordained minister, he was an influential leader throughout both California and Hawai'i. Miyama organized other young immigrant students to create the first voluntary Japanese American organization and later founded the first Japanese American church of any religious affiliation. In fact, his Japanese Methodist Mission in San Francisco was founded in 1886, thirteen years before the first Japanese American Buddhist Temple was constructed. In an effort to replicate Christian successes, Buddhists eventually adapted to their social setting and "made adjustments to soften their differences from Protestant Christianity. Leaders recoded much of the terminology and outward practices—temples were called 'churches' and priests, 'reverends'" (Yoo 2002, 125).

The issei attending Christian churches eventually encouraged the younger nisei to become involved as both participants and leaders in order to practice "a brand of Christianity that spoke to their specific needs as a racial-ethnic group as well as a generation." Within two generations of living in the United States, Japanese Americans were able to develop a number of church-based programs that became tightly integrated into the ethnic community. Summer conferences specifically targeted for youths are just one example of the Japanese American churches as an ethnic legacy. Thus, the issei and nisei began a cycle of ministry to new generations of Japanese Americans that continues to this day (Carnes and Yang 2004, 24).

As a result of certain historical events and the passage of several generations, Japanese America has become further diversified in several areas such as class, industry, geography, and even ethnic makeup. It is unfair—if not impossible—to make generalizations about this community that is pioneering the late-generation Asian American experience. Yet despite the multiple forces that could tear the community apart, Japanese American churches continue to serve their community and to adapt in order to address the needs of future generations.

A Brief History of Japanese American Christian Youth Retreats

As described in the following subsections, several long-established conferences, retreats, and camps have sustained Japanese American youths for generations.

The Young People's Christian Conference

The Northern California Young People's Christian Conference was the first Japanese American Christian youth conference. It took place on October 24–25, 1925, "to promote leadership, inspire a return to religion and fellowship . . . [and] share religious experiences and community concern" (Koga 1977, 108). While it was primarily the effort of Presbyterian missionary Dr. Ernest Adolphus Sturge, the leadership was composed of Japanese Americans such as Rev. Suzunosuke Kato, who "enabled the second generation to meet and to discuss issues that they faced together as Japanese Americans and as Christians" (Yoo 2002, 132). By 1926, "sectional YPCC's began to grow in the Bay Region, Sacramento Valley, Coast Region, Santa Clara Valley and Fresno areas" ("The 40 years I spent at the Lake" 1986). These conferences occurred regularly and fostered the congregation of young Japanese Americans that most likely would not meet otherwise. YPCC's popularity peaked during the late 1930s and early 1940s when they attracted from five to eight hundred attendees. Unfortunately, YPCC retreats were put on hold during World War II, since all of the Japanese Americans who would attend the retreats were interned.

The Lake Sequoia Retreat

Immediately after the internment years, young Japanese American Christians in California reestablished their annual retreats. While YPCC retreats continued until the 1960s, a new youth summer camp quickly rose in popularity for Japanese American youths. Former YPCC leaders organized the first annual Lake Sequoia Retreat on August 1–4, 1946. According to the Lake Sequoia Retreat Forty-Year Reunion event program, "the theme of the first camp was 'Teach Us to Build,' an appropriate message for young nisei who were struggling to rebuild their lives in the aftermath of the war." In 1960, the Lake Sequoia Retreat attracted one hundred ten nisei from sixteen churches across Northern California. By the 1970s, the annual camp had grown to over two hundred sansei—many who were children of the original YPCC or early Lake Sequoia Retreats—who came together from all part of California "to deepen one's spiritual life; to learn to help others to be Christian; and to promote Christian fellowship and friendship."

The Lake Sequoia Retreat had a history of adapting to the current social needs of its campers. For example, while the early camps addressed postwar nisei concerns, camp themes in the 1960s and 1970s were conscious of the rising issue of drugs while those of the 1980s spoke to a pan-ethnic Asian American identity. When the Lake Sequoia Retreat held its last annual camp in the mid-1980s, attendance had declined to around fifty. By then, a demographic shift began to dramatically change the ethnic complexion of Japanese American youths. After three or four generations of acculturation in the United States, rising intermarriage rates, and a heightened ethnic consciousness—as a result of both the emergent field of Asian American studies and the ongoing struggle for redress and reparations—encouraged young Japanese Americans to begin to explore different routes toward understanding and developing their dynamic ethnic identity. Despite attempts to continue updating the camp, the Lake Sequoia Retreat eventually gave way to a new, pan-Asian Christian youth summer camp.

United Methodist Asian American Summer Camp

In 1974, Rev. Peter Chen of San Jose Japantown's Wesley United Methodist Church and Rev. Harry Murakami of Livingston United Methodist Church created United Methodist Asian American Summer Camp (commonly referred to as "Asian Camp"). The new camp fulfilled a need that other summer camps of that era did not—in "speak[ing] to their unique experiences as ethnic minorities" ("About," n.d.). Chen also believed that "Asian-American youths could become a dynamic, powerful force within church once they became united as a group." Chen and Murakami collaborated with other Asian American United Methodist churches, rather than just Japanese American churches, in their efforts to contribute to the development of Asian America.

By 1980, Asian Camp's attendance reached over two hundred participants that represented churches from California, Hawai'i, Oregon, Colorado, and even some parts of the East Coast. Although the majority of the camp was of Japanese ancestry, Chinese, Fijian, Korean, Filipino, and Samoan ethnic groups were also present. According to the 1980 Asian Camp booklet,

Asian-Camp's rapid growth and success can be attributed to the fact that it is a Christian camp which dares to implement non-traditional Christian means in helping young people deal with the issues and problems which confront them in today's ever-changing world. The learning experiences presented at camp challenge each individual to critically examine his/her Asian identity, personal feelings towards self and others, and one's social responsibilities, all form a Christian perspective. While we may not necessarily be a "religious" camp, we have found a way to carry the message of Christianity in contemporary forms to Asian-American youths. ("History of Asian Camp" 1980)

Asian Camp's growth mirrored the development of the pan-ethnic Asian American identity that spawned during the late 1960s. However, attributable in large part to the different immigration patterns of non–Japanese Asian Americans and their subsequent growth in the United States, Asian Camp's target demographic has since changed from a pan-Asian group to primarily youth from Japanese American churches. Yet, Asian Camp's pan-Asian roots are instrumental in helping address issues that face today's increasingly multiethnic and multiracial Japanese American youths. Despite declining attendance during the mid- to late-1990s, when camp rosters regularly listed sixty to seventy campers, Asian Camp had a resurgent phase when 112 campers attended Asian Camp 2006. The increase in camper attendance can be attributed to increased participation from churches outside of California. This swing in geography has made Asian Camp less "California-centric" and is just one example of how Asian Camp is constantly evolving.

Despite structural changes in Asian Camp, its primary goal of creating a safe space for identity formation and social dialogue to occur has remained constant. This voice of fostering community growth is reflected in its current mission statement:

In its 42-year history of empowering and inspirational ministry, Asian Camp has developed a reputation amongst its participants as a family-like community, yielding lifelong relationships and faithful servants of God.

The mission of "Asian Camp" is to reach out to youth and young adults in our Asian American churches and communities, in an effort to lead them toward a closer relationship with Christ. Through worship, fellowship, prayer, growth groups, community builders, and other outdoor activities, Asian Camp encourages campers, as well as staff, to explore their faiths, reflect on their personal identities, and use their spiritual gifts for God's glory. With special focus on equipping for the future, Asian Camp seeks to instill pride in each camper's spiritual, cultural, and ethnic identity.

A hallmark of Asian Camp that sets it apart from other Christian summer camps is a tradition of creating its own programming, with inclusion of activities that focus on our Asian heritages and social justice issues relevant to today's youth. With every aspect of programming, Asian Camp aims to foster an atmosphere of love and acceptance, where youth feel secure in their personal identities, but are still challenged to be all that God has created them to be. Within this context, our intent is to create life-affirming experiences that will root Asian Camp participants in understanding of their relationships with God and their identity. (NJAUMC 2016)

By comparing the two Asian Camp quotations—separated by thirty-six years—one could argue that the voice of Asian Camp has become more "religious" in the 2006 mission statement. Yet, regardless of how the rhetoric concerning Asian Camp has evolved, socially positive messages that encourage community development and civic engagement have carried over through the decades as cultural boundaries that cannot be neglected.

NCJCCF Junior High Camp and Senior High Camp

During the 1960s, the Northern California Japanese Christian Church Federation sponsored a Junior High Camp and a Senior High Camp. Some of the churches that were instrumental in the development of these camps included Wesley United Methodist Church in San Jose, Aldersgate United Methodist in Palo Alto, Buena Vista United Methodist Church in Alameda, and Sacramento Japanese United Methodist Church in Sacramento. By creating two different camps to address the different issues facing junior high school–age youths versus high school–age youth, both of these camps quickly attracted significant groups of Japanese American youths from Northern California. Junior High Camp and Senior High Camp generally followed the formulas for a weeklong summer camp laid before them by predecessors such as the Lake Sequoia Retreat. In the 1980s, these two camps were primarily targeted for the new yonsei who were now reaching adolescence in their Japanese American Christian churches. By the late 1990s, Senior High Camp suffered from low camper attendance and ultimately folded because of competition with Asian Camp. Eventually, most of those involved with Senior High Camp aligned with Asian Camp. Meanwhile, Junior High Camp continued to operate and grow. In 2002, it began to outreach heavily to Southern California churches. In fact, in recent years, the campers from Southern California outnumbered those from Northern California at Junior High Camp.

Other Japanese American Christian Youth Camps

Some other examples of Japanese American Christian youth camps include the United Methodist Pacific Northwest Winter Youth Conference and the Mount Hermon Conference hosted by the Japanese Evangelical Missionary Society (JEMS). Both of these conferences have histories that span over half a century and continue to thrive to this day.

The United Methodist Pacific Northwest Winter Youth Conference originally catered to the Japanese American United Methodist churches in the Pacific Northwest Caucus, but has recently increased its outreach efforts to include the large numbers of Japanese American Christian youths from sister churches in California. Aside from occurring in December instead of the summer, Winter Youth Conference is unique in two key aspects. Rather than being held in California, the conference is hosted by one of five active Japanese American United Methodist Churches in the Pacific Northwest Caucus: (1) Blaine Memorial United Methodist Church in Seattle, Washington; (2) Epworth United Methodist Church in Portland, Oregon; (3) Simpson United Methodist Church in Arvada, Colorado; (4) Highland Park United Methodist Church in Spokane, Washington; and (5) Community United Methodist Church in Ontario, Oregon. Also, since the conferences take place at the churches rather than at remote campsites, the conference organizers usually coordinate a homestay with the church members.

Despite these differences, most of the structure for Winter Youth Conference is similar to the summer camps. For example, the junior high school– and high school–aged youths are assigned to small groups led by counselors, daily worship services are held, and a dance is given on the last night. Since Winter Youth Conference always takes place between Christmas and New Year's Day, it serves as a chance for those who attended the summer camps to reunite and rebuild their friendships without having to wait until the following summer.

As for the Mount Hermon Conference, it is now in its sixty-seventh year and hosts about fifteen hundred attendees from North America, Hawai'i, and even Japan (Koga 1977, 250; "Mount Hermon Conference" 2017). According to one Japanese American senior pastor, a falling out occurred between JEMS leadership and Japanese American United Methodist leadership. Thus, the Japanese Americans that attend Mount Hermon represent several other non–United Methodist denominations, such as Free Methodist, Holiness, Baptist, and Christ churches. Although the Mount Hermon Conference is beyond the scope of this study, it is significant to note that other Japanese American Christian youth camps exist outside of those associated with the United Methodist Church.

Japanese American Christian Summer Camps Today

The following subsections highlight the relevance of Christian camps to Japanese American youths and discuss camp profiles, reasons for attending, and the lasting effects of the camps.

Addressing the Needs of the Japanese American Youth Community

Perhaps the most vital ingredient in a successful youth camp or conference is a critical mass of people to help create a memorable experience. For Japanese American Christian youth camps in particular, the young people and the adult leaders are not just the participants; they are also the reason for participating. They are extremely diverse in terms of ethnicity, class, gender, and sexual orientation. However, all of the participants are somehow connected to a Japanese American Christian church and thus contribute the future of Japanese America.

The attendees of Japanese American Christian youth camps represent several geographic areas with a strong Japanese American history. They offer a place for young Japanese Americans to meet others like themselves from different parts of the country. Because of the widespread nature of Japanese America, it is often difficult for them to even meet other Japanese American youths in their daily lives. "At camp, they have each other, unlike [in] their public schools," says Rev. Michael Yoshii of Buena Vista United Methodist Church in Alameda, California. One recent Asian Camp attendee attests to this point with her own personal account: "I never had many Japanese American friends before camp. Well, just one at school, and we were friends because we were the only two Japanese girls there, and she invited me to the basketball league. That's where I met Asian American girls for the first time, and one of them was the one that took me to Junior High Camp for the first time." By going to the camps and being able to create a wide social network, the camps "make the community seem so much closer and accessible," says Ryan Acuña, who is half Mexican American and half fourth-generation Japanese American. Acuña further states, "A lot of times like where these kids are from, like Fresno or rural, less populated areas, they don't have the chance to really interact with fellow Japanese Americans, or I guess even in places like some parts of San Jose, so I believe that Junior High Camp and Asian Camp are the place where they can go to meet fellow Japanese Americans from all parts of California, Northern California, Southern California, even Seattle and Colorado." In addition to attendees from the large, metropolitan areas of Seattle, Denver, San Jose, and Los Angeles, substantial contingents come from smaller agricultural towns such as Spokane, Washington; Ontario, Oregon; and Dinuba, California.

Although the youth camps do not collect personal data on race or ethnicity, I was able to make some generalizations on the camp population based on the surnames listed in camp rosters. Of the 112 campers at a recent Asian Camp, 71 had a Japanese surname, 24 had a non-Japanese Asian surname, and 17 had a non-Asian surname ("One2One" 2006). However, these statistics can be misleading since surnames represent only one side of an individual's nuclear family and do not represent factors such as intermarriage and adoption. For example, some of the campers with non-Japanese Asian last names have Japanese American mothers, and others may be full Chinese. Also, two of the 17 campers with non-Asian surnames had Japanese first names, while only four of the 71 campers with Japanese surnames had Japanese given names, perhaps indicating a possible shin-issei parent. Although a survey of given names and surnames of a highly multiethnic group can be problematic—especially when considering intermarriage and the nonexclusive policies of the historically Japanese American churches— these numbers help illustrate the dominant Japanese American presence.

Profiles of the Camps

The two summer camps researched in this study, Asian Camp and Junior High Camp, share much of the same structure, but are geared for different age groups. Junior High Camp accepts campers from incoming sixth through ninth grade, while Asian Camp accepts campers from incoming ninth grade through second-year college. Essentially, campers would naturally progress from Junior High Camp to Asian Camp as they get older. Today, the two camps collaborate and work around each other's schedules in order to give more Japanese American youths greater opportunities to become involved.

Both of the summer camps take place at retreat locations in rural areas that are generally a few hours driving distance away from metropolitan areas. Some examples of previous campsites include Ponderosa Pines Christian Camp in Rolling Springs, California (near San Bernadino, California), and Camp Cazadero in Cazadero, California (near Santa Rosa, California). By having the summer camps in these rural areas, directors assume that the campers can better remove themselves from their daily routines and concentrate on the camp community.

Asian Camp and Junior High Camp share a similar schedule for the week. Each year, the camps' respective directing teams create a theme and spend several months training counselors. The counselors work in pairs to facilitate small groups during the week of camp. These coed small groups can range in size from approximately six to twelve campers and are based on age.

Also, campers are assigned to single-sex cabins supervised by counselors and other camp staff. Both camps adhere to a strict schedule in order to maximize their week. Mandatory worship services—which include contemporary Christian songs, sermons, and announcements—take place once or twice a day. A large portion of the week is spent in the small groups, which gives the youth an opportunity to dialogue with others in a much more personal setting. Also, both of the camps have camp-wide programs that involve everyone, regardless of age or sex. Some examples include a camp-wide dance featuring a DJ, as well as a talent-sharing show to give the campers an opportunity to share their unique skills. Each activity is designed to encourage interaction and fellowship between the campers. Even for meals, campers are randomly assigned tables to sit at in an effort to minimize social cliques.

Since Asian Camp and Junior High Camp are geared for different age groups, they also have programming that is specific to their campers. Junior High Camp features a water balloon fight and an evening program that introduces concepts such as diversity. Likewise, Asian Camp schedules a program on social justice that is more appropriate for high school students. Previous social justice programs have covered issues such as the 9/11 tragedy and the Columbine High School massacre. For the program on 9/11, Japanese American filmmaker Lina Hoshino was invited to present and discuss her film *Caught in Between*, which illustrated parallels between post–September 11th Muslim Americans and post–Pearl Harbor Japanese Americans. As for the program on the Columbine massacre, some of the campers and camp staff who attended, several of whom are alumni of Columbine High School, shared their personal connections to the shootings.

Aside from the religious and identity lessons that are learned at camp, many of the youths also benefit from the inherent social opportunities, such as the development of romantic relationships. The campers can find people whom they can connect to in new ways, stemming from their multiple points of commonality. Several stories of prom dates and even future spouses have come from past Japanese American Christian youth camps.

Despite the innocent adolescent mischief that takes place at the camps, the camps still retain their Christian background and serve as a place for ethical lessons to be taught. Besides the counselors and directors, ministers and/or youth pastors are always present to enforce the integrity of the camps. Parents generally have few concerns with putting their trust in these individuals concerning the safety of their children throughout the week. According to Rev. Roger Morimoto, a sansei from Aldersgate United Methodist Church in Palo Alto, California (who himself was a product of the camps), "Japanese American camps do things in a style or a way that are very effective, that are very positive in the moral standpoint."

Reasons for Attending the Camps

"I first went to camp because of all the great stories I'd heard from my older brothers," says Mariko Yamazaki, a fourth-generation Japanese American from Los Angeles, California. She continues, "It's only a week long, but the friendships I formed there are more intimate than almost any other friendships I've ever made." Like Yamazaki, each of my interview subjects stressed that it was the people that made the youth camps so memorable. This naturally leads to the question: What is it about these Japanese American Christian campers that makes their friendships so special?

I contend that Japanese American Christian youth camps and the friendships created there are special because the campers are finally introduced to people that they can connect to on multiple levels of their identity. Since so much of Japanese America is widely dispersed, the youth camps present a rare opportunity to be in a community of others like themselves. Rather than meeting new people and having first to navigate through identity issues such as race, ethnicity, and language spoken, all of those primary introductions can be easily bypassed to make room for deeper dialogue since almost everyone at the Japanese American youth camps comes from a similar historical situation. Furthermore, the structure of the camps is extremely conducive to inclusion, teaches the youths that they have a voice as Japanese Americans, and urges them to use that voice. By giving them an opportunity to speak and be heard in their small groups, the camps offer positive steps to build individual confidence and skills that can later be used in public situations. This combination of community education and individual empowerment encourages Japanese American community development beyond just the camps.

Since many of the youths have similar backgrounds as Japanese Americans, they tend to be more comfortable with opening up and sharing their personal stories. Acuña refers to the camps as "a place where you can be yourself and do things, be funny, be silly, and people won't sit there and judge you for it. More than anything, you can be honest." Thus, the Japanese American youths can begin to develop both a personal and a group identity by observing those around them. "Many of the kids . . . don't even realize they're different until the camps. It becomes a self-reflective mirror on themselves that they don't have otherwise," says Rev. Morimoto. These similarities help create the same environment where everyone can feel more relaxed and comfortable. According to Kristi Hoshibata, a half-fourth-generation, half-fifth-generation Japanese American from Seattle, Washington: "I think a lot of it has to do with the comfortability of knowing [everyone else is] Japanese American. And I think for me, it's easier to talk to someone who's Japanese American, rather than someone who's not. I just don't know why. And I've come to realize that just going throughout college I can talk to people who are not Japanese American just as easily, but I feel more comfortable and myself." As Hoshibata's statement attests, it is easy to see how much Japanese American youths can develop not just individually as Christians but also as a community of Japanese Americans. According to Rev. Morimoto, "I think camp does provide this place for youth to gather and ask spiritual questions, but also identity questions. And also what I call identity experiences. . . . Much of it comes from unspoken cultural norms in the Japanese American culture. The sense of belonging and acceptance I think is different than the mainstream conference camps."

Japanese American Christian youth camps foster group identity in that they enable the campers to find others with similar characteristics as themselves. They learn that instead of being a marginalized individual, they are part of a group that can join together, empower each other, and help dictate the future of Japanese America. For example, instead of being the only Asian American on their basketball team, or the only Asian American in their school that can't speak an Asian language, they can find other Asian Americans on basketball teams and other Japanese Americans that don't speak Japanese. Although they recognize their marginalization in American society, they also realize that they have the power and support of others to positively change their situations.

Yonsei Tim Shimizu mentions that part of the camps' popularity is because of their "low price of entry." Although Japanese American United Methodist churches host the youth camps, they do not require the campers to be Japanese American, United Methodist, or even active Christians. He continues, "You can go there without any social skills or knowledge about Christianity, and the camps are so geared to those things that they will make up for any individual deficiencies, and pretty much anyone can go." All that is asked of them is to enter with an open mind, an open heart, and to obey the camp rules. Since the majority of the campers grew up in their churches, they are already accustomed to the ethnic and racial diversity within Japanese America. The unspoken rule of accepting one another despite a number of differences, such as ethnicity, sexual orientation, and even social standing, serves as the foundation for unique relationships and, ultimately, the development of a new generation of Japanese America.

The Lasting Effects of the Camps

The camps are important not just because they are a week of enjoyment, but because the impact from the week carries over for the rest of the campers' lives. The newly formed friendships serve as the core to the legacy of the camp community. Since the camps are aligned with the Japanese American churches—which are the historic centers of the Japanese American community—the camps directly affect the next generation of Japanese America. It is important to stress that even after the week of a youth camp is over, the newly created friendships persist, especially by means of online social networks such as Facebook and Instagram.

Of the 106 campers that attended Asian Camp in 2005, 58 returned in 2006. If we disregard the 18 college-aged campers in 2005 that were too old to be campers in 2006, we can calculate that roughly 66 percent of the campers returned. Since two-thirds of the campers who were able to return did, they are also able to renew and build on previously established relationships. The one-third of campers who are new can continue the camp's legacy of creating community networks by following the examples all around them. In other words, a majority of campers have enjoyed their experiences enough to continue to attend camp, year after year, until they are too old to be campers.

Once campers become too old for camp, they are welcome to take on a leadership position. As with being a camper, one does not have to be Japanese American or a baptized Christian become a counselor, but one does have to be willing to dedicate roughly half of a year to counselor training sessions. At these training sessions, which are led by the camp directors, the counselors learn leadership methods, discuss the themes of the camp, plan the programs, and bond with each other throughout the entire process. By the time camps start in the summer, most of the counselors are already good friends with one another, and these friendships serve as examples for the campers.

The youths who attend the Japanese American Christian church camps consider the counselors as role models. Many campers have mentioned how they looked up to and followed the examples of their counselors. Thus, when the youths are too old to be campers, several of them choose to emulate their role models and become leaders for the next generation of Japanese American youths. This creates a cycle of leadership to ensure the success and survival of the camps. Counselors have no upper age limit, but generally, the Junior High Camp counselors are older high school students, while the Asian camp counselors range from college sophomores to individuals in their late twenties.

Despite multiple generations of assimilation and acculturation into American society, youths from Japanese American churches persist in identifying themselves as part of the Japanese American community. However, the defining points of Japanese American history—most notably the internment experience—are slowly fading out of the consciousness of today's youths. The results of this study reaffirm the real effects of racial formation on the psyche of today's Japanese American youths who are often racialized by the dominant white American society. Furthermore, they are often othered by first- or second-generation Asian American youths for lacking language skills and other cultural markers common to most Asian immigrant groups. Finally, this study illustrates the inherent human desire to discover one's own community based on commonality as opposed to difference, not just as a form of resistance against racialization but as a form of individual empowerment through group membership. When Japanese American youths can realize that are part of a community and understand their shared past, they can better decide on a direction for the future.

Conclusion

This study has examined today's Japanese American Christian youth camps in an effort to raise the consciousness of today's fourth- and fifth-generation Japanese American youths and to maintain hope that this historically significant community will continue to embrace Christian youth camps as a physical space for community building for future generations of Japanese Americans. In understanding this model for the future, it is also important to return to the starting point of this phenomena: the Young People's Christian Conference. Although the actual YPCC has been defunct for decades, its remaining participants—who are now senior citizens—refuse to let its legacy fade away. Each summer, these Japanese American Christian senior citizens from different churches congregate at the annual Japanese Fellowship at the Zephyr Point Conference Center for a weeklong retreat of fellowship, spiritual growth, and reminiscing on their past experiences as a young Japanese American Christian. As they continue to make these community-building camp experiences a priority in their old age, they continue to benefit from the legacy of Japanese American Christian youth camps.

Japanese American Christian youth camps have positively affected thousands of Japanese Americans over multiple generations in the United States. Essentially, these camps created a cycle of bringing together a critical mass of Japanese Americans, putting them in an isolated environment for them to grow as a community, and sending them back to their respective geographic locations as empowered individuals with a new understanding of their identity. In some ways (albeit definitely a bit of a stretch), these Japanese American Christian youth camps parallel the internment experience. While this study in no way attempts to condone the grave injustices of Japanese American internment, I bring this point up to illustrate the "ties that bind" any community together. After four, five, and even six generations in the United States, demographic shifts have caused the Japanese American community to evolve into one based less on physical proximity and more on maintaining personal connections in spite of distances. Is this continuous cycle of coming together and dispersing, to borrow former camper-turned-minister Rev. Michael Yoshii's phrase, "a collective Japanese American experience transferred in time?"

The findings from this study illustrate that despite its extremely diverse nature, Japanese America maintains its own unique cultural traditions that are specific to their lives and histories in the United States. Japanese American Christian youth camps are one such example of a specifically Japanese American tradition that has adapted over the years to the changing face of

Japanese America. Today, it is the responsibility of the next generation of Japanese American leaders to ensure that this legacy endures. As Japanese American Christian youth camps continue to thrive, I have faith that the next generation will live up to its responsibilities and continue to redefine what it means to be Japanese American.

REFERENCES

"About." n.d. NJAUMC Asian Camp Home Page. Accessed March 31, 2019. http://njaumc.org/asiancamp/about.html.

Asakawa, G. 2004. *Being Japanese American: A JA Sourcebook for Nikkei, Hapa . . . & their Friends*. Berkeley, CA: Stone Bridge Press.

"Asian Americans: A Mosaic of Faiths." 2012. Pew Research Center Home Page. Accessed March 15, 2016. http://www.pewforum.org/2012/07/19/asian-americans-a-mosaic-of-faiths-overview.

"The 40 Years I Spent at the Lake." 1986. Lake Sequoia Retreat reunion program booklet. Burlingame, CA.

Fugita, S., and D. O'Brien. 1991. *Japanese American Ethnicity: The Persistence of Community*. Seattle: University of Washington Press.

Ichioka, Y. 1988. *The Issei: The World of the First Generation Japanese Immigrants, 1885–1924*. New York: Free Press.

———. 1989. *Views from Within: The Japanese American Evacuation and Resettlement Study*. Los Angeles: University of California Asian American Studies Center.

Japanese Evangelical Missionary Society. 2016. Japanese Evangelical Missionary Society Home Page. Accessed March 15, 2016. http://jems.org/mt-hermon.

Jeung, R. 2002. "Asian American Pan-Ethnic Formation and Congregational Culture." In *Religions in Asian America: Building Faith Communities*, edited by P. G. Min and J. H. Kim. Walnut Creek, CA: AltaMira Press.

———. 2005. *Faithful Generations: Race and New Asian American Churches*. New Brunswick, NJ: Rutgers University Press.

Koga, S. 1977. *A Centennial Legacy: History of the Japanese Christian Missions in North America, 1877–1977*. Chicago: Nobart.

Kurashige, L. 2002. *Japanese American Celebration and Conflict: A History of Ethnic Identity and Festival in Los Angeles, 1934–1990*. Berkeley: University of California Press.

Lein, P., and T. Carnes. 2004. "The Religious Demography of Asian American Boundary Crossing." In *Asian American Religions: The Making and Remaking of Borders and Boundaries*, edited by T. Carnes and F. Yang. New York: New York University Press.

"Mount Hermon Conference." 2017. JEMS: Japanese Evangelical Missionary Society Home Page. Accessed March 31, 2019. https://www.jems.org/mt-hermon/.

NJAUMC (National Japanese American United Methodist Caucus). 2016. Asian American Summer Camp. Accessed March 15, 2016. http://njaumc.org.

Omi, M., and H. Winant. 1994. *Racial Formation in the United States: From the 1960s to the 1990s*. 2nd ed. New York: Routledge.

"One2One." 2006. Asian Camp program booklet. Cazadero, CA.

Sano, R. I. 1982. *From Every Nation without Number: Racial and Ethnic Diversity in United Methodism*. Nashville: Abington.

Spickard, P. R. 1996. *Japanese Americans: The Formation and Transformations of an Ethnic Group*. New York: Twayne.

Strong, E. 1934. *The Second Generation Japanese Problem.* Stanford, CA: Stanford University Press.

Suzuki, L. 1977. "History of the Japanese United Methodist Church in America." *A Centennial Legacy: History of the Japanese Christian Missions in North America, 1877–1977.* Chicago: Nobart.

Yoo, D. 2002. "A Religious History of Japanese Americans in California." In *Religions in Asian America: Building Faith Communities,* edited by P. G. Min and J. H. Kim. Walnut Creek, CA: AltaMira Press.

5

Religious Nones?

Increasing Unaffiliated and Christian Religiosity among Japanese American Millennials

BRETT J. ESAKI

As we have seen in other chapters, Japanese Americans have followed patterns of assimilation similar to other American groups, yet no pattern in particular. The same is also the case for religion, where Japanese Americans have crafted their own way to adapt to the American religious landscape. For example, Japanese American religions follow the so-called "spiritual marketplace," which involves religious organizations "supplying" spiritual goods such as ideals, and communities and individuals shopping around for organizations that fit their spiritual "demands." Over time, this exchange undergirded the evolution of contemporary spirituality, characterized by individuals assembling their own spirituality from pieces of multiple religious traditions. Even non-Christian Japanese Americans have adopted American Protestant practices, such as naming Jodo-Shin Buddhism the "Buddhist Churches of America," which has democratically elected "reverends" and utilizes Protestant hymnody and organ music in Buddhist worship. Given this longer history, one might wonder whether the trajectory of Japanese American religiosity is to split into individuals without religious tradition and community or to become like white Protestants. Using recent sociological data on Japanese American millennials, I illustrate how the answer may be both and more.

I analyzed the Pew Forum (2012a) survey of Asian American religion, *Asian Americans: A Mosaic of Faiths*, with particular interest in Japanese American millennial "religious nones."[1] Since the 1960s, sociologists of American religion have detailed the steady increase in the number of people not identifying with a religion, a phenomenon called "religious nones." As noted in the ominously titled *"Nones" on the Rise*, also published by the Pew Forum (2012b), the number of those not affiliating with religion continues to grow, and the youngest generation does not affiliate at the highest rate, 32 percent. I wanted to investigate whether Japanese American millennials followed this larger trend, especially given that (1) in surveys of American racial groups, Asian Americans have consistently had the highest percentage of religious nones, and (2) among Asian American ethnic groups, Japanese Americans have had the second-highest percentage of religious nones.

I illustrate that instead of simply following this trend, Japanese American millennials have a religiosity that is increasingly unaffiliated *and* Protestant Christian. I situate the data within other survey results and examinations of Japanese American religion and argue that their religiosities match the highly embedded racial position of Japanese Americans as well as a Japanese religious practice of cultivating harmony and the "ordinary."

Overview of Asian American Religion and Youth

This study builds upon existing studies of young Asian Americans and their religions, with most work on Protestants and how religion intertwines with race (Alumkal 2003; Busto 1996; Iwamura and Spickard 2003; Chen 2008; Chen and Jeung 2012; Jeung 2005; Joshi 2006; Kim 2006; Suh 2004; Yang 1999). For example, Rebecca Kim (2006) and Sharon Suh (2004) have respectively examined Korean American Evangelical and Buddhist youth and argued that their religious affiliations in some ways both enable and preclude Korean Americans from relationships with different racial, ethnic, and religious groups. Similarly, Khyati Joshi (2006) examined Indian American youth and illustrated how they face bigotry of both race and religion and so empathize across race and religion.

Several studies of Asian American college students demonstrate that religion can amplify the effects of the model-minority myth, leading to highly productive and pressured individuals who strive for the best in academics, economic status, and moral behavior (Busto 1996; Kim 2006). Members of this "moral model minority" are predominantly Protestant, raised in middle-class households, upwardly mobile, and identify equally as Asian American and Christian. Hence, they are not merely conforming to white American Protestantism and the model-minority myth, but at the same time outperforming standards and rejecting white American norms. That is, Asian American Christians recognize the crucible of American racism, and they value Asian traditions and community, yet in some ways presume the uprightness of Protestant morality and the assured rewards of an American meritocracy.

In these ways, the study of Asian American religions has argued that traditional religions (Christianity, Buddhism, and Hinduism) have helped young Asian Americans in the formation of self and community, leading them to affirm ethnic identity, to network across racial lines, and to contest and to conform to norms.

Russell Jeung (2012) has been researching young Chinese American religious nones and uncovers a connection between nonaffiliation and Chinese culture (also see Jeung, Esaki, and Liu 2015). Across his research, he argues young Chinese American religious nones retain familial traditions of Chinese popular religion, especially its rites and responsibilities (feng shui, Lunar New Year rituals, funeral responsibilities, and so on). Thus, not affiliating with religion facilitates the practice of Chinese religion.

To my knowledge, little to no work has been completed on the religions of Japanese American millennials, and most studies are on issei and nisei. These studies focused on questions of acculturation and survival and largely argue that religion has mitigated racial oppression with ethnic solidarity and selective assimilation (Hayashi 1995; Yoo 2000; Williams and Moriya 2010). Given that millennials can be of fourth or higher generation as well as new immigrant generations (*shin-issei* and *shin-nisei*), it is not clear how these studies apply. Jane Iwamura (2007) has studied the transformation of Japanese American religion after the 1980s and demonstrated that they have adopted a "critical faith," or an alternative to American patriotic religion that is based in spiritual solidarity in protest of injustice, much like other cultural nationalist groups. Additionally, as Dana Y. Nakano illustrates in Chapter 3 ("To Be Yonsei in Southern California") of this book, Japanese American millennials utilize ethnic organizations, including houses of worship, to feel stable under marginalization. These studies suggest that religion continues to mitigate racial oppression with selective assimilation. I argue accordingly, except I find that millennials' reaction to racial oppression is less oppositional and more about utilizing pieces of religions to embed themselves within multiple groups, thus forming solidarity and a sense of "ordinariness"—both of which can be traced to Japanese popular religion. In this way, Japanese American youths are like other young Asian American youths who have used religion to develop community with other races and religions and also like young Chinese American religious nones whose nonaffiliation allows them to practice Chinese popular religion.

Data and Analysis

These conclusions are based on my analysis of the Pew Forum (2012a) survey, *Asian Americans: A Mosaic of Faiths*. The survey is the most comprehensive data set on the religiosity of Asian Americans, involving over 65,000 in-depth interviews of Asian Americans across the country, with a final representative sample of 3,511 interviewees. I analyze the subset of Japanese Americans, which totals 523 interviewees.[2]

TABLE 5.1. GENERAL CHARACTERISTICS OF SURVEY RESPONDENTS: AGE, RELIGIOUS AFFILIATION, GENERATION

Age Group	Total Number	Unaffiliated by Percent	Buddhist by Percent	Christian by Percent	3rd gen+ by Percent	2nd gen by Percent	1st gen by Percent
18–32	44	38.6	18.2	40.9	45.5	40.1	13.6
33–49	125	48.0	16.0	24.8	25.6	20.8	54.4
50–65	184	31.0	22.3	41.8	47.8	14.1	37.5
66–79	108	25.9	38.9	35.2	20.4	20.4	59.3
80+	55	9.1	29.1	61.8	9.1	50.9	40.0

Note: Percentages based on responses divided by total number in age group. Figures do not include those who chose not to respond, therefore the percentages do not add to 100%. Generation figures deciphered by interpreting where born and where parents born. Those who had both parents born in the United States are at least 3rd generation, those born in the United States with one or no parents born in the United States have been labeled 2nd generation, and those not born in the United States are labeled 1st generation.

Source: Asian Americans: A Mosaic of Faiths (Pew Forum 2012a).

This study is unique in that it focuses on millennials in comparison to other generations within one ethnic group and looks across religious affiliations. I separated Japanese Americans by age into five sets of roughly fifteen years per group: ages 18–32 (millennials, or those born in 1980 and later), 33–49, 50–65, 66–79, and those older than 80. Besides the millennials that comprise the first age group, the other groups do not necessarily correspond to generations, though they could be superimposed by the reader. For example, sansei and baby boomers are found within the age groups between 50 and 79. However, as Table 5.1 indicates, the varying generational makeup of the age groups contests these generalizations. Forty-four millennials constitute 8.4 percent of the sample, which is enough to draw several significant conclusions about this generation. I also divided the data into four religious affiliations—unaffiliated (or religious nones), Buddhists, Christians, and Other—and further broke down these categories when needed for additional detail. Table 5.1 illustrates the number of interviewees within the age groups, along with religious affiliation and generation statistics.

These figures reveal that though Japanese American millennials have a sizable percentage of religious nones, they are certainly not defined by the lack of religion. Compared with those age 33–49, millennials have increased the percentage of Christians and decreased the percentage of religious nones. The percentage of Buddhists is similar to the age group just older, both of which are more than 20 percent lower than those age 66–79. In these ways, compared with other age groups, millennials have a strong percentage of religious nones, a steady percentage of Buddhists, and a rising Christian affiliation. As I explain shortly, the religiosity of Buddhists is connected to that of religious nones in several aspects and contrasts with the religiosity of Christians.

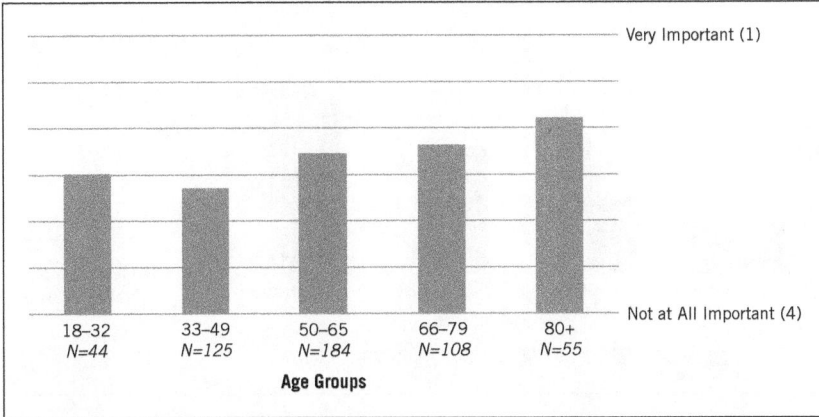

Figure 5.1. Likert Scale Responses to "How important is religion to your life?" by Age Group. (Source: Pew 2012.)

We can begin to illustrate the two religiosities by examining responses about the importance of religion. To the question "How important is religion to your life?" millennials responded that religion was more important than did those 33–49 but less than those 50 and older. Figure 5.1 illustrates the mean of the responses (rating of 1 to 4), separated by age.[3]

One reason that millennials overall place more importance on religion compared with those 33–49 is that significantly more Christians are part of the millennial generation (16.1 percent more). As Table 5.1 illustrates, Japanese Americans are Christian as often as they are Buddhist, and significant percentages have been Christians since first immigration. The Christian composition stems from missionary schools in Japan that assisted early emigration and from conversion in the United States (Azuma 2005; Hayashi 1995; Spickard 2009; Yoo 2000). Christians in every age group responded that religion was more important to their lives, as Figure 5.2 illustrates.

In addition, Figure 5.2 illustrates that for each religious affiliation, the millennial generation (marked by the darkest bar on the left) generally considers religion least important to their lives. The difference in importance between the unaffiliated and Christians is a characteristic distinction between the millennials' two religiosities. Figure 5.3 provides more detail on the effect of religious affiliation, and it charts the mean of the responses for all Japanese Americans, separated by religious affiliation and arranged from least importance to greatest.

To understand why religious affiliation might affect responses, we should consider how respondents might interpret two terms in the question: "important" and "religion." Those who identify as religious nones often consciously reject belonging to a religious organization or do not have interest in joining a religious organization; in both cases, "religion" implies an or-

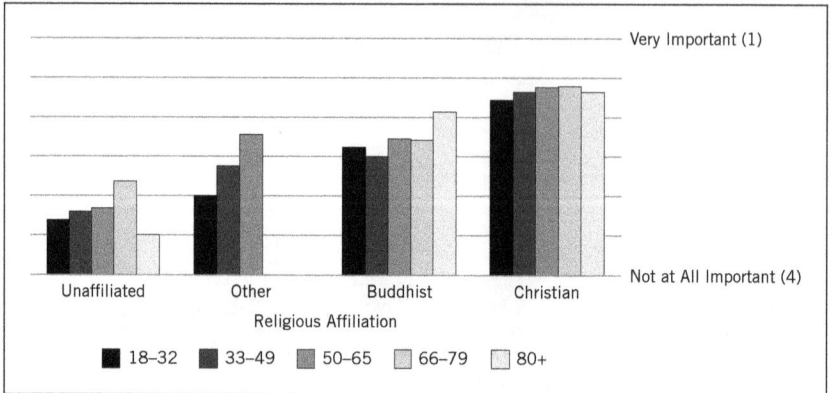

Figure 5.2. Likert Responses to "How important is religion to your life?" by Age Group and Religious Affiliation. (Source: Pew 2012.)

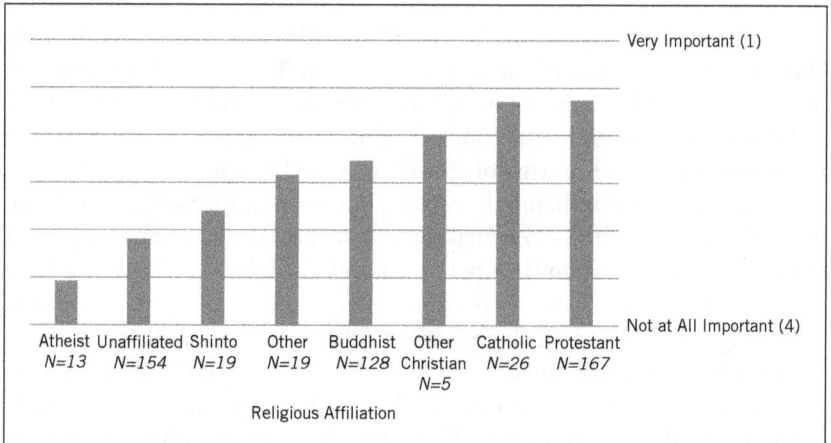

Figure 5.3. Likert Scale Responses to "How important is religion to your life?" by Religious Affiliation. Detail: "Unaffiliated" includes Agnostic, Nothing in Particular. "Other" includes Jewish, Muslim, Something Else, Don't Know/Refused. "Other Christian" includes Mormon, Orthodox. (Source: Pew 2012.)

ganization, which is clearly not important for the unaffiliated.[4] Atheists specifically reject forms of belief, so it is not a surprise that they responded with the least importance. For others with religious affiliations, the question may refer to the degree of impact that the affiliations have on their lives. Christians value their specific denomination of Christianity, so it makes sense that their specific affiliation is important to them. By contrast, Buddhists hold a common perspective that one's way of life is more important than specific affiliation.[5] This perspective explains why they value their religious affiliation but less than Christians.

With this explication, the picture of Japanese American millennials becomes clearer. For each affiliation, religion is less important to millennials' lives; this finding shows a quality of the unaffiliated religiosity. Christians place the most importance on religion out of all of the affiliations, even for millennials; this finding shows a quality of the Christian religiosity. Other results illuminate why millennials made polarized responses while attributing lower importance to every religion.

For example, responses to questions about the absolute correctness of one's religion illustrated the polarization and decreasing importance. The questions were the following: (A) whether the holy scriptures are the word of God; and (B) if so, whether they are literally true; (C) whether the teaching of their religions can be interpreted in only one true way; and (D) whether their religions are the one true path to enlightenment or eternal life.

To all of these questions, millennials asserted the following options at the highest percentage of all age groups (though in one case, 1 percent below). They responded that holy scriptures were written by men and were not the word of God. Even those who responded that their scriptures were the word of God asserted that not everything in their holy scriptures should be taken literally. They also felt that "there is more than one true way to interpret the teachings of my religion" and that many religions can lead to enlightenment or eternal life. Figure 5.4 illustrates the percentages of people who responded in these ways, broken down by age group.

As age decreases, the more likely respondents felt that holy scriptures were written by people and should not be taken literally, that religious teachings may be interpreted in multiple ways, and that many religions are effective. These findings indicate that millennials are the most contextual interpreters of holy scriptures, meaning that they feel that religious writing was created by people based on their "contexts" and are not to be taken literally. Further, they are the most empathetic to others' religious beliefs and practices in the sense that they feel that other religions are also valid and that their own religion can be correctly interpreted in multiple ways.

When the data on these questions are broken down by religious affiliation, it becomes clear that millennials' religiosity displays a broad trend of contextual and empathetic beliefs. Millennials who responded differently to questions A, C, and D were nearly all Christians. However, it should be noted that the majority of Christians were contextual and empathetic. By contrast, Buddhists and religious nones were nearly unanimous in their contextual understanding of religious ideas and their empathy with other religious views.

The overarching trends of contexuality and empathy are qualities of the unaffiliated religiosity, yet a minority of millennial Christians believes that there is only one true version of their religion, which is a quality of the Christian religiosity. The Christian religiosity is further illustrated by the responses to questions about belief in heaven, hell, angels, and evil spirits. Millennials

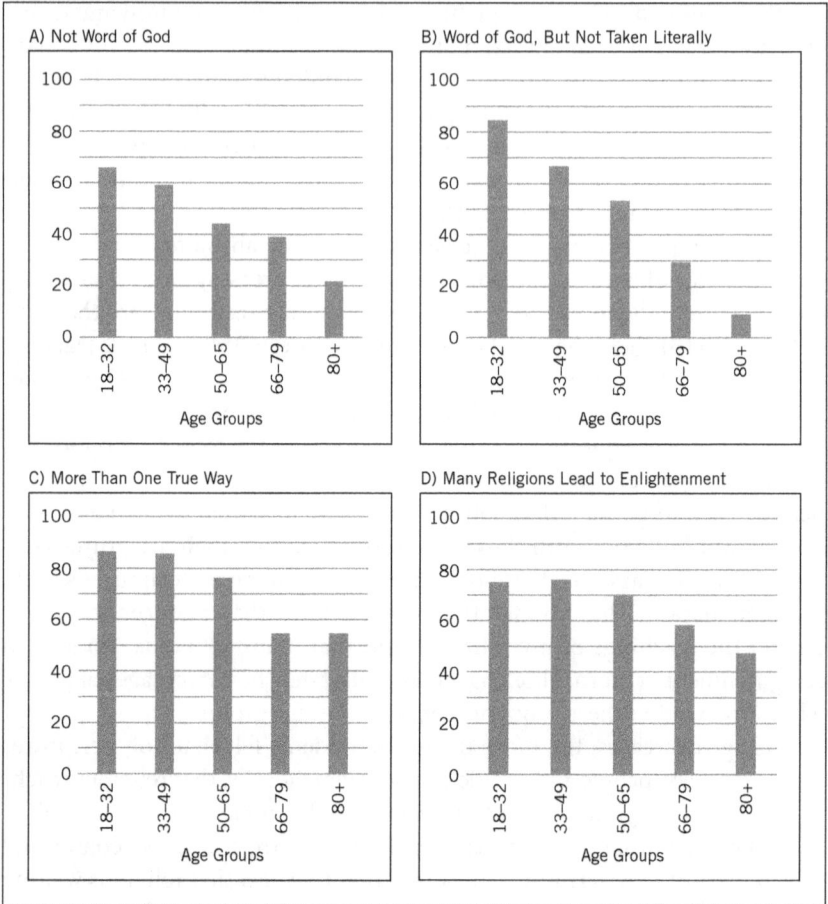

Figure 5.4. Contextual and Empathetic Responses to Questions on the Correctness of One's Religion, Percentage by Age Group. (Source: Pew 2012.)

responded in the highest percentage of all age groups that they believed in heaven, hell, angels, and evil spirits. For these questions, only one response was made with a higher percent (and only by 0.7 percent), which is about the percentage of one respondent in both age groups. Figure 5.5 illustrates the responses by age group.

These results can be explained with a few considerations. When broken down by religion, Christian millennials responded at high rates that they held these beliefs. This finding is significant because, as described earlier, this age group has a large percentage of Christians. However, other age groups have higher percentages of Christians and their average belief rates were lower. This finding indicates that being a millennial Christian involves a high degree of belief in certain religious ideas, which is one quality of their religiosity.

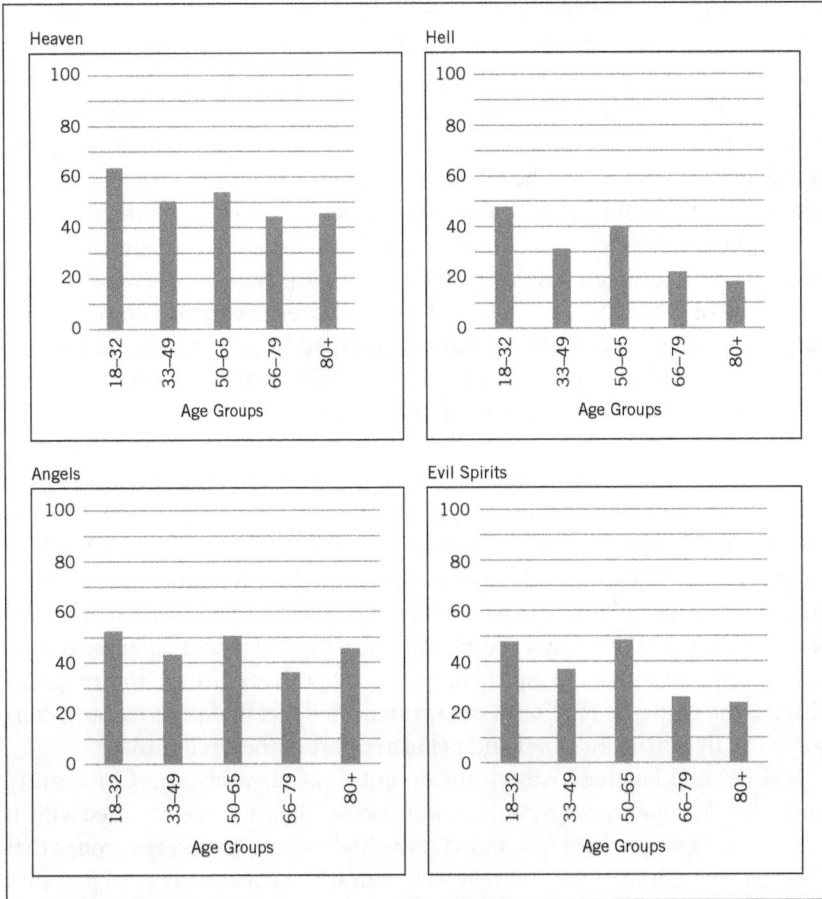

Figure 5.5. Affirmative Responses to Belief in Heaven, Hell, Angels, and Evil Spirits, Percentage by Age Group. (Source: Pew 2012.)

On the other hand, millennial Buddhists had relatively high rates of the religious beliefs just described, responding at about the same percentage as the overall average for Japanese Americans (which is more than some age groups containing many Christians). Religious nones had the lowest rate among millennial religious affiliations, yet the percentage who hold the beliefs ranged from 23.5 to 35.3. This finding indicates that though polarization exists between Buddhists and religious nones on the one hand and Christians on the other, millennials of each affiliation have a high rate of belief in heaven, hell, angels, and evil spirits.

One possible explanation is the degree of empathy that this generation has toward other religions; consequently, they may leave open the possibility that other religious ideas, including heaven and angels, are valid. They may frequently encounter Christians, since they have a relatively high percentage of Christians in their age group, and millennial Christians hold their beliefs strongly. Another possibility is that this generation's popular culture frequently asserts the existence of the afterlife and supernatural beings. The prevalence of these beliefs may expose the unaffiliated to these ideas and may push the percentages higher across the board. Thus, a mutual push of empathy and belief may occur for millennials, along with other factors of exposure to beliefs.

In these ways, Japanese American millennials have two rising religiosities: (1) an unaffiliated religiosity defined by a low importance of religion, a high level of contextual reading, and a high degree of empathy toward other religions, and (2) a Christian religiosity defined by strong belief in heaven, hell, angels, and evil spirits. Each religiosity has a core of strong adherents *and* affects the overall religiosity of millennials.

Other data confirm how the religiosities mutually reinforce one another. One example is the celebration of Christmas, which for millennial Japanese Americans was a unanimous 100 percent, whereas other age groups were 90 percent and below. They also celebrated Thanksgiving and the Lunar New Year at higher rates than older age groups, even though neither are Japanese. In fact, all three holidays are part of broader American and/or Asian American cultures. In these ways, the empathetic nature of young Japanese Americans could be seen to bring them to practice other cultural and religious rituals; the empathy facilitates engagement in belief and practice, and consequentially Christian ritual and belief are part of their religiosity.

Millennial Japanese Americans do not limit themselves to Christianity and other Asian American cultures, but also see themselves embedded within other racial groups. They responded at the highest rate among age groups that they get along pretty well and very well with white Americans (95.5 percent), black Americans (77.3 percent), and Latinos (84.1 percent). Similarly, 86.4 percent asserted that "homosexuality should be accepted by society," which is 4.8 percent higher than the next age group and 13.0 percent higher than the one after that. With the exception of one respondent, millennials who did not support homosexuality were Christians. One may argue that younger generations are more liberal, but they hold that abortion should be legal in most or all cases at about the same level as the two next older age groups.

In these ways, the data point to millennial Japanese Americans being closely associated with racial groups, Asian ethnic groups, and sexual orientations, and this finding is reflected in the mutual influence of unaffiliated and Christian religiosities.

Discussion: Embedded Religiosity

Now that these two trends have been articulated by survey data, we can speculate why they may exist. First, I contend that they connect Japanese

TABLE 5.2. COMPARISON OF RELIGIOUS COMMITMENT: JAPANESE AND
JAPANESE AMERICAN UNAFFILIATED

Importance of Religion	Japanese by Percent	Japanese American by Percent
Very Important	2	7
Somewhat Important	13	18
Not too/Not at all (combined)	84	73

Source: *Asian Americans: A Mosaic of Faiths* (Pew Forum 2012a).

American millennials to Japanese religion. The Pew Forum surveyed Japanese religion, and some overall figures of unaffiliated Japanese and unaffiliated Japanese Americans are alike. For example, Table 5.2 illustrates the importance of religion.

In Japan, the concept of "religion" is narrower because it was created to capture the Western conflation of religion with holy texts, and so the Japanese word is nearly synonymous with "doctrines" (M. Ama 2007). This narrower definition might explain the high percentage of unaffiliated in Japan who overall rank "religion" of lower importance in their lives. However, among Japanese American age groups, millennials have the lowest percentage of immigrants (see Table 5.1), so it is not place of birth that affects their lack of affiliation. Rather, I suggest that it is the empathetic connection to Japanese perspectives. Specifically, it seems to match the cultural religion of Japan, which Japanese scholar Toshimaro Ama (2005) calls "natural religion" and the value of being "ordinary." In Japan this religion is not considered a "religion" for reasons just stated, but it includes ritual obligations, folkloric beliefs, and ideals of humility and communal harmony. Like Russell Jeung (2012), who illustrates that young Chinese Americans utilize nonaffiliation to practice Chinese popular religion, Japanese American millennials may be using their unaffiliated religiosity to practice natural religion, including exchanging rituals and beliefs and acting to maintain harmony with others.

With the goal of harmony and the "ordinary" in mind, millennials' Christian religiosity may not only cultivate harmony across Japanese American religions but may also help to intertwine them with other American racial groups who are predominantly Christian. As the Pew Forum demonstrated, 75 percent of the American public identifies as Christian, 58 percent respond that religion is very important in their lives, 56 percent pray daily, 36 percent attend worship services weekly or more, and 92 percent believe in God.[6] The Christian religiosity of Japanese American millennials can connect them not only to the general public but also to minority groups who are predominantly Christian; consider how millennials asserted that they "get along well" with African Americans and Latinos. Jane Iwamura (2007) describes how Japanese Americans developed a "critical faith"—or spiritual solidarity—after internment, but the impulse for harmony and ordinariness could also have influenced them to adopt aspects of racial minorities' Christianity, like their passion for social justice. Hence, their Christian religiosity is not a mere mimicking of other groups, but an extension of their (Japanese religious) practice of unifying with as many groups as possible.

I also emphasize that this "religiosity" is not a Christian "affiliation," especially in light of common Asian American Protestant practices and beliefs. In comparison with white Evangelical Protestants—one of the most conservative Christian blocks—Asian American Evangelical Protestants respond more conservatively that "my religion is the one, true faith" (72 to 49 percent), "there is only one true way to interpret the teachings of my religion" (53 to 43 percent), and that the Bible is the word of God (94 to 92 percent).[7] By contrast, Japanese American millennials respond in the inverse to these comparisons, even the Christians. Consequently, Japanese American millennials are not fully assimilating the Protestantism of the general population, white Evangelical Protestants, or Asian American Evangelical Protestants. Their Christian religiosity asserts selected beliefs that facilitate harmony among other American Christians.

One way to understand these connections without affiliation is by examining other trends in American religious nones. As Michael Hout and Claude S. Fischer (2014) demonstrate, the greatest factor for the overall rise in religious nones is the backlash against the rise of the religious right, or the uniting of conservative Evangelical moral goals with political goals (such as pro-life and antihomosexuality agendas). As Americans increasingly associated religion with conservative politics, many liberal Americans increasingly rejected religious affiliation along with conservativism. Japanese American millennials' unaffiliated religiosity follows a similar pattern: it rejects affiliation with rigid doctrines and conservative political views. However, unlike the majority of religious nones in the United States who are predominantly white, unaffiliated Japanese Americans millennials are increasing their Christian beliefs.

This distinction from other patterns in American religion makes sense from a longer historical view. Japanese Americans have been forced into mixed neighborhoods and have chosen to integrate with other groups. Their history of integration includes the World War II–era race hiding such as that of Takao Ozawa, Fred Korematsu, and Henry Kitano; the postwar insertion into mixed-race urban neighborhoods, including Little Tokyo and Chicago; and the cultural nationalism of the 1960s and beyond (see Kurashige 2008; Palumbo-Liu 1999; Spickard 1989). In these social and physical locations as well as economic statuses from wealthy to poor, Japanese Americans have allied with different political perspectives, such as both sides of the San Francisco State University conflict that helped to define the Asian American movement. Japanese Americans have also frequently intermarried (41.3 percent) and identified as multiracial (30.5 percent), according to the 2000 Census (Lee and Boyd 2008, 321; Min 2006, 49). For these reasons, Japanese Americans have repeatedly found ways to integrate with the other groups, however tentatively, and do so because they have multiple political, cultural, economic, and personal reasons. Rejecting others' rituals and beliefs would betray the history of diverse solidarity.

Fumitaka Matsuoka (2012) further articulates how Japanese Americans' translocal racial position affects their religiosity. Existing in an in-between social location, Japanese Americans live in a place of precariousness and insecurity, yet this cultivates empathy for others and the combination of multiple religious perspectives. He calls this religiosity "holy amphiboly," which is "a non-singular vision with an unresolved state of non-complimentary cosmologies and faith traditions" (Matsuoka 2012, 22). Given that today's larger American religious landscape includes an increasing percentage of religious nones and a strong Christian affiliation, it makes sense that Japanese Americans would be expressing their holy amphiboly by adopting religious characteristics of religious nones *and* Christians. While a small percentage of Japanese American millennials strongly adheres to one affiliation, most do not adopt these affiliations in their entirety; I suggest that exclusivity would fray connections to other groups, or would cease the "non-singular vision" and "unresolved state" of multiplicity.

In other studies of Japanese American religion, I have further discovered that for many decades a nonspecific "spirituality" has enabled Japanese Americans simultaneously to cultivate multiple religious traditions, including indigenous religions, traditional Japanese religions, and new religions (Esaki 2013a, 2013b). Likewise, Japanese American millennials can be seen to elaborate on this process with empathy and practical, selective assimilation— continuing a tradition that adapts to the cultural landscape while deepening ties to multiple communities and cultivating Japanese religions. Whether the religiosity of Japanese American millennials is conceived as holy amphiboly or natural religion, this generation is engaging their embeddedness, in part, by utilizing others' beliefs and practices as well as preserving their own. Japanese Americans are increasing their unaffiliated and Christian religiosities, and in doing so express that they value multiple religious views and choose to affiliate with this multiplicity, appearing "ordinary" while promoting harmony through rich multireligious and multiracial ties.

NOTES

1. Note that the percentages in the generational analyses are unweighted, whereas the percentages from the Pew Forum (2012a) report itself and other Pew reports are weighted; weighting will be cited in endnotes. All comparisons presented are statistically significant.

2. The total number of Japanese Americans is larger than the figure provided in Pew (2012a) because they omitted Japanese Americans who did not primarily identify as Japanese American, thereby excluding multiracial and multiethnic Japanese Amer-

icans who identified equally with their backgrounds and those who chose another identification as primary.

3. Figures for my analyses are unweighted.

4. For a deeper analysis of nonaffiliation and belonging, see Baker and Smith (2009, 719–733).

5. In *Being Buddhist in a Christian World*, Sharon Suh (2004) even demonstrates that Korean American Buddhist parents allow children to try out Christianity, under the belief that life will eventually convince them that Buddhism is better.

6. Figures weighted by Pew researchers (Pew Forum 2012a, 14, 17).

7. Figures weighted by Pew researchers (Pew Forum 2012a, 21).

REFERENCES

Alumkal, Antony W. 2003. *Asian American Evangelical Churches: Race, Ethnicity, and Assimilation in the Second Generation*. New York: LFB Scholarly Publishing.

Ama, Michihiro. 2007. "Immigrants to the Pure Land: The Acculturation of Shin Buddhism in Hawai'i and North America, 1898–1941." Ph.D. diss., University of California, Irvine.

Ama, Toshimaro. 2005. *Why Are the Japanese Non-religious? Japanese Spirituality: Being in a Religious Culture*. Lanham, MD: University Press of America.

Azuma, Eiichiro. 2005. *Between Two Empires: Race, History, and Transnationalism in Japanese America*. New York: Oxford University Press.

Baker, Joseph, and Buster Smith. 2009. "None Too Simple: Examining Issues of Religious Nonbelief and Nonbelonging in the United States." *Journal for the Scientific Study of Religion* 48:719–733.

Busto, Rudy V. 1996. "The Gospel according to the Model Minority?" *Amerasia Journal* 22:133–147.

Chen, Carolyn. 2008. *Getting Saved in America: Taiwanese Immigration and Religious Experience*. Princeton, NJ: Princeton University Press.

Chen, Carolyn, and Russell Jeung, eds. 2012. *Sustaining Faith Traditions: Race, Ethnicity, and Religion among the Latino and Asian American Second Generation*. New York: New York University Press.

Esaki, Brett J. 2013a. "Embodied Performance of Folklore in Japanese American Origami." *Amerasia Journal* 39(2): 71–90.

———. 2013b. "Multidimensional Silence, Spirituality, and the Japanese American Art of Gardening." *Journal of Asian American Studies* 16(3): 235–265

Hayashi, Brian Masaru. 1995. *"For the Sake of Our Japanese Brethren": Assimilation, Nationalism and Protestantism among the Japanese of Los Angeles, 1895–1942*. Stanford, CA: Stanford University Press.

Hout, Michael, and Claude S. Fischer. 2014. "Explaining Why More Americans Have No Religious Preference: Political Backlash and Generational Succession, 1987–2012." *Sociological Science* 1:423–447.

Iwamura, Jane N. 2007. "Critical Faith: Japanese Americans and the Birth of a New Civil Religion." *American Quarterly* 59(3): 937–968.

Iwamura, Jane N., and Paul Spickard, eds. 2003. *Revealing the Sacred in Asian and Pacific America*. London: Routledge.

Jeung, Russell. 2005. *Faithful Generations: Race and New Asian American Churches*. New Brunswick, NJ: Rutgers University Press.

———. 2012. "Second-Generation Chinese Americans: The Familism of the Nonreligious." In *Sustaining Faith Traditions: Race, Ethnicity, and Religion among the*

Latino and Asian American Second Generation, edited by Carolyn Chen and Russell Jeung, 197–221. New York: New York University Press.

Jeung, Russell, Brett Esaki, and Alice Liu. 2015. "Redefining Religious Nones: Lessons from Chinese and Japanese American Young Adults." *Religions* 6:891–911.

Joshi, Khyati. 2006. *New Roots in America's Sacred Ground: Religion, Race, and Ethnicity in Indian America*. New Brunswick, NJ: Rutgers University Press.

Kim, Rebecca. 2006. *God's New Whiz Kids? Korean American Evangelicals on Campus*. New York: New York University Press.

Kurashige, Scott. 2008. *The Shifting Grounds of Race: Black and Japanese Americans in the Making of Multiethnic Los Angeles*. Princeton, NJ: Princeton University Press.

Lee, Sharon M., and Monica Boyd. 2008. "Marrying Out: Comparing the Marital and Social Integration of Asians in the US and Canada." *Social Science Research* 37:311–329.

Matsuoka, Fumitaka. 2012. "My Faith Journey: Grace in an Entangled Story." *Journal of Race, Ethnicity, and Religion* 3(2): 1–26.

Min, Pyong Gap, ed. 2006. *Asian Americans: Contemporary Trends and Issues*. 2nd ed. Thousand Oaks, CA: Pine Forge Press.

Palumbo-Liu, David. 1999. *Asian/American: Historical Crossings of a Racial Frontier*. Stanford, CA: Stanford University Press.

Pew Forum on Religion and Public Life. 2012a. *Asian Americans: A Mosaic of Faiths*. Pew Research Center: Washington, DC.

———. 2012b. *"Nones" on the Rise*. Pew Research Center: Washington, DC.

Spickard, Paul. 1989. *Mixed Blood: Intermarriage and Ethnic Identity in Twentieth-Century America*. Madison: University of Wisconsin Press.

———. 2009. *Japanese Americans: The Formation and Transformations of an Ethnic Group*, 2nd ed. New Brunswick, NJ: Rutgers University Press.

Suh, Sharon. 2004. *Being Buddhist in a Christian World: Gender and Community in a Korean American Temple*. Seattle: University of Washington Press.

Williams, Duncan Ryuken, and Tomoe Moriya, eds. 2010. *Issei Buddhism in the Americas*. Urbana: University of Illinois Press.

Yang, Fenggang. 1999. *Chinese Christians in America: Conversion, Assimilation, and Adhesive Identities*. University Park: Pennsylvania State University.

Yoo, David K. 2000. *Growing Up Nisei: Race, Generation, and Culture among Japanese Americans of California, 1924–1949*. Urbana: University of Illinois Press.

6

"I Am Trailblazing"

Young Adult Japanese American Shin Buddhists
Negotiating Complex Identities

CHENXING HAN

Walking into the lobby of the Jodo Shinshu Center (JSC) in Berkeley, California, I met the familiar gaze of the close-to-life-size bronze statue of Shinran Shonin, thirteenth-century founder of Shin Buddhism, before glancing up at the twelve-foot wide dharma wheel suspended from the lofty ceiling. This weekend in March 2013, I was at the JSC not in my usual capacity as a graduate student at the Institute of Buddhist Studies, but as a first-time attendee of the Sixth Annual TechnoBuddha Conference for Buddhists between the ages of twenty-one and thirty-nine. Enthusiastic greetings filled the air as other young adults arrived, sleeping bags and duffels in tow. Many commented on how they had not seen each other (outside of Facebook, of course) since last year's conference. In spite of their busy schedules, attendees came from near (Bay Area) and far (other parts of the West Coast and even Canada) for the opportunity to convene in person.

TechnoBuddha is sponsored by the Buddhist Churches of America (BCA), the U.S. branch of the Nishi Hongwanji subsect of Jodo Shinshu (aka Shin) Buddhism.[1] Steven Tamekuni (2012) explains the impetus for the annual gathering in an article for the BCA website:

The TechnoBuddha conference started out as just a networking conference for those who grew up in the Jodo Shinshu community. From there, it was discovered that all of us had the same mentality—that we wanted to be active in the temple still, but that it was very hard to do. This is because it seemed that there was no community for our age group within the larger temple community. People would go to temple up until they graduated from high school and then would disappear until their first child was born. The conference became a way for all of us who existed in this "gray area" to reconnect with fellow Jodo Shinshu Buddhists, and, of course, to make some new friends along the way.

As Steven alludes to in his mention of "new friends," TechnoBuddha reaches beyond the ethnic boundaries of Japanese Americans and the sectarian boundaries of Jodo Shinshu. Though most of the participants are Japanese Americans raised in the BCA, several are of mixed heritage, and those of us not of Japanese heritage and/or not Jodo Shinshu were still warmly welcomed to participate.

Young adult Japanese American Shin Buddhists (JASBs) are largely absent from scholarly literature about Japanese American Buddhists, which tends to focus on the experiences of first- (issei) and second-generation (nisei) Japanese American Buddhists. Tension between assimilation and resistance appears as a common theme in studies of Shin Buddhist community and identity in America. The pioneering issei navigated becoming American as racial Others who belonged to a religion widely regarded as un-American; Buddhist organizations and perspectives helped their nisei children construct Japanese American identities during the interwar years (Yoo 1996). Duncan Ryūken Williams (2002, 198) points to how the "Camp Dharma" of World War II internment camps "had the paradoxical task during the war of simultaneously serving as a repository for Japanese cultural traditions and as a vehicle for becoming more American" for both issei and nisei.

Michael Masatsugu's (2008) research reveals how nisei Japanese American Shin Buddhists in 1950s America engaged scholars and artists beyond their ethnic community in articulating a uniquely Japanese American vision of Buddhism while challenging Orientalist representations of Buddhism by white Americans such as the Beat poets. Despite the efforts of these nisei Buddhists more than half a century ago, Shin Buddhists continue to be lumped together with other Asian American Buddhists and dismissed as "perpetual foreigners," as evidenced by a "two Buddhisms" typology in academic and popular literature that contrasts convert, white, middle-class, "Western" Buddhists with their nonconvert, Asian, immigrant, "ethnic" Buddhist counterparts.[2] As Scott Mitchell (2010, 109–110) points out, a "narrative of decline" hangs like a pall over American Shin Buddhism, which the academic literature depicts as "traditional, conservative, and static." Thus, Shin Buddhists are cast—and cast aside—as clannish foreigners, their religious communities relegated to "ethnic enclave" status.

The experience of JASBs exemplifies the innovation and resistance required of Asian American Buddhists as a group who must negotiate their ethnic and Buddhist identities while "doubly marginalized by virtue of race and religion" (Yoo 1999, 6). In this chapter, I focus on the perspectives of young adult JASBs to explore how they continue this tradition of innovation and resistance as they support the diversification of Shin Buddhism in America and counter its marginalization. I draw on interviews with eleven Shin Buddhist young adults of full or partial Japanese heritage,[3] part of a broader research project in which I conducted eighty-nine one-on-one, semi-structured interviews with young adult Asian American Buddhists about their Buddhist practices, communities, and beliefs; perceptions of Buddhism in America; and opinions about the representation of Asian American Buddhists.[4]

In this chapter, I first consider Shin Buddhism's invisibility within the mainstream media and the contested debates around this lack of representation. I go on to highlight how religious and cultural identity are intertwined for many JASBs, even as the contours of their spiritual journeys differ. Next, I consider how various factors that contribute to the diversification of the BCA also lead to a decoupling of Shin Buddhist identity and Japanese American ethnicity. These factors create tension between a desire to preserve the tradition, on the one hand and to embrace a more diverse community, on the other. Ultimately, the young adult JASBs I interviewed draw upon Buddhist teachings such as impermanence and interconnectedness to help them navigate this tension in their own lives, while also calling for more accurate and diverse representations of Buddhism in popular media.

Shin Buddhism's Invisibility within the Mainstream

The Shin Buddhists I interviewed matter-of-factly acknowledged their tradition's invisibility to the mainstream. As Kaila notes, "When people ask me what kind of Buddhist I am I usually don't say Jodo Shinshu because I don't think that most people know what that is."[5] Even Naomi confesses that she had heard before coming to study in the United States that Jodo Shinshu was not well known here; in her native Japan, as the country's dominant sect of Buddhism, Shin was "like air: it was there all the time for me."

When asked what they thought were the best-known types of Buddhism in America, none of the JASBs I interviewed named Jodo Shinshu. David reflects on how exotification and stereotypes of Buddhism in popular culture contributes to a lack of awareness about Shin Buddhism in America: "I think when Americans think of Buddhists or Buddhism they think of Zen or Tibetan Buddhism. This is probably because these two are the ones that come up the most in popular culture. The Dalai Lama is probably the most famous living Buddhist figure in the world right now so there has been a lot of coverage on his particular sect of Buddhism. Zen seems to have gotten a lot of press as well when Japanese Buddhism is depicted in TV and movies. I want to say that the American idea of Buddhism is focused more on the monastic sects of Buddhism—the 'mysterious and mystical' East and their ancient knowledge."

Jane Iwamura (2011, 22) argues that tropes such as the Oriental Monk serve white hegemonic desires to make Asian American religions palatable "for dominant culture consumption." It may be the unpalatability of Shin Buddhism within narrowly defined "American Buddhist" tastes that renders the tradition so invisible within American Buddhism. For one, American Shin Buddhists fail to conform to the Oriental Monk stereotype, since temple services are led by ministers/reverends who are often married. The absence of celibate monastics traces back to founder Shinran, who practiced for two decades as a monk on Mt. Hiei before breaking with tradition by marrying (and eating meat). Furthermore, mindfulness meditation, upheld as the Buddhist practice par excellence and often uncritically equated with Buddhism in mainstream media, has little doctrinal support within Shin Buddhism. "Practice" is a problematic descriptor in that it may imply a "self-power" (jiriki) effort that Shinran believed to be an unnecessary arrogance in light of the salvific power of Amida Buddha. It is noteworthy that American Shin Buddhist communities have made adaptations to this expectation of meditation, though the issue is not without controversy.[6]

Finally, while the emphasis on chanting over meditation and the reverence for Amida Buddha may mark Japanese American Shin Buddhists as "devotional" immigrants within the "two Buddhisms" typology, they can hardly be said to be recent immigrants with limited English proficiency. After all, they belong to the only Asian ethnic group in the United States that is majority American-born (Pew Research Center 2013, 8), and English is the predominant language at BCA temples. Forcing Japanese American Shin Buddhists to choose between being "Asian" or "Western," "Japanese" or "American," "traditional" or "modern" obscures the dynamic history of change within the American Shin Buddhism community and ignores the complex ways in which the community's members have constructed their identities over multiple generations.

As a tradition with noncelibate, nonvegetarian priests—and without an emphasis on meditation practices—Jodo Shinshu defies popular expectations of American Buddhism. David observes, "I think it is difficult explaining my particular sect of Buddhism to people because there is so little awareness of Buddhism that isn't Zen or Tibetan. When people think of Buddhism they think of vegetarian, pacifist monks so when they see a 'normal' meat-eating American like me it kind of clashes with that idea." For David, the appeal of Shin Buddhism is that it is ordinary and accessible, "a religion for lay people or the everyday person," part of the mainstream rather than something exotic and mysterious for an elite group. Kaila insists, "I would like to see Asian American Buddhists represented, as we are, diverse. I do not want to see all Asian American Buddhists represented as bald monks who air bend."

Toward the end of my interview with Rachel, I ask whether she associates Japanese people with Zen, given the tradition's Japanese origins. She pauses before exclaiming, "I don't! I don't think of Japanese Americans in Zen; I think of Caucasians." Pointing to a photo collage from a blog post entitled "Why Is the Under 35 Project So White?" (Arun 2012b), Rachel adds, "When I think of Zen Buddhists, I think of the people pictured here."

Rachel was pointing to a collage of twenty faces—almost all of them white—created by the young adult Asian American blogger Angry Asian Buddhist, who used the image to critique the lack of Asian American writers featured in a Shambhala SunSpace project aimed at promoting a new generation of Buddhist voices. The Angry Asian Buddhist created similar collages in critiquing the 2011 and 2012 Buddhist Geeks Conferences (Arun 2011; Arun 2012a). Buddhist Geeks, an online Buddhist media company founded in 2006, boasts that their inaugural conference in 2011 was "received extremely well with nearly 200 people in attendance, and end[ed] up being featured in several publications including *Fast Company, Tricycle*, and the *Los Angeles Times*" ("A Brief History of Buddhist Geeks" 2016). In her interview, Holly, a Vajrayana Buddhist of mixed ethnic (including Japanese) heritage, offers a more nuanced perspective as an attendee of the conference:

> I remember the first Buddhist Geeks conference held at my school in Los Angeles, titled "The Emerging Face of Buddhism in America." I was drawn to its brand as a sangha for young-ish, technology-minded Buddhists. Overall, I enjoyed the conference and valued the motivations of the organizers and participants. Yet I pointed out to the audience that there are actually multiple 'faces' of Buddhism in America, and I didn't particularly see that embodied in the content or representatives at the conference. Some people became defensive while others were receptive to my critique. . . . I noticed that the following year, the conference was amended to the more inclusive title: "The Emerging Faces of Buddhism in America." However, the presenters remain primarily Caucasian.

Discussing her response to the conference, Holly clarifies her intention to "help Buddhist Geeks be an ally" and promote public dialogue about "the homogeneous representation and cosmetic fixes to lack of diversity" (in this case, adding the "s" in "faces") within American Buddhism. Ann Gleig (2014, 20) also comments on the lack of racial diversity in her study of the 2012 and 2013 Buddhist Geeks Conferences.

Like TechnoBuddha, Buddhist Geeks is a Buddhist conference started by young adults and billed for the tech-savvy, with an emphasis on inclusivity and diversity. One could, conceivably, critique TechnoBuddha as "too Asian," just as Buddhist Geeks is criticized for being "too white"—though the fact that TechnoBuddha does not purport to represent the future of American Buddhism lessens the force of this argument. Buddhists Geeks's language of self-promotion contrasts with the community-oriented ethos of TechnoBuddha. Some of the JASBs I interviewed see the contrast between the visibility of the two conferences as evidence that white Buddhists are better at outreach than Asian American Buddhists: "If the Asian Buddhists have a problem with it, they should step up and be more active." Katrina offers the following explanation for the invisibility and decline in numbers of Asian American Buddhists based on her experience growing up biracial: "I think it may in part be due to Asian culture. My Japanese grandmother always instructed me to work hard and stay focused. . . . My white father always told me to speak up. While just a difference in culture, it can be a recipe for disaster. This creates a huge disconnect and ultimately contributes to the decreasing Asian American Buddhist population. If people don't see people like them, or see something they don't relate to, they won't embrace it." Katrina's comment suggests that the BCA needs to be more inclusive of non–Japanese Americans in order for others to embrace it. Ironically, her final sentence could also be used to corroborate the Angry Asian Buddhist's critique of predominantly white groups such as Buddhist Geeks for excluding Asian Americans. The young adult JASBs I interviewed did not see themselves represented in the "emerging faces" of American Buddhism. However, many JASBs were untroubled by these issues of representation growing up— perhaps because they found a sense of belonging in the BCA with others who shared their ethnic and religious identity.

Growing Up with Other Japanese American Shin Buddhists

Religion and culture are intertwined for the young adult JASBs I interviewed who grew up in the Buddhist Churches of America. "I almost find Buddhism synonymous with my Japanese American identity," remarks Lesli, who, like Rachel, went to weekly Sunday school at a BCA temple in California. Lesli describes her church's "Japanese cultural school" for youth during the summer as a turning point in her Buddhist journey. She appreciated the opportunity to question her Buddhist identity at a time when she and her peers faced more questions about identity in school: "It was always nice to reflect and have each other during the summer. . . . That's where all of us got close."

Religious life and social life are also inextricably connected for young adults raised in the BCA. Rachel, who was "born into the religion" and grew up attending a BCA temple in California, explains, "I never thought of myself as 'highly religious.' It was just a part of my life." Her fondest memory of temple is playing basketball with the church league, where she made friends with other followers of the dharma. The networked nature of BCA communities, which have more than sixty temples/churches across the United States, meant that Rachel's interactions with other Shin Buddhists were not limited to her hometown.[7] Conferences with other middle- and high-school-age Shin Buddhist youth, holiday celebrations such as Obon, sports tournaments, and memorial services took her to BCA communities across California and even to New York. When I asked Rachel what drew her to these activities, she replies, "The sense of community. . . . I can't imagine not being a part of my temple. You know, my heart is there." The "huge social aspect" of the temple, rather than detracting from her religious life, was all the while enhancing it through the creation of lasting memories and friendships.

The annual festival of Obon, hosted by various BCA temples throughout the summer, illustrates the way culture and religion are interwoven for JASBs. Lesli notes that many of her Japanese American Christian friends also attend "Obons, which are Buddhist festivals," leading her to muse, "I'm not sure at what point it's cultural, and at what point it's religious." For Kaila, the festival is a way to connect with her cultural heritage and her family. Growing up, she loved the opportunity to wear traditional clothing and dance the Bon Odori; only when she was older did Kaila understand the festival's origins in the Japanese Buddhist custom of honoring ancestors who have passed away.

Most of the JASBs I interviewed admit to having limited knowledge about other forms of Buddhism. The Shin Buddhist, majority–Japanese American religious communities they grew up in are their primary reference point for understanding Buddhism. These were the temples where they had listened to countless dharma talks with their families and attended Sunday school with their peers. These were the churches where they recited English- and Japanese-language chants and sang Buddhist songs. These were the communities where they had observed older Shin Buddhists until bowing and *oshoko* (incense offering) became second nature—"just something you do" and "part of the ceremony of being Buddhist," as Lesli described it.

While my JASB interviewees share many experiences in common—attending Obon, New Year's services, and dharma talks at BCA churches with family members; taking BCA-sponsored trips to Japan and visiting the BCA "mother temple" in Kyoto; making friends through youth groups and conferences—their spiritual journeys are far from homogeneous. Landon, for example, was hardly an enthusiastic youth member of his church and readily admits he did not care about Buddhism growing up: "I told the teacher this is stupid, this is not applicable to my life." Personal challenges led him, still rather skeptically and begrudgingly, back to the church. After reading a book about the important Shin Buddhist concept of *akunin*, the evil person or one who cannot be saved, Landon acknowledged that perhaps there were things he had missed or could not appreciate when he was younger. When he returned to his home temple, he found that "it was nice just to find a place to belong." Landon now spends much of his free time as a volunteer adviser for numerous BCA youth groups.

Katrina's relationship with Shin Buddhism shifted from a reluctant inheritance as a young child to a more active engagement as she got older, recalling the trajectory of Landon's spiritual path. She too went to church at the instance of her mom, who felt she and her sister lacked exposure to their Japanese heritage. Katrina confesses, "I went to church because I had to—I didn't usually look forward to it." In high school, she reluctantly took up her YBA (Young Buddhist Association) adviser's recommendation to attend YAC (Youth Advocacy Committee) training. Through this process, she "learned so much about the religion" and became closer to the home temple minister, who convinced her to take a class from professor Mark Unno, a scholar and Shin Buddhist minister. The girl who dragged her feet to church ended up minoring in religious studies in college.

While personal crisis after college deepened Landon's engagement with the BCA, it caused Rachel to turn her back on her temple for a time. Already, Rachel's involvement with her home temple had diminished after going away for college, an experience shared by other JASBs in the "gray area" that Steven Tamekuni described. Lesli also experienced a shift after high school: "It's a completely different experience of going to church when it's not the same church you knew." Though church is no longer a part of her weekly routine, Lesli still sees Shin Buddhism as an important part of her life. Family, culture, and "my own happiness" motivate Lesli's ongoing engagement with the tradition of her upbringing. She remembers going home during a break from college and attending an evening class at her home temple after a long time away. On the car ride home, she experienced a moment of contentment in which she realized "it's okay that I haven't gone to church, because I can always go back to it.... Whatever I'm doing, it's always there. I can always turn to it when I need to." "Buddhism is "part of me," Lesli explains, even if she is not visibly "practicing" every day.

While growing up in the BCA offers cherished connections to their Japanese American heritage and fellow JASBs, a number of factors also threaten the close association between culture and religion within the BCA community. These include factors external to the community, such as the pressure to assimilate, as well as factors internal to it, such as increasing rates of intermarriage, as I discuss in greater detail in the following section.

A Diversifying Community

Though they understand their religion to be deeply rooted in Japanese American culture, the Shin Buddhists I interviewed also emphasize the diverse and diversifying nature of their religious communities. As Rachel puts it, "The face of Jodo Shinshu Buddhists is changing. We're lucky enough to have a lot of people coming from different religions and different ethnic backgrounds.... It's a stereotype that they're [all] Japanese, Japanese American."

Lesli echoes this observation: "I said [earlier in the interview that] I grew up in a completely Japanese American community at church, but really it's becoming much more diverse now." Landon too remarks on how "our families are not pure Japanese" as in the past. Thus, even as growing up in the BCA offers valuable connections to fellow Japanese American Shin Buddhists, the diversification of the community enables Shin Buddhism to be decoupled from Japanese ethnicity to a greater extent than in the past.

Studies of issei and nisei Shin Buddhists in America emphasize the importance of the BCA as a spiritual, cultural, and social center for Japanese Americans who faced discrimination as racial and religious minorities. While the BCA still serves these functions, many options for meaning and connection exist outside of the community. For the young adult Shin Buddhists I spoke to, religious affiliation and involvement are more of a choice than an inheritance compared with previous generations of Japanese Americans. As part of the most racially diverse (Pew Research Center 2014, 4) and "least religious" generation (Chee 2015) in U.S. history, my interviewees acknowledged the unprecedented number of options afforded them. Katrina notes, "Religion for the younger generation is a choice. . . . It's not that generation Y is faithless, it's just that it's no longer required." Patricia Usuki (2005, 164) observes the absence of sansei (third generation) and yonsei (fourth generation) Japanese Americans from the *fujinkai* (Buddhist Women's Association), a trend she attributes to younger women having more spiritual and social options than older generations. These expanded options reflect how Shin Buddhists who came of age half a century after the end of internment are spared the levels of discrimination and segregation their forebears faced. Landon contrasts his generation with that of his parents: "Growing up, my parents didn't have anywhere to go, because Japanese people were discriminated pretty strongly against after the war. So the temple was like a safe place. And so all your sports and all your friends were with the youth group, were with the church basketball team or kendo club or judo club." Landon posits that decreased pressure to stay in the BCA and increased pressure to assimilate lead to a decline in the number of JASBs: "I would say that [the Buddhist] religion leaves, because it's not important now, because you don't have to be with the Japanese people, because you can have any other group of friends, whether it's another Asian group, or Caucasian, or African-American, or Latino. . . . There's no need to come back to church, because you have your outside friends."

Many of my interviewees note the challenge of being Buddhist in a majority-Christian country. In response to statistics indicating the decline of Buddhism in the Asian American community (Pew Research Center 2012, 51), Kaila underscores how Christianity has impacted multiple generations of JASBs:

I think that a lot of this could be due to the pressures of Asian American Buddhists to assimilate into American society, which means becoming Christian. I think a lot of this pressure stems from the incarceration of people of Japanese ancestry during World War II and society telling them that in order to be a good American you must be Christian. For other Asian American groups, I think that this could be because of the importance of fitting into American culture where the dominant group of people are Christian. I think that Asian American Christians might think that Asian American Buddhists are too old school and haven't really tried to become "American."

For Aiko, the growth of Christianity is matter of course: "I'd have to say that we live in a predominantly Christian country. The tendency in many cultures is to assimilate to the dominant one, whether in custom or language. Christianity is much more heavily promoted, advertised, and readily available, so it's no surprise that Christian numbers are growing." She adds that "Buddhism and its beliefs are in some ways counter to, or at least not in line with, American 'values' of self-sufficiency and independence and self-promotion." Interestingly, the Pew Research Center report indicates that 44 percent of Asian American Christians think of themselves as "a typical American" compared with just 32 percent of Asian American Buddhists.[8] Conversely, 59 percent of Asian American Buddhists consider themselves to be "very different from a typical American" compared with 49 percent of Asian American Christians.

David's response to the Pew Research Center report tempers concern with understanding: when Asian American Christians have tried to convert him, he has politely declined, though he understands the motivation behind their proselytizing efforts. Like David, many JASBs I interviewed evince both open-minded acceptance of, and personal resistance toward, Christianity. Ironically, Shin Buddhism has been critiqued for being too similar to Christianity with its weekly services at "churches" and doctrinal emphasis on *tariki*, or "other power." While Shin Buddhists may be the majority within the BCA, they are well aware of the pressures of assimilation as minorities within the broader religious landscape of America.

While pressures to assimilate may encourage Japanese Americans to leave the BCA, increasing rates of intermarriage are changing the face of the community itself. Shin Buddhist millennials are more likely than previous generations of Japanese Americans to marry outside of their ethnic group.[9] The fact that a number of young adult Japanese American Shin Buddhists are themselves multiethnic/multiracial shows that their generation is accelerating rather than pioneering this pattern of intermarriage. In his study of interracial-interreligious families at a Thai Buddhist temple in the Bay Area,

Todd LeRoy Perreira (2004, 328) laments the lack of studies on cross-cultural marriage in Buddhism in America studies, arguing that this overlooked line of inquiry points to a uniquely American universalism in Buddhist communities that reveals the limits of traditional "scholarly categories [that] are too dichotomous, inflexible, and exclusive to account for interracial couples and their offspring." Katrina evokes a "distinct yet complementary" approach to her different heritages that Perreira also found among Thai Buddhists of mixed heritage in describing her ethnic and religious identity: "I identify myself as multiracial, and a huge part (literally 50 percent) of that is being Japanese American. I grew up slightly different than most of my 'Buddhist Buddies' in that my father is white. Going to church was a way to immerse myself in one side of my heritage. . . . I don't identify with my Japanese side any more than I identify with my white side. Furthermore, I don't associate Buddhism with being primarily an Asian religion anymore." For Katrina, the diversification of the BCA is an opportunity to expand Buddhism's associations to include more than a single racial or ethnic group.

Kaila's pride in her JASB heritage is by no means diminished by the fact that she has a Cambodian American Buddhist fiancé. To the contrary, she has delved deeper into understanding her own tradition through visits to the Theravada Buddhist temple with her fiancé and his family. She has embraced their religious and ethnic differences as an opportunity "to think about Buddhism more critically," and hopes to raise her children in both sects. Kaila is learning Khmer and has discovered "some chants in common between Theravada and Jodo Shinshu Buddhism that I am able to follow along with and chant since they are in the Sanskrit language." In discovering these similarities, Kaila is making pan-ethnic (Japanese and Cambodian) and pan-Buddhist (Mahayana and Theravada, Jodo Shin and Khmer) connections between purportedly parallel, nonintersecting groups. Simplistic binaries of Asian/white, Japanese/American, traditional/modern, ethnocentric/universal run the risk of confusing more than clarifying increasingly complex ethnic and religious identities.

In the ever-diversifying millennial generation, it is becoming untenable to make the assumption that Asian Americans are invariably "cradle" Buddhists born into a form of Buddhism that matches their ethnic/cultural identity. Consider Gabrielle, who was raised in Seattle with exposure to an eclectic mix of religious influences by family members who were "predominantly white and Japanese American." Gabrielle identifies as "Asian American, because, as someone who is half Filipina, a quarter Japanese (and 100 percent culturally Japanese), that's the lens with which I've grown up seeing the world." She also identifies as "hapa, or mixed-race Asian American" as well as "gosei, or fifth-generation Japanese American" and "a second-generation Filipino-American by blood only." Gabrielle was not born into Shin Buddhism but sought out the religion in college in response to a longing for "my own community and religious identity" like the one her boyfriend had with his Christian friends. She also credits her Japanese American Zen Buddhist grandfather with helping her carve her own religious path during this time of spiritual seeking.

Gabrielle's religious and even ethnic identities are to a large extent a matter of personal choice, though a choice deeply influenced by inherited culture. She finds no contradiction in being a quarter Japanese American (by blood) and "100 percent culturally Japanese," or between identifying as both a Jodo Shinshu Buddhist and as a "nondenominational Buddhist" who sits zazen with her grandfather and sees the Dalai Lama as one of her religious teachers. Though not raised in the BCA, Gabrielle, like other JASB young adults I interviewed, feels "my Japanese Buddhist faith (Jodo Shinshu) often goes hand-in-hand with my Japanese American values and identity."

Gabrielle's flexible approach to identity calls to mind a comment by Holly, who is "'multiethnic,' which includes an Asian-American identity" that was "very influenced by Japanese culture, as well as by Jewish and Alaskan culture." Holly writes, "I think young Asian American Buddhists I know, including myself, face challenges in integrating and expressing multiple cultural identities—as young, American, Buddhist and Asian. Yet I think we are all moving toward a more pluralistic world in which multiplicity of identity will be the norm. As a Buddhist, I know that the self is always inconstant and interdependent, so in a way my Buddhist practices help me be at peace in the midst of the tensions in multiplicity and diversity." Like Gabrielle, Holly carved her own spiritual path in college, though her explorations led to a different form of Buddhism. The diversification of the BCA can be seen as a broader trend among millennial Asian American Buddhists. Yet this trend poses challenging questions for the future of Shin Buddhism in America.

Navigating the Tension between Tradition and Innovation

In his interview, Rev. Kuwahara, a Jodo Shinshu minister from Japan who now serves at a temple in the Bay Area, wonders whether the BCA can maintain a Japanese American ethnic community in the face of increasing intermarriage. Some JASBs interviewees respond to this question/challenge by redoubling their efforts as proud representatives of their ethnicity and faith, while others concede that Shin Buddhism's expansion in America cannot rely solely on the Japanese American community. Landon, for all his involvement with BCA youth, suggests, "It's going to have to be other ethnic populations to keep the religion going in the next hundred years." If this prediction were to pan out, would it represent a dilution or decline of the religion—or just another development in Jodo Shinshu's adaptation to the United States? Would these future members value the preservation of Japanese American culture? Would they, to use Cristina Rocha's (2010) term, "creolize" Shin

Buddhism with other ethnic or religious practices? Would they reform it entirely—say, by doing away with all Japanese language in the temples? These questions encapsulate the tension Japanese American Shin Buddhists face between the ethnically specific, sectarian roots of their religion and the universal nature of the BCA's mission "to promote the Buddha, Dharma, and Sangha as well as to propagate the Jodo Shinshu teachings." This tension is not new for JASBs, though many of my interviewees face challenges unique to their generation because, as expressed by Gabrielle, they "carry on the legacy of [our] ancestral and religious heritage amid globalization, growing technology, and the threat of losing our culture."

It is unlikely that the connection between Jodo Shinshu and Japanese American culture will be severed altogether. Even Landon, who perceives older BCA members' unwelcoming behavior toward non–Japanese Americans in the BCA as a form of "reverse racism," defends his community against complaints by Caucasians who think there is too much Japanese in church services; as Landon sees it, many of these Japanese terms contain key Buddhist teachings. For Landon, these concepts include *okagesama desu,* which he translates as "because of you, I am who I am," and *ichi-go ichi-e* ("one time, one meeting"), which reminds him to "be mindful of now." "Ichigo ichie, Always Changing, Always Flowing," was the theme of the 2014 TechnoBuddha Conference; which Landon cochaired with a Caucasian coworker he had invited to the previous year's conference. Landon clarifies that his prediction that other ethnic groups will carry Shin Buddhism into the next century is less an expression of pessimism than a realistic assessment of the needs of a changing community. He advocates for finding a "middle ground" between the extremes of, on the one hand, clinging to fixed expressions of Japanese Americanness based on a fictive notion of cultural purity/essence and, on the other hand, destroying the deep Japanese American cultural/historical roots of American Shin Buddhism.

The Japanese Americans who participated in my project grapple with a desire to respect their cultural heritage and Buddhist ancestors and a recognition that their generation's adaptations of Buddhism are likely to emphasize Japanese traditions less and less. When reanalyzing her 2014 survey research to focus only on respondents of full or partial Asian heritage, the first statistically significant difference researcher Anne Spencer (personal communication) found among the 18- to 29-year-olds was that they were more likely than any other age group to agree with the statement "I go to the temple because it is important to keep the Japanese cultural traditions alive" and to indicate that "Japanese/Asian cultural activities" were an important factor in their involvement in the BCA during the previous year.[10] Spencer also found, however, that 18- to 29-year-olds were the least likely age group to tend to a *obutsudan* (a Buddhist altar) or say the *nembutsu* (the central contemplation in Shin Buddhism, "Namo Amida Butsu") out loud.

Several young adult JASBs I interviewed acknowledge that they are not well versed in the Japanese language, chants, and rituals important to Shin Buddhism. Nevertheless, it is clear that religious objects such as the *obutsudan/onaijin* (Buddhist altar) and *onenju/ojuzu* (prayer beads) still hold strong symbolic significance for them. Rachel, Landon, and Lesli all name their onenju when asked what object they owned best represents their Buddhist practice. Their collections, accumulated over the years, range from simple strings of beads made during Sunday school to special ojuzus purchased for special occasions. Rachel associates hers with reciting the nembutsu. Landon tries not to forget to wear his when he goes to temple; the one he was wearing during our interview reminds him of the Buddhist teaching of impermanence since the beads resemble skulls. In high school, Lesli had a Buddhist friend who wore a different ojuzu every day: "[I remember thinking] I like that idea because it portrays that you're Buddhist by having it on, [even if] most people think it's just an accessory." She recalls feeling amused when power beads became popular in high school: "I was like, cool—I have this thing that looks like power beads, but really, in secret, it's like my own thing to have, it had so much meaning and I could identify with other people wearing them." After her sister told her that their grandfather would get a new ojuzu each time somebody close to him passed away, Lesli began to wear special ojuzu when she wanted to remember loved ones.

Landon told me how he justified buying an expensive onaijin as a way to support his mom (who was helping run the silent auction where he bought the onaijin) and his home temple (knowing the money would go back to the church)—even though he does not know how to make the traditional offerings. Even Aiko, a Japanese American who describes Buddhism as a "cultural form of engagement" (she went to family memorial services and New Year's services as a child with her parents, but they stopped going to the Shin Buddhist temple after the reverend left), wears a Buddhist prayer bead that her grandmother bought for her in Japan. When visiting her parents, Aiko "will *omairi* (pray) at the obutsudan soon upon entering the house, and we offer water every morning, rice whenever we eat rice at dinner, and make offerings of the first food of what we eat." The Buddhist objects mentioned by my interviewees are more than just accessories: they serve as reminders of Buddhist teachings, opportunities for practice, and links to ancestors.

If "devoutness" is measured by continuation of chanting and ritual offerings, it would appear that Shin Buddhists are becoming less engaged in their religion with each passing generation. But what of other measures of engagement with religious engagement? Could Landon, who spends more time volunteering at the BCA than his parents and who was the one persuading his parents to see the Nishi Hongwanji main temple (not the other way around) when they took a family trip to Japan, represent a generational invigoration rather than a dilution of Shin Buddhism across generations? Would not Gabrielle, whose parents are skeptical of religion, not represent the same?

While the transmission of tradition is clearly important, the young adult JASBs I interviewed also express appreciation that their religion appeals to those outside the Japanese American community. For Lesli, the diversification of her rural home temple is "a positive change." She speaks admiringly of her church's Caucasian minister as "one of the most devout Buddhists I've ever met" and adds, "When I was in high school the minister was Caucasian, and he had great dharma talks, because he broke it down for outsiders. . . . Even though I had been exposed to Buddhism my whole life, there may have been things that were part of the ceremony of it, but I had never analyzed. . . . It made [me] reflect, so I especially liked listening to those dharma talks." In her appreciation for both the traditional and innovative elements of Shin Buddhism in the twenty-first century, Lesli demonstrates how the religious lives of young adult JASBs are marked by both transmission and disjuncture. Many acknowledge their indebtedness to BCA "insiders"—parents, siblings, friends, youth group leaders, ministers—while also crediting "outsiders"— college professors whose courses gave them a greater awareness of Asian American and Buddhist history, non–Japanese American converts who brought a different perspective to the BCA, even Christian classmates—as important teachers along their Buddhist paths. As such, they agree with Gabrielle that "Buddhist communities and the dharma should be open to all people regardless of background or skin color."

Resisting Marginalization, Pluralizing the Mainstream

Faced with the challenge of adapting the intersecting inheritances of Shin Buddhism and Japanese American culture to a rapidly diversifying society, the young adults I interviewed unsettle the binaries of Asian/American, ethnocentric/universal, and traditional/modern that are often used to marginalize Asian American Buddhists as racial and religious Others. In articulating a vision for diverse, inclusive Buddhist communities that honor but are not reducible to their cultural origins, these young adults trouble the narrative of American Shin Buddhism as an "ethnic" religion in decline, expanding the possibilities of what it means to be Japanese American Buddhist, Asian American Buddhist, and, simply, American Buddhist.

Several months after our interview, Gabrielle sent me photos from her wedding. As I read about how her wedding wove together Japanese, Shinto, Buddhist, Christian, and Irish elements, I recalled a line from her interview: "I often feel like I am trailblazing how to incorporate Buddhism into life as a soon-to-be wife, future mother, and career woman." Gabrielle's dance/theater/taiko piece "Farewell Shikata ga nai," which premiered in spring 2014 at the Ninety-Second Annual Japanese American Citizens League Banquet at

Seattle University, is an intergenerational drama that tells the story of the World War II Japanese American experience and its aftermath on the Nikkei community. The presentation integrates a dharma message on compassion from former internee John Nomura—Gabrielle's grandfather. Gabrielle's projects and aspirations stand in sharp contrast to portrayals of Asian American Buddhists as being sequestered away in "ethnic enclaves" that are "virtually 'invisible' to the broader civic space of America" (Williams and Moriya 2010, 41). Gabrielle writes, "Many people say that my generation, the millennials, are similar to the Greatest Generation. We made headlines when we all came out to vote for Barack Obama, for example, and we're known for being a group who truly cares, who are truly invested in our communities and our world. I very much see myself as being a part of this group. And me growing into an active Buddhist and proud representative of the Asian American community seems fitting as someone of my age."

The Japanese American millennials I interviewed do not allow Buddhism in America to be reduced to a cultural war between the figure of the "passive, silent, insular, and largely disengaged" (Masatsugu 2008, 427) Asian American Buddhist and the implied counterfigure of the active, vocal, open-minded, and engaged white convert Buddhist. They also challenge the argument that "disparate Buddhist immigrant groups" are unlikely "to forge a shared Asian American and Buddhist identity" (Seager 2012, 271).

Aiko believes that "young adult Buddhists have a different set of world views and experiences that they can use to meld their Buddhist values with modern society." Young adult Shin Buddhists are trailblazing in myriad ways: as the first female Shin Buddhist ministers in their families, as youth group advisers and conference organizers finding creative ways to make Buddhism relevant for younger generations, as socially engaged innovators of their inherited traditions. In articulating a vision for inclusive sanghas, the young adult Shin Buddhists I interviewed present a challenge to the dichotomous logic behind "two Buddhisms." They see fluid boundaries instead of stark delineations between Asian and American/white, traditional and modern, ethnocentric and universal, social/cultural and religious. In lieu of polarized and reductionist representations, they advocate for pluralizing the cultural mainstream in a way that accurately reflects the complex reality of Buddhist millennials.

The open-minded and flexible ways in which young adult Shin Buddhists relate to their cultural and religious practices, beliefs, identities, and communities expand rigid and dualistic categories that fail to capture the multifaceted reality of their spiritual lives. Ultimately, the dissonance between the lived reality of young adult Shin Buddhists and stereotyped portrayals of Asian American Buddhists in the media can point us in productive directions. With their religious and ethnic identities in a constant state of flux, young adult Japanese American Shin Buddhists are constantly exploring the limits of what it means to be Japanese American and Asian American and American, Shin Buddhists and millennial Buddhists and American Buddhists. Buddhist teachings on impermanence and interdependence help them negotiate the multiplicity and diversity of these identities. When I ask how she would categorize American Buddhists, Katrina responds with an emphasis on interconnectedness: "I wouldn't separate us. That seems to introduce an element of exclusivity that doesn't belong in my eyes. I would rather be inclusive." Her ideal Buddhist community? "A diverse group of individuals that both embraces its Asian history and looks toward its diverse future."

NOTES

1. For information on the history of Jodo Shinshu in America, see Prebish (1999, 130), Yoo (2000, 41–57), Masatsugu (2008), Iwamura (2011, 11–13), Kerstetter (2015, 169–170), and Nagata (2006).

2. For critiques of the Orientalist and racist logic behind "two Buddhisms," see Quli (2009), Hickey (2010), Cheah (2011), and Spencer (2014).

3. Eight of these interviewees were born in the United States; those who subscribed to generational labels called themselves fourth- (yonsei) or fifth-generation (gosei). It is important to note that three of these interviewees—all Shin Buddhist ministers— identified more strongly as Japanese than Japanese American: though living in the United States and fluent in English, they were born and raised in Japan. Nevertheless, I consider their perspectives valuable for this chapter; as an interviewee of Chinese heritage noted, "I do not identify as Asian American because I do not think that I have been in America long enough to be considered as part of this group [but] I have been reconsidering my definition of 'Asian American' as more inclusive, because all Asians living in America encounter similar issues related to race and identity."

4. These eighty-nine interviewees hail from a diverse range of ethnic and Buddhist backgrounds. For more details about my research methods, see Han (2017).

5. Throughout this paper, I use real names or pseudonyms depending on interviewees' stated preferences.

6. The Berkeley Buddhist Temple, for example, incorporates a few minutes of "quiet sitting" before services, and the Midwest Buddhist Temple in Chicago even has regular "Zen Shin Meditation" sessions.

7. Scott Mitchell (2010, 111) explains that "BCA-affiliated sanghas are alternately labeled churches, temples, and betsuin, and for all intents and purposes, there is little substantive differences between these types of institutions."

8. Only Asian American Hindus were less likely to think of themselves as typical Americans, at 27 percent (Pew Research Center 2012, 30).

9. Among Asian Americans, Japanese Americans have the highest rates of intermarriage, with nearly two-thirds of newlyweds between 2008 and 2010 marrying a non-Asian (55 percent) or other Asian American (9 percent) (Pew Research Center 2013, 106).

10. I am indebted to Anne Spencer for her generosity in statistically reanalyzing for data on 18- to 29-year-olds, a group she did not analyze in her original publication.

REFERENCES

Arun. 2011. "The Emerging Face of Buddhism." *Angry Asian Buddhist*. Accessed March 24, 2016. http://www.angryasianbuddhist.com/2011/04/emerging-face-of-buddhism.html.

———. 2012a. "Discovering the Emerging Faces of Buddhism (Are Mostly White)." *Angry Asian Buddhist.* Accessed March 23, 2016. http://www.angryasianbuddhist.com /2012/08/discoveremerging-faces-of-buddhism-are.html.

———. 2012b. "Why Is the Under 35 Project So White?" *Angry Asian Buddhist.* Accessed March 24, 2016. http://www.angryasianbuddhist.com/2012/08/why-is-under-35 -project-so-white.html.

"A Brief History of Buddhist Geeks." 2016. *Buddhist Geeks.* Accessed March 23, 2016. http://web.archive.org/web/20160309221926/http://www.buddhistgeeks.com/history.

Cheah, Joseph. 2011. *Race and Religion in American Buddhism: White Supremacy and Immigrant Adaptation.* New York: Oxford University Press.

Chee, Beth Downing. 2015. "The Least Religious Generation." *San Diego State University News Center.* Accessed September 25, 2015. http://newscenter.sdsu.edu/sdsu_news center/news_story.aspx?sid=75623.

Gleig, Ann. 2014. "From Buddhist Hippies to Buddhist Geeks: The Emergence of Buddhist Postmodernism?" *Journal of Global Buddhism* 15:15–33.

Han, Chenxing. 2017. "Diverse Practices and Flexible Beliefs among Young Adult Asian American Buddhists." *Journal of Global Buddhism* 18:1–24.

Hickey, Wakoh Shannon. 2010. "Two Buddhisms, Three Buddhisms, and Racism." *Journal of Global Buddhism* 11:1–25.

Iwamura, Jane Naomi. 2011. *Virtual Orientalism: Asian Religions and American Popular Culture.* New York: Oxford University Press.

Kerstetter, Todd M. 2015. *Inspiration and Innovation: Religion in the American West.* Hoboken, NJ: Wiley-Blackwell.

Masatsugu, Michael K. 2008. "Beyond This World of Transiency and Impermanence: Japanese Americans, Dharma Bums, and the Making of American Buddhism during the Early Cold War Years." *Pacific Historical Review* 77(3): 423–451.

Mitchell, Scott A. 2010. "Locally Translocal American Shin Buddhism." *Pacific World,* 3rd Ser., No. 12, 109–126.

Nagata, Brian. 2006. "History of the Buddhist Church of Oakland." *Buddhist Church of Oakland.* Accessed March 30, 2016. http://web.archive.org/web/20160118031958/www .buddhistchurchofoakland.org/BCOhistory.htm.

Perreira, Todd LeRoy. 2004. "*Sasana Sakon* and the New Asian American: Intermarriage and Identity at a Thai Buddhist Temple in Silicon Valley." In *Asian American Religions: The Making and Remaking of Borders and Boundaries,* edited by Tony Carnes and Fenggang Yang, 313–337. New York: New York University Press.

Pew Research Center. 2012. "Asian Americans: A Mosaic of Faiths." Accessed August 9, 2015. https://www.pewresearch.org/wp-content/uploads/sites/7/2012/07/Asian-Amer icans-religion-full-report.pdf.

———. 2013. "The Rise of Asian Americans." Accessed August 9, 2015. http://www.pew socialtrends.org/files/2013/04/Asian-Americans-new-full-report-04-2013.pdf.

———. 2014. "Millennials in Adulthood: Detached from Institutions, Networked with Friends." Accessed August 9, 2015. http://www.pewsocialtrends.org/files/2014/03 /2014-03-07_generations-report-version-for-web.pdf.

Prebish, Charles S. 1999. *Luminous Passage: The Practice and Study of Buddhism in America.* Berkeley: University of California Press.

Quli, Natalie E. 2009. "Western Self, Asian Other: Modernity, Authenticity, and Nostalgia for 'Tradition' in Buddhist Studies." *Journal of Buddhist Ethics* 16:1–38.

Rocha, Cristina. 2010. "'Can I Put This Jizō Together with the Virgin Mary in the Altar?': Creolizing Zen Buddhism in Brazil." In *Issei Buddhism in the Americas,* edited by

Duncan Ryūken Williams and Tomoe Moriya, 5–26. Urbana: University of Illinois Press.

Seager, Richard Hughes. 2012. *Buddhism in America*. Rev. ed. New York: Columbia University Press.

Spencer, Anne C. 2014. "Diversification in the Buddhist Churches of America: Demographic Trends and Their Implications for the Future Study of U.S. Buddhist Groups." *Journal of Global Buddhism* 15:35–61.

Tamekuni, Steven. 2012. "TechnoBuddha Conference 2012: Who Am I? The Search for Spiritual Self in the Digital Age." *Buddhist Churches of America*. Accessed February 2, 2016. http://web.archive.org/web/20170322162558/http://buddhistchurchesofamerica.org/technobuddha-conference-2012/

Usuki, Patricia Kanaya. 2005. "American Women in Jodo Shin Buddhism Today: Tradition and Transition." *Pacific World*, 3rd Ser., No. 7. Accessed March 2, 2016. http://www.shin-ibs.edu/documents/pwj3-7/09KanayaUsuki37.pdf.

Williams, Duncan Ryūken. 2002. "Camp Dharma: Japanese-American Buddhist Identity and the Internment Experience of World War II." In *Westward Dharma: Buddhism Beyond Asia*, edited by Charles S. Prebish and Martin Baumann, 191–200. Berkeley: University of California Press.

Williams, Duncan Ryūken, and Tomoe Moriya, eds. 2010. *Issei Buddhism in the Americas*. Urbana: University of Illinois Press.

Yoo, David K. 1996. "Enlightened Identities: Buddhism and Japanese Americans of California, 1924–1941." *Western Historical Quarterly* 27(3): 281–301.

———. 1999. "Reframing the U.S. Religious Landscape." Introduction to *New Spiritual Homes: Religion and Asian Americans*, edited by David K. Yoo, 1–15. Honolulu: University of Hawai'i Press.

———. 2000. *Growing Up Nisei: Race, Generation, and Culture among Japanese Americans of California, 1924–49*. Urbana: University of Illinois Press.

PART III

REDEFINING ETHNICITY

7

Of Transgression

Zainichi Korean Immigrants' Search for
Home(s) and Belonging

KYUNG HEE HA

Take my daughter, for example. Her mother is a Zainichi person
and her father is from South Korea, and she was born and raised
in America. Is she neither Zainichi nor Korean, but merely Korean
American? I want her to come to terms with the complex
socio-historical contexts, which have made her who she is today,
and to develop her identity as such.—SUN-HEE

During the interview, Sun-hee, a second-generation Korean woman in her
fifties from Osaka, emphasized her desire for her daughter's identity development.[1] She wished her daughter to embrace complex and multiple
belongings rather than simplified and singular ones that equate nationality,
identity, and sense of belonging with one's physical location. Her narrative
also reveals that being physically transplanted outside of Japan, that is, no
longer *Zainichi* (residing in Japan) in a literal sense, does not automatically
mean that one stops being Zainichi politically, culturally, or otherwise. On
the contrary, as this chapter will demonstrate, many contemporary Korean
immigrants from Japan to the United States continue to hold onto, (re)dis-
cover, and strengthen their Zainichi Korean heritage and identity years after
their immigration despite the lack of availability of such an identity in the
United States.

According to the 2010 U.S. Census, people of Japanese heritage numbered
1,304,286, and people of Korean heritage 1,706,822. For the year 2017, naturalized American citizens included 1,713 Japanese, 14,643 South Koreans,
and 15 North Koreans.[2] Sun-hee and others that I will introduce in this
chapter do not fall neatly into these statistical categories because they are
ethnically Korean, born and raised in Japan, and usually hold a South Korean passport at the time of immigration. They are virtually nonexistent in
these official numbers. This chapter discusses the experiences of these "invisible" Koreans from Japan, generations of postcolonial exiles also known

as "Zainichi Koreans." As someone with Korean and Japanese backgrounds now residing in the United States, I explore different ways in which Zainichi Korean immigrants engage in the process of "home-making" (Espiritu 2003) in what follows. In *Home Bound*, Yen Le Espiritu (2003) defines "home-making" as "the process by which diverse subjects imagine and make themselves at home in various geographic locations" (2). How then do Zainichi Koreans imagine home(s)? What constitutes home(s), and in what ways do Zainichi Koreans assert their sense of belonging? I am interested in different means and tools through which Zainichi Koreans gain agency and make themselves at home.

This chapter employs interviews as the primary methodology. I conducted thirteen in-depth interviews with Zainichi Koreans who had been residing in the United States for more than ten years. Specifically, this chapter focuses on the third-generation Zainichi Koreans who were in their twenties and thirties at the time of interview over a span of four years between 2006 and 2010, and the number of years in residence and their resident status vary from citizen and permanent resident to nonimmigrant visa holder. I define "Zainichi Korean millennials" as those who were born in Japan to at least one Korean parent and grew up in the 1990s and 2000s in Japan and the United States. Examining Zainichi Koreans in the United States as the analytical site will help us better understand how immigrants retain ties and memories of home(land)s while physically relocating to and spending extended time in the United States. This study on recent Korean immigrants from Japan to the United States sheds lights on alternative Nikkei experiences that are neither the so-called grand narrative nor those of shin-nisei as discussed extensively in this volume, and allows us to explore the questions of citizenship and belonging for multiply displaced postcolonial subjects. I hope this essay will encourage us to better understand how "Japanese America" has been shaped and defined not only in relation to a larger American society, but also to the differences and diversity that have always existed within communities.

Living as "Quasi-Refugees"

At the end of Japanese colonization of Korea (1910–1945) and upon Japan's defeat in the Pacific War, some two million Koreans were living in Japan. Although the end of the war brought the dispersed Koreans hope for repatriation, this hope lasted only for a brief moment until the two mutually antagonistic ideologies, communism and capitalism, started to collide in their homeland, which eventually escalated into the Korean War (1950–1953). The instability and uncertainty in the Korean Peninsula consequently left some six hundred thousand Koreans behind on their former colonial master's soil. These immigrants became the primary group that constitutes today's diasporic community.[3] Those first-generation Koreans and their descendants later came to be known as "Koreans residing in Japan" or "Zainichi Koreans," in which "*zai*" means "residing in" and "*nichi*" means Japan in Japanese. The term "Zainichi" means more than one's physical location in Japan or a mere identity category. It also represents one's subject position as the marginalized within the sociohistorical and cultural context of Japan.

More than 90 percent of Koreans in Japan are born in Japan today (Ryang 1997).[4] Because Japanese nationality law employs *jus sanguinis,* or the principle of blood, one is not automatically given Japanese nationality by having been born in Japan. In 2015, 491,711 Koreans were registered as "aliens" in the Alien Registration System.[5] Of those, 411,547 hold permanent residency,[6] constituting a group of what Suh Kyung-sik (2002) terms "quasi-refugees,"[7] without official citizenship or full civil rights (such as suffrage), not only in Japan but also in either state of the Korean Peninsula.[8]

While rendered "aliens" *at home,* Koreans in Japan have employed various ways to deal with the sense of displacement and dispossession. A total of 92,749 Zainichi Koreans (and 6,600 Japanese nationals, mostly female spouses) were "repatriated" to North Korea under the "humanitarian" arrangement between the North Korean Red Cross and the Japanese Red Cross between 1959 and 1984 (Morris-Suzuki 2007; Ryang 2008); and more than 350,000 were naturalized as Japanese between 1952 and 2013.[9] Furthermore, for the majority of Zainichi Koreans—whether naturalized or not—"passing" has been a "default option," as sociologist John Lie (2008, 20) writes, "For second-generation ethnic Koreans in Japan—in fact, even for any first-generation Koreans who were being busily Japanized in the prewar period—passing was a default option. Many ethnic Koreans are willy-nilly in the closet because in everyday interaction they pass as ordinary Japanese. In other words, unlike African Americans, *not* passing for Zainichi requires a decision to be out of the ethnic closet: one must consciously assert ethnic identification by divulging one's Korean name or ancestry (emphasis in original)."

Although "passing" produces "anxiety from the omnipresent threat of exposure and the ethical conundrum of leading a life of deception" (19), Zainichi Koreans continue to engage in the practice of "passing." The 2000 Mindan statistics reveal that nearly 90 percent of Zainichi Koreans use Japanese aliases to hide their Korean background, thereby avoiding possible discrimination and prejudices.[10] International forums such as the United Nations Commission on Human Rights have noted that the "deep" and "profound" racism and xenophobia have continued to prevail in Japan to this day.[11]

Born as "quasi-refugees," some choose naturalization while others choose repatriation to the Korean Peninsula in their efforts to find home. Yet others fight for their civil rights as "foreign residents" without naturalizing as Japanese nationals (Chung 2010). In addition, a group of Zainichi Koreans immigrated to the United States, a "country of freedom," hoping to cultivate a sense of belonging. While my previous works (Ha 2016; Fischer and Ha 2012) have focused on both second- and third-generation Zainichi Korean immigrants to the United States, this chapter focuses on the third-generation young adults who were in their twenties and thirties at the time of interview, the so-called millennials.

Unlike the second-generation Zainichi Korean immigrants who all testified that they had experienced severe racism and sexism in Japan, most of the third-generation individuals that I introduce in this chapter did not experience racism in a blatant form. Instead, as Jinsuk (male in his twenties) notes, racism in Japan was "hidden like people wouldn't acknowledge." In addition to their different experience of racism in Japan, millennial Zainichi Korean immigrants also varied greatly from the older generation in terms of their gender component, class/educational background, and purposes and means of their immigration. Specifically, the older generation Zainichi Korean immigrants that I interviewed in the past were predominantly women without a college degree at the time of immigration. To escape from racism and sexism in Japan, they married American men and eventually moved to the United States, leaving their families behind. In contrast, among the younger Zainichi Korean immigrants that I interviewed were an almost equal number of men and women (seven males and six females), all of whom have at least a four-year college degree. The majority of them had immigrated with their middle-class family members who were to enroll in graduate schools and research institutions or start businesses in the United States. The number of years of residence (except one who grew up in Canada and immigrated to the United States as an adult) varied from ten to twenty-five years. While some have kept South Korean or Japanese nationality with permanent residency status in the United States, others have naturalized as U.S. citizens.

As Multiply Displaced Subjects

The earliest scholarship on Korean immigrants from Japan in the United States traces back to the 1978 master's thesis of Dae-kyun Chung, a Zainichi Korean sociologist who studied at the University of California, Los Angeles, from 1976 to 1978. In his thesis, "Japan-born Koreans in the United States: Their Experiences in Japan and the United States," Chung delineates life experiences of thirty-two second-generation Zainichi Korean individuals who immigrated to the United States because of the anti-Korean racism and discrimination. Unable to see their future in Japan despite their middle-class background and college-level education, they decided to immigrate to the United States. While some initially came as sojourners, others came to settle permanently in the country they associated with freedom and equal opportunity. According to Chung, being Korean changed its meaning and significance from being negative to neutral in relation to Japanese, eventually leading to "Koreanization" among Zainichi Korean immigrants. One of his interviewees said that she is only seen as an Asian uniformly regardless of her ethnicity and that Koreans and Japanese have become "equally foreigners" in the United States. As a result, she feels much easier being Korean and using her Korean name, not only with Americans but also with Japanese.

Other studies reveal more diverse reactions amongst Zainichi Korean immigrants. Eika Tai (1999) conducted interviews with people from Japan in the San Francisco Bay Area that included several Zainichi Koreans as well as other ethnic minorities from Japan. Some of her interviewees also experienced the Koreanization process that Chung discussed, but others contrarily moved toward a more Japanese identity because they have realized how culturally Japanese they are as a result of being exposed to a large number of Koreans from South Korea who were very different from them. Others have started to hold a more cosmopolitan identity, refusing the ethnic labeling and adopting U.S. multiculturalism that at least in theory celebrates different cultures equally.

Chung's and Tai's innovative works on Zainichi Korean immigrants in the United States suggest that overall they find it easier to be who they are (that is, Koreans by ancestry and Japanese by culture and upbringing), in their new host country because of its liberal and egalitarian policies toward racialized minorities. The interviews they conducted generally construct the United States as a benevolent nation, the idea juxtaposed with their firsthand negative experiences of being Korean in Japan. As a result, many of them seek legal and political inclusion through naturalization.

United States as Benevolent Nation

Similar to the previous studies by Chung and Tai, interviews that I conducted also reveal the shared perception that the United States is much more liberal and democratic than Japan among Zainichi Korean young adults. They feel more comfortable being a minority in the United States because of the larger population of (visible) minorities—a direct result of the imperialism that the United States seeks to forget—and the recognition of issues related to these groups. Jinsuk (male in his twenties) compares the minority situation between Japan and the United States and points out a critical difference in the way that racism is treated in each country: "[In Japan,] I always felt it [racism] was hidden like people wouldn't acknowledge. . . . In America, it's opposite of Japan. . . . People say there's so much racism here. It might be true, but at the same time, at least it's acknowledged and we see it when it's happening." Likewise, Junko (female in her twenties) raises a (re)naming practice as an indicator of the U.S. benevolence that tolerates and even celebrates different racial and ethnic backgrounds and cultural practices. When Junko's family moved to Hawai'i, they "ditched" their Japanese last name, Kaneda, and started to use Kim. She considered switching her last name to Korean was "cool" because she now knew that "people here won't care" as opposed to in Japan where she and her sister were raised to hide their Korean identity. As Junko's account indicates, being able to use their Korean name more easily signifies not simply having a choice of the name that one uses but also the fact one can be "open" about being Korean without any negative consequences.

Despite the importance of these examples of social and cultural acceptance, the starkest difference between the United States and Japan that my interviewees emphasized was access to citizenship and civil rights. As an example, Rika (female in her thirties) finds it extremely powerful to have laws to protect individual rights against racism: "I think that it's easier to live in the United States . . . [even though] there are a lot of things about this country that is not really minority friendly, or that a lot of it are [sic] dominated by white people. . . . I think at least you feel like that law is there to protect your individual rights. I think coming to America, a lot of things happened, but in the end, I think that it's given me the sense of identity that I am proud to be actually Korean with my Japanese background." Rika believes that citizenship and constitutional protection in fact grant her the right to embrace her ancestral and cultural backgrounds, the right she was never allowed to have while living in Japan.

Significantly, Jinsuk, Junko, and Rika talk about U.S. benevolence in explicit and specific comparisons with their and their parents' experiences in Japan—societal acknowledgment of racism, tolerance toward different cultural practices to citizenship, and protection of rights for minorities—none of which was afforded in Japan. Specifically, Jinsuk (male in his twenties) clearly remembers how segregated his high school in California was by "color lines." Nami (female in her thirties) also shared her experience of being treated as a "delinquent" by her neighbors growing up in the Midwest just because she was not white. Nami was later politicized during her college years as a "woman of color" because of the racism and sexism she experienced in different parts of the country she had resided. Even when people like Jinsuk and Nami share their experience of being discriminated against for being Asian (American), they emphasize that these incidents were primarily interpersonal and acknowledge that the U.S. society strives to be "as politically correct as it can."

Although they are aware of the issues and their positionality as racialized minority and immigrants, they still feel more comfortable in the United States where they feel racism is acknowledged and their individual rights are protected by laws. Furthermore, many reported that they felt strongly supported being Asian and American at the same time. In other words, being

"American" does not necessarily mean the total negation of their ethnic and cultural heritage, unlike in Japan where being Korean and Japanese were considered to be mutually exclusive. In this way, the idea that the United States is a liberal democratic country is developed and reinforced among Zainichi Korean immigrants.

Perpetual Aliens in Japanese and Korean America

Although the majority of the interviewees have expressed that they felt somewhat "liberated" about being Korean, their sense of alienation does not disappear completely because they are faced with a lack of recognition and space for their unique ethnic Zainichi background in their new host country. As Junho (male in his twenties) expressed, "I feel that my identity is best characterized as an 'ethnic minority.' This may be an idiosyncratic way of defining ethnic identity but I feel that this is the only way to encompass everything that I am. . . . I feel this way because in every community that I lived in, I was a minority. The fact that I was and still am an ethnic minority is the only thing that has been consistent throughout my life as far as my identity is concerned." Some of my interviewees reported their unpleasant interactions with Korean immigrants and Korean Americans. For example, Masato (male in his twenties) talked about his experience at a Korean church[12] where one of the members tried to test his loyalty by invoking the recent dispute over Dokdo (Takeshima in Japanese), a group of islets between South Korea and Japan. Other interviewees including Chang-ho (male in his thirties) and Rika (female in her thirties) have also noted that they felt that their authenticity is always being checked. What it means to be Korean is determined and regulated by Koreans from Korea or Korean Americans who consider themselves culturally and linguistically more authentic.[13] In diasporic Korean communities, Zainichi Koreans are generally seen as not "Korean enough" culturally, linguistically, politically, and ideologically, and thus made to feel alienated in Korean diasporic spaces.

Naturally, many of my interviewees associate with Japanese immigrants because of their shared linguistic and cultural background. While none of them reported an incident of explicit racism when interacting with Japanese communities and individuals, some commented on ignorance and limitations. For example, Hyemi (female in her twenties) shared the frustration she felt when she realized that the Japanese community can only be helpful to a certain extent; for example, it cannot address specific legal issues, such as reentry permits to Japan and retaining Japanese permanent residency, with which Zainichi Koreans outside of Japan are confronted.

Several of my interviewees started to regard themselves in a more "cosmopolitan" way, an identity alternative to having to choose between Japanese and Korean. Satoshi (male in his thirties) still uses his Japanese name in the United States, but identifies himself as an "international Zainichi Korean." Satoshi says he does not want to naturalize as a Japanese national because he thinks having as many ethnic affiliations as possible is to his advantage. Similarly, Eric (male in his twenties) identifies himself as someone who has "Korean nationality, born in Japan and living in the United States." Eric says, "Three cultures (Korean, Japanese, and American) accumulate and influence each other and make who I am." Both Satoshi and Eric appreciate their unique paths and describe who they are as a mixture of these cultures that they have lived with, without negating any of them.

However, a handful of my interviewees showed concerns about these identity categories that are unable to fully encompass their unique upbringing as a minority in their home country *and* new host country. Their narratives resonate with the experiences of Koreans who immigrated to the United States from Latin American countries, such as Brazil, Argentina, and Paraguay. Anthropologist Kyeyoung Park's (1999) study explicates dilemmas and challenges experienced by yet-another group of multiply displaced subjects who are "floating in the air." Her research on Korean–Latin Americans demonstrates that they do not form a strong sense of belonging to any ethnic group. As one of her interviewees said, "I feel always torn apart, feeling that I don't fit in any of these three cultures perfectly. I am uprooted completely." Similar narratives were found among my interviewees, feeling "uprooted" as an ethnic minority no matter where they live. In the next section, I discuss different ways in which Zainichi Korean young adults deal with the sense of "homelessness." In the words of Seokyung (male in his thirties), "No matter where I go, I am an ethnic minority. I am homeless."

Homing Desire, Homing Practices

Sociologist Avtar Brah (1996, 180) distinguishes "desire for a 'homeland'" and "homing desire" among diasporic populations in which the former presupposes the fixed origins to which they desire to return to, while the latter focuses on desire to make home(s) in places that are not necessarily their ancestral homelands. Moving away from "original homeland," Hamid Naficy (1999, 6) defines home as "anyplace; it is temporary and it is moveable; it can be built, rebuilt, and carried in memory and by acts of imagination." Similarly, Yen Le Espiritu (2003, 10) defines home as "not only a physical place that immigrants return to for temporary and intermittent visits but also a concept and a desire—a place that immigrants visit through the imagination." Borrowing their ideas of locating home(s) as unfixed conceptual space that can exist temporarily in, between, and around the "homeland" and the host country, I examine different means and tools through which Zainichi Koreans gain agency and make themselves at home. I argue that they engage in "home-making" by creating space and gaining recognition in the context of American society, as well as by retaining multiple legal statuses that allow them to be "flexible citizens" who are able to transgress multiple national, cultural, and linguistic borders.

Zainichi Korean American Communities

One way Zainichi Koreans make themselves at home in the United States is through creating a group for themselves. Lim Bangja, a second-generation Zainichi Korean woman from Osaka founded Zainichi-no-Kai, L.A. (hereafter Zainichi-no-Kai) in 1998. The members of the group included Zainichi Koreans of various age groups whose years of residency in Japan and the United States greatly varied (Zainichi-no-Kai newsletters). In an interview (*Asahi Shimbun* article of April 6, 1998), Bangja explains that after twenty-four years since her migration in 1974, she was finally able to come to terms with being "Zainichi, nothing else." Since the inauguration of the group, more than twenty participants gathered at Bangja's restaurant located in West Hollywood. In their monthly meeting, participants would introduce themselves and their family backgrounds, share personal issues such as marriage and employment, and together think about what it means to "remain Zainichi" while their physical location make them "Zaibei" (residing in the United States). The generational difference was stark between the second-generation who experienced blatant racism and the third-generation who benefited from economic prosperity and political stability in Japan that eventually led them to expand the horizons beyond the Japanese borders. Even among the same age groups, members found their experiences to be very diverse, depending on where they grew up and what kind of schools they attended. As the Zainichi-no-Kai newsletter of November 1, 1998 concludes, "There are as many ways of living as Zainichi as there are people." Despite these differences, the Zainichi-no-Kai members together created a space that provided legal advice and emotional support, as well as celebrated their unique ethnic and cultural background.

While Zainichi-no-Kai mostly focused on social and cultural gatherings, a newer Zainichi Korean group, Eclipse Rising, emphasizes its political involvement in promoting "Zainichi community development, peace and re-unification in the Korean Peninsula, and social justice for all oppressed groups in Japan, the United States, and beyond, through transnational education, advocacy, and solidarity."[14] Founded in 2008, not all core members and other community members necessarily had identified as Zainichi Koreans before joining the group. Rather, many of them started to perceive themselves as part of a larger Zainichi Korean community when they "discovered" shared histories and memories as young adults, since this knowledge was not always available to them in the United States. Members of Eclipse Rising include mixed-race Zainichi Koreans with Japanese and white American heritage, as well as queer-identified individuals with differences in age, nationality, first language, and knowledge of Zainichi Korean history and culture. In her groundbreaking master's thesis, "Uri Transnational Movement Building," Kei Fischer (2011, 100) argues that Eclipse Rising has successfully created a space of "home" for those Zainichi Koreans with diverse backgrounds who have a "sense of shared networks, mutual support, and common ideology" rather than mere ethnic authenticity. Considering the issues that racialized minorities face in Japan and the United States as comparative and relational, as well as issues connected to militarism, globalization, and indigeneity, Eclipse Rising has employed a transpacific approach and played a bridging role between the two sides of the Pacific. As a significant example, Eclipse Rising has cofounded the Japan Multicultural Relief Fund along with the Japan Pacific Resource Network in the immediate wake of the March 11, 2011, Great Tohoku Earthquake that triggered a tsunami and nuclear meltdown in northeastern Japan.[15] These organizations assessed damages on the ground with particular focus on vulnerable communities, including migrant workers, single mothers, and Zainichi Koreans, and identified the community organizations that work with these populations, delivering a total of $44,435.34 in relief funds raised within the United States. This experience has had a significant impact on one of the Eclipse Rising members. Mihwa (female in her thirties) said, "This was personally the most rewarding experience I've ever had, being able to send the fund to the organizations that support 'people of color' in Japan such as Koreans, Filipinos, and people with disabilities. . . . They had been so isolated and deprived. [When I met one of the fund's recipient organizations] I was really happy because I knew this task could only probably be done by us, Eclipse Rising." Most recently, Eclipse Rising helped mobilize support from Japanese civic organizations in support of the resolution introduced by Supervisor Eric Mar in San Francisco that urges the City and County of San Francisco to establish a memorial for so-called comfort women—the victims and survivors of Japan's sexual slavery during the World War II and to educate the broader public about ongoing global human trafficking.[16] Members of Eclipse Rising have increasingly placed their focus on building and strengthening transpacific solidarity as a way to claim and celebrate their unique experiences and consciousness in collaboration with diverse communities both in the United States and Japan.

Transgression as Homing Desire and Practice

While on a collective level, Zainichi Koreans in the United States have come together to create their own community as a way to establish "home" and claim a sense of belonging in metropolitan cities such as Los Angeles and the San Francisco Bay Area, some interviewees considered becoming U.S. citizens as a way to establish full membership in the society, particularly through exercising voting rights. Others engage in homing practices in a form of literal and discursive transgression of national, cultural, and linguistic borders on a daily basis. One significant way to secure the means of transgression is to have legal statuses in multiple nations, namely the United States (gaining citizenship or permanent residency), Japan (retaining permanent residency), and South Korea (retaining nationality). By retaining as many legal statuses as possible, they attempt to have "multiple homes" between which they have means to move and make a living with flexibility, thus creating another way to engage in homing desire and home-making practice. Here's what Yuna (female in her thirties) had to say about why she had recently decided to become a U.S. citizen: "I'm applying for the citizenship. . . . There is a pragmatism that I didn't really have before. In the United States, even if you become a citizen, [y]our connections with Korea or Japan are not going to be jeopardized. . . . I go back to Japan regularly. My family is there. My grandparents are buried there. I want to be able to go back to Japan infinitely, but I would rather die [than] become a Japanese national."

While living in Japan, none of my interviewees actively sought naturalization as a solution to ending their life as "quasi-refugees" because they were aware of the process that required total assimilation, a legacy from the colonial era, or simply did not see the urgent necessity to do so. However, after living in the United States, some of my interviewees started to view naturalization as an effective way to end the condition as an ultimate stranger as well as to retain their ties with Japan through obtaining an American passport (i.e., freedom of mobility). For many who have lived in the United States for twenty or thirty years, it is likely that they had to give up their Japanese permanent residency at some point because of Japanese immigration regulations.[17] Upon losing permanent residency in Japan, all South Korean nationals, whether or not they were born in Japan, had to obtain a tourist visa—the inconvenience and source of frustration expressed by my interviewees.[18]

On the contrary, U.S. nationals were not required to have a tourist visa to Japan for ninety days or less, which in and of itself reflects how powerful U.S. hegemony is in the world. The desire for a U.S. passport implies that they regard having ties with Japan as a critical element for them to retain their Zainichi Korean identity while they are no longer Zainichi (residing in Japan) in a literal sense. U.S. citizenship allows them to overcome the sense of alienation in *and* beyond the U.S. context by providing legal rights in the United States where they currently reside as well as means for easier travels to Japan—connections that remain critical to their identity as Zainichi Koreans today.

Similarly, Junho who has lived in the United States for sixteen years, held permanent residency in the United States and Japan as well as South Korean nationality because he believed that it was "a privilege very valuable for someone who wishes to work internationally"; it allows him to legally live and work in any of those countries. My interviewees seemed to have come to the conclusion that it is impossible to feel completely "at home" in a single geographical location. Instead, they make attempts to have multiple homes between which they had means to move with flexibility through gaining as many legal statuses as possible. They negotiate and maneuver between different nationality and immigration laws in order to maintain access to a passport and permanent residency. For example, Kwang-il (male in his thirties) returns to Japan every few years to retain Japanese permanent residency in part because South Korean nationals with permanent residency in another country are exempted from the compulsory military service. Similarly, some of my interviewees intentionally refuse to naturalize as U.S. citizens and remain mere permanent residents because South Korean nationality law does not allow dual citizenship by principle. All of these regulations and responsibilities upon acquiring citizenship or losing permanent residency can potentially limit flexible mobility of Zainichi Koreans. Interestingly, some of my interviewees described having noncitizen status in multiple nation-states as a "privilege very valuable for someone who wishes to work internationally." Indeed, to be able to remain noncitizen subjects while having means to travel transnationally may be a privilege, but the privilege also involves the inconveniences and disadvantages of not having citizenship or protection of civil rights in any country. In other words, their flexibility is at the expense of not having protection of their rights.

This difference is probably the most important one between Zainichi Koreans with multiple noncitizen statuses and those who are often described as "flexible citizens" by Aihwa Ong (1999) and others. While the latter denotes the elite global businessmen who accumulate passports as safeguards in times of political uncertainty and economic instability, Zainichi Korean immigrants negotiate different kinds of governmentality while rejecting to be fully incorporated into any single nation-state. It may be inevitable for Zainichi Koreans, as subjects of multiple displacement who are divided by national borders, ideologies, languages, and cultures to imagine and have homes in and between various geographical locations. In this regard, those who naturalize as U.S. citizens and those who refuse naturalization are rather similar in the sense that both of them make their choices based on the same desire to have means for flexible and fluid mobility.

Conclusion

I have attempted to show the different ways in which Zainichi Koreans in the United States responded to their homing desire—overcoming a sense of displacement. Whether they choose to become citizens or remain stateless, maintaining and regaining ties with Japan seem central to their motives because what it means to be Zainichi Korean is still very much rooted in the space of Japan. Material and symbolic ties with Japan play a crucial role in constructing their subjectivity and identity as transnational Zainichi Koreans. For some, it meant to remain noncitizen subjects with multiple permanent residencies and nationality, and for others, it meant to become a U.S. citizen because U.S. nationality allows them to have easier transnational movement.

NOTES

1. All of names of the interviewees in this chapter are pseudonyms, and the generations of the interviewees reflect their generations in Japan, not in the United States. In other words, "second-generation" means that they were born to Korean immigrant parents in Japan, and "third-generation" means that they were born to second-generation parents.

2. U.S. Department of Homeland Security, *Yearbook of Immigration 2017, Persons Naturalized by Region and Country of Birth: Fiscal Years 2015 to 2017*, accessed June 16, 2019, https://www.dhs.gov/immigration-statistics/yearbook/2017/table21.

3. In addition to the chaos in the Korean Peninsula, restrictions on carrying property out of Japan, the shortage of return ships to Korea, and the fact that they had established families and businesses in Japan led some Koreans to decide to remain in Japan. However, most of them thought their stay in Japan would be temporary and were still going back to Korea, as they hoped the reunification would be realized shortly. Koreans in China, as well as Sakhalin and other parts of the former Soviet Union, whose displacement is rooted in Japanese colonial rule, remained in these respective regions after the liberation for many different reasons. Like Zainichi Koreans, they have created distinct diasporic communities.

4. Out of those who originally came from (colonial) Korea, more than 97 percent are from southern parts the Korean Peninsula such as Kyong Sang province, Cholla province, and Jeju Island (Ryang 1997, 3).

5. According to the Japanese Ministry of Justice Statistics (December 2015), registered foreign residents in Japan number 2,232,189, making up 1.75 percent of the total Japanese population. The majority are Chinese (665,847) and Koreans (491,711), followed by Filipinos (229,595) and Brazilians (173,437). See https://www.e-stat.go.jp/stat-search/files?page=1&layout=datalist&toukei=00250012&tstat=000001018034&cycle=1&year=20150&month=24101212&tclass1=000001060399.

6. Ibid.

7. See Suh Kyung-sik, *Han-nanmin no Ichikara* [From the standpoint of quasi-refugees] (Tokyo: Kage Shobo, 2002).

8. Zainichi Koreans with South Korean nationality were granted partial suffrage in South Korea in 2012 as a result of the South Korean constitutional court ruling that determined that overseas South Korean nationals being deprived of voting rights was a violation of human rights.

9. *Human Rights and Life* 39 (December 2014), 67–68. Since the mid-1990s, approximately 10,000 Zainichi Koreans naturalize as Japanese each year.

10. *2000-nen do Zainichi Kankokujin Ishiki Chosa Chukan Hokoku* [The 2000 Zainichi Korean Survey Interim Report] (Tokyo: Zainichi Kankoku Mindan, 2001).

11. Doudou Diène, *Report of the Special Rapporteur on Contemporary Forms of Racism, Racial Discrimination, Xenophobia and Related intolerance, Doudou Diène, on His Mission to Japan.* UN Commission on Human Rights (January 24, 2006). See http://www.debito.org/UNdienereport012406.html.

12. Korean churches have long functioned as a "gatekeeper" for Korean communities in the United States, providing a space to nurture one's faith and to build kinship and business partnership among the members.

13. The 2000 Mindan Survey reveals that less than 10 percent of Zainichi Koreans are foreign-born as opposed to 57 percent among Korean Americans according to the 2000 Census. In terms of language proficiency, while over 70 percent of Korean Americans speak Korean at home, more than 90 percent of those born after 1976 said they are not able to carry basic conversations in Korean. These numbers may suggest that Zainichi Koreans are more assimilated into the host society linguistically and culturally than Korean Americans.

14. Eclipse Rising website, accessed August 1, 2015, https://sites.google.com/site/eclipserising/about-us.

15. The Great Tohoku Earthquake, the strongest earthquake known to have hit Japan in over 140 years, resulted in nearly 16,000 deaths and an estimated $200–300 billion in property damage. See "The Great Tohoku, Japan Earthquake and Tsunami: Facts, Engineering, News and Maps," Multidisciplinary Center for Earthquake Engineering Research (MCEER), accessed June 1, 2016, http://mceer.buffalo.edu/infoservice/disasters/Honshu-Japan-Earthquake-Tsunami-2011.asp.

16. The San Francisco Board of Supervisors unanimously passed the resolution on September 22, 2015.

17. As special permanent residents of Japan, Zainichi Koreans with a foreign passport need to retain a "reentry permit" from the Japanese Ministry of Justice if they wish to retain the legal status. The permit could only be renewed at a local office of the Japanese Ministry of Justice every year before 1991 and every four years after that (confirmed with the Osaka Immigration Bureau [Kyoto Branch] on February 1, 2015). For detailed discussion on the history of the reentry permit system and Zainichi Koreans, please refer to Chung Yeong Hwan, "'Sainyukoku Kyoka' Seido no Rekishi to Genzai" [History and Present of the 'Reentry Permit' System], *PRIME* 33 (2011): 31–46.

18. It was not until March 2006 that South Korean nationals were allowed to visit Japan for ninety days or less without a tourist visa.

REFERENCES

Brah, Avtar. 1996. *Cartographies of Diaspora: Contesting Identities.* London: Routledge.

Chung, Dae-kyung. 1978. "Japan-born Koreans in the United States: Their Experiences in Japan and the United States." M.A. thesis, University of California, Los Angeles.

Chung, Erin Aeran. 2010. *Immigration and Citizenship in Japan.* Cambridge, UK: Cambridge University Press.

Espiritu, Yen Le. 2003. *Home Bound: Filipino American Lives across Cultures, Communities, and Countries.* Berkeley: University of California Press.

Fischer, Kei. 2011. "Uri Transnational Movement Building." M.A. thesis, San Francisco State University.

Fischer, Kei, and Kyung Hee Ha. 2012. "Zainichi Koreans (Koreans in/from Japan): Replanting Our Roots." In *Koreans in America: History, Culture, Identity,* edited by Grace Yoo, 119–130. San Diego: University Readers.

Ha, Kyung Hee. 2016. "Zainichi Koreans [Koreans from Japan] in the U.S.: Negotiating Multiple Displacement and Statelessness." *PAN JAPAN: The International Journal of the Japanese Diaspora* 11 (1–2): 41–67.

Lie, John. 2008. *Zainichi (Koreans in Japan): Diasporic Nationalism and Postcolonialism.* Berkeley: University of California Press.

Morris-Suzuki, Tessa. 2007. *Exodus to North Korea: Shadows from Japan's Cold War.* Asian Voices. Lanham, MD: Rowman and Littlefield.

Naficy, Hamid. 1999. *Home, Exile, Homeland: Film, Media, and the Politics of Place.* London: Routledge.

Ong, Aihwa. 1999. *Flexible Citizenship: The Cultural Logic of Transnationality.* Durham, NC: Duke University Press.

Park, Kyeyoung. 1999. "I Am Floating in the Air": Creation of a Korean Transnational Space among Korean–Latino American Remigrants." *Positions* 7(3): 667–695.

Ryang, Sonia. 1997. *North Koreans in Japan: Language, Ideology, and Identity.* Boulder, CO: Westview Press.

———. 2008. *Writing Selves in Diaspora: Ethnography of Autobiographics of Korean Women in Japan and the United States.* New Asian Anthropology. Lanham, MD: Lexington.

Suh, Kyungsik. 2002. *Han-Nanmin no Ichi Kara* [From the standpoint of "semi-refugee"]. Tokyo: Kage Shobo.

Tai, Eika. 1999. *Tabunka Shugi to Diasupora* [Multiculturalism and diaspora]. Tokyo: Akashi Shoten.

U.S. Department of Homeland Security. 2017. *Yearbook of Immigration Statistics 2017, Persons Naturalized by Region and Country of Birth: Fiscal Years 2015 to 2017.* Accessed June 16, 2019. https://www.dhs.gov/.

8

Millennial Shin-Issei Identity Politics in Los Angeles

AKI YAMADA

The U.S. West Coast and Hawai'i exhibit a rich history of Japanese immigration over the last century and a half. Many descendants of the original Japanese immigrant communities are already transitioning to the fifth generation and are increasingly assimilating toward mainstream American culture and lifestyle. Aside from this first wave of early Japanese immigrants, a group of contemporary Japanese who recently arrived from Japan also reside in the United States. Today, a yearning for betterment of socioeconomic status no longer motivates emigration from Japan. Rather, modern Japanese migrants have a diverse range of reasons for immigrating to the United States. Economic, cultural, and academic globalization has facilitated the arrival of transnational Japanese individuals, families, and groups to the United States.

The postwar movements of these "New Japanese" (also known as *shin-issei* in Japanese) overseas are closely linked to the transnational economic expansion of Japanese industries starting in the 1960s (Adachi 2006). During the mid to late 1960s, the Japanese economy grew drastically, expanding both domestically and internationally. The first significant wave of New Japanese individuals, transnational corporate sojourners, and other groups began to arrive to the United States after the Immigration and Nationality Act of 1965 relaxed restrictive immigration quotas. This trend of Japanese economic expansion continued into Japan's bubble economy during the 1980s, resulting in numerous waves of New Japanese settling in the United States. I understand globalization as the transnational movement of economic goods and knowledge and as the increased mobility in the people following these trends. Modern globalization plays a strong role in the creation of New Japanese communities in the United States.

As contemporary Japanese immigrated to the United States, their experiences created a distinct group of migrants. I differentiate between these New Japanese immigrants because their circumstances differ from the previous, pre–World War II Japanese immigrants in terms of globalization factors, education, economic background, and reception in American society. Being a diverse group of people, some of the major groups of New Japanese migrants include cultural migrants, specialized professionals, corporate sojourners and their families, blue-collar workers, and small business entrepreneurs. The New Japanese hail from many socioeconomic backgrounds, but mostly they belong to the middle class and are not motivated by poverty. The arrival of New Japanese immigrants in the United States provides an opportunity to look at migration through the lenses of modern globalization and transnational identity. Linda Basch, Nina G. Schiller, and Cristina Blanc (1994, 6), define transnationalism as the "process by which immigrants forge and sustain multi-stranded social relations that link together their societies of origin and settlement." As modern immigrants, shin-issei enjoy the benefits of Japan's new economic strength, readily accessible ties to their homeland through globalization and technological advancement, and in some cases, belonging to international corporate or academic entities providing support. These factors are very important points of analysis in understanding the characteristics of shin-issei.

This chapter begins to fill the void of discourse on millennial New Japanese immigrants in the literature. I explore the unique characteristics of millennial New Japanese (immigrants born between 1980 and 2000) in the United States, specifically Los Angeles, and their integration into their American host society. To help the reader understand the shin-issei categorization and the diversity within it, I examine three major shin-issei groups: (1) cultural migrants, (2) specialized professionals, and (3) corporate sojourners and their children. Each group helps demonstrate the reasons that shin-issei are being pushed and pulled abroad. Drawing from in-depth interviews with members from each of these groups I examine Angeleno shin-issei identity and community, both as migrants and immigrants. The introduction of transnationalism and globalization are essential to researching contemporary Japanese with the aim of truly identifying the modus operandi of the New Japanese in Los Angeles. While transmigrant identities prevail in specialized professionals and corporate sojourner families, their social spheres are close-knit and generally demonstrate a preference to associate with other shin-issei over Americans or even Japanese Americans. This research examines the influence and impact of transnationalism and globalization by focusing on characteristics of New Japanese communities and how these themes factor into their sense of identity and culture, lifestyle, and means of living in the United States. Additionally, I analyze the roles of Japanese identity and culture and the central themes that arose from my research. However, I do not explore the relationship of these immigrants with the broader Japanese American community as I did not gather relevant data.

A Case Study of Angeleno Shin-Issei

Los Angeles County provides a robust New Japanese presence to study. Among all the places Japanese migrate to, it is easy to find examples of Japanese corporate sojourner subjects who migrated to the United States in the Los Angeles area and became issei immigrants. Japanese corporate internationalization in the Americas began in the 1960s—Southern California was a primary expansion point in the United States (Yasuike 2005). Torrance was home to the U.S. headquarters of major Japanese companies like Honda, Toyota, All Nippon Airways, as well as the native Mitsuwa supermarket chain. The creation of these major connections is indicative of the Japanese business preference toward this area. According to the 2010 Census, the population of Torrance was 10.6 percent Japanese, making Japanese the most common recorded racial ancestry (U.S. Census Bureau 2010). Furthermore, it is estimated that the average payroll for Southern California–based Japanese firms is 48 percent higher than the California average (Consulate General of Japan 2011), indicating that Japanese corporate sojourners and longer-term business workers associated with Japanese companies have significant economic means that isolate them from ethnic enclaves and ghettos usually associated with new immigrant groups.

From 2012 to 2014, I conducted research to learn more about the New Japanese and their lifestyles in Los Angeles. Primary methodologies for this case study included participant observation, ethnography, and in-depth interviews while spending time with the New Japanese community in Los Angeles. Qualitative methodology enabled a personal understanding of their lifestyles, motivations, and mindsets. During this period, I took part in the Japanese Graduate Student Association in Los Angeles, and through this association I could connect with and interview many fellow graduate students. Additionally, I worked as a teaching assistant at a Japanese weekend supplementary school, where I met and interviewed shin-issei staff members, parents, and their friends in the New Japanese community. I established rapport with many shin-issei individuals and acquainted myself with the community from an insider's perspective. I recorded, transcribed, and translated more than twenty-five interviews of millennials and non-millennials in Japanese, the preferred language of all my shin-issei interviewees. I refer to each participant using fictitious names throughout this chapter.

Terminology

In this section, I briefly discuss the basis for positing that millennials are people born between 1980 and 2000. A global employee survey conducted by PricewaterhouseCoopers, London Business School, and the University of Southern California counts those born between 1980 and 1995 as millennials (Finn and Donovan 2013). A similar study done by Goldman Sachs expands the scope of millennials to include those born between 1980 and 2000. Finally, the U.S. Census, a demographic authority, defines millennials as those born between 1982 and 2000 (U.S. Census Bureau 2015). As I demonstrated multiple data points on both ends of the spectrum, I posit that the millennials generation includes anyone born between 1980 and 2000.

In Japanese, members of the first generation of these New Japanese immigrants are called *shin-issei*, and their American-born second-generation children are called *shin-nisei*. To break down these terms, in Japanese *shin* means "new" and *issei* means "first generation," or "immigrants from Japan" (Ichioka 1990), and *nisei* means "second generation." Japanese terminology for generational qualifiers further extends to the third generation as *sansei*, the fourth generation as *yonsei*, the fifth generation as *gosei*, and so on. These Japanese words are used to distinguish new versus old and generational differences, and they are frequently used within the Japanese American community as part and parcel of their attempt to define and maintain their cultural and ethnic identity. While the usage and accuracy of generational categorizations between old Japanese American issei, nisei, sansei, yonsei (etc.) has been questioned in Japanese American studies, I posit that sufficient differences exist between the old and new Japanese groups in the United States to warrant a distinct categorization as shin-issei.

Cultural Migrants

One unique phenomenon among shin-issei is that many come to the United States, and Los Angeles in particular, because of an affinity to Western culture. These "cultural migrants" are mostly young Japanese who were exposed to American culture in Japan and decided to travel abroad to immerse themselves in American culture and lifestyle. Many cultural migrants simply experience a vague dissatisfaction with remaining in Japan and thus possess a desire to experience America based on media imagery they encountered in Japan. This media typically depicts America as a culture of freedom, with relatively fewer societal pressures and restrictions than are associated with Japanese society. As an iconic American city associated with Hollywood and media industries, Los Angeles is a common destination for Japanese cultural migrants. Some of the Japanese youths I encountered during my ethnographic research in the Sawtelle neighborhood of Los Angeles indicated that they wanted to participate in American "cultural production," such as film, photography, graphic design, and music. Cultural migrants differentiate themselves from prior generations because they do not immigrate to the United States in pursuit of Western modernity or for better living standards outside Japan. These young Japanese come from the Japanese middle class, and they already enjoy the same economic standard of living in Japan as middle class Angeleno residents. Notions of foreign culture motivate the cultural migrant group of shin-issei.

One cultural migrant I interviewed, Samantha, was a college student in her mid-twenties who had been living in the United States for seven years. In high school, she decided that she did not want to attend a Japanese college and instead came to the United States to attend community college in Los Angeles, later transferring to a four-year college. Samantha explained her strong ambition to study in the Unites States: "I always wanted to come to Los Angeles, not any other city, only Los Angeles. Because I am from Tokyo, I was raised in a big city and an urban place was a must for me. During my school years in Japan, time spent on education was very restrictive and I had so many pressures from my family. As a result, I wanted to go to another country with a different atmosphere, which led to the thought that my destination had to be Los Angeles. And now I'm grateful to be here, meeting new friends and exposing myself to a different culture, but moreover to wean myself from my parents' support." Yet, despite her desire to experience and participate in American culture, the friends she studies and lives with are all shin-issei studying in the United States. When asked to reflect on her seven years in the United States, Samantha replied, "It has been quite challenging, but I think I found a new part of me. There are many kinds of Japanese people here, such as Nikkei Japanese people who don't speak Japanese and haven't lived in Japan, but they are Japanese, Japanese who are from Japan like me, and people who are interested in Japanese culture even though they are not Japanese at all. Both being Japanese and Japan itself are quite the brands!" Samantha solidified her self-identification as Japanese in a global setting, contextualizing herself amongst the broader Japanese community in the United States. However, her tight-knit shin-issei social circle indicate an even stronger identification with her direct Japanese heritage, expressing cultural experience and language ability as factors that differentiate herself from Japanese Americans or other groups she might identify with.

Another shin-issei I met, Dorothy, a mother in her early thirties, moved to the United States after graduating from high school. Dorothy came to the United States because she wanted to explore the world outside Japan, but after five years she remained and wed a non–Japanese American husband. When asked why she migrated and about adjusting to an American lifestyle, Dorothy responded,

I came to the United States after graduating high school, because I always had a dream that I wanted to come to the United States, to California, where I had the idea that Los Angeles would be sunny and welcoming to everyone. I was always watching American movies when I was growing up in Osaka, and after graduating high school I decided to not go to university in Japan, and instead to come to the United States. I came by myself and went to the community college, where I met many friends like me, who were Japanese and came to the United States based on their own personal desires. . . . I do think I am not a typical Japanese because Japan was sometimes boring and I wanted to challenge myself, so I came to the United States.

However, she never gained confidence in English, and instead integrated into a largely shin-issei social circle. Despite living in the United States almost fifteen years, Dorothy relies heavily on her husband to help her as she still struggles with English and other aspects of daily life in the United States. Becoming a housewife, Dorothy was largely insulated from American culture and falls back to Japanese language and culture whenever possible, especially at home, even though her sojourn was long term. Because of her strong Japanese-centric identity, Dorothy only communicates with her children in Japanese and teaches them her Japanese culture and identity. Dorothy's identification preference surfaced in her relationship with her son and his upbringing at home, as she described, "Because my husband is very busy with work, he is not at home much and I am spending more time with my children, always speaking and texting to them in Japanese and not in English. I think this pattern will continue until they really get tired of me speaking to them in Japanese, but so far, I think they will keep growing toward having a Japanese identity, and I myself will keep thinking that I am a Japanese mother and will try to have a strong influence nourishing their Japanese identity." Dorothy's identity was so rooted in her Japanese language and culture that her son excelled at Japanese and was thoroughly engaged in studying for his weekend Japanese supplementary school. However, this preference resulted in some difficulties; referring to her son, she explained, "Of course, as you talked about [my son], he always watches Japanese TV, but his English is not that good. . . . I'm also a bit concerned that he is not trying as hard toward his American school studies and assignments. Maybe he became interested in Japanese culture a lot because I myself cannot speak English very well. I always communicated to him in Japanese, and we both watched many Japanese TV shows together, exposing him to Japanese culture more often and thoroughly than American culture." Dorothy's son illustrates the degree to which many shin-issei still maintain a strong Japanese identity, going so far as to pass it on to their children, even after spending many years in the United States. Interestingly, as cultural migrants, both Samantha and Dorothy had similar paths for coming to the United States, and both sought to leave behind aspects of Japan in favor of foreign experiences and culture. Yet, in both cases there were disconnects between the imagery that motivated their desire to leave Japan and the reality they encountered in the United States, which forced them to reevaluate and negotiate their identity in a global context. Like all the shin-issei I met over the course of my research, they adapted and learned from their experiences, but nonetheless clearly positioned themselves and lived as Japanese living in the United States. Thus, despite choosing to leave Japan because of dissatisfactions with aspects of their life there, they still chose to maintain a largely Japanese lifestyle and identity, making conscious choices to abstain from fully integrating with or assimilating into American culture and language.

Specialized Professionals

Somewhat like the cultural migrants, another group of shin-issei I met in Los Angeles can be categorized as specialized professionals. This group consists of shin-issei who came to the United States to pursue specialized professions or interests that are not available in Japan, or where Japan is not conducive to successful career development in their chosen profession. Depending on their field of interest, Japan may not be able to provide job positions, funding, or support they can receive by studying or working in the United States. One such group of specialists is composed of academic scholars, such as university students who aspire to study in the United States, earn a degree, and subsequently find work in the United States. Specialized professionals differ from cultural migrants in that they are not motivated solely by cultural interests, but rather by being in an environment better suited to pursue their given field of study.

Another interviewee, Regina, a female student in the late twenties, who completed her undergraduate degree and was attending graduate school in the United States, explained, "It is quite well known that life science and engineering students in fields such as STEM [science, technology, engineering, and math] will pursue higher education in the United States for research opportunities or to attend a worldwide top-ranked school or program. On the other hand, students majoring in humanities or Japan-centric studies, it is rare for them to leave Japan and come to the United States." Regina also explained that she does miss Japan, but after coming to the United States, she has gained new perspectives and understanding from her experiences abroad. Again, like cultural migrants, the specialists I talked to did not consider themselves to be immigrants, but did not have concrete plans to return either. They have a strong pride to be Japanese, and they network and collaborate with other shin-issei in their fields of interest.

Acquiring specialized knowledge not only motivates millennial shin-issei to immigrate to the United States; specialization lures older shin-issei as well. One interviewee named Michael, a millennial shin-issei in his early thirties, came to the United States to earn a graduate degree in a specialized engineering field. He explained, "I came to the United States because I already knew I wanted to work in a very specific field where work cannot be promised in Japan. To challenge myself, I knew coming to the United States was the right choice and destination." The desire to acquire specialized knowledge through institutions of higher education did not motivate Michael to immigrate to the United States. Rather, his desire to apply his existing specialist skills drove him to migrate from Japan to the United States.

Unintentional Migration: Corporate Sojourners and their Millennial Children

Some New Japanese are migrants who intend to reside in the United States permanently, and other New Japanese do not intend to stay permanently. Temporary business workers and other New Japanese migrants who are in the United States for a set period are often referred to as corporate sojourners. Because of economic expansion stemming from globalization, various Japanese and multinational corporations began establishing branches all over the world, sending employees abroad to set up base as the frontline of Japanese economic imperial expansion (Befu and Guichard-Anguis, 2003, 5). Corporate sojourners gradually decreased after the rapid economic contraction resulting in the 1991 bubble burst. This practice was commonly seen in experienced corporate personnel belonging to those generations before the millennial generation, as being experienced in the ten years following the 1991 asset price bubble burst implies a birth year well before 1980 (the older end of the millennial generation). Again, the generational positioning of the Japanese corporate sojourner places their children in the millennial shin-issei category.

Corporate sojourners' families are sent abroad on a temporary basis, generally staying a few years before returning to their post of origin in Japan. These professionals have specific educational plans for their children, both while they are in the United States and after their return to Japan. Japanese companies, closely knit with elite private schools, supported sojourners' millennial children. Corporate sojourners usually intend to return to Japan, maintaining a transnational identity instead of integrating into American society. Shin-issei families who fall under the corporate sojourner category prefer a transnational Japanese identity, culture, and lifestyle like the cultural migrants and specialized professionals. The corporate sojourners' assimilation in existing shin-issei communities, support from corporate sponsors, and their employers' expectation to return to Japan further amplifies this preference.

Employers do not expect corporate sojourners selected and sent abroad to have prior working knowledge or skills to assist the transition. Thus, corporate sojourners are often ill-prepared for life in the United States outside their ethnic support network. An interviewee named Amanda, who was in her early fifties, illuminated many of the unique challenges and characteristics of shin-issei corporate sojourner families and their millennial shin-issei children. Not knowing what the future held for her family, Amanda questioned whether she should consider herself an immigrant or a temporary visitor. Amanda faced a great deal of uncertainty in her early years in the United States. First and foremost, Amanda did not know how long she was going to stay in the United States, and thus, she constantly faced the challenge of trying to help her sons adapt to their lives in the United States but also be prepared for the possibility of a sudden return to Japan. She explained the plan was clear at first, but hinted at later ambiguity: "In the beginning, I heard from my husband's Japanese company that our family was going to be sent to the United States temporarily, not permanently, so my mind was clear that I had to teach and make children maintain their Japanese to prepare for returning to Japan. In the beginning, it was clear that we were going to the United States temporarily, and that I would eventually return one day to Japan. At least that was the original plan and endgame that I understood."

Another important characteristic of corporate sojourners' families is that they often plan to, or feel pressured to, return to Japan, but as time progresses, it becomes unclear whether that will occur. The passage of time damages their ability to operate in the United States. If sojourner families assume that they will eventually return to Japan, they may opt into Japanese bubble communities and forgo integration. Many interviewees, not just corporate sojourners, faced the same ambiguity in their status as migrants, simply choosing to claim that they are Japanese living in the United States for a long time, even if their presence is habitual and permanent. Amanda's shin-issei millennial children made the decision for her family. Amanda's husband eventually asked her to stay in the United States permanently for their children's sake, all having adapted to American life: "Looking at our two sons who were becoming more American than Japanese, speaking English more easily and fluently than Japanese, and making new friends and enjoying their new lives, we both started to feel it would be better for my husband and our sons. However, when I asked myself whether I wanted to stay in the United States longer than the original plan, it was very difficult, because I faced, and still face, several issues adjusting to life in the United States. For instance, I miss my parents and family back in Japan, but the strongest concern was speaking English, which is still very difficult for me."

To sum up, shin-issei families that are relatively certain of their future residence in the United States often choose to provide a Japanese education by choice, but there is no level of Japanese proficiency that must be attained beyond any personal expectations that they themselves set. On the other hand, corporate sojourners face the daunting task to educate their children in Japanese so they are prepared to return to Japan. However, some millennial shin-issei children of corporate sojourner families integrated into their American host society so much that they effectively forced their shin-issei families to remain in the United States, despite parental efforts to educate the children in the Japanese language and original plans to return to Japan. In this case, both the parents and children are shin-issei.

Shin-Issei Communities and Social Circles

As I alluded to in my interviews with the various shin-issei groups, many shin-issei choose to socialize and form support networks semiexclusively with other shin-issei encountered in their work or social circles. All the shin-issei I met and interviewed in Los Angeles self-identified strictly as Japanese, rather than Japanese American, or American, even those that lived in the United States for decades. The desire for shin-issei to socialize with other Japanese often stemmed from wanting to be able to communicate comfortably, in Japanese, and with those who could understand and relate to their circumstances.

Previous studies on ethnic communities indicated that ethnic communities play a significant role for immigrants and especially for women as they provide helpful resources, advice, and information for them and their families as they adapt to their new host society. Nukaga (2008) found that shin-issei mothers who recently moved to Los Angeles had trouble adapting to American life. As an active participant in a supplementary Japanese Saturday school, I witnessed how important the school was for shin-issei parents to meet other Japanese people with similar backgrounds. The school allowed parents to share information relating to their unique circumstances as new immigrants and migrants trying to raise their children bilingually and biculturally. For these parents, it was important to socialize with other shin-issei who could relate to their parenting goals.

In one explanation for the seemingly self-imposed ethnic isolation of shin-issei, Roger Goodman and others (2003) propose that current corporate out-migratory patterns result in "environmental bubbles" that isolate the emigrants within Japanese-centric communities built around them. Such bubbles specifically cater to the needs of temporary Japanese expatriates and allow them to operate as if they were in an extension of Japan. For example, such community infrastructure can include corporate-supplied housing and activities, Japanese schools for their children, and prearranged Japanese social circles offering support. As Japanese expatriates constantly rotate between Japan and America, these communities stay intact for new migrants to bring family and immediately reside within a community containing Japanese schools, stores, and opportunities to meet other Japanese expatriate families with similar backgrounds. Their social circles and lifestyles allow them to operate as if still in Japan as much as possible. Goodman and colleagues (2003, 9) described Japanese communities outside Japan as "the encapsulation and isolation of Japanese migrants within their host cities and countries. The creation of a series of Japanese cultural and social landscapes in cities in various parts of the world enables migrants to remain within a Japanese social milieu, operating according to rules and expectations that are familiar from Tokyo, Nagoya or Osaka."

To a large extent aspects of these same bubble communities are shared with long-term shin-issei migrants and immigrants, but are more pronounced for the corporate sojourner group. Essentially, New Japanese, especially corporate sojourners, create their ethnic communities as an extension of their previous lifestyles in Japan. In a sense, this isolates them further from their host society and limits expectations for mainstream assimilation. Zhou (1997) points out that assimilation theory has dominated sociological thinking, and recent studies now question whether assimilation translates to upward social mobility, as was once thought. Transnational migration, enabled by today's globalized and interconnected world, requires a reevaluation of these established interpretations of migration and assimilation.

I attended meetings with groups of shin-issei mothers to learn more about their social networking. The topics that Japanese shin-issei mothers frequently discussed included difficulties with English, the lifestyle and cultural gaps they faced while living and raising their children in the United States, information on schooling in the United States and Japan, and educational concerns regarding their children. One shin-issei mother in her early thirties, Persephone, explained, "We mostly met each other through our children's Japanese school and we started to talk to each other. For example, we discussed how we teach Japanese at home, how we make our children keep up with their Japanese homework, and how we encourage the use of Japanese language despite many of us being married to non-Japanese husbands." In this sense, the exclusivity of closely knit shin-issei social networks is a pragmatic solution to address their desire for Japanese societal norms and to find support among like-minded individuals sharing their circumstances.

Shin-Issei Identity and Cultural Maintenance

Transnationalism allows us to see how immigrants live in two different nations, how globalization affects their identity and lifestyle, and the processes they use to maintain ties with their motherland. Transnationalism is closely tied to contemporary immigration because of the technology supporting and providing readily accessible means for long distance travel and communication. Immigrants are no longer considered "uprooted and transplanted migrants who will be assimilated into the receiving societies, but 'transmigrants,' who will keep close ties and be identified with both their original and receiving countries and beyond" (Li 2009, 26). Through the collective opinions of my shin-issei subjects, I found that rather than fully integrating their American and Japanese cultural identities, these New Japanese maintained separate identities and switched appropriately for a given context. All shin-issei I interviewed identified themselves with a strong affinity to their native Japanese language and cultural identity.

Even when shin-issei live in the United States for a decade or more, establishing a sense of permanence in the United States, those subjects whom I interviewed exhibited a consistent pattern of forgoing significant attempts of assimilation into American culture, social groups, and English fluency. While living in the United States, shin-issei find ways to maintain their Japanese identity and culture, often allowing them to maintain many aspects of their former lifestyles in Japan. Shin-issei maintain aspects of their Japanese lifestyles through ethnic communities that provide both concrete (e.g., food consumption) and abstract (e.g., communication and media) opportunities for cultural consumption.

The advent of readily accessible global transportation and shipping networks and of instantaneous communication via video, text, message, email, and the internet provides international access to homeland culture and news. An interviewee named Daphne, in her early thirties, told me, "I miss Japan, but I know that I can easily go home anytime because my family is still there. Japan does not seem that far anymore because I can get news and updates from my family easily through SNS." Daphne also referenced her own consumption of Japanese cultural media and how this cultural media has become essential to raising her son to communicate with her in Japanese and instill in him a Japanese identity. Referring to her son, she further stated, "Despite being born and raised in Los Angeles, he always watches Japanese TV and seems to identify himself as being a Japanese more than being an American. Also, he always speaks to me in Japanese and always asks me to show him more Japanese TV shows such as Japanese anime and comedies, and to get Japanese books for him." I recognize that globalization and the established Japanese communities in Los Angeles have given rise to the availability of ethnic media, books, and other cultural goods and allowed Daphne to raise her son with a strong Japanese identity matching her own. Furthermore, shin-issei mothers like Daphne cited their use of ethnic community markets and supplementary learning institutions to provide Japanese instruction for their children. Technological advancements in media and communication allow a much greater degree of transnationalism in shin-issei identity and lifestyle.

International Ties

Despite living in the United States, shin-issei do not feel physically or emotionally disconnected from Japan. Almost all the millennial shin-issei I met indicated that they returned to Japan for vacation or to visit family at least once a year, and thus there is no clear breakage with their homeland or Japanese cultural identity. Because most shin-issei fall within the Japanese middle class (Gordon 1993), they have the financial resources able to support frequent return trips to Japan. Furthermore, it must be recognized that as transnational migrants, shin-issei maintain family and friendship relationship ties internationally and return frequently to Japan to visit their social circles left behind in Japan. I interviewed a shin-issei mother in her early thirties named Shannon, and she stated that "she always would take her daughter with her back to Japan during summer and winter breaks to allow her to gain familiarity with her heritage and family in Japan." Ties to family in Japan were a common theme, even among shin-issei families with long stays of 20 or 30 years in the United States. These ties can have a profound pull-effect toward rooting the Japanese identity in shin-issei families. Shin-issei mothers saw their strong social ties to family in Japan as important motivators and resources for raising their children in a Japanese-identifying household and lifestyle. During my research, several families indicated that their relatives in Japan would send Japanese language materials and cultural products with the primary purpose of providing ethnic education for shin-nisei children being raised in the United States. Rather than give up their Japanese identity when immigrating to the United States, shin-issei systematically engage in relationships and activities that cultivate a strong Japanese identity. This trend continues strongly in the first and second generation children of shin-issei.

Limitations

This research focused specifically on the New Japanese in Los Angeles from 2012 to 2014. The limited aim of the research is to give the reader insight into shin-issei lifestyle, culture, and identity, as evidenced through a limited number of interviews. I stressed that the shin-issei are a very diverse group and have tried to capture a variety of interviewee cases to demonstrate this quality. However, because of limited space, I only provide a small representative sampling from the interviews captured during this period. I conducted interviews with corporate sojourners, temporary visitors, and permanent immigrants to the United States; however, I still cannot claim to have presented nearly the full breadth of variety in this community, especially because I did not find examples of millennial shin-issei corporate sojourners, even though their children became millennial shin-issei immigrants. Further breaking down shin-issei groups by period may help identify subtle trends not captured by this study. More geographic sampling and quantitative polling could help draw further conclusions about shin-issei patterns at larger regional or national levels, which cannot be validated by my research alone.

Conclusion

The subject of millennial shin-issei in the United States has not received much attention, as they comprise a small and somewhat hidden presence. The millennial shin-issei category, despite being simple and concise in the general sense as "new first-generation" Japanese in the United States, is quite vague and open to much interpretation when applied to its members at the individual level. To provide an accurate examination of millennial shin-issei, this study first looked millennial shin-issei subgroups, their characteristics, and the diversity that makes this group hard to succinctly define.

New Japanese and their presence in the United States are heavily influenced by contemporary trends toward globalization and transnationalism. It is quite common that their reasons for being in the United States are directly tied to global networks affected by these trends, as is the case for corporate sojourners, entrepreneurs, academics, and many other occupations and pursuits. Modern transnationalism, globalization, and technological advances all allow millennial shin-issei to access Japanese culture, news, and carry out Japanese lifestyles, even while living in the United States. These factors push their case beyond historical assumptions such as immigration patterns from poor to rich countries or models that define assimilation as an unavoidable and desirable pathway to economic and social advancement. A significant number of New Japanese migrants, millennial or otherwise, stay in the United States for extended periods of time with plans to return to Japan and after such a long stay some end up as permanent immigrants, albeit unintentionally.

Shin-issei home life and inner social circles are often centered on a Japanese lifestyle, regardless of exposure to American lifestyle outside the home. Attitudes toward favoring a Japanese transnational identity like these interviewees were prevalent among shin-issei in my own research and previous studies (Nukaga 2008; Yasuike 2005). Although the shin-issei I interviewed came to the United States of their own volition and remained in the United States for decades, they do not self-identify as Americans or even as immigrants. Instead, they prefer a transnational Japanese identity that reflects a lack of both cultural and social assimilation toward the American mainstream. With a strong Japanese community presence providing access to Japanese culture and language and an inner social circle of other shin-issei, it is possible for shin-issei to imagine their personal lifestyle as Japanese and their homes as Japanese spaces within the United States.

The more globalization and transnationalism expand in everyday life, the more the transfer of information and cultural exchange becomes increasingly rapid and pervasive. Even though one century ago, Japan and the United States would be considered extremely far apart, both geographically and culturally, today Japanese migrants can travel back and forth with ease. Furthermore, it is now possible to live a cosmopolitan lifestyle, allowing them to choose to forgo assimilation into American culture and society. We see how evident transnationalism is among shin-issei, socializing within Japanese communities and institutions and raising their children to be proficient in Japanese language and culture—all despite having left Japan itself. Given the pervasive globalization we see today, processes of immigration and living abroad do not necessitate a break from one's homeland culture and ways of life. In many respects, shin-issei are representative of a new form of migratory patterns and lifestyles that are enabled through our modern context, and I believe these studies will soon be applicable to other emergent groups that are forgoing the strict historical patterns of immigration and assimilation.

REFERENCES

Adachi, Nobuko. 2006. *Japanese Diasporas: Unsung Pasts, Conflicting Presents, and Uncertain Futures*. London: Routledge.

Azuma, Eiichiro. 2005. *Between Two Empires: Race, History, and Transnationalism in Japanese America*. New York: Oxford University Press.

Basch, Linda, Nina G. Schiller, and Cristina Blanc. 1994. *Nations Unbound: Transnational Projects, Postcolonial Predicaments, and Deterritorialized Nation-States*. New York: Psychology Press.

Befu, Harumi, and Sylvie Guichard-Anguis. 2003. *Globalizing Japan: Ethnography of the Japanese Presence in Asia, Europe and America*. London: Routledge.

Consulate General of Japan in Los Angeles. 2011. *Japan-Southern California Economic Relations*. Los Angeles, CA: Consulate General of Japan.

Finn, Dennis, and Anne Donovan. 2013. *PwC's NextGen: A Global Generational Study*. London, England.

Fujita, Yuiko. 2009. *Cultural Migrants from Japan: Youth, Media, and Migration in New York and London*. Lanham, MD: Lexington.

Goldman Sachs. 2016. *Millennials Coming of Age*. Accessed March 3, 2017. http://www.goldmansachs.com/our-thinking/pages/millennials.

Goodman, Roger, Ceri Peach, Ayumi Takenaka, and Paul White, eds. 2003. *Global Japan: The Experience of Japan's New Immigrant and Overseas Communities*. London: Routledge Curzon.

Gordon, Andrew. 1993. *Postwar Japan as History*. Berkeley: University of California Press.

Hyodo, Hirosuke. 2012. *"The Japanese New Yorkers": "Adventurers in Adventure Land" in Globalized Environments*. Doctoral diss., New York: The City University of New York. Accessed April 1, 2013. ProQuest, UMI Dissertations Order No. 3499247.

Ichioka, Yuji. 1990. "Japanese Immigrant Nationalism: The Issei and the Sino-Japanese War, 1937–1941." *California History* 69(3): 260–275.

Li, Wei. 2009. *Ethnoburb: The New Ethnic Community in Urban America*. Honolulu: University of Hawai'i Press.

Nukaga, Misako. 2008. *Motherhoods and Childhoods in Transnational Lives: Gender and Ethnic Identities Among Japanese Expatriate Families in Los Angeles*. Los Angeles: University of California.

Robertson, Roland. 1992. *Globalization: Social Theory and Global Culture*. London: Sage.

Sassen, Saskia. 1994. "Economic Internationalization: The New Migration in Japan and the United States." *Social Justice* 21(2): 73–102.

———. 1998. *Globalization and its Discontents: Essays on the New Mobility of People and Money*. New York: New Press.

Takahashi, Jere. 1998. *Nisei/Sansei: Shifting Japanese American Identities and Politics*. Philadelphia: Temple University Press.

UNESCO (United Nations Educational, Scientific and Cultural Organization). 1997. *Adult Education in a Polarizing World*. Paris, France: UNESCO.

U.S. Census Bureau. 2010. "Profile of General Population and Housing Characteristics: 2010." Accessed March 24, 2019. https://factfinder.census.gov/bkmk/table/1.0/en /DEC/10_DP/DPDP1/1600000US0680000.

———. 2015. *Millennials Outnumber Baby Boomers and Are Far More Diverse, Census Bureau Reports*. Washington, DC: U.S. Census Bureau.

Yasuike, Akiko. 2005. "Maternalism: Japanese Patriarchal Bargaining in the Era of Globalization: Corporate Transnational Wives and Shin Issei Women in Southern California." Doctoral diss., University of Southern California, Los Angeles.

Yui, Daizaburo. 2006. *The World of Transnational Asian Americans*. Tokyo: Center for Pacific and American Studies, University of Tokyo.

Zhou, Min. 1997. "Growing Up American: The Challenge Confronting Immigrant Children and Children of Immigrants." *Annual Review of Sociology* 23:64–95.

PART IV

INTERSECTING IDENTITIES

9

Mixed-Race Japanese American Millennials

Millennials or Japanese Americans?

REBECCA CHIYOKO KING-O'RIAIN

At the beginning of the millennium, the Nikkei 2000 (N2K) Conference was held in San Francisco to mark the beginning of a new century for Japanese Americans. Many Japanese American community organizations attended to debate the theme of the conference: "Will there be a Japanese American Community in 2020?" The "future," in that provocative and worrying question about the Japanese American community, was highly dependent upon what we now recognize as multiracial millennials—mixed-race Japanese Americans born in the 1980s and 1990s. As we now stand just a year or so away from that predicted timeline, "the future is now" with people still predicting that "by 2020 . . . the majority of Japanese Americans will be multiracial/multiethnic" (Chan 2016). With all this mixing, is it safe to say that there is a Japanese American Community? Undoubtedly, yes, there is a Japanese American community, but it may look a little different than it did in the past. Japanese American communities in places like San Francisco, Honolulu, and Los Angeles have no doubt undergone significant demographic changes, and some well-loved Japanese American institutions like the *Rafu Shimpo* newspaper are in decline. Given these conditions, this chapter asks: How is the nature of Japanese American communities changing? What are the changes that have taken place, and what effects are they having on Japanese American community and identity? More specifically, how do demographic shifts affect Japanese American millennials (JAM), and how do these shifts make millennials different from Japanese Americans of past generations?

This chapter begins by examining the demographic shifts taking place in the Japanese American community, focusing in particular on the comparison between Japanese Americans of older generations and Japanese American millennials. The second section of the chapter looks at the growing multiracial Japanese American population to analyze their identity and connections to Japanese Americanness and Japanese American communities. The third section concludes the chapter with an analysis of the ways in which some mixed-race JAMs remain strongly connected to Japanese American communities while also engaging with mainstream white, African American, other Asian American, and global Japanese culture. Mixed-race JAMs are clearly not fully "assimilating" (even if half white) so that they are just seen as the same as white millennials—in practice, their racial and ethnic "work" at the boundaries of these identities and communities ensures that they are uniquely Japanese American and multiracial. This example of the formation of "flexibly racialized" identities (King-O'Riain et al. 2014) demonstrates how identities are carefully shaped by fluctuating local and global contexts through the social interaction between asserted (what mixed individuals say they are) and ascribed (what others identify them as) identities.

Shifting Japanese American Demographics

Younger Japanese Americans, those born since 1980 and referred to in this chapter as Japanese American millennials, have been raised in the midst of a major demographic shift for Japanese Americans as a whole.

Generational Identification

Many JAMs are mixed-race—signaling not only a major shift in the demographic composition of the community but also in the definitions of who is Japanese American and how that term is defined. JAMs can also be yonsei/gosei generationally, but some are also shin-nisei, binational, or of mixed generational statuses. Not only are the generational labels of the past problematic for some JAMs but also shifts in the cultural and ethnic identification as Japanese American. In moving from a predominantly monoracial community to a predominantly multiracial community, the socially understood "essence" of Japanese Americanness itself is changing. Table 9.1 summarizes some of the demographic changes that foreground this shift.

Japanese Americans within Asian America

In terms of immigration, JAMs increasingly live in a predominantly American-born context, with only 32 percent of the community foreign-born compared with other Asian American groups with an average of 74 percent foreign-born. While this difference might lead one to think that Japanese Americans are completely assimilated, they are still distinct from

TABLE 9.1. DEMOGRAPHIC COMPARISONS OF PRE-MILLENNIAL AND MILLENNIAL JAPANESE AMERICANS

	Pre-Millennial Generations (born before 1980s)	Millennials (born after 1980)
Immigration	Immigration slowing relative to other Asian American (AA) groups	Immigration even slower; 32% foreign-born compared to 74% of all Asian Americans (AA) who are foreign-born
Marriage	Increasing intermarriage rising to 50% in 1980s	Japanese Americans (JA) now the most likely of all AA to be intermarried with non-Asians and non-JAs (2008–2010: JA 55% married to non-Asians, 9% to other Asians, and 36% to other JAs), so pan-Asian ethnic marriage has not panned out and interracial with whites still the most common outmarriage
Multiraciality	Increasing interracial marriage; increasing acceptance of interracial marriages (more so than Koreans, Vietnamese, or Indians)	Now JA most likely of all AA groups to be multiracial, with 41% of JA population identifying as mixed; most in the West Coast (CA and HI); and 2020s could see the first generation of JAs to be majority mixed
Size of group	1910–1960 largest AA group	By 2010, the 6th-largest AA group; other AA groups growing faster; JA growing slower due to aging population and low immigration; shrinking relative to other AA groups
Geographic location	HI and CA with scatterings across the U.S. post–WWII	71% in the West—concentrated geographically, but not locally

Abbreviations: Asian American (AA), California (CA), Hawai'i (HI), Japanese Americans (JA).

Source: All data in this table are from Pew Research Center (2017).

the white population in terms of being born in the United States. Japanese Americans still have a higher percentage of foreign-born members than other fourth- and fifth-generation Americans such as Irish Americans, so ties to Japan can still be strong for some in the JAM cohort such as binational and shin-nisei JAMs. Interestingly, Japanese Americans are different from other fourth-generation immigrant groups and are also different from most other Asian and Pacific Islander groups.

Geographically, 71 percent of Japanese Americans live in the western part of the United States, predominantly in Hawai'i and California, indicating a strong geographic concentration; however, many tend to be locally geographically dispersed within the West Coast and are likely to have neighbors who are not Japanese American (Hoeffel et al. 2012). Their dispersion has increased contact (including intimate contact) with non–Japanese Americans and may be the reason for increased interracial and interethnic marriage rates. Japanese Americans are the most likely of all Asian American groups to be interracially married with non-Asians, with a 55 percent outmarriage (Pew 2012). JAMs are also less likely to be interethnically married (9 percent are married to other Asians), so the predicted spread of Asian pan-ethnicity through interethnic marriage (Shingawa and Pang 1996) is somewhat limited in these data. However, multiethnic Japanese Americans also marry Chinese, Koreans, and Asians of other backgrounds, not just black and white.

The high interracial marriage rate means that multiraciality is much more common amongst JAMs; in fact, they will be the first generation of Japanese Americans to have a majority of mixed-race, instead of monoracial, individuals. Of the overall Japanese American community, 41 percent identifies as mixed, and some predict that by the 2020 Census the Japanese American community will report being more mixed than monoracial. In the 2010 Census, Japanese Americans had the highest proportion reporting multiple detailed Asian groups and/or another race(s) relative to the largest detailed Asian groups (Pew Research Center 2017). This finding indicates that Japanese Americans were more likely than other Asian American groups in the census to indicate multiraciality. Among the detailed Asian groups with "alone-or-in-any-combination" populations of one million or more, the Japanese population had the highest proportion reporting multiraciality, with 6 percent reporting monoraciality, 28 percent reporting Japanese and another race, and 7 percent reporting multiple detailed Asian groups and another races (see Figure 9.1). Combining these groups, 41 percent of the Japanese American population identified with multiple detailed Asian groups and/or another race(s)—in other words, 41 percent said they were of mixed race. By contrast, Indians and Vietnamese were found to be 11 percent mixed in comparison for the same time period and less tolerant of intermarriage as well.

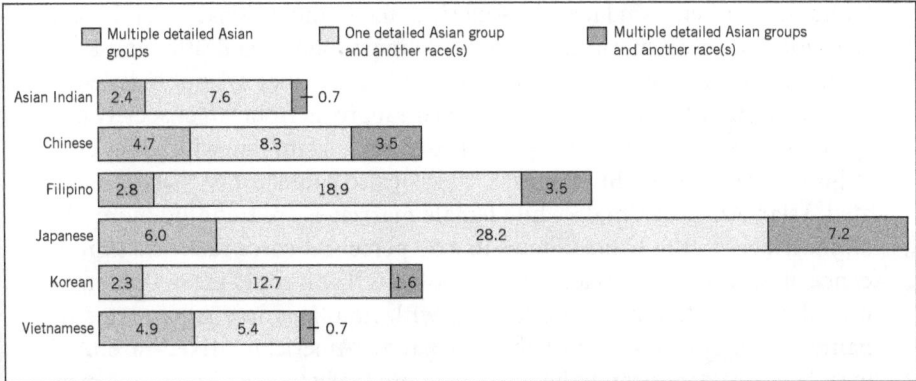

Figure 9.1. Percentage of Largest Detailed Asian Groups Alone or in Any Combination by Number of Groups and Races, 2010. Note: Percentages are based on the alone-or-in-any-combination population for each group. People who reported two or more detailed Asian groups, such as Korean and Filipino, and no other race group are represented in the "Multiple detailed Asian groups" category. People who reported one detailed Asian group and another race(s), such as Korean *and* White are represented in the "One detailed Asian group and another race(s)" category. People who reported two or more detailed Asian groups and another race(s), such as Korean, Filipino, *and* White are represented in the "Multiple detailed Asian groups and another race(s)" category. Together, these three categories represent the Asian in any combination percentages for each detailed group. (Source: Hoeffel et al. 2010.)

Why Intermarriage? What Is the Effect?

It may be that Japanese American intermarriage is just assimilation in progress, but it may be more as well. As Pawan Dhingra and Robyn Magalit Rodriguez (2014, 101) write, "White men come to represent the ideals of material security and modernity within a global hierarchy, especially compared with Asian women (Nemoto 2006). Furthermore, the fact that both Asian American women and men feel assimilated means they could choose one another but instead see their race as too foreign and instead seek out whites. This is again, an instantiation of having internalized dominant racist ideas about Asian Americans." Intermarriage to whites, especially to white men, may be shaped by racialized and gendered perceptions of power, but these perceptions may not materialize or be true in every case of intermarriage. Jenifer Bratter and Rosalind King (2008) showed that Asian women married to white men had a 4 percent higher chance of divorce than white/ white couples, but Asian men/white women marriages had a 59 percent higher chance of divorce, so outmarriage in the Asian American community appears to be strongly gendered in terms of marriage and divorce. It is not clear if Japanese Americans specifically fall into this same pattern, but high rates of gendered outmarriage (Japanese American women marrying with whites more often than Japanese American men) might signal lower divorce rates for Japanese American female/white male couples as Bratter and King found. Asian American men may find that because they are not married to a co-ethnic they face discrimination and disapproval from larger society and perhaps even within their own possibly patriarchal families, which may contribute to the stress within their marriage. It also could just be that acculturated Asian American male/white female marriages are trending more like all marriages in the United States to a 50 percent divorce rate. The significance of the divorce rates for this discussion is that it could mean that many mixed-race JAMs have white fathers, with non–Japanese American surnames and may be less identifiable as Japanese American. Mixed-race JAM with Japanese American fathers will be more likely to have Japanese American surnames, but may or may not have continuous contact with their Japanese American fathers if their parents are separated or divorced and if they reside primarily with their non–Japanese American mothers. If this situation is the case, then mixed-race JAMs may have a Japanese name, but perhaps no contact with or knowledge of Japanese American relatives or culture and may not feel they are Japanese American.

On Being Mixed

The effects of all of these demographic changes mean that those Japanese American millennials born in the 1980s and 1990s are growing up and living now as adults in a different demographic, cultural, and social situation than past generations. The biggest growth in young people in the Japanese American community are those with mixed heritage, and the identification and participation of those young mixed folks in some ways determines the passing on Japanese American culture and the sustainability of its long-held traditions and community organizations. Are JAMs integrated into existing cultural practices and organizations? Or have they departed from community ties altogether? Or are they reformulating the practices and organizations of the community while still remaining tied to Japanese American identity and networks? The first step in answering these questions is to investigate how mixed-race Japanese Americans identify, which I analyze in the next section.

The Identity of Mixed-Race Japanese American Millennials

Given that 41 percent of Japanese Americans identify as mixed-race, it is important to understand the experiences and identities of mixed-race Japanese American millennials. The contexts of where they grow up, the racial/ethnic background their non–Japanese American parent, as well as their physical appearance and their acceptance (or not) into the Japanese American community—all may play a role in identity development.

Meanings of Mixed-Race

While data on mixed-race Japanese Americans are limited, if we examine data on multiracial Asian/whites (of which mixed-race Japanese Americans make up a large part), we can draw some possible conclusions. Studying multiracial Americans in greater depth than the U.S. Census Bureau, the Pew Research Center (2015, 5) found that most multiracial Americans were proud of their mixed-race backgrounds (60 percent) and felt that they were more open to other cultures (59 percent). However, many also said that they had been subjected to racial slurs or jokes (55 percent). Being mixed Japanese American and white may not always give one safe passage into whiteness, and one may or may not be seen and treated as white. It is also reasonable to think that African American/Japanese American mixed-race people may never be given passage into whiteness, but instead may be treated as and/or solely identify as black.

Mixed Black, White, or Other?

Multiracial Americans are also a diverse bunch. Their experiences were shaped by their backgrounds. Of those with a partly black background, 69 percent reported that they thought people saw them as black or African American, and their attitudes were much more closely aligned with the black community. Asian/white mixed people felt more closely connected to whites than Asians (perhaps because they did not feel accepted by Asians), but 60 percent of them also reported experiencing the discrimination of racial slurs and jokes—almost the same as black/white individuals (Pew 2015, 8). So, while many Asian/white people identify with whites, they are often not seen by others as white and experience discrimination at rates much closer to monoracial Asians than to monoracial whites. As one of the largest constituents of the mixed-race community (growing 87 percent from 2000 to 2010), 70 percent of Asian/white mixed-race people say they identify as multiracial. Of all mixed-race people, 21 percent indicated that they experienced pressure to identify as a single race, and this identification can be shaped by "feeling that they look like" one race, being raised by someone of one race, or closely identifying with a single race (Pew 2015, 12).

Past research on racial eligibility rules in Japanese American community beauty pageants and basketball leagues (King-O'Riain 2006) indicates that these statistics may seem valid and applicable to the mixed-race Japanese American experience. Mixed-race Japanese Americans often want to identify not only as white or black or another Asian ethnicity—to which there are obvious racial limits if one does not look white or black or Chinese—but also to identify as Japanese American. Again, racial limits to identification exist if one is "not Japanese American enough" in appearance to be considered as an authentic and legitimate Japanese American within cultural institutions such as Japanese American ethnic beauty pageants or basketball leagues (see King-O'Riain 2006 for more on this topic). While the focus is often on the choices that mixed Japanese Americans make, research shows that flexible racialization suggests that perhaps the social action is really present within the interaction between identification and the racial and ethnic "limits" imposed by others and structured by interactions with individuals and institutions around them. Many mixed Japanese Americans, as reflected in the data given earlier, chose to identify as multiracial *and* Japanese American, and the acceptance of this type of identification within the Japanese American community is growing. In fact, we have now reached a point where most white/Asian (58 percent) mixed people say that their racial background has not been a disadvantage compared with single-race whites (32 percent) and single-race Asians (15 percent) (Pew 2015, 14). These findings indicate that definitions of who is and what constitutes being Japanese American is shifting away from racial toward more cultural definitions of what it means to be Japanese American. This shift is also accompanied by a problematization and possible expansion of generational labels such as issei, nisei, sansei, since some of these labels may not apply to shin-nisei, mixed generational, or binational folks. The dominant generational narrative of Japanese American history may need to be rethought as JAMs offer new cultural categories (mixed, binational, etc.) to capture their unique experiences and identities. While the Japanese American community persists, some of the cultural categories that were the building blocks of Japanese American identities in the past are shifting.

An Aging Community

The Japanese American community is aging faster than most other Asian Pacific Islander (API) communities, but, again, this finding does not imply that young people in the community are not important. In fact, multiracial people are more likely to be young; 46 percent are under eighteen years of age, compared with 23 percent of the overall U.S. population under eighteen (Pew 2015, 11). For Japanese Americans, this shift means that the age profile of long-standing community groups, like the Japanese American Citizens League, largely composed of older Japanese Americans, is shrinking. JAMs are more likely to participate in younger and newer community groups (Cherry Blossom Festival committees); social media (Ryan Higa or NigaHiga on YouTube); and on digital media discussions (#JapaneseAmerican on Twitter popularized by groups such as the Young Adults Club of the Venice Japanese Community Center in Los Angeles [@VJCCYAC]); all of which are beginning to spring up to represent the interests of younger Japanese Americans, JAMs, and mixed-race JAMs.

Mixed-Race Multiculturalism or a Disappearing Japanese American Community?

The discussion about the "end of the Japanese American community" may have been premature as it is clear that JAMs and mixed-race JAMs are not diluting Japanese Americanness or Japanese American community organizations; however, they may be transforming them. Many multiracial Japanese Americans are crucial to the continuing legacy of Japanese American communities. In many ways, mixed-race millennials feel the pressure of being both the harbingers of multiculturalism *and* the symbol of the dissolution and disappearance of the Japanese American community. Of multiracial Asian people, 19 percent reported that they have felt like a go-between, or bridge, of interracial understanding (Pew 2015, 18). Multiracial Japanese Americans feel this pressure, as well as that of being symbols of racial and cultural blending and at the same time the results of intermarriages and the potential loss of culture (King-O'Riain 2006).

Mixed-Race Beauty

Often this quality is implied in contrasting images of multiracial Japanese Americans. One stereotype that often befalls them is that mixed-race Japanese American babies/people are more beautiful than single-race Japanese Americans. For some, mixed-race Japanese Americans (sometimes referred to as "hapa" or "hafu"; see Yamashiro 2008) are considered beautiful because they are the blending of East and West in Japanese American communities in Hawai'i and California. In the wider society, an obsession with "mixed-race babies" also exists and tends to focus on the blending of racial/bodily features (such as dark curly hair with light green/blue eyes) often photographed or visually represented online (in such places as http://www.mixed racebabies.org/fan-feature-s.html or Instagram and Facebook). The objectification and possible rejection of mixed people based on their "unusual" phenotypes have shaped how mixed-race people experience the social world. These experiences can often lead to a gathering of mixed people, some of whom may experientially know what it feels like to have been asked "What are you?" all of their lives.

Collective Hapa Identifications

One such gathering became a group based on a collective identification as mixed JAMs around the term "hapa." In the early 1990s, Hapa Issues Forum was founded at the University of California, Berkeley, as a mixed-Asian student group. Building on the word "hapa," which had come from Hawai'i, meaning "half white/foreigner," the group reappropriated the word to mean "anyone of part Asian ancestry." Native Hawaiians who argued that "hapa" was a Hawaiian word that should not be used outside of Hawai'i criticized the move at the time. In spite of these criticisms, the use of "hapa" grew across California and, by the mid-1990s, several chapters of Hapa Issues Forum had formed. The term "hapa" and the organization, Hapa Issues Forum, grew at that particular historical moment because it identified, particularly in the Japanese American community, a growing recognition that mixed-race Japanese Americans were growing in number and coming of age; they did not need their parents to speak for them within the community but could speak for themselves on social, cultural, and political issues. In addition, Japanese American organizations, such as the Japanese Culture and Community Center of Northern California, recognized the need to engage with hapas as an untapped resource for their membership and cultural continuation.

This growing acceptance was also reflected in artistic and cultural expressions such as the *100 Percent Hapa* exhibit by Kip Fulbeck (2008). This exhibition, made up of photographs and expressions of identity by various mixed people, turned the ubiquitous question that mixed-race people often encounter about "what they are" in terms of percentages or blood quantum, into an affirmative statement that one could be more than 50 percent Japanese and 50 percent white by being instead 100 percent hapa (or mixed). The exhibit, and later the book, questioned and played with the stereotypes of mixed-race Japanese Americans as "bridges" and "beautiful." The exhibit was made up of headshot photographs of mixed-Asian-descent people with their *own* statement of their identity underneath.[1] The objectification of mixed people was often embedded in scientific racism studies of the early twentieth century that often pictured mixed people as zoological specimens with their "mixes" written underneath (see Spickard 1989). Fulbeck's exhibit turned this on its head to allow the mixed people in the photos to assert how they see and identify themselves. This exhibit ran at the Japanese American National Museum in Los Angeles for several months and was one of the most successful exhibits to date. The response to the exhibit within the Japanese American community reflected the growing wish to understand mixed-race experiences better and to show public acceptance of the growing population of younger mixed people within the community. Japanese American multiracials were now a recognized category of Japanese American in many ways, paving the way for mixed JAMs.

Going Global

But it was not just within the United States that mixed-race Japanese Americans were coming of age in the millennium. Across the Pacific Ocean, a growing movement for recognition of racial mixing was also taking place in Japan, thus creating a transnational connection between people of mixed Japanese descent in the United States and Japan.

Mixed-race JAMs also seem more connected, often through social media, to other mixed people the world over, perhaps shaping a global mixed-race identity. Japanese American mixed-race identity is increasingly shaped and informed by this multinational mixed-race discourse.

One example of this discourse that reflected increasing diversity within the Japanese American mixed millennial community occurred when mixed-race people from Japan and mixed-race Japanese Americans (many of them latter generations) started to find things in common and to form communities around those cultural and experiential commonalities, regardless of being born in the United States or Japan. The Hapa Japan Conferences organized and hosted by Professor Duncan Williams at the University of California, Berkeley, in 2011 and again in 2017 at the University of Southern California, are good examples of the joining of these two groups, in this case across Japan and the United States. While their experiences took place and often were shaped by different nations and racial situations, they still had much in common. With the advent of the hapa community came a growing recognition that being of mixed race within Japanese communities in Japan was particularly challenging—as acceptance was not as easy as in the U.S.-based Japanese American communities. Conference topics examined the history of mixed people in Japan and Okinawa from the 1500s to the pre– and post–World War eras. They also included papers such as Cynthia L. Nakashima's (2011) "The New Nikkei: Towards a Modern Meaning of 'Japanese American'" and films on representing and representations of mixed-race Japanese in the United States and Japan.

Other, more recent examples include the debate around the African American and Japanese heritages of Miss Universe Japan 2015, Ariana Miyamoto, and the Indian and Japanese ancestry of Miss World Japan 2016, Priyanka Yoshikawa. Debates about the ability and appropriateness of Ariana Miyamoto's ability to be Miss Japan not too surprisingly broke down over racial lines and racial debates. Although fluent in Japanese and having been raised predominantly in Japan, questions about her "Japaneseness" surfaced quickly after she was awarded her title. "One Twitter user wrote that 'Even though she's Miss Universe Japan, her face is foreign no matter how you look at it," while another said, "Miss Universe Japan is. . . . What? What kind of person is she? She's not Japanese, right?" (Ward 2015).

Again in 2016, when Priyanka Yoshikawa was crowned Miss World Japan, people wrote to express their concern at the "advantage" that mixed-race queen candidates had. By not "looking" Japanese, she was not Japanese "enough" to represent Japan, despite having the cultural capital of Japaneseness, having been raised in Japan, speaking the language, and knowing the culture and customs. Readers couldn't understand why they couldn't "pick a proper Japanese" (Ryall 2016). Her racial appearance still mattered to signal her Japaneseness.

While criticisms of beauty pageants abound, one cannot ignore the fact that for some they are seen as symbolic representations of their community and, in this case, their nation. Miyamoto's response has been interesting, and she has spoken openly about how a mixed-race friend of hers faced racial discrimination in Japan causing him to commit suicide. The response within the United States and particularly by mixed-race Japanese American multiracials has been one of unanimous support—they strongly related with her exclusionary experiences in the United States and Japan.

In other places, such as Canada, we also see the growth of artistic and digital media production of the mixed experience. Canadian film maker Jeff Chiba Stearns is a prime example of how the changing demographics of Japanese Canadians have changed the face of the community in Canada but have also contributed to a growing awareness of the mixed experience. Stearn's film *One Big Hapa Family* astutely examines how few monoracial Japanese are left in Canada, but shows how this trend has created mixed-race family ties to many different types of people. As a part of an international film and digital media festival, these contributions in Canada have come together for five years now in *Hapalooza*, a celebration of mixed-race heritage and hybrid cultural identity (http://www.hapapalooza.com).

Again, international connections through social media, film, and artistic expression flow quite effortlessly over national boundaries and time zones and allow connections to be made faster and more easily than before between those of mixed Japanese descent. This allows mixed JAMs to connect to other mixed Nikkei—not just Japanese American, but Japanese Canadian, mixed Japanese Brazilian, mixed Japanese in Hawai'i, and mixed Japanese from Japan (hafu). Through Twitter and Facebook, they discover that they all have things in common in terms of their cultural backgrounds and lived experiences as mixed people. This online communication allows for the creation of a network of global mixed-race Japanese millennials. Social media also create a transnational, younger, more tech-savvy generation of Nikkei, many of whom are less wedded to pure racial ideas of Japanese Americanness. This network not only substantiates the linking of virtual and embodied communities across the United States but also solidifies transnational links to Brazil, Europe, and Japan. Social media networks also illustrate how mixed-race Japanese American experiences across the globe lead the way in expanding community membership by eliminating an either/or choice and supporting multiple choices within specific contexts—an example of flexible racialization at work.

Japanese American Mixed-Race Millennials and the Future of Community

Demographic, technological, and cultural change means that the context of Japanese American community and identity development is shifting drastically. These structural changes also shape new forms of Japanese American culture, identity, and community—many of which are linked to multiraciality.

Challenging "Community"

The Japanese American community is now mostly middle class and contains both aging monoracial and growing young multiracial components (the latter including both Generation Y/millennials and Generation Z born 1995 and later). Furthermore, the transnational dimension remains important as Japanese Americans continue to be seen within the context of United States/ Japan relationships and are closely tied to Japan or Asia more generally in important ways. Even more permeable national and racial boundaries apparent in mixed-race lives do not mean that race and nation cease to exist in the cultural politics of race—as is clear in the case of Ariana Miyamoto. Increasing globalization and transnationalism affects Japanese Americans, but Japanese Americanness has not disappeared and is still grounded in cultural and racial "performances" (Schechner 2013) strongly linked to Japanese American history in the United States, including internment. However, within that legacy, both continuity and change play a role in the terms defining Japanese Americanness, which are increasingly becoming more fluid and flexible. Multiraciality is increasingly legitimate and widely accepted as a way forward for "the community." Therefore, these changes do not mean that Japanese Americans are now without culture or without a community because of a young and growing mixed-race community within its boundaries.

Changing Notions of Millennialism

Ideas of race and mixed-race flow across racial and national boundaries—but so too do ideas about millennialism. When one hears the word "millennials," it conjures up images of young (born post-1980s), self-involved slackers who lack motivation, cannot find work, live with their parents too long, are not interested in marriage, and have short attention spans as a result of technology overuse. But are all millennials like this? Are they all the same? Or has the homogeneous image of all millennials been overplayed? Do Japanese American millennials have more in common with other millennials or more in common with fellow co-ethnics who have gone before them? How does religion, generation, migration status (and the context of that migration), ethnicity (and growing multiethnicity within the Japanese American community) and gender come to play a role in how Japanese American millennials identify themselves and their culture and community? Japanese American millennials are significantly different from their white counterparts and also different from Japanese Americans of past generations, and this difference is played out in terms of changing identity, culture, and community.

Slackers or Adapters?

The stereotypes of millennials described earlier are tested in this section of the chapter to see if Japanese American millennials fit these stereotypes. For the most part, JAMs are similar to their white counterparts in that the structure of the job market has affected them negatively, including having more debt, less job security, and having to grapple with a fast-changing skill set. For many JAMs, these challenges may mean that they are finding it increasingly difficult to maintain the standard of living that their sansei/yonsei or shin-nisei parents have achieved; that is, by living the American Dream in terms of education and income. Mixed-race JAMs may be finding it more difficult than monoracial JAMs. For example, Arthur Sakamoto, Isao Takei, and Hyeyoung Woo (2011, 1445) found that "single-race Japanese Americans tend to have higher schooling than multirace Japanese Americans and 1.5 generation Japanese Americans, who migrated as young people to the US from Japan, tend to have higher schooling than native-born Japanese Americans." This finding would seem to imply that groups closer to Japan (or migration from Japan) and monoracials are doing better in terms of educational outcomes, not necessarily those in the United States longer or those of mixed-race descent. However, caution must be taken when analyzing data such as that just given. It is true that in 2014, 36.4 percent of all women and 42.8 percent of all men in the United States of ages 18–34 were still living at home mainly based on economic reasons (Fry 2015; Alter 2015). However, the fact of living at home and depending on parents may not always be an indication of lower social mobility or economic distress. For cultural reasons, Japanese American parents have historically always been involved in their young adult children's lives, and many Japanese American young adults lived at home in the past until marriage and/or financial security (ability to buy a home) was attained—this pattern is not new. Living at home also did not mean that JAMs were just slackers or downwardly mobile. Most worked and many also provided family support as well as elder and child care in multigenerational home situations.

A second stereotype is that JAMs are self-involved. Perhaps some JAMs are self-involved, but no signs have indicated that Japanese American community involvement is declining because JAMs are only able to think of themselves. Even with the geographic dispersal of most Japanese Americans, JAMs continue to work hard to remain connected to cultural festivals and events such as the Nisei Week Festival in Los Angeles, now in its seventy-fourth year. Young people in the San Francisco Cherry Blossom Festival chose "Heritage, Tradition and Legacy" as their theme in 2014, and later-generation Japanese Americans have shown increased interest in taking up Taiko drumming and other Japanese cultural arts. Japanese American sports leagues, especially basketball leagues, continue to thrive, as has participation in Japanese American Christian Youth Camps by later-generation Japanese Americans because they provide a venue for building Japanese American social networks and discovery of individual and group expressions as Japanese Americans through them. In 2000, it looked like Japanese American community organizations might be disappearing. And yet, that has not happened in large part because of JAMs' commitment and participation.

Thirdly, it is assumed that JAMs are not interested in marriage. Of Japanese Americans, 53 percent are married compared with 59 percent of all Asian Americans, and, interestingly, compared with 51 percent of all U.S. adults (Pew Research Center 2012). Japanese American are clearly interested in marriage and do marry. It may be true that some Japanese Americans do marry later, as do their white counterparts, but this pattern is historically not new for Japanese Americans and not unique to the millennial generation. Some may also not marry at all and, again, this lifestyle is not new. Two or three generations ago, singletons existed and almost every Japanese American family had a bachelor uncle or auntie. Marriage trends simply reflect a combination of historical community patterns with widespread national trends.

Do JAMs overuse technology? JAMs do make good use of technology in their social relationships, but they also increasingly use social media for political mobilization and community involvement. JAMs of all genders are more likely to be involved in flexible, but what they describe as "more meaningful," work. They tend to be more egalitarian and to be striving for a better work/life balance (even in the high-tech sector), and they are more globally aware, perhaps because of the flow of digital information across the world (Kotkin 2013).

Japanese American millennials may be different from others of their generation. It would not be accurate to say that they are the same as white millennials. As Russel Jeung, Brett Esaki, and Alice Liu (2015) found when studying the difference between religious belief and religious practice: "It is not just what they believe, but what they 'do.'" It is how they practice and "do" Japanese Americanness that matters. They are also different from Japanese Americans of previous generations. What does this mean then for Japanese American identity, community, and culture? In Table 9.2, I have summarized some of the ways that Japanese American identity, culture, and community have changed in the millennial generation.

TABLE 9.2. IDENTITY, COMMUNITY, AND CULTURE SHIFTS AMONG
JAPANESE AMERICAN MILLENNIALS

	Pre-Millennial Japanese Americans (JAs)	Japanese American Millennials (JAMs)
Identity	Stable social identity based on generational cohorts	"shin" generations + Global Bricolage
Community	Race as community membership	Young, mixed-race/multicultural Transnational (non-U.S. Nikkei diaspora)
Culture	Monocultural assumptions WWII internment "101 Ways to Tell You Are JA"	Digital identities practiced and produced in cultural forms (sports leagues, beauty pageants) and Online Transnational movement Global flow of cultural ideas and political/social movements

If we look closely at JAMs today, we see that the basis of their identity and the ways that they identify are changing. They are different from Japanese Americans in the past and are shifting from more stable generational cohorts of identities to more global, diasporic, even culturally diverse notions of identity, which seem to move away from the idea of "core racial" identities. These identities could be seen as more "flexibly racialized" (King-O'Riain et al. 2014). They are asserted mixed-race identities that interact and are shaped by local as well as global contexts. Mixed-race JAMs, where they are accepted as Japanese American, may unseat "race" then as a core (although not unimportant) identifier not just for individuals, but for communities as well. The criteria for membership and participation in the Japanese American community may be shifting more toward a transnationally negotiated multiracial/multiethnic and flexible sense of who is Japanese American.

Finally, we may be moving away from racially codified experiences of what makes us Japanese American to a sense of culture that is shaped not only by social but also digital identities in online virtual communities, as well as practiced and produced in cultural forms such as Taiko, sports leagues, and beauty pageants. Digital communities are able, in some ways, to capture the transnational movement of culture and the global flow of cultural ideas, all of which serve to shape new cultural, social, and political movements.

Conclusion

Has an increasing mixed-race population meant that the Japanese American community is being racially diluted into nonexistence? Other racial and ethnic communities have dealt with this issue in the past, and while no two groups are the same, it is possible that we may see the Japanese American community follow in the path of communities such as Native Americans or African Americans. Both of these communities grappled with cultural and identity issues when a large proportion of their community members became mixed race. Perhaps the Japanese American community, as it becomes more mixed race than monoracial, will go the way of the African American community, where anyone with one drop of Japanese blood is considered a member of the community, or perhaps they will go the way of Native American communities, where blood quantum is measured carefully and those who do not have enough Japanese blood will not be considered Japanese American.

While Japanese Americans still live the experience of internment and the international relationship between Japan and the United States, which in the past has strongly shaped their experiences, they have not experienced slavery, legal racial segregation, or genocide in the same way the African Americans or Native Americans have. But as they increasingly accept mixed-race Japanese Americans as full members of the Japanese American community, the racial contours of the Japanese American cultural landscape are shifting away from an exclusive or primary focus on race. What will the connection of their children, "quapas" (defined by Urban Dictionary as an "individual who is 1/4 Asian or Pacific Islander"), be to the more traditional Japanese American community structures? Will they identify as Japanese American, hafu, or something else all together? Already evidence supports that in some Japanese American basketball leagues and beauty pageants, those with 25 percent Japanese ancestry are welcome and considered legitimate participants and representatives of the Japanese American community.

Initially, the mixed-race JAM generation mobilized through existing Japanese American community structures such as the Japanese Culture and Community Center of Northern California, but now JAMs are—with changed economic circumstances (less opportunity), changed culture (more acceptance in the JA community and possibly among whites), and changing technologies (new opportunities for communities not bound by place)—reinventing the form of community itself. This transnational and more fluid approach to Japanese American identity and culture is reenergizing the community even as the structural challenges of outmarriage, reduced colocation, and other social and cultural changes are increasing.

In the first section, we saw that the demographics of the Japanese American community are changing in important ways with a new, predominantly mixed-race generation on the rise. In the second section, we saw that these changes did not bring about the end of the Japanese American community, but instead generated a wide range of cultural innovations involving multiracial Japanese American millennials, even while they faced "racial limits" imposed from within and outside the community. The third section examined the further innovations in the practice and form of Japanese American community building that have been associated with the millennial generation. These changes have not resulted in the dissolution or destruction of Japanese American culture, identity, or community, but instead have created a transnationalizing, digitizing, and, vitally, a more fluid notion of race within the JAM generation that expands rather than contracts cultural membership in and the borders of the Japanese American community today.

NOTE

1. The term "hapa" became conflated with not just those of partial Japanese American descent, but all of those with mixed Asian and Pacific Islander descent.

REFERENCES

Alter, Charlotte. 2015. "Millennials Are Setting New Records—for Living with Their Parents." *Time* magazine. http://time.com/4108515/millennials-live-at-home-parents.

Bratter, Jenifer, and Rosalind King. 2008. "But Will It Last?": Duration of Interracial Unions Compared to Similar Race Relationships." *Family Relations* 57 (2): 160–171.

Chan, Louie. 2016. "Hapas Soon to Be the Majority in the Japanese American Community." *AsAmNews*. April 6. Accessed March 21, 2019. http://www.asamnews.com/2016/04/06/hapas-soon-to-be-the-majority-in-the-japanese-american-community.

Dhingra, Pawan, and Robyn Magalit Rodriguez. 2014. *Asian America: Sociological and Interdisciplinary Perspectives*. Hoboken, NJ: John Wiley and Sons.

Fry, Richard. 2015. "Record Share of Young Women Are Living with Their Parents, Relatives." PEW Research Center. Accessed March 21, 2019. http://www.pewresearch.org/fact-tank/2015/11/11/record-share-of-young-women-are-living-with-their-parents-relatives.

Fulbeck, Kip. 2008. *100 Percent Hapa* (exhibit). Japanese American National Museum, Los Angeles, California.

Hoeffel, Elizabeth M., Sonya Rastogi, Myoung Ouk Kim, and Hasan Shahid. 2012. "The Asian Population: 2010." *2010 Census Briefs*. March. Washington, DC: U.S. Census Bureau. Accessed March 21, 2019. https://www.census.gov/library/publications/2012/dec/c2010br-11.html.

Jeung, Russell, Brett Esaki, and Alice Liu. 2015. "Redefining Religious Nones: Lessons from Chinese and Japanese American Young Adults." *Religions* 6:891–911.

King-O'Riain, Rebecca C. 2006. *Pure Beauty: Judging Race in Japanese American Beauty Pageants*. Minneapolis: University of Minnesota Press.

King-O'Riain, Rebecca C., Stephen Small, Minelle Mahtani, Miri Song, and Paul Spickard, eds. 2014. *Global Mixed Race*. New York: New York University Press.

Kotkin, Joel. 2013. "Are Millennials Turning Their Backs on the American Dream?" *New Geography*. November 10. Accessed March 21, 2019. http://www.newgeography.com/content/004043-are-millennials-turning-their-backs-american-dream.

Mixed Race Babies. Accessed March 21, 2019. https://www.pinterest.ie/jadejerrico/mixed-race-babies/.

Nakashima, Cynthia L. 2011. "The New Nikkei: Towards a Modern Meaning of Japanese American." Paper presented at the Hapa Japan Conference. April. University of California, Berkeley.

Pew Research Center. 2012. "Social and Demographic Trends: Japanese Americans." Washington, DC: Pew Research Center. Accessed March 22, 2019. http://www.pewsocialtrends.org/asianamericans-graphics/japanese.

———. 2015. "Multiracial in America: Proud, Diverse, and Growing in Numbers." Washington, DC: Pew Research Center. Accessed March 22, 2019. http://www .pewsocialtrends.org/2015/06/11/multiracial-in-america.

———. 2017. "Japanese in the U.S. Fact Sheet," Washington, DC: Pew Research Center. Accessed March 22, 2019. http://www.pewsocialtrends.org/asianamericans-graphics /japanese.

Ryall, Julian. 2016. "'Just Pick a Proper Japanese': Purists Question Miss Japan's Indian Heritage." Accessed March 21 2019. https://www.telegraph.co.uk/news/2016/09/06 /just-pick-a-proper-japanese-purists-question-miss-japans-indian/.

Sakamoto, Arthur, Isao Takei, and Hyeyoung Woo. 2011. "Socioeconomic Differentials among Single-Race and Multi-Race Japanese Americans." *Ethnic and Racial Studies* 34 (9): 1445–1465.

Schechner, Richard. 2013. *Performance Studies: An Introduction*. 3rd ed. New York: Routledge.

Shinagawa, Larry Hajime, and Gin Yong Pang. 1996. "Asian American Panethnicity and Intermarriage." *Amerasia Journal* 22:127–152.

Spickard, Paul R. 1989. *Mixed Blood: Intermarriage and Ethnic Identity in Twentieth-Century America*. Madison: University of Wisconsin Press.

Urban Dictionary. 2019. Accessed March 20, 2019. https://www.urbandictionary.com/ define.php?term=Quapa.

Ward, Alexander. 2015. "Miss Japan Gets Online Abuse 'Because She Doesn't Look Japanese Enough.'" *The Independent*. June 7. Accessed March 22, 2019. https://www.inde pendent.co.uk/news/people/miss-universe-japan-has-to-put-up-with-abuse-from -online-bullies-because-she-doesnt-look-japanese-10302115.html.

Yamashiro, Jane H. 2008. "Hafu." In *Encyclopedia of Race, Ethnicity and Society*, ed. Richard T. Schaefer. Thousand Oaks, CA: Sage.

10

The New Second Generation

*Biculturalism and Transnational Identities among Japanese
American Shin-Nisei*

TAKEYUKI TSUDA

R esearch on second-generation Japanese Americans focuses exclusively
on nisei who were born before World War II (e.g., Hosokawa 1992; Matsumoto 2014; Takahashi 1997; Tamura 1994; Yoo 2000), and their historical struggles have become part of the dominant narrative about Japanese
Americans. In contrast, almost no research has been done on the "new"
second generation of Japanese Americans ("shin-nisei"),[1] who are descendants of Japanese who immigrated to the United States after 1965.[2] Although
their experiences are not as dramatic as those of the prewar nisei, their stories have not yet been told.

A New Generation of Nisei

Because the total volume of Japanese immigration since 1965 has been limited because of Japan's postwar economic prosperity, the number of shin-
nisei is not large, but it continues to grow.[3] Along with fourth-generation
Japanese American youth ("yonsei"), they represent the future of the Japanese American community. Most shin-nisei are part of the historical millennial generation who were born in the 1980s and 1990s and were raised in a
pro-Japanese, multicultural, and globalized environment. As a result, they
have retained their Japanese cultural heritage, their ethnicity and identities
tend to be bicultural, and they are transnationally engaged with their ethnic
homeland of Japan.

Because my shin-nisei interviewees partly grew up in the postwar Japanese expatriate community and are much more connected to Japan and Japa-

nese culture, a good number of them did not identify much with the broader Japanese American community (see also Takahashi 1997, 208–209; Yamashiro 2008, 258). As a result, they felt quite different from prewar nisei, third-generation sansei, and fourth-generation yonsei. In fact, only a couple of shin-nisei had ever been a member of any Japanese American organizations.

"I've never had any contact with the Japanese American community and know nothing about them," one of them remarked. "I grew up with Japanese kids from Japan [in the Japanese expatriate community]. So my life was much more oriented toward Japan, and I feel much more culturally Japanese than most Japanese Americans."

Matt Honkawa[4] had similar experiences: "When I say I'm Japanese American, I'm not identifying with Japanese American history or anything like that. I'm identifying mainly with Japan. It's not that I don't relate to Japanese Americans. I have sansei and yonsei buddies. But I feel different from them because my understanding of Japanese culture is greater." Although he was a student at the University of California, San Diego (UCSD), he never bothered to attend Nikkei Student Union (Japanese American student organization) events on campus. "They're yonsei. They don't speak any Japanese," he noted. "The purpose of the club isn't to continue Japanese culture. For me, it's just not important that I surround myself with other Japanese Americans."

"I actually never used the word 'Japanese American' when I grew up," Yuki explained. "It's not a term I really became aware of until college. I just thought of myself as Japanese. Actually, a group of us used the term 'American-born Japanese,' or ABJ."

The only shin-nisei I interviewed who was currently active in the Japanese American community was Steve, who was a past board member of the Nikkei Student Union and past president of Asayake Taiko (a Japanese American drumming group at UCSD). However, even he did not consider himself Japanese American when he was growing up and thought of himself more in Japanese nationalist terms. He described his reaction when he went to Japan as a child and was called *nikkeijin* (a Japanese ethnic term that refers to Japanese descendants born abroad, such as Japanese Americans): "I was like 'Hey, that's f—d up! I'm not nikkeijin. I'm *nihonjin* [Japanese].' So that was my first major culture shock, and I really felt bad back then." However, over time, he came to identify more with the Japanese American community and now calls himself "nikkeijin" in Japan. He also began to use the ethnic term "Japanese American" in college. Nonetheless, he described to me how he does not always feel like a true Japanese American and sometimes struggles to be included in the community:

> Sometimes I feel like I'm not an authentic Japanese American, because I'm not a product of their history of internment and redress

[the movement to seek reparations for wartime internment]. I'm much more connected to the history of Japan. But I'm trying to understand and identify with Japanese American experiences too.... When I say I'm "shin-nisei," I'm making a political statement saying, "You know what? Being Japanese American is not just about being sansei and yonsei. It's about being shin-nisei too." And to deny this distinction within the community is absolutely unacceptable. There are minority elements in the bigger community.

This chapter is based on one-and-a-half years of fieldwork and participant observation with Japanese American communities in San Diego and Phoenix from 2005 to 2006 and in 2009. Fifty-five in-depth interviews (two to three hours each) were completed with Japanese Americans (twenty-four of them were with Japanese American millennials, and thirteen were with shin-nisei). Initial contacts were made with the Japanese American Historical Society of San Diego, the Nikkei Student Union (at UCSD), and the Japanese American Citizens League (in Phoenix), but through snowball sampling, I also interviewed Japanese Americans who did not participate in these organizations. My sample consists of Japanese American men and women of all ages from the second to fourth generations. I also conducted participant observation by attending meetings and community activities of these three Japanese American organizations (plus the Japanese American Buddhist Temple in San Diego) and socialized with various Japanese Americans on many occasions. I should note that my sample includes only Japanese Americans living in a limited part of the American Southwest. I make no claims that my description and analysis also pertains to those living in the Midwest, East Coast, or Hawai'i, although I would suspect that some similar ethnic experiences would be found among them as well. However, my research does illuminate the experiences of millennial Japanese Americans who live outside the main Japanese American communities of Los Angeles and Hawai'i.

Being Japanese American in Postwar America

A number of obvious but significant changes have occurred since World War II that have caused shin-nisei millennial youth to remain strongly connected to their ethnic heritage and homeland (see also Kitano 1993, 202–203; Takahashi 1997, 211). In contrast to the mainly white, assimilationist world in which the prewar nisei came of age, the postwar nisei are a product of a much more ethnically diverse and multicultural America that tolerates and even encourages the second generation to maintain their native cultures and languages and transnational commitments (see Foner 2002; Levitt 2001, 203). A couple of my shin-nisei interviewees spoke of how the current ethnic diversity in the United States allowed them to become bicultural instead of adopting a singular American nationalist identity. Yuki Sumimoto spoke about his past experiences in this respect as follows: "I don't remember feeling too much pressure to assimilate and become Americanized. I was already pretty Americanized at that point, and in the United States, there are so many different peoples of different backgrounds. So I didn't have to consciously decide to become either American or Japanese. I could kind of be both." According to another shin-nisei, Takehiro Watanabe, "I grew up in a really diverse community: there were blacks, Mexican people, and Japanese Americans. So I just blended into the local community and tried to fit in. There wasn't that much pressure to show that you're really American. For me, Japanese American identity was more hybrid, a mixture of cultures. It wasn't just defensively asserting your Americanness. I like the notion of fluid, flexible identities."

Meanwhile, American attitudes toward Japan have been completely transformed as a formerly despised, enemy nation has become an economically prosperous and respected First World country that is the United States' oldest and closest East Asian ally (O'Brien and Fugita 1991, 127; Fujitani 2011, 230–231). As a number of Asian American scholars have noted, ethnic minority status is not only shaped by the socioeconomic location of the group in the United States, but by the position of its ethnic homeland in the global order (Kim 2008, 2–3; Tsuda 2009b; Wu and Song 2000). Thus, Japanese Americans have been significantly influenced by America's changing relationship with Japan (Kitano 1993, 3). Because of the currently positive images about the country, some Americans have considerable fascination about Japan, including its culture, history, food, global commodities, technology, and popular culture. This has encouraged postwar second-generation Japanese Americans to identify strongly with Japan and their cultural heritage (see also Takamori 2010, 224).

The shin-nisei youth I spoke with generally felt that American images of Japan were quite positive, and they could not think of many negative images. They noted how the country is regarded as a modern, highly advanced, and rich nation that is a pro-American ally. They also mentioned favorable perceptions of the country's technology, electronics, cars, computer games, and anime, as well as the American fascination with historic images of Japan based on samurais, ninjas, geishas, and Japanese art. A few of them also spoke of perceptions of Japan as an orderly and harmonious society based on social obligations and hierarchical respect. The shin-nisei seemed to feel that any negative American reactions toward Japan were mainly a thing of the past. A number of them mentioned prejudice against Japanese based on Pearl Harbor and World War II, but felt it was mainly confined to elderly people and old war movies and not really relevant today. Another example mentioned by a couple of shin-nisei was American resentment toward Japanese economic prosperity and competition in the 1980s,[5] but they again felt it was no longer an issue. "Americans used to be concerned about Japan kicking our ass economically," one of them observed. "But now, most of this [resentment] is directed toward China. No one complains about Japan anymore." The only negative contemporary perceptions of Japan that the shin-nisei mentioned were Japanese tourist behavior and the patriarchal nature of the country.

Therefore, the dynamics of racialization for Japanese Americans in the United States have completely changed, so that being "Japanese" no longer has the unfavorable meanings it did in the past nor leads to serious discrimination or racism. The postwar nisei felt that they are no longer subject to much prejudice or discrimination. Most of them could not remember an instance when they were directly mistreated or personally discriminated against because of their ethnicity, except when they were children and were teased by other kids.

"You hear instances of discrimination against other people, like blacks, or Muslims after 9/11," Steve Okura noted. "That gets me upset. And I definitely have this awareness of institutionalized discrimination against Japanese in the past. But personally, I've never experienced anything that I consider discrimination."

Yuki, one of my shin-nisei interviewees, had been called "Jap" once by elderly World War II veterans at a state fair in California. However, he recalled that "I didn't make much of it because I knew it was from the war long ago."

In contrast to the prewar era, most discrimination against Asian Americans today seems to be structural or relatively hidden (such as the glass ceiling) and is rarely overt. In fact, studies show that second-generation Asian Americans are less likely to experience direct discrimination than other nonwhite second-generation groups (e.g., see Kasinitz et al. 2008, 37). Even my most socially aware shin-nisei interviewees, such as Takehiro (a university faculty member), found it difficult to attribute possible unequal treatment directly to racial discrimination: "Professionally, I can't say there was an incident that was blatantly racist or discriminatory. It's very hard to say. If I don't get an academic job that I felt I was qualified for, is that because I wasn't white? Or because I didn't have a Ph.D. from Harvard? When I started new faculty positions, I felt the staff [members] weren't treating me well, or they gave me a really terrible office until I made a big fuss about it. Is that because of my race, or because I was still a junior faculty member? I don't know."

Matt, a college student, noted, "It's probably more perceived on my part than anything. . . . It's like when I was looking for a job on campus, or even interviewing for some internships, I feel like if I was a white guy, I'd probably have a better shot of getting the position because my interviewers tend to be white. But I just feel like it's a slight disadvantage, not a major hurdle."

Doug Ishimura, who was 2.5 generation (his mother was from Japan, his father was second generation), actually felt his ethnicity was an advantage at times on the job market in a multiethnic society: "I think a lot of times, my ethnicity benefits me. It's not like there's a lot of Affirmative Action for Asians or anything. But when I apply for a job, I notice there aren't many Asian workers at a company. I figure that may be a plus for me."

As a result of these postwar changes, the shin-nisei feel that Japanese Americans are generally well regarded today. When asked about American perceptions of Japanese Americans, they referred to positive stereotypes about Asian Americans in general. Almost all of them mentioned that they are seen as model minorities who are smart and hard-working academic overachievers and are good at math, science, and computers.[6] Some felt they are regarded as socioeconomically well-to-do, as well as quiet, good citizens. Others mentioned more ambivalent gendered images of Asian American women as traditional, submissive, as well as sexually attractive, and Asian men as wimpy computer nerds who are asexual and effeminate. "I've never heard of a Japanese American firefighter, for example," one woman re-marked. "They don't go into those types of masculine occupations." Nonetheless, the shin-nisei generally felt that being Japanese American was a much more positive than negative experience.

Finally, second-generation Japanese Americans today have had significant opportunities to maintain active transnational ties to their ethnic homeland of Japan. As a number of researchers have noted, today's second generation live in a globalized world characterized by the greater ease of international travel, global mass media, and the internet, which enable them to stay connected with their parents' country of origin (Kasinitz, Mollenkopf, and Waters 2004, 5–6; 2008, 4). In addition, because of the postwar economic prosperity of Japan, the parents of the shin-nisei immigrated to the United States generally as well-to-do students, businessmen, and professional expatriates who often travel back and forth between the United States and Japan as part of their careers. As high-skilled, relatively elite immigrants, they have the economic means to live transnational lives and have been able to pass on their transnationalism to their children. As Cecilia Menjívar notes (2002, 537–538), children of immigrants with middle-class backgrounds are more likely to develop transnational ties to the ethnic homeland compared to those from poor backgrounds. Most shin-nisei have therefore visited Japan numerous times during their lives with their parents, and some of them had actually lived there by themselves in order to work, go to school, or teach English.

Ethnic Heritage and Biculturalism

Because shin-nisei Japanese Americans of the millennial generation grew up in a multicultural and transnational world where being ethnically Japanese is positively regarded and no longer leads to significant ethnic and socioeconomic discrimination, they have developed a strong attachment to their Japanese heritage and have become fully bicultural. It is important to remember that members of the second generation do not always strengthen their ethnic minority identity or affiliation with their national origins as a "reactive ethnicity" against increased majority discrimination and socioeconomic marginalization (cf. Espiritu and Wolf 2001; Portes and Rumbaut 2001, chap. 7). They may also do so as an affirmative reaction to the positive meanings that can be associated with their heritage and homeland.

A couple of my interviewees explicitly mentioned that they felt a certain pride in their Japanese cultural background. "I wouldn't say it's a nationalistic pride, or anything," Matt remarked. "But I do take a bit of pride in being Japanese, or maybe satisfaction is a better word. I enjoy being Japanese, like the food, culture, and being able to speak the language. I don't proudly assert it, but it is part of who I am."

Likewise, Doug felt he was "sort of proud to be Japanese American." He elaborated further: "Because of the community here, there is a sense of pride in who you are. The Japanese are humble and have some good qualities. And being Japanese American, even though it's been a short time, has a pretty good history.... I don't say 'I'm Japanese American,' just to clear up ambiguity or confusion. I'm more proud to say it."

"I really like the Japanese culture and the language," another commented. "I see my heritage in a positive way and feel pretty attached to it."

A few of my shin-nisei informants were more ambivalent about their Japanese ethnicity when they were children but eventually came to embrace it. Like other young Japanese Americans, Matt was raised in a white middle-class suburb in the 1990s. He faced assimilationist pressures at school and distanced himself from his ethnic background as a child. "Growing up, a lot of my friends were white," he recalled. "My close friends weren't Asian. So I wanted to Americanize more." He spoke about how his mother would make Japanese lunches to take to school. "I'd be like, 'Oh man, I don't want to . . . Make me a sandwich.' The other kids would be like, 'What's that?' I felt embarrassed a bit." Eventually, his mother began making him sandwiches because he wouldn't eat Japanese lunches at school. "My Japaneseness wasn't like the bane of my existence or anything," he added. "But the pressure to be American was definitely there. So I didn't enjoy it and wasn't too proud of it." As a result, Matt did not want to go to Japanese school but did so because of parental pressure. "But it was bearable because I had a lot of friends there and they didn't all want to be there either. So we kind of just stuck together," he remarked. However, as he grew older and entered college, he came to value his ethnic heritage to a greater extent and eventually took pride in it. "You start realizing that being Japanese is a good thing, that it's fine to be different. I also met more nisei like me, especially in college, who had similar experiences."

Doug, who was 2.5 generation, also had a somewhat similar experience. He spoke about how his parents wanted to take him to Japan as a child but he did not want to go. "I would just fight it," he recalled. Also, he did not want to study Japanese at that age. "There was this sense of me being an American and I was like 'Why am I studying Japanese? None of my friends speak Japanese. Why do I have to speak it?'" However, as he grew older, he developed a positive perception of Japanese culture and a greater appreciation of his ethnic heritage.

It was rather remarkable that all the shin-nisei I spoke with were fully bilingual and bicultural. Although biculturalism is similar to the concept of selective acculturation that is used in the second-generation segmented assimilation literature, I prefer the concept of biculturalism. Selective acculturation refers to the children of immigrants who grow up in large, cohesive co-ethnic communities that allow them to partially retain their parents' home language and culture, therefore slowing down their cultural assimilation to mainstream society (Portes and Rumbaut 2001, 54). This slowing down is seen as promoting their socioeconomic success because it preserves parental authority over their children and provides a bulwark against discrimination. However, selective acculturation theory implies that ethnic heritage retention is opposed to assimilation in a zero-sum game, so that the more second-generation individuals maintain their parents' language and culture, the less they will be assimilated to mainstream culture and vice versa.

However, very few of the second-generation Japanese Americans I spoke with mentioned that all the effort they put into studying Japanese had hindered their English language acquisition or performance in American schools. The concept of biculturalism does not assume that the persistence of cultural heritage gets in the way of cultural assimilation (or vice versa), since both can happen simultaneously. In fact, although my interviewees had partly grown up in Japanese immigrant expatriate communities and went to Japanese Saturday school for many years, these circumstances did not seem to have impeded their simultaneous cultural assimilation (almost all spoke English without an accent, for example).

Because of their bicultural and bilingual backgrounds, the shin-nisei generally rated their Japanese as quite fluent. They could also read and write with some facility. Takehiro gave a somewhat typical assessment of his Japanese: "I'd say I'm pretty fluent. I can more or less speak like a Japanese and don't stand out as a foreigner in Japan. I don't really have an accent in Japanese. But I don't write very well and don't like to write in Japanese. If I read a [Japanese] book, it would take me at least twice as long as a book in English."

Most of the shin-nisei explicitly spoke about how their parents pressured them to study the Japanese language. "There was a lot of pressure in my family about the language thing," Takehiro recalled. "My parents really wanted me to study the language. They were pretty proud Japanese nationalists, especially my dad." Since a good number of the Japanese parents of the shin-nisei were professionals and businessmen who initially came to the United States as temporary sojourners and planned to return to Japan, they seemed to have insisted that their children study Japanese and maintain their cultural heritage. Even when they became permanent settlers, they retained strong transnational ties with their homeland and sometimes continued to entertain the notion of eventual repatriation. One shin-nisei woman described her experiences as follows: "My parents always said they would return to Japan. At the beginning, it was after my dad got his Ph.D. When that didn't happen, they said my dad would eventually get a job in Japan and they'd return. When that didn't happen, they said they would return after my dad retired. After a while, it became really obvious that they would never return. But that didn't stop them from insisting that we go to Japanese school and keep studying Japanese."

In general, it seems that the shin-nisei complied with their parents' wishes. Most of them attended Japanese Saturday schools, which were created for the children of Japanese businessmen and other professionals in large American cities with significant Japanese expatriate communities. Since most of these Japanese children intend to repatriate in a matter of years, these schools can be quite rigorous and attempt to keep up with the curriculum in Japan. The shin-nisei I interviewed generally attended these schools for many years (sometimes from first grade to the end of junior high school or even high school) and therefore took classes mainly with students from Japan, although there were other Japanese Americans in their classes.

The shin-nisei attended Japanese Saturday school not simply because of parental pressure but also because it was something they wanted to do. This dual motivation may be related to the positive meanings and experiences attached to their Japanese heritage and ethnic homeland as well as the current multicultural climate. A couple of them also mentioned that being bilingual may help them for their professional careers later in life. According to Yuki, "I don't think [my parents] forced the Japanese on me. I mean, they did make me go to Japanese school, but I didn't mind it too much. I just naturally did it. Actually, it was mostly for the friends. I wasn't too crazy about having to study such a difficult language every week. But in hindsight, I'm glad I did it."

"I had very strict parents, so quitting [Japanese school] was not an option," Steve said. "But I didn't really complain. Actually, I didn't want to quit myself. The thought never really crossed my mind. I had a lot of Japanese friends [from Japan] in Japanese school and enjoyed going." In fact, Steve even contemplated applying to Japanese universities.

In addition to learning the Japanese language, the shin-nisei youth also largely felt culturally Japanese and spoke about aspects of themselves that they positively attributed to their cultural heritage and upbringing. Yuki felt he was more group-oriented like the Japanese in Japan and had a communal attitude compared to other Americans: "I think more about the good of the community and about forgoing individual gains for the group. I think that stems [from] my going to Japan and the schools there. Students there have to do everything themselves, like clean the school and serve themselves. Here, I think people tend to be more selfish and take it for granted that other people will do things for them and they don't have to give back. Sometimes that annoys me. Because of my experience in Japan, I realize the importance of conforming and doing things for the benefit of others." Doug also spoke about the value of "sacrificing for others and the betterment of other people" as well as his ability to compromise and his respect for elders, which he attributed to his Japanese upbringing. He appreciated the respect and politeness of Japanese culture and the ability to preserve and live in harmony with the environment, which he observed during his stays in Japan. In contrast, he had a rather unflattering assessment of American culture. "Americans are so wasteful and just a bunch of pigs," he claimed. "And we've thrown away our elderly, instead of taking care of them."

In fact, Steve was the only shin-nisei who did not regard his Japaneseness in simply positive terms. He does love the Japanese language and its expressiveness and felt his Japanese respect for elders empowered him when he worked with seniors and was able to relate to and assist them better than other American youth. However, he felt limited by what he perceived were other Japanese cultural characteristics he had acquired: "I grew up Japanese and get really mad at myself that I have these Japanese tendencies that are built into how I was raised. Like if I see a stranger on the street, I'll bow. I won't smile or make full eye contact when I meet someone and instead look down. I have this pretty ridiculous attachment to hierarchy. I won't disrespect someone who is above me and am too apologetic. I've realized recently that once I get a job and start worrying about promotions and stuff like that, this type of behavior may drag me down and I might create my own glass ceiling. I have to work hard to break these stereotypes."

At Home in the Ethnic Homeland

In addition to having a strong bicultural background, the shin-nisei millennials have also been transnationally engaged with their ethnic homeland of Japan.[7] Their transnationalism has been inherited from their immigrant parents, who have taken them to Japan on numerous occasions. However, they have also sustained their transnational lives on their own, and some had lived in the country for extended periods for personal, educational, or professional reasons.

In general, the shin-nisei had quite positive experiences in their ethnic homeland. They reported that their cultural adaptation to Japan is quite smooth and they feel comfortable living there. This contrasts with other ethnic return migrants, who are often not fully bicultural and can have alienating experiences as cultural foreigners in their ancestral homeland (see Tsuda 2003, 2009a, 2009b). For the shin nisei, Japan was never truly a foreign country and they are able to sufficiently speak and "act Japanese" to the point where they have little trouble being socially accepted. As a result, they felt very much "at home" in their ethnic homeland. "Homeland" is a place of origin to which one feels emotionally attached, whereas "home" is a place of residence that feels secure, comfortable, and familiar (Tsuda 2009a, 242–243). Although the two places do not correspond for many ethnic return migrants who feel ethnically and socioeconomically marginalized in their ancestral homeland, this was not the case for the shin-nisei.

For instance, consider the experiences of Matt, who had lived and worked in Japan as a completely bicultural shin-nisei and tries to "act as Japanese as possible" in the country:

> My experiences in Japan are quite positive. I can easily switch to a Japanese identity. Otherwise, if you stick out, you make things difficult for yourself there. I know how to be Japanese because growing up, my mom taught me Japanese manners, customs, and spoke both languages to me. I had plenty of Japanese friends growing up and related well to my teachers and peers at Japanese school, so knew what Japanese culture was like. Interacting with Japanese in general is pretty natural for me. So in terms of living in Japan, it was very easy and comfortable for me. . . . It was sort of a reproduction of my Japanese school experiences in the United States.

"I can be totally accepted as Japanese in Japan if I want," Steve remarked. "I used to be really sensitive about acting Japanese in Japan. It used to bother me when the Japanese saw me as different. So I felt I had to be more Japanese than other Japanese people."

"I make a conscious effort to blend in Japan and speak mostly Japanese," said Yuki, who attended school in Japan. "When I talk loudly with my sister in English in the subway, people start looking at you."

Although the shin-nisei are bicultural, because they are not Japanese from Japan nor native speakers, a number of them noted that they introduce themselves as Americans in Japan partly to avoid any initial confusion and disorientation among the Japanese.[8] For instance, Takehiro, who lived in Japan for years and became fluent in the language, spoke about this as follows: "For short conversations, it's not noticeable that I'm a foreigner. So if I go into a store, I just act like a Japanese. But if I get into a longer conversation, I like to tell people I'm American. It makes things so much easier that way because otherwise, you become an idiot if you don't know something all

Japanese are supposed to know or make a mistake speaking the language." Likewise, Steve mentioned that he introduces himself in Japan as a "Nikkei Amerikajin" (an American of Japanese descent).

Nonetheless, my shin-nisei interviewees generally felt that Americans are well regarded and treated in Japan. For them, their Americanness was more of an ethnic asset and a source of interest than a disadvantage because of the cultural affinity and favorable perceptions Japanese have toward the United States (see also Yamashiro 2011, 1512–1513). Takehiro's comments supported this viewpoint: "I didn't feel any prejudice being a foreigner in Japan, except the language thing. The Japanese friends I choose were really interested in America and American pop culture. I was their informant about America and they seemed to like me for that. My Americanness was therefore more of an asset than anything else."

Although Yuki was a bit more ambivalent about how Japanese reacted to him as an American,[9] he had similar favorable experiences in Japan: "I think Japanese attitudes toward Japanese Americans are positive. A lot of [Japanese] people wish they could go to the United States. There's even a sense of awe. Japanese like to come here and go to Las Vegas. They like American popular culture, American movies, and American franchises are everywhere, so they are pretty aware of Americans. So having an American background is quite positive." Indeed, Steve even felt a sense of superiority in Japan as an American. "In Japan, my ethnicity isn't really an issue because in the end, I'm like, 'Sorry, America is above you Japan,'" he said. "You don't tell me what to do, I tell you what to do. I'm arrogant and egotistical. I feel this superiority in Japan as an American. In fact, I make a point that I'm American."

In contrast to other Japanese Americans, whose exposure to Japan is often limited to brief vacations as tourists, a few shin-nisei who lived in Japan for extended periods tended to give more balanced and ambivalent accounts of the country. Consider the comments of Takehiro, who had lived in Japan as both a student and researcher:

Over time, I started getting disenchanted with the romantic visions I had of Japan, because you start seeing all the warts, in addition to the cherry blossoms. I had this image of [Japanese] aesthetics that I was attracted to, so I used to love going to temples and gardens. Also museums to see the artwork. I was attracted to the exotic part of Japan. But being in Japan longer, you get this critical distance—not just how beautiful the artwork is. I was struck by things that are Japanese characteristics that I didn't like, such as the overexcessive social hierarchy, and I distanced myself from that. That was what was the most disturbing. And also the racialized nationalism.

"At first, you think everything is perfect in Japan," said Yoko, a biracial Japanese American who had gone to Japan continuously since she was three years old. "Then, when I'd go to Japan later on, I started to see the negative aspects, such as the alcoholism and the strong racism there, which I sense personally, even among my family [relatives in Japan]." Another shin-nisei woman who had lived in Japan for a long time expressed frustration over the gender expectations that constrain women in Japan, especially the pressure to dress up with makeup and "look perfect." "I felt like rebelling," she recalled. "I was like, 'I'm not going to wear *any* makeup. I'm going to wear everyday sweatshirts and jeans.'"

Despite some ambivalence about their experiences living in Japan that arose from their greater immersion in Japanese society, most of the shin-nisei strengthened their identification with Japan, especially over time. Although some of them felt more American in Japan because of the cultural differences they encountered, they also developed a transnational ethnic consciousness based on a dual affiliation with both America and Japan to some extent. For instance, Yuki spoke about his experiences: "In Japan, I definitely feel my Americanness more because I notice more differences than similarities [with the Japanese], even though I can do a decent job of getting by. But I also have a Japanese side I can activate, and a lot of times, I do, for courtesy's sake. I don't need to advertise that I'm from the United States." Although Takehiro mentioned that he distanced himself from aspects of Japanese culture that he did not like, he was ultimately conflicted as he vacillated between his Japanese and American sides. "It was a sense that I could never completely fit in there. Would never be like them. It was a combination of distance but also intimacy with the Japanese." Likewise, Matt also initially reinforced his American identity as a partial reaction to those aspects of Japan he disliked when he was younger. However, he was quite explicit about how he eventually came to adopt a more accommodating, transnational ethnic consciousness as a gradual maturational process:

When I was younger, it [his trips to Japan] probably reinforced my Americanness. I could relate to the culture and it was not hard for me to fit in, but I didn't like it. I preferred American culture—it's more free and not as strict. But as I got older and mature, I realized that's just how it is. It's not necessarily bad, just different. I went [to Japan] the past summer, and the year before, and came to reinforce my sense of relating to my Japanese side, because by that time, I had grown and can appreciate Japan. I don't act defensively anymore and say I'm American. I just totally fit in and embrace Japan. When I'm in Japan, I feel great, like I could live there for a long time. But when I get back to the United States, I feel great being back home. I can operate fine in both cultures.

Transnational Ethnic Consciousness

The postwar shin-nisei have developed ethnic identities that are more transnational in orientation because of their bicultural background as well as their experiences in Japan, as previously noted. Transnational ethnic identities are based on a simultaneous, dual identification with the host and origin countries (Tsuda 2012c, 462–463). Some confusion exists in the immigration literature about the nature of such identities. Examples of immigrants identifying with their home country across borders is often referred to as a "transnational" identity (e.g., Carling 2008, 467; Glick Schiller and Fouron 1999; Guarnizo and Díaz 1999, 414–415; Levitt and Glick Schiller 2008:287; van Niekerk 2007; Vertovec 2004, 978–980). However, immigrants' affiliations to their homelands are simply transborder (or long-distance) *nationalist* identities (since they involve identification with only one nation-state) and are not transnational unless they simultaneously identify with the host country.

First-generation immigrant parents often do not identify in transnational ways since they continue to maintain a strong nationalist identification with their home countries and do not develop as much attachment to the host society. In contrast, their second-generation children naturally come to identify with their country of birth, while they may simultaneously develop a significant affinity to their ancestral homeland because of the influence of their parents and trips they take to their parents' country of origin. In addition, increased access to information about their ethnic homeland through the mass media and the internet has given them new opportunities to develop a more expansive transnational ethnic consciousness.

The shin-nisei have developed quite prominent transnational identities based on a dual affinity with both the United States and Japan. Although they identify nationally with Japan and even sometimes think of themselves in Japanese nationalist terms, they also strongly and simultaneously identify as American nationals. This is quite a contrast to their parents, whom some of them described as "Japanese nationalists," "gung ho Japanese," or "patriotic toward Japan." Michiko Kawamura reflected on this generational difference: "My mother never really assimilated in America and doesn't speak much English. She's forever Japanese in her thinking. The thought of becoming an American citizen has never even crossed her mind, although she's been here for decades and will never go back to Japan. In fact, it bothers her because I've recently started to call myself Japanese American. When I grew up, she kept saying I'm 'pure Japanese.' Of course, I have both cultures inside of me and am connected to both countries. I don't think of myself as just one or the other. I'm actually a dual national."

A number of scholars have used the concept of "hybridity" instead of transnational identities to understand the ethnic consciousness of the second generation (Brettell and Nibbs 2009; Hickman et al. 2005; Potter 2005).

The children of immigrants are sometimes portrayed as caught between the two competing and opposing cultures of their parents and mainstream society (see e.g., Hickman et al. 2005; Portes and Rumbaut 2001, chap. 7), and the notion of hybrid identities seems to offer an alternative third path. Instead of choosing to emphasize one identity over the other, second-generation individuals are blurring the boundaries of difference by bringing together two separate and incompatible identities (Brettell and Nibbs 2009, 680). This "lived hybridity" prevents them from experiencing identity fragmentation that pulls them in opposite directions.

However, the concept of hybridity also has a number of problems (see also Robbins 2004, 327–333). First, it assumes the prior existence of two separate and pure cultural identities (based on the country of origin and the country of birth) that somehow become synthesized and integrated as a hybrid mixture among those of the second generation. However, both of these initial identities are often based on cultures that are themselves hybrid combinations of various cultures (especially American culture) and are not self-contained, homogeneous entities. In addition, hybridity implies that the conflict between the two incompatible identities is resolved through a dynamic balance and stable equilibrium, producing a coherent self. This obscures the inherently unequal, hierarchical ordering of these identities and the continuing tension between them.

Instead of presuming some kind of smooth hybrid integration and balance between two conflicting identities (which is often difficult to achieve), the concept of transnational identities emphasizes how they simultaneously coexist within the individual as multiple selves and are deployed at different times in different situations. The two identities can certainly struggle for supremacy, with one becoming more dominant during certain occasions or periods of time. Nonetheless, the dynamic tension between the incompatible identities often persists and is not resolved. However, this tension does not always fragment the subject because the different selves are not always manifested at the same time and are often compartmentalized.

Because of their biculturalism, my shin-nisei interviewees had developed a dual, transnational affiliation with both the United States and Japan and therefore had fluid, multiple identities. However, the two parts of their bicultural selves were not in some type of hybrid balance but inherently unequal, since one side was privileged over the other (usually the American side). For instance, according to Michiko, "I would say culturally I'm much more American than Japanese. I feel more natural in terms of the way I behave when I'm with Americans versus Japanese. With Japanese I have to be more conscious of like, 'I shouldn't be saying this because this is Japan.' Or 'I shouldn't act this way because I'm in Japan.' Whereas in the United States, I can just act naturally and be myself. So if you were to ask, it's natural that my American side is much stronger because I was born and raised here." Others such as Yuki had similar assessments of their transnational identities: "I wouldn't say my American side completely overrides my Japanese side, but I think in general, I identify as American first, although there are a lot of things about me that are still based on my Japanese heritage. So I think in English more than Japanese. I grew up Japanese, so everything in my mind was Japanese in the past. But I think it slowly transitioned to American as I grew older." In contrast, only a small number of shin-nisei felt more Japanese than American. For instance, according to Steve, "I can be Japanese or American. But if I had to choose sides, I'm inevitably more Japanese than American."

Although the shin-nisei generally felt that their American and Japanese cultural identities were incompatible, they were not that concerned about reconciling them by somehow creating a coherent, hybrid integration of their two selves. Instead, their two identities coexisted simultaneously as multiple, transnational affiliations that were appropriately deployed on different occasions and countries. Michiko described her experiences in this regard: "I'm fully bicultural, but that doesn't mean I act American and Japanese at the same time. That's not possible. My identity is a very situational thing. When I'm with white Americans here [in the United States], I consider myself fully American. I feel like I'm accepted as an American and I can act and speak like one and I have no trouble. When I go back to Japan or I hang out with Japanese from Japan here in the United States, I feel very Japanese. I can speak like a native. I can bow. I can mix in with Japanese well enough that I don't stick out. So I can use both sides of my identity completely proficiently."

Likewise, Matt also spoke about how he "switches identities" from American to Japanese when he goes to Japan, which he found is quite easy to do. "Depending on which country I'm in, I can feel pretty Japanese or feel quite American," he remarked. "I can totally fit in and embrace Japan. When I'm in Japan, I feel great, like I could live there for a long time. But when I get back to the United States, I feel great being back home. I can operate fine in both cultures."

For Steve, who felt he "can be Japanese or American," this type of transnational ethnic identity was more a product of being caught between two different cultures and countries: "Ultimately, I feel more shin-nisei than either American or Japanese. I'm in a bind because I'm not Japanese, but I'm more Japanese than most Japanese Americans since I have these Japanese cultural tendencies inside me that I keep fighting. I can easily be Japanese and go to Japan and get a job and seriously be Japanese. But then, I'm here and I want to be here and stay here and want my children to stay here. So I've got to be more American or it's going to hurt me in the United States." Steve seemed to favor his American side, not in a restrictive, nationalist sense, but because of its more cosmopolitan, global nature compared to an insular Japanese national identity. "I get mad at myself that I have these Japanese tendencies, which don't help me," he remarked. "We live in a global community, and if you want to step out and compete with the Western world, you need to be more Western. I try to break stereotypes. In Japan, I don't have to be Japanese, even if I can. It's a global community, so I'm going to act as whatever."

Finally, a few shin-nisei conceived of themselves in even more flexible and cosmopolitan ways that went beyond simply a dual transnational identification. For instance, Takehiro was not comfortable thinking of himself simply in nationalist terms as American and said he "like[s] the notion of fluid, flexible identities." However, what he was thinking of was an even more radical, multiple subjectivity. Consider the following exchange I had with him during our interview:

> Takehiro: I think when I was much younger I used to be more on those terms, kind of a binary, like American, Japanese. But as we know from people who work on identity, identity is a much more complicated matter than that. So what is an American? What is a Japanese? So I like the idea of not being stuck in some kind of category.
> Author: So you no longer think of yourself in those kinds of binary terms?
> Takehiro: No, no. As I said, I probably used to, but I don't think that way any more at all. I think of myself as having these real complicated relationships with a lot of different communities. There was a time when I identified a lot with black culture. I liked black culture.
> Author: So you see yourself as a true cosmopolitan.
> Takehiro: I don't know if I'm a true cosmopolitan, but I feel like I have these multiple affiliations and I'm kind of a composite at the intersection of all these different kinds of identities. And not just one identity to the exclusion of the other ones. I don't even think in terms of like, "Oh, I'm one-third this, and one-third that. . . ." Or whatever.

A couple of other shin-nisei also had an ethnic consciousness that superseded transnational affiliations, but not because their subjectivity could not be contained in binary terms, but because they did not fit any of the essentialized, ethnic categories that are available to them. In other words, they felt they were ethnically unclassifiable. According to Steve, "My experience is so unique and it's so distinct. I'm not really Japanese American. I'm not really Japanese. I'm not white. I'm always struggling to find my identity within the different communities that affect me and that I affect."

Another good example of an individual with such experiences was Karla Jones, who was biracial (she was second-generation Japanese descent on her mother's side and fourth-generation Welsh descent on her father's side).[10] An excerpt from our interview is again quite illustrative:

> Author: So have you ever identified as an Asian American?
> Karla: No. In high school I was part of the Asian American Club, but I never participated. I've never called myself Asian American.
> Author: So you see yourself as kind of distinct from all these groups. Do you also not see yourself as Japanese American? Or are there times when you just act like you're a white American? Or do you just go around saying "I'm American"?
> Karla: Culturally, I am American. I recognize that. But I do have other aspects of me which I cannot attribute to being white American. When I was teaching high school, I was telling my students that I use anthropology: I'm a liminal person. I'm betwixt and between.
> Author: Victor Turner.
> Karla: And that's how I describe myself. I'm betwixt and between because I'm not really accepted by either. And I don't really accept either in a way. Because I feel like I'm somewhat of both but not fully. And so I can't just be categorized as one or the other.
> Author: That's interesting. So you really see yourself as between these two groups. So what about the word "hapa" [half Japanese, half white]? Is that something you use a lot or does it have a lot of meaning for you? Or is it just something that Japanese Americans kind of use to refer to you?
> Karla: I notice the Asian community using it. It has more meaning to them than to the white American community. But I think it is because it kind of means a person who is half, and a person who isn't really either. I've only used the word occasionally, and only with Asians.

Conclusion

In contrast to the experiences of other Japanese Americans, the shin-nisei have developed a much more bicultural and transnational ethnic orientation. As members of the historical millennial generation, they are descendants of transnational Japanese professionals and grew up in an increasingly multicultural and globalized America where their ethnic homeland is now regarded in favorable terms. As a result, they have retained their Japanese ethnic heritage, and their bicultural lives and identities are based on a transnational sense of belonging that simultaneously encompasses both the United States and Japan. Theirs is not a reactive ethnicity asserted against a discriminatory mainstream society, but an affirmative identification with a heritage and homeland that are now positively construed. As a result, the shin-nisei have successfully inherited the Japanese language, cultural heritage, and transnationalism of their parents. Although they are culturally assimilated, this has not prevented them from simultaneously retaining their ancestral culture and remaining transnationally involved.

This chapter has also argued that the experiences of the new second generation are better understood through the concept of biculturalism (the simultaneous maintenance of two cultures) instead of the oft-cited concept of selective acculturation from the segmented assimilation literature, which implicitly assumes that cultural assimilation and ethnic heritage are opposed and incompatible. In addition, I have examined how the shin-nisei have developed transnational identities (a simultaneous affiliation with the two countries of the United States and Japan). The concept of simultaneity avoids the problems associated with the concept of hybrid identities, which presupposes a dynamic balance and integration of two conflicting identities. In contrast, the inherent tension between the "American" and the "Japanese" identities of the shin-nisei often persists and is not resolved. These multiple and hierarchically ordered selves simply coexist simultaneously within the individual and are deployed on different occasions and countries.

When we examine the strength of ethnic heritage among different generations of Japanese Americans, we must not neglect the important factor of age. The shin-nisei are more bilingual and engaged with their Japanese heritage than other generations of Japanese Americans, not only because they are members of the multicultural and transnational historical millennial generation but also because most of those in my sample were still young. Much of the learning of cultural heritage and native languages as well as visits to the ethnic homeland occur under the auspices of parents when the second generation are still children or youth. In addition, college is when a number of Asian American youth explore and fully discover their ethnicity (e.g., see Espiritu 1994; Kibria 2002; see also Levitt 2002, 140), partly because of the tolerant, multiethnic social environment that prevails on university campuses, the presence of large numbers of other Asian American students, and opportunities to study abroad in the ethnic homeland. As Peggy Levitt (2002) points out, transnational (and I would also say ethnic heritage) activity does not remain constant throughout the life cycle, but ebbs and flows at different stages.

Therefore, the issue of age becomes relevant to the ethnic future of the new second generation. Although the shin-nisei youth are currently bicultural and transnationally engaged, will they eventually become more detached from their ethnic heritage and from Japan as they grow older? It is quite evident that second-generation ties to heritage and homeland are very much dependent on transnational immigrant parents, who foster, if not insist, on the maintenance of the native language and culture and take their children with them for their return visits to their country of origin. There-fore, it is possible that the second-generation millennials of today will be-come less ethnic and transnational as their first-generation parents pass away and they become busy adults preoccupied with their professional ca-reers (see, e.g., Smith 2006, chap. 8) and their own children, who will be another generation removed from the ethnic homeland.

Although the lives of current second-generation Japanese American youth may indeed unfold in this manner as they grow older, I would argue that they will continue to remain connected to their cultural heritage to a notable extent. Two of my older, middle-aged shin-nisei informants were still fluent in Japanese, and one continued to conduct research in Japan. The other had become more detached from Japan over time and did not travel there as often as in her youth, but mentioned a continued desire to visit or even live there in the future. Therefore, the shin-nisei youth of today will probably continue to be influenced by their multicultural and transnational upbring-ing as part of the millennial generation as they grow older. This indicates that the formative experiences that members of a historical generation have when they are young can shape their ethnic consciousness for the rest of their lives.

NOTES

1. This chapter is a shortened and modified version of a chapter published in *Japanese American Ethnicity: In Search of Heritage and Homeland across Generations* (Tsuda 2016).

2. The author has not found any research that focuses specifically on the shin-nisei. Studies that have some coverage of the contemporary status of Japanese Americans either do not mention the shin-nisei or do so only briefly (e.g., Kitano 1993; O'Brien and Fugita 1991; Spickard 1996; Takahashi 1997).

3. Although it is difficult to estimate the population of shin-nisei, it may be bigger than the yonsei population.

4. All names are pseudonyms.

5. This resentment included trade friction between the United States and Japan, public concern about Japanese corporations buying up American properties such as Rockefeller Center, and backlashes in response to the success of the Japanese auto industry in the United States, which was illustrated by the murder of Vincent Chen (who was mistaken for a Japanese) by a Detroit autoworker and his stepson. The anti-Japanese sentiment of the time was even exploited in movies, such as *Rising Sun* (1992), based on a Michael Crichton novel.

6. Most of my informants spoke of this perception as an ethnic stereotype, but only two were directly ambivalent or critical of it.

7. Part of this section uses material from an edited book chapter (Tsuda 2009b).

8. One of my interviewees noted that the Japanese can tell he is a foreigner in Japan. However, they also sometimes assume he is an uneducated Japanese person, because he does not speak Japanese like a native.

9. "It depends on the person," he noted. "I think sometimes, I got some resentment, although I wouldn't say hostility, but it wasn't much. I think Japanese hide it quite well. But I never let that worry me too much, and no one ever mistreated me."

10. The biracial individuals (called "hapas") in my sample generally do not identify as Japanese American nor are they involved in the Japanese American community. Half of my four shin-nisei hapa interviewees had experiences more similar to their Japanese American shin-nisei counterparts in terms of ethnic heritage. The others did not (see Tsuda 2016, conclusion).

REFERENCES

Brettell, Caroline, and Faith Nibbs. 2009. "Lived Hybridity: Second-Generation Identity Construction through College Festival." *Identities: Global Studies in Culture and Power* 16:678–699.

Carling, Jørgen. 2008. "Toward a Demography of Immigrant Communities and Their Transnational Potential." *International Migration Review* 42(2): 449–475.

Espiritu, Yen Le. 1994. "The Intersection of Race, Ethnicity, and Class: The Multiple Identities of Second-Generation Filipinos." *Identities* 1(2–3): 249–273.

Espiritu, Yen Le, and Diane Wolf. 2001. "The Paradox of Assimilation: Children of Filipino Immigrants in San Diego." In *Ethnicities: Children of Immigrants in America*, edited by Rubén Rumbaut and Alejandro Portes, 157–186. Berkeley: University of California Press.

Foner, Nancy. 2002. "Second-Generation Transnationalism, Then and Now." In *The Changing Face of Home: The Transnational Lives of the Second Generation*, edited by Peggy Levitt and Mary Waters, 242–252. New York: Russell Sage Foundation.

Fujitani, Takashi. 2011. *Race for Empire: Koreans as Japanese and Japanese as Americans during World War II*. Berkeley: University of California Press.

Glick Schiller, Nina, and Georges E. Fouron. 1999. "Terrains of Blood and Nation: Haitian Transnational Social Fields." *Ethnic and Racial Studies* 22(2): 340–366.

Guarnizo, Luis Eduardo, and Luz Marina Díaz. 1999. "Transnational Migration: A View from Colombia." *Ethnic and Racial Studies* 22(2): 397–421.

Hickman, Mary, Sarah Morgan, Bronwell Walter, and Joseph Bradley. 2005. "The Limitations of Whiteness and the Boundaries of Englishness: Second-Generation Irish Identifications and Positionings in Multiethnic Britain." *Ethnicities* 5(2): 160–182.

Hosokawa, Bill. 1992. *Nisei: The Quiet Americans: The Story of a People*. Niwot: University Press of Colorado.

Kasinitz, Philip, John Mollenkopf, and Mary Waters. 2004. "Worlds of the Second Generation." In *Becoming New Yorkers: Ethnographies of the New Second Generation*, edited by Philip Kasinitz, John Mollenkopf, and Mary Waters, 1–19. New York: Russell Sage Foundation.

Kasinitz, Philip, John Mollenkopf, Mary Waters, and Jennifer Holdaway. 2008. *Inheriting the City: The Children of Immigrants Come of Age*. New York: Russell Sage Foundation.

Kibria, Nazli. 2002. *Becoming Asian American: Second-Generation Chinese and Korean American Identities*. Baltimore: Johns Hopkins University Press.

Kim, Nadia. 2008. *Imperial Citizens: Koreans and Race from Seoul to LA*. Stanford, CA: Stanford University Press.

Kitano, Harry. 1993. *Generations and Identity: The Japanese American*. Needham Heights, MA: Ginn Press.

Levitt, Peggy. 2001. "Transnational Migration: Taking Stock and Future Directions." *Global Networks* 1(3): 195–216.

———. 2002. "The Ties That Change: Relations to the Ancestral Home over the Life Cycle." In *The Changing Face of Home: The Transnational Lives of the Second Gen-*

eration, edited by Peggy Levitt and Mary Waters, 123–144. New York: Russell Sage Foundation.

Levitt, Peggy, and Nina Glick Schiller. 2008. "Conceptualizing Simultaneity: A Transnational Social Field Perspective on Society." In *The Transnational Studies Reader: Intersections and Innovations*, edited by Sanjeev Khagram and Peggy, 284–294. New York: Routledge.

Matsumoto, Valerie. 2014. *City Girls: The Nisei Social World in Los Angeles, 1920–1950.* Oxford: Oxford University Press.

Menjívar, Cecilia. 2002. "Living in Two Worlds? Guatemalan-Origin Children in the United States and Emerging Transnationalism." *Journal of Ethnic and Migration Studies* 28(3): 531–552.

O'Brien, David, and Stephen Fugita. 1991. *The Japanese American Experience.* Bloomington: Indiana University Press.

Portes, Alejandro, and Rubén Rumbaut. 2001. *Legacies: The Story of the Immigrant Second Generation.* Berkeley: University of California Press.

Potter, Robert. 2005. "'Young, Gifted and Back': Second-Generation Transnational Return Migrants to the Caribbean." *Progress in Development Studies* 5(3): 213–223.

Robbins, Joel. 2004. *Becoming Sinners: Christianity and Moral Torment in a Papua New Guinea Society.* Berkeley: University of California Press.

Smith, Robert Courtney. 2006. *Mexican New York: Transnational Lives of New Immigrants.* Berkeley: University of California Press.

Spickard, Paul. 1996. *Japanese Americans: The Formation and Transformations of an Ethnic Group.* London: Prentice Hall International.

Takahashi, Jere. 1997. *Nisei/Sansei: Shifting Japanese American Identities and Politics.* Philadelphia: Temple University Press.

Takamori, Ayako. 2010. "Rethinking Japanese American 'Heritage' in the Homeland." *Critical Asian Studies* 42(2): 217–238.

Tamura, Eileen. 1994. *Americanization, Acculturation, and Ethnic Identity: The Nisei Generation in Hawaii.* Urbana-Champaign: University of Illinois Press.

Tsuda, Takeyuki. 2003. *Strangers in the Ethnic Homeland: Japanese Brazilian Return Migration in Transnational Perspective.* New York: Columbia University Press.

———. 2009a. "Diasporic Homecomings and Ambivalent Encounters with the Ethnic Homeland." Conclusion to *Diasporic Homecomings: Ethnic Return Migration in Comparative Perspective*, edited by Takeyuki Tsuda, 325–350. Stanford, CA: Stanford University Press.

———. 2009b. *Diasporic Homecomings: Ethnic Return Migration in Comparative Perspective.* Stanford, CA: Stanford University Press.

———. 2009c. "Global Inequities and Diasporic Return: Japanese American and Brazilian Encounters with the Ethnic Homeland." In *Diasporic Homecomings: Ethnic Return Migration in Comparative Perspective*, edited by Takeyuki Tsuda, 227–259. Stanford, CA: Stanford University Press.

———. 2012. "Whatever Happened to Simultaneity? Transnational Migration Theory and Dual Engagement in Sending and Receiving Countries." *Journal of Ethnic and Migration Studies* 38(4): 631–649.

———. 2016. *Japanese American Ethnicity: In Search of Heritage and Homeland across Generations.* New York: New York University Press.

van Niekerk, Mies. 2007. "Second-Generation Caribbeans in the Netherlands: Different Migration Histories, Diverging Trajectories." *Journal of Ethnic and Migration Studies* 33(7): 1063–1081.

Vertovec, Steven. 2004. "Migrant Transnationalism and Modes of Transformation." *International Migration Review* 38(3): 970–1001.

Wu, Jean, Yu-wen Shen, and Min Song. 2000. Introduction to *Asian American Studies: A Reader*, edited by Jean Wu, Yu-wen Shen, and Min Song, xiii–xxiv. New Brunswick, NJ: Rutgers University Press.

Yamashiro, Jane. 2008. *Transnational Racial and Ethnic Identity Formation among Japanese Americans in Global Tokyo*. Ph.D. Dissertation, University of Hawai'i at Manoa.

———. 2011. "Racialized National Identity Construction in the Ancestral Homeland: Japanese American Migrants in Japan." *Ethnic and Racial Studies* 34(9): 1502–1521.

Yoo, David. 2000. *Growing Up Nisei: Race, Generation, and Culture among Japanese Americans of California, 1924–49*. Urbana-Champaign: University of Illinois Press.

11

Techie, Gender Queer, and Lesbian

Interview with Shin-Nisei Mioi Hanaoka

AMY SUEYOSHI

E ach year in April, more than two hundred Asian Pacific Islander queer
women and transfolks in the San Francisco Bay Area gather for a banquet
to celebrate community. They compose just a third of a notably larger
group of six hundred people loosely tied together on the electronic mailing
list APIQWTC (Asian and Pacific Islander Queer Women and Transgender
Community).[1] I remember vividly the first time I attended. I had just moved
from Los Angeles and six years had passed since I had come out. Packed in a
room with so many queer API women literally took my breath away. The attendants, nearly all visibly queer, clearly lived their lives out and proud. Many
sported meticulously styled buzz cuts, and about a third wore pressed shirts
and ties. A handful donned a men's suit for the special occasion. All of them
walked with confidence, as if they could change the transmission in their car,
build a bridge that spanned the San Francisco Bay, and put together a quinoa
salad all at the same time. I met couples with kids in tow, activists whose feminist writings had inspired me as a student, and older lesbians in wheelchairs.
All of them had made it a point to attend the banquet that year. I suddenly
saw myself as part of something larger, a queer with a past as well as a future.
That evening, I felt strength bursting from inside of me, simply in the very
existence of other queer API women and transfolks.

Although at that time, I stood at the younger end of the attendants, today
I sit firmly as a middle elder at the table. And, as each year passes, millennials are increasingly making up the majority. In contrast to a previous generation, they are more likely to be in a dance crew, design an app, and subject
themselves to a cleanse, all the while posting on Facebook. They are defining

a new "queer and Asian," not so unlike how my generation likely diverged from an older Asian lesbian cohort who initiated nonprofits and marched on Washington just as I was learning how to ride a tricycle.

For sure, millennials are on the forefront of technology and the vast cultural change it brings. Yet queer millennials in particular are pushing forth new ways of thinking about gender while reviving old ways of pressing for social change. As did their forebears who called themselves "third world women," they believe in multi-issue political organizing by building coalitions across race and ethnicity. Yet they more expansively use social media to garner an explosion of supporters across the nation (Burstein 2013; Mohanty, Russo, and Torres 1991; Moraga and Anzaldua 1983). Additionally, many queer millennials assigned female at birth have discarded the utility of identifying as women even in their commitment to feminism, sparking a national shift in how we understand gender. No doubt, we are in the midst of a radical reconfiguration of bathrooms and pronouns that no longer abide by the male and female gender binary (Darr and Kibbey 2016; Scherer et al. 2016; Steinmetz 2015).

It was through APIQWTC that I met Mioi Hanaoka more than seven years ago. Mioi, a female-identified gender queer who prefers the gender neutral "they" pronouns, had a quiet-yet-committed engagement to community.[2] Without complaint they worked in the male-dominated technology industry that no doubt impacted their everyday well-being. I had great admiration for Mioi. As a technology professional, they held the magical key to a broadening world in which I felt increasingly disabled. And, while successful at work, I imagined that Mioi endured countless insults in a professional environment not known to be feminist nor antiracist. By comparison, my own workplace in higher education seemed like a softer lesson in patriarchy, since academics—while mostly men—at least try to appear concerned with women and people of color at a public university.

Moreover, Mioi, who apparently had never felt compelled to change their name to a more Americanized "Michelle" or maybe even "Mike," stood out as an individual of great-yet-unassuming queer and undeniably Japanese American (JA) courage. Rather than shouting at rallies or scowling with vocal pronouncements at every straight person's misstep, Mioi seemed to work more unobtrusively to change the world. They tended to wait to become centrally part of a group, whether at work or in the community, before initiating change. Even when fellow queers attempted to impose new engagements around pronoun use at one API queer conference during introductions, I remember Mioi declaring, barely audible to the group, "I think pronouns are stupid."

Mioi remains intensely familiar to me, as if they were a younger queer sibling for whom I have felt simultaneously protective of as well as inspired by, when considering how I myself as a queer JA with immigrant parents might thrive. They appear as if a forward-looking mirror, both reflecting my existence and offering new possibilities for a future. For sure, it seems almost impossible to find works in Japanese American studies or queer studies that illuminate what it means to be queer and Nikkei, particularly for shin-nisei, in America today. Within a twenty-first-century Asian American population in which three-quarters of adults are foreign-born, the existing literature oddly seems to have forgotten that Japanese Americans can be immigrants, let alone queer, as well (Pew Research Center 2013).

Mioi Hanaoka, born in 1980, is the youngest daughter of Nobuaki and Ayako Hanaoka. Nobuaki Hanaoka served as pastor of Pine United Methodist Church in San Francisco's Richmond District from 1979 to 1991, which became one of the earliest Japanese American reconciling churches to openly accept the lesbian, gay, bisexual, and transgender (LGBT) community into their congregation.[3] Their mother, Ayako Hanaoka, worked as a teacher at a Japanese bilingual preschool called ABC Preschool. Mioi's parents immigrated to the United States in 1970 so that Hanaoka's father could attend Colgate Rochester Crozer Divinity School, an institution committed to transformational ministry for the advancement of social justice.[4] The Hanaoka family remains prominent in the San Francisco Japanese American community as well as the larger Christian JA community. I interviewed Mioi via email in August 2016.

On Being a Millennial

Millennials are often understood as anyone born between 1977 and 2000. What do you think it means to be a millennial and where do you fit?
I don't really identify as a millennial even though I guess technically I am. I definitely feel like a 80s kid. I grew up watching Sesame Street and a variety of other children's programming on PBS [Public Broadcasting Service]. I guess I'm not familiar enough with understanding what a millennial is to be able to identify as such. My friend, who is the same age as me, and I took an online quiz to try to determine "how millennial are you?" Oddly enough, according to the quiz, my friend wasn't a millennial. I was though! The quiz knew how old we were but didn't take into consideration our ages to determine if we were millennials or not. The quiz asked about our daily habits of how much TV we consume, if we read a daily newspaper or not, if we have a landline, if we have piercings or tattoos. I wonder what sets my friend and me apart. We both spent our childhoods in the Bay Area. We both have very stable careers in the tech industry. But she is in a hetero marriage and has two kids. She reads the *New York Times* every day. She does not use Snapchat. Her politics are progressive but not radical. She listens to NPR [National Public Radio] and podcasts.

After reflecting on our similarities and differences, I came to realize two things. First, I was an extremely late bloomer. I was very shy as a child, so shy that some people thought I was unable to speak. I think this was partly due to having a very extroverted older sister who always spoke on my behalf as well as just my inherent personality of being quiet. Trying to bust out of that shyness in my early twenties led me to feel very vulnerable and awkward. I opted to just be a loner. What also might have contributed to this was the fact that I lived at home with my parents all through college at San Francisco State University and beyond. I really only started socializing several years after graduating college in 2006, when I was twenty-six years old. This is when I met Ayumi, who eventually became my first girlfriend. I got an opportunity to work the box office as a cashier for CAAMFest, presented by the Center of Asian American Media and previously known as the San Francisco International Asian American Film Festival.[5] Ayumi was an intern. Somehow, for some reason, I became very extroverted in this newfound group of young Asian creative types. And, it turned out that I wasn't as awkward as I thought I was, because people actually liked me. My self-confidence grew and I felt like I finally came into my own being. In fact, on my twenty-sixth birthday, Ayumi and some friends threw me a "twenty-first birthday party" at a bar. In the same year, I also started my professional career in the tech industry. In 2007, when I was twenty-seven, I finally moved out of the house with Ayumi and my sister, into a small in-law unit in San Francisco's Oceanview District, not too far from my parents in Daly City. I felt like I was finally an adult. It's possible that this late blooming is what caused me to slip a few years behind and relate more with the younger crowd. I mostly hung out with Ayumi and her friends, who were all four years my junior.

Second, I believe that my queerness has strongly contributed to my millennial traits and habits. I wonder if I would be married and have kids right now at the age of thirty-six had I turned out straight. I probably would have. Most of my straight friends are married with kids, including my friend who took the millennial quiz. It's not that gay marriage had been illegal up until three years ago, or that it's logistically much harder for same sex couples to have kids, that as a queer person, I'm not married with kids. I believe that my queerness has shifted my perception of all things heteronormative. I question the institution of marriage; I question the societal expectation of couples having kids. I think it is this shift of perception, as well as having free-thinking parents who, despite being Asian, have never pressured me to get married or have kids, that sets me apart from a Mioi who turned out straight.

Can you talk about your first interest in computers or other things that are millennialesque?
My very first interest in computers came when I was about nine years old in 1989. My dad had a really old computer that had WordPerfect and MS-DOS. This was back in the day when computers weren't at all popular. I just remember thinking that they were really cool. Through my early teenage years,

I got to play with my older brother's personal computer (PC). I think I used to play games on it. The thing that really got me hooked was when I discovered chat rooms in 1995 when we got AOL. I found chat rooms for lesbians. I wasn't out yet, but I learned that I could be out and talk openly about being queer on the internet. This was when I was in high school, right around the time when I was coming to the realization that I might be queer. I was having strong attractions toward people in band who happened to be women. While my peers were starting to date people of the opposite sex, I remember only being attracted to other girls. I couldn't talk to anyone or reveal anything about this to anyone in person, but I was able to be open on the internet. It felt liberating to be able to put on a different persona online and be able to meet all kinds of people. The shyness and social anxiety I felt when I meet people in real life disappeared online. I felt free to be my funny, witty, and smart self online. I was so addicted that I remember, one month, I racked up a $200 phone bill. My mom was not pleased.

What do you do now, and how did you develop an interest in computers develop into a career?
I am a software engineer in the tech industry. I have always been really into making things, as in I enjoyed fabricating replicas of things, like Federal Bureau of Investigation (FBI) badges back when I was into the X-Files (TV series). I enjoyed drawing Super Bowl logos and creating mix compact discs (CDs) with really nice-looking covers. So when the internet came around, I was really interested in designing websites. I was obsessed with it at some point. I pretty much picked up HTML (the markup language that most web pages are written in) on my own, by looking at how others did it and doing it on my own. This eventually lead to me teaching myself an actual scripting language (Perl) to create dynamic content for the web. After I got a hang of this, I wanted to go deeper, which led to my interest in administering a website. These skills allowed me to do contract work doing web design for a few years after graduating college. I studied broadcasting (audio engineering) at San Francisco State University, and they had a couple of classes for web design where we learned CSS, Javascript, Flash, and Actionscript. This helped a lot too. Eventually, I got an internship in the Site Operations team at Ask.com. I was fortunate enough to have a brother working there already.

On Being Japanese American

In what kind of household did you grow up?
We grew up in a pretty socially progressive family. We were surrounded by many Japanese Americans since we were part of a JA church. We lived in San Francisco across from Pine Methodist in a parsonage with my beloved purebred beagle named Joy, until I was eleven. With a father who was the pastor

of a church, we had a lot of favors done for us. A lot of our belongings such as clothes and cars were blessed upon us by members of the church. I don't know if it was the Christian aspect or the Japanese aspect of the community that fueled that generosity and/or sense of obligation. Maybe it was both. We didn't grow up rich or anything. We were definitely living on a budget and learned to value hard work, humility, and community. We moved to the Westlake neighborhood of Daly City in the summer of 1991 after my dad had been reassigned to a JA church in Sacramento and my parents decided to buy a house. For the most part, my father lived in the parsonage in Sacramento and traveled back to Daly City on the weekends.

I remember my mom always clipping coupons. We appreciated what we had and we never really wanted more. When I say "we," I mean mostly my sister and me, since we were close in age. We didn't grow up with a lot of toys or resources. Our childhood was pretty modest. We respected our parents and their decisions. We grew up with the practice of *touban* where we all took turns doing household chores.[6] I distinctly remember [that] I was around six at the time, polishing the wooden furniture and piano with Pledge and Windexing the windows and not even questioning it or complaining about it. I remember that it was my duty, so I did it. Somehow my parents instilled in me the value of working hard and working together and the importance of maintaining a clean and tidy house.

I loved to please my parents. As a small child, I hated mushrooms. I remember one time when I was about eight, in order to please my mother, I decided to eat mushrooms, despite my dislike of the flavor. I showed her that it was in my mouth. It was worth it, because I made her proud. Since we were such well-behaved kids, we never or hardly ever got punished. This is probably what allowed us to live pretty freely. My parents trusted us and we took responsibility in the trust they put into us. We used to live on 33rd Avenue in the Richmond District of San Francisco. Our elementary school, Alamo Elementary School, was on 23rd Avenue so we would walk ten city blocks by ourselves. I think back now and wonder how we got away with that. Maybe streets were safer back then. There were definitely some sketchy moments where we almost got abducted. For the most part though, it was totally fine.

Even though we grew up in a very Christian family and community, my parents were very open-minded. Some churches preach hate, but ours only preached love and to "love everyone for who they are." With that way of thinking, my dad would not hesitate to allow homeless people to take shelter in the church. In the 1980s, when acquired immunodeficiency syndrome (AIDS) was a big thing, I remember seeing signs up in the church about how we should help people with AIDS and not be scared of them.

In the 1990s, the leaders at the church invited people who identified as LGBTQ to speak to us about what it meant to be LGBTQ. I think I was about eleven or so. John Oda, the pastor who came after my dad in 1991, was the pastor when Pine became reconciling. My dad had planted the seed to get the church members to start thinking about becoming reconciling without any knowledge that I might be queer. I was still too young to really understand the implications one might face in life for being LGBTQ. I also didn't identify as LGBTQ at the time so it did not resonate with me.

I know you have some excellent Japanese language skills, better than most JAs. Do you identify as Japanese or Japanese American? Why or why not?
I identify as Japanese American. I was born in San Francisco and never lived in Japan. Apparently, Japanese was my first language. It's weird now to think that my first words were Japanese. My parents were both born in Japan and came to the United States after the war, so that makes me shin-nisei. Growing up, there weren't that many nisei who were my age. Most JAs that I know are third or fourth generation. My grandparents were not interned during the war. I do not have aunts, uncles, and cousins living in the United States. I feel like my family story is a bit different [from] most other JA stories. I've come to realize somewhat recently that our personal stories (of the journey of our parents or grandparents and how they ended up in the United States) are an important part of the American fabric. I think being JA means I have a family heritage that goes deeper than American roots. Our stories don't just begin when we landed here, but start from the homeland. My parents never gave up their Japanese identities; they still maintain their Japanese citizenship and continue to live in the United States as permanent residents. I think that when they were younger and the kids were still young, they considered moving back to Japan. At one point, before I was born, they did try to live in Japan for about a year. I think it was due to Japan's rigid societal rules and homogenous way of thinking that made my parents want to move back to the United States. This in-between status of my parents influenced my identity of being American but being raised by Japanese people and in a Japanese household. Many of my friends are API, but are considered to be part of a diaspora. When a significant population moves from their homeland to some other land, it is usually due to some sociopolitical reason. The parents of my current girlfriend are refugees, literally forced out of their home in Vietnam not just to seek a better life, but for survival in another land. I sometimes identify myself as API. Other times, I identify as JA. When I set myself apart from other APIs, it's mostly out of respect, showing respect that our family histories of how we ended up here are quite different, rather than out of pride or something. JAs have a different story from how Vietnamese Americans ended up here.

I understand that I could identify as Japanese, even if I was born in the United States. I guess technically I am Japanese since I have dual citizenship. However, I don't think I could ever live in Japan. The Japan I am familiar with is the Japan that exists within my parents. Since they left Japan in the 1960s, I might feel more at home in 1960s Japan than twenty-first-century

Japan. I am not even sure if my parents would feel at home in twenty-first-century Japan. A lot of Japan has become modernized, and Japanese is one of those languages that can change rapidly. Apparently, some very common words I know in Japanese are outdated. For example, the color pink to me is *momo iro*.[7] Umbrella is *koumori*.[8] I never learned that the verb for taking a shower is *abiru*. Since my parents left Japan before showers were introduced, they always used the verb *toru* to describe the act of taking a shower. I think even to this day, they would say *shawa o toru* instead of *shawa o abiru*.[9] I remember traveling to Japan with them—the most recent time was two summers ago—and on multiple occasions, people corrected them on using outdated or incorrect words! It's kind of fascinating.

My parents always spoke to me in Japanese. My father eventually started speaking to me in English when English became my primary language, but my mother still speaks to me in Japanese. They enrolled my sister and me in *nihongo gakko*, which was a Saturday school taught strictly in Japanese.[10] We learned all of the subjects including Japanese, math, and science. Most of the kids were either Japanese or Japanese American and had the intention of moving back to Japan someday. I hated it. My sister hated it too. We just wanted to play on Saturdays! I guess it was due to my parents giving us a lot of freedom that we decided to drop out. We soon started speaking to our parents only in English. We never even tried to learn Japanese again until high school/college when we regretted dropping out of nihongo gakko. I can't say why or how this pivotal moment in our adolescence contributed to our overall identities growing up. I think a part of us wanted to fit in with our peer groups at school. And we didn't see the connections between language, culture, and family. To us, English was the more natural language, we wanted to fit in, and we still benefited from my mom's home-cooked Japanese food.

I got fairly decent in Japanese in 2009–2010 when I took classes at Soko-Gakuen, another Japanese language school in San Francisco. But after I finished the classes, I stopped speaking/reading/writing in Japanese, so I lost my fluency in the language, unfortunately. I think I was so good at it back then, because my girlfriend at the time was Japanese and so I was able to practice with her. Also, my mom speaks to me in Japanese so it's pretty easy for me to understand the language.

What do you think it means to be JA, and how do you think you fit?
I am a pretty literal person, so when I say I am Japanese American, I guess what I mean is I'm an American with Japanese ancestry. Beyond the literal meaning, I think being JA means I have a family heritage that goes deeper than American roots. I have samurais and ninjas in my ancestry! When I say I am second generation, it seems to erase the many generations of Japanese people that came before me. I still very much feel the importance of being connected to that lineage.

I sometimes fantasize about how I might have turned out if my parents never moved to the United States. Would I look the same? Would I have the same values? Would my mannerisms be totally different? I wonder how growing up in the United States has affected all aspects of my identity. I don't really know the answer to that. I want to say that I grew up American, but even "growing up American" is not easily definable due to the ethnically diverse makeup of this country. My parents decided to leave Japan for a reason. I can imagine how hard of a decision that was to make, but they also decided not to go back. I think that they found something special in the culture of the United States that wasn't back home in Japan. I believe that they were somehow able to cultivate a hybrid culture in which they were able to raise their kids. I realize now that the identity which I claim is the one that came out of the culture that my parents created. It sounds kind of weird, but I remember not feeling too culturally connected to the other JAs in our lives. Compared to other Japanese families, if the parents were issei, my parents weren't as strict nor [did they] have expectations of us that other Japanese parents had of their kids. Also, many Japanese families had different traditions based in Shintoism and/or Buddhism that we didn't have. I don't ever remember celebrating *obon,* for example.[11] We never had a *kagami mochi* during New Year's.[12] And, compared to some of the JAs we grew up with who had already been in the United States for multiple generations, no one in our family had been incarcerated in the camps.

What does it mean to be a JA millennial?
For someone to define themselves as a JA millennial, I think it means to be politically conscious. They embody a young and energetic inheritor of a long and uniquely JA history, a history that started in Japan and continued into the United States. They know about the anti-Asian racism that their ancestors had to endure, that they still endure today, as well as what makes our stories different from other API stories. I still feel like I am in the minority, in terms of being politically conscious, when it comes to JA millennials.

Can you talk more about your other identities that make up who you are and tell us your definition of your identities?
In addition to identifying as Japanese American, I also identify as Asian American. I grew up in the Richmond District of San Francisco where my elementary school was mostly Asians. Even though growing up, I did not feel like I had anything in common with my Chinese counterparts since our cultures are pretty different; I realized later in life that the thing that we have in common is how we navigated a white supremacist society. We were subject to the same flavor of racism and microaggressions. For those reasons and for solidarity, I also identify as Asian American.

Additionally, I identify as a lesbian. I'm a woman who is attracted to other women. I also identify as queer. I define "queer" to mean someone who does not conform to heteronormativity. The distinction between queer and lesbian or gay is that it goes beyond describing someone who is attracted to the same sex. So many systems, other than attraction, can and should be challenged. As a queer person, I question societal norms like the institution of marriage, patriarchy, and capitalism. I have been on my "gender journey" for some time, but now, I identify as a gender-nonconforming cis woman.[13] I present more masculine of center. I wear men's t-shirts and have a more gender-neutral wardrobe. I keep my hair short and do not wear makeup. I was born female and identify as being female, but I reject gender norms. I prefer people use female or gender-neutral pronouns when referring to me, although I don't like pronouns in general, because pronouns, specifically gendered pronouns, are a vehicle for discrimination and perpetuating heteronormativity. I remember being taught to use male pronouns when referring to a nonspecific singular person. Grammatical rules like these promote the notion that men are the norm and women are "others." Even today, when people are more careful and attempt to be inclusive by saying "he or she," they are excluding people who do not identify as either, such as people who might identify as transgender or intersex.

We are at a point in history now where we know that gender is a social construct. People may fall anywhere on the gender spectrum; they may even fall somewhere completely outside of the spectrum. For language to be inclusive of all people, something as basic as pronouns should be reexamined. The Japanese language, for example, [doesn't] have gendered third-person pronouns in the same way that English does. It is more common to use a person's name than to use a pronoun. Also, pronouns are often omitted since it's implied. If you think of it, once the subject of a topic has been set, why keep referring to it with a pronoun? It seems inefficient to me.

My newest identity is "techie." I believe that there is a stigma around being someone in the tech industry, especially in activist spaces. "Techies" especially in the Bay Area are known to be a part of the gentrification problem. Therefore, they can be seen as oblivious to problems within local communities, oftentimes communities of color, and therefore seen as classist and/or racist. I want to claim "techie" as one of my identities, because I believe it is important to defy the stereotype so that some dialogue can happen between techies and the local communities that are being displaced in order to solve the problem of gentrification.

On Community Engagement

I always see you everywhere in the community, carrying heavy stuff for events as well as donating significant amounts of money. Can you tell us about your activism?

Growing up in a Japanese American Christian family, I remember being obligated to give to charity, specifically to those less fortunate than us. It wasn't so much out of generosity or because our hearts were big. It was our duty to be charitable, as Christians. That value stuck with me into my adulthood. My earliest donations as an adult were to KQED, the member-supported public radio and television station in the San Francisco Bay Area. I was a daily listener so I felt some sense of obligation for giving back. I received a full four-year academic scholarship through San Francisco State University's Presidential Scholars Program, so I was not in debt after college, which I think probably contributed to me being able to give. I also donated to places like Oxfam America, Doctors without Borders, and Mercy Corps. I was a monthly donor to these organizations, giving probably about $20 per month to each organization. I took my sense of duty to give to those less privileged literally and gave to organizations that provided relief to poor countries that really needed aid. I gave what I could. And I gave, because it was an easy way to help.

I didn't really embrace my Asian American identity until I was twenty-six. I grew up watching the same mainstream media as all other young Americans, and I believed that being beautiful and successful meant being white. It wasn't until I worked for CAAMFest with a bunch of other Asian Americans that I started feeling empowered and proud of my Asian American identity. I wasn't even attracted to Asian women until I started working for CAAMFest! I started feeling attracted toward some of the interns. Anyway, I wouldn't say that CAAM politicized me, but it did make me start owning my Asian Americanness. After CAAMFest ended, I started living a comfortable life with a stable income as a techie. People would have probably called me a yuppie, or young urban professional, and for the most part, I was. I was aware of social inequities and homelessness and such, but didn't really do anything about it.

Fast forward to the summer of 2011. I had just broken up with Ayumi after she moved back to Japan. I had a huge divot in my heart that I needed to fill with something. I decided to go back to church after an extremely long hiatus. I started going back every Sunday to my home church, Pine United Methodist Church. There, I befriended a familiar face. Oneida Chi was a friend of my father's and was so warm and welcoming. One day she invited me to the closing night screening of Queer Women of Color Media Arts Project (QWOCMAP) Film Festival.[14] I had no idea what to expect. I went and it completely blew my mind. I had never been in a space where I felt like I could be my full and authentic self. I was surrounded by queer women of color who embraced, empowered, and celebrated each other. I did not realize what I had been missing my whole life. I had never found an LGBTQ space in which I felt comfortable. And, most of my friends were straight. It wasn't until QWOCMAP that I began seeking queer friends of color.

My QWOCMAP experience in 2011 also kicked my charitable giving up to a wholly different level. I had been working at LinkedIn at the time, and the IT department was selling outdated work computers, four-year-old Mac

Pros, at about 50 percent of retail value to employees. I had secretly wished that LinkedIn would have just donated the equipment to charity, but since that wasn't happening, I decided to purchase two of the Mac Pros and donated them to QWOCMAP. This was the start of my charitable giving toward organizations and communities in which I actually felt like I belonged.

Fast forward again to 2013, I had just purchased a house in Berkeley and soon realized that I was pretty much done achieving all of my goals since I didn't see marriage and kids in my future. I started questioning the purpose of life. What was life after I had achieved all of my goals? I told myself that I was ready to die. I wasn't suicidal or anything. I just knew that if I did die, at that point in my life, at the age of thirty-two, I would have no regrets. Then, another thought came into my head, "That was a selfish and privileged way of thinking." What about other people less fortunate than me? What about organizations that could use help? I realized a new life mission, to volunteer, continue my philanthropy, and to serve others.

Right around that time, I was introduced to an organization called API Equality—Northern California. They work to empower and uplift LGBTQ and API voices by increasing visibility of our communities. I found a place where I could volunteer as well as donate. I also decided to volunteer my time to other organizations like APIQWTC and QWOCMAP.

I was fortunate enough to land a career in tech that pays quite well, especially to engineers and especially in the San Francisco Bay Area. With this disposable income and an obligatory duty to give back to the community, I have been giving to many nonprofit organizations, mostly LGBTQ and/or people of color (POC) groups. I have also joined the Red Envelope Giving Circle, a philanthropic group who pool their money together to give yearly grants to projects and organizations that work in the LGBTQ and API communities. A giving circle is a small group of people who collect their money together to be able to fund community organizations and projects. The idea of a giving circle comprising my own queer and API community really resonated with me. The Red Envelope Giving Circle demonstrates how there is abundance in our community and we can sustain ourselves in terms of funding and resources. We have funded a wide range of projects, such as the Dragon Fruit Project, an intergenerational oral history project documenting and disseminating queer and API activism from the 1960s through the 1990s. We have also funded multiple film projects, youth leadership development projects, and the first API Transmasculine Retreat.

I've noticed that as active as you are, you don't take up a lot of space. You're not making a lot of noise or trying to hog the spotlight. Can you tell us more about your style, and why you're comfortable with it?
I'm naturally just a shy and introverted person. Most of the time, in big group settings, my goal is to take up as little space as possible. I like helping

in the background. I have done panels and workshops on JA gender diversity, diversity and inclusion in tech, and what it means to be a techie in social justice spaces where I have to literally be the center of attention. But I have discovered that it takes a toll on me physically and mentally. I would like to try to do more public speaking, however, I just need to take huge breaks in between.

In the philanthropy world, white folks claim that Asians are too cheap to donate. What would you say to them?
I am not familiar with that stereotype! I guess I would say that those white folks don't know what they're talking about. That said, I do wonder if I would be this philanthropic if I were straight. I notice that people tend to give more to causes they care about. I believe that being queer, a gender-nonconforming woman of color, has heavily influenced the lens of how I see the world. I see the huge wealth gap between whites and communities of color. Another reason I give is because I believe one of the solutions to the huge wealth gap is redistribution of wealth. I know that I can't do it alone, but I would like to inspire others to understand that the marginalized remain marginalized due to the inaccessibility of wealth in this country.

Do you think it's your millennial side that informs your engagement with community? Why or why not?
I sometimes find myself on Facebook several times a day. Many of my Facebook friends are younger than me and post a lot about police brutality, racism, sexism, and homophobia. At one point, I realized I was probably addicted to Facebook, so I deactivated my Facebook and tried to live without it for about a half a year. It was actually kind of a nice mental break. But anyway, I think that a big part of my identity, my queerness, and my millennial side, are intrinsically tied together. So I'm not sure if it's due to my queerness or due to my millennial side. Probably both!

We are in the midst of a tremendous technological revolution as well as a sociopolitical reconfiguring. Some feel as though we are back in the civil rights turmoil of the 1960s. What do you see as the current state of affairs for someone like yourself, and what do you think the future holds for folks coming up after you?
I think what has really defined this moment in U.S. history is the Black Lives Matter movement. Five years ago, I thought Occupy Wall Street might be the defining movement. I do believe that the Occupy movement galvanized a lot of Americans (i.e., the 99 percent) who would have otherwise been complacent with the status quo. However, the police killings of Michael Brown and Eric Garner really got the movement rolling. People started organizing against police brutality and antiblack racism. More recently, with the police

killings of Alton Sterling and Philando Castile, we have been reminded that systemic change is slow. But it's also good to keep in mind that the civil rights movement spanned over a decade. Sometimes I wonder why I am on Facebook so much. There is just so much negativity in this world that I don't know how to deal [with it]. I have been to protests and marches. I do feel a bit like I'm getting too old for it, though. I think that it's just important to remember that there is this huge population of young people, the millennials, who are more socially conscious than previous generations, who know racism exists, and who know that things have to change.

Being a part of the tech industry, I see that there are many privileged young folks who don't seem to care that much. They surface-level care by celebrating marriage equality and voting for Obama, but I think that a lot of young people in the tech industry need to be politicized. I'm trying to do what I can, but it's challenging, since it's hard to talk about politics at work. Luckily, there are new companies coming up that understand the role of tech in this society. The tech boom in San Francisco has caused many thousands within the local community to be displaced. The demographics, storefronts, [and] rent/housing costs have all changed drastically in the last ten years. I believe there is this momentum that is trying to counter this. Tech companies like Slack, Pandora, Indiegogo, are proponents of increasing diversity and inclusion in tech. It is awesome to see companies take a stance, saying that there is a big problem, and then actively trying to fix it.

Finally, what do you think about being a queer JA millennial activist? Is it a contradiction in terms?
I don't think that it is a contradiction in terms. I think "queer" and "millennial" and "activist" overlap pretty well. If anything, the "JA" part seems a little out of place. I guess when I am in queer POC activist spaces, my JA identity doesn't stand out too much. I definitely own my nonwhite identity in those spaces though. There is this social group call O-Musubi, for queer JA women. I think it is great, but for some reason, I am not drawn to this group. I don't feel like it is necessary for me anyway. Just because someone is JA, it doesn't make me want to connect with them. There are some really tightly organized queer groups in the Bay Area for other ethnic groups, like for Vietnamese folks, Korean folks, and Filipino folks. It's interesting how there isn't one for JAs. I kind of touched on it earlier, but groups of Asian folks who were displaced due to war seem to be more tightly organized and politicized in the Bay Area. I think the closest thing that JAs have experienced is the incarceration camps. My grandparents never left Japanese soil, so it is hard for me to understand the internment experience during the war. I do think modern-day racism, racism against black people, specifically by the police, is a problem. This is something that is blatant and something that I can see happening right now. So I think what it means to be a queer JA millennial activist, I guess it means

showing solidarity with the Black Lives Matter movement. As a queer JA millennial activist, I have also witnessed the mainstream LGBT movement shut out certain groups, specifically transgender people of color. I've marched in the San Francisco Trans March for a couple of years now after witnessing the shrinking of the API contingent in the main pride parade. In some ways, I think of this transition of presence of our community into the trans march from the main pride parade as a handing off to the millennials. Many trans people of color are still killed, and it is important for us to stand up against the racist transphobia that is still very much present in this country.

NOTES

1. APIQWTC (pronounced "API cutesy") provides opportunities for Asian and Pacific Islander queer women and transgender people to socialize, network, build community, engage in intergenerational organizing, and increase community visibility. See Asian and Pacific Islander Queer Women and Transgender Community (APIQWTC), accessed February 6, 2017, http://www.apiqwtc.org.

2. The use of "their" in this introductory section signifies a gender-neutral, first-person pronoun that can refer to Hanaoka as well as its more conventional use as a third-person plural pronoun. Darren Lascotte (2016), "Singular They: An Empirical Study of Generic Pronoun Use," *American Speech* 91(1): 62–80.

3. Methodists in Boston in 1982 developed a program in which local churches could declare their support of the LGBT community so that "reconciliation" between the United Methodist Church and gays and lesbians could begin. See Reconciling Ministries Network, accessed February 6, 2017, http://www.rmnetwork.org/newrmn/who-we-are/history.

4. According to Mioi, their father Nobuaki Hanaoka had chosen Crozer Theological Seminary because Martin Luther King had received his degree from there. For more on King's time at Crozer, see Clayborne Carson (1997), "Martin Luther King Jr: The Crozer Seminary Years," *Journal of Blacks in Higher Education* 16 (July): 123–128.

5. CAAM was originally NAATA or National Asian American Telecommunications Association when it formed in the early 1980s. For more on CAAM/NAATA's history, see Jun Okada (2009), "'Noble and Uplifting and Boring as Hell': Asian American Film and Video 1971–1982," *Cinema Journal* 49(1): 20–40.

6. *Touban*, or 当番 (とうばん), literally translated means "being on duty."

7. *Momoiro*, or 桃色 (ももいろ), literally means "peach-colored" and was in more common usage to signify the color pink before pinku, or ピンク, came to replace it.

8. Hanaoka's use of *koumori*, or 蝙蝠 (こうもり), which also means "bat" and is more frequently written as コウモリ, is likely an abbreviation of *koumori kasa*, or こうもり傘. Today, the abbreviated *kasa*, or 傘 (かさ), is in more common use.

9. *Shawaa o toru*, or シャワーをとる, which means "to take a shower," has been replaced by *shawaa o abiru*, or シャワーを浴びる.

10. Hanaoka's *nihongo gakko* began in 1968 with support from the Japanese government and is currently known as the San Francisco Japanese School, or サンフランシスコ日本語補習校 (さんふらんしすこほしゅうこう). See San Francisco Japanese School, accessed February 6, 2017, http://www.sfjs.org/about.

11. *Obon*, or お盆, is a Japanese Buddhist festival that honors the dead. "Gathering of Joy: A History of Japanese American Obon Festivals and Bon Odori," SFJapantown,

accessed February 6, 2017, http://sfjapantown.org/news/gathering-of-joy-a-history-of
-japanese-american-obon-festivals-and-bon-odori.

12. *Kagami mochi*, or 鏡もち(かがみもち), is a traditional New Year's decoration with Shinto origins composed of a stack of mochi rice cakes.

13. "Cis woman" is a person who was assigned female at birth and also identifies as a woman.

14. See Queer Women of Color Media Arts Project (QWOCMAP), accessed February 6, 2017, http://www.qwocmap.org.

REFERENCES

Burstein, David. 2013. *Fast Future: How the Millennial Generation is Shaping Our World.* Boston: Beacon Press.

Darr, Brandon, and Tyler Kibbey. 2016. "Pronouns and Thoughts on Neutrality: Gender Concerns in Modern Grammar." *Pursuit: The Journal of Undergraduate Research at University of Tennessee* 7(1): 71–84.

Mohanty, Chandra Talpade, Ann Russo, and Lourdes Torres, eds. 1991. *Third World Women and the Politics of Feminism.* Bloomington: Indiana University Press.

Moraga, Cherrie, and Gloria Anzaldua, eds. 1983. *This Bridge Called My Back: Writings by Radical Women of Color.* New York: Kitchen Table Press.

Pew Research Center. 2013. *The Rise of Asian Americans.* Washington, DC: Pew Research Center.

Scherer, Michael, Charlotte Alter, Belinda Luscombe, Melissa Chan, Philip Elliott, Elizabeth Dias, Maya Rhodan, and Katy Steinmetz. 2016. "Battle of the Bathroom." *Time* 187(20): 30–37.

Steinmetz, Katy. 2015. "This Gender-Neutral Word Could Replace 'Mr.' and 'Ms.'" Time. com. Accessed April 7, 2019. http://time.com/4106718/what-mx-means/.

PART V

CROSSING AND BRIDGING BOUNDARIES

12

Japanese American Millennials in Contemporary Japan

JANE H. YAMASHIRO

This chapter adds to our understanding of Japanese American millennials by examining their experiences in Japan. The larger edited volume demonstrates how Japanese American millennials are diverse in terms of phenotype, ancestry, geographic upbringing, gender, and sexual orientation, shaping their experiences in the United States. I argue that this diversity among Japanese American millennials continues to shape their experiences as they migrate to live in Japan.

Japanese American millennial experiences in Japan challenge the idea that Japanese American social generations can be described interchangeably with ethnic generational labels, as my interviewees ranged from sansei, yonsei, and gosei to shin-nisei.[1] Japanese American millennial experiences in Japan disrupt the notion of stable social identities by showing how identification is contextual and can shift over time and across place. While some shared understandings of Japaneseness do exist, this chapter illuminates how ethnic Japanese communities in different societies have constructed "Japanese" identities in multiple, sometimes conflicting ways.

The chapter is organized in the following way: first, I review my research methods and the backgrounds of my interviewees. Then, I discuss how, in order to understand the structure of Japanese American millennial migration to Japan, it is useful to think about their social positioning, which I explain in terms of social generation; stage in the life course; and mixed-ethnic generations, including people of multiple ancestries. Next, to understand the larger social contexts from which and into which Japanese

American millennials migrate, I review constructions of Japaneseness in the United States and in Japan. The second half of the chapter analyzes Japanese American millennial experiences of living in Japan, particularly regarding phenotype and ancestry; the construction of Japaneseness in Hawai'i as different from on the U.S. continent and in Japan; different constructions of Okinawanness in Hawai'i, the U.S. continent, and Japan; and gender, class, and sexuality.

Methodology

Findings in this article are based on eighteen long, semistructured interviews, as well as many informal interviews, conducted in the United States and Japan with fifteen Japanese American "millennials" born between 1980 and 1989 who were living in or had previously lived in Japan (see Table 12.1). Interviews took place where participants were residing at the time. When I interviewed Japanese Americans in the United States, they had previously lived in Japan. I interviewed five people only in Japan, three in both Japan and the United States, and seven only in the United States.

Since I used snowball sampling to find interviewees, they are not a representative sample, but still reflect the ethnic and racial diversity of the younger Japanese American population in the United States. Eight interviewees claimed only Japanese ancestry, while six additionally claimed Okinawan, Italian, English, Scottish, Taiwanese, and Irish ancestries. One person identified as being of only Okinawan ancestry, but was aware that my study was about "Japanese American experiences."[2]

Before I met with interviewees face-to-face, most of them had filled out my five-page questionnaire asking for basic background information, such as age, where they grew up and had lived, current occupation, and exposure in the United States to Japanese language and culture (see Hays 1996). Interviews averaged about two hours. During the interviews, I took notes and also audio-recorded while reviewing their questionnaire responses and asking follow-up questions.

These data are part of a larger ethnographic fieldwork project I carried out for five years (2004–2009) in the greater Tokyo area. I interviewed over fifty Japanese Americans who were living in Tokyo (most between 2004 and 2007) and over thirty Japanese Americans who were living in the United States after having returned from Japan (most in 2013). I limited my interviewees to people living in Japan for at least one year in order to omit tourists, but included students and Japan Exchange and Teaching (JET) Program participants since they represent a significant part of Japanese American experiences in Japan. (For more about my methods, please see Yamashiro 2017, 157–173).

TABLE 12.1. BACKGROUND DATA FOR JAPANESE AMERICAN MILLENNIAL INTERVIEWEES

	Name	Year of Birth	Ancestries	Raised	Generation(s)	Occupation while Living in Japan
1	Aaron	1985	Japanese	Southern California	*Shin-nisei*	college exchange student
2	Brent	1981	Japanese, Okinawan	Hawaiʻi	*Sansei, Yonsei*	language student
3	Dave	1984	Japanese	Northern California	*Yonsei*	JET Program participant
4	Emma	1985	Japanese, Italian, English, Scottish	Southern California	*Shin-nisei*	college exchange student
5	Erin	1980	Japanese	Northern California	*Yonsei*	JET Program participant
6	Glenn	1989	Japanese, Filipino	Hawaiʻi	*Gosei*	JET Program participant
7	Jay	1980	Japanese	Southern California	*Sansei, Yonsei*	JET Program participant
8	Kenji	1985	Japanese, Taiwanese	Northern California	*Shin-nisei*	JET Program participant
9	Kim	1985	Japanese	Hawaiʻi	*Yonsei*	JET Program participant
10	Leo	1981	Japanese	Northern California	*Yonsei*	college exchange student
11	Melody	1981	Okinawan	Hawaiʻi	*Yonsei*	language student
12	Nancy	1982	Japanese	Hawaiʻi	*Yonsei*	JET Program participant
13	Saori	1986	Japanese	Northern California	*Shin-nisei*	JET Program participant
14	Scott	1980	Japanese, Irish	Northern California	*Yonsei*	JET Program participant
15	Ying	1983	Japanese, Taiwanese	Northern California	*Sansei, Yonsei*	college exchange student

Abbreviation: JET = Japanese Exchange and Teaching Program.

The Structure of Japanese American Millennial Migration to Japan

The structure of Japanese American millennial migration to Japan can be understood in terms of their social positioning as millennials. Since Japanese American millennials are a social generation at a particular stage in the life course, their experiences in Japan take place at a particular historical moment and also differ from contemporary older Japanese American experiences in Japan. Generational differences exist not only among Japanese Americans, but also among Japanese in Japan; so, comparisons of Japanese and Japanese American millennials and older generations also vary.

Social Generation

Several concepts related to the idea of "generations" require explanation, as they are sometimes used in overlapping and unclear ways (Mortimer and Shanahan 2007). Dictionary definitions point out that "generation" can refer to groups of people in terms of kinship ties or shared historical experiences (e.g., Merriam-Webster 2015). More specifically, then, "social generation" refers to people who are born during the same time period and experience historical periods together at the same stage in the life course (see Mannheim 1952).[3] Japanese American millennials are a social generation. "Ethnic generation" refers to kinship generation; generations are defined by how far removed descendants are from the first generation of immigrants (see Hansen 1996). Examples of Japanese American ethnic generations are issei (prewar first generation), nisei (prewar second generation), sansei (prewar third generation), yonsei (prewar fourth generation), shin-issei (postwar first generation), and shin-nisei (postwar second generation). While Japanese American millennials constitute a social generation, as discussed in the following section, they are mixed in terms of ethnic generation.

Life-Course Stage

A sociological life-course approach emphasizes how age and stage in life structurally shape experiences (Wingens et al. 2011, 5).[4] "In its simplest form the life course refers to a series of life stages through which an individual passes. Each stage of the life course is associated with unique relationships, roles, and responsibilities, and the transition from one life stage to another marks a qualitative shift in these" (Lauer and Wong 2010, 1055). Using this framework highlights how people migrate for different reasons at different ages and how, depending on where one is in the life cycle, different priorities become salient to affect decision making, as well as interpretations of experiences.

The Japanese American millennials I met were not married and did not have children, in contrast to the older Japanese Americans living in Japan whose decisions about where to live were heavily shaped by the pull of spouses and family connecting them to Japan.[5] For example, for my book, I interviewed a number of Japanese American men in their forties and fifties who worked in international business and law and were married to Japanese women. Many of them commented that, in addition to the social and business networks that they had developed over time living in Tokyo, they were motivated to live in Japan long-term because it was easier for their wives to raise their children in Japan owing to cultural familiarity, as well as the practical benefits of having her parents and other relatives close by. The majority of these older Japanese Americans were utilizing work visas or the "spouse or child of a Japanese national" visa to legally reside in Japan. As predominantly men married to Japanese women, the gendered dimension to these international marriages reflects larger patterns among marriages between U.S. and Japanese citizens. My Japanese American millennial interviewees were dating Japanese men and women, but none of them were engaged or talking about marriage in the near future.[6]

All of my Japanese American millennial interviewees were shorter-term migrants without plans to stay in Japan long-term, as opposed to long-term migrants or permanent residents who are generally older. Since millennials went to Japan in occupations and on visas that were for one to five years, they did not plan to stay beyond those maximum terms. If they did want to stay in Japan longer, they would have had to find new visas since their activities and related visa statuses would change.

The Japanese American millennials I spoke with were migrating to Japan as college exchange and language students and as members of the Japan Exchange and Teaching (JET) Program. The four college exchange students I met were based at International Christian University (ICU) and Sophia University, which are both known for their international curriculum (e.g., well-developed Japanese language programs for nonnative speakers, content courses offered in English) and student bodies that include many *kikokushijo,* or Japanese "returnees" who were raised partly abroad, and many exchange students.[7]

The two full-time language students were in a ten-month intensive Japanese immersion program at the intermediate and advanced levels. All conversation on the campus premises (even with fellow Americans) was supposed to be in Japanese to provide the fullest immersion experience possible.

The JET Program was established in 1987 by the Japanese government (Council of Local Authorities for International Relations [CLAIR] 2015) and, thus, has only in recent decades been an option for finding employment in Japan. Without the JET Program as an option, Japanese Americans in earlier periods did not have the same kind of institutional and structural support (e.g., visa, guarantor provision) in finding work in Japan from abroad. Of the nine JET program participants I interviewed, eight were Assistant Language Teachers (ALTs); Jay was the only Coordinator of International Relations (CIR), which requires intermediate fluency to conduct daily work in Japanese.

Related to occupation are visas, which dictate legal length of stay in Japan. Student visas are typically for one year and are not renewable. So if a foreign national resides in Japan on a student visa, after one year the student must then either leave or find another way to obtain a new visa status in Japan. JET Program participants utilize the corresponding visas that support their work activities. ALTs have "instructor" visas, while CIRs have "specialist in humanities/international services" visas. The JET Program provides visas initially for one year, renewable for up to five years[8] total based on mutual consent of employer and JET Program participant.[9]

Since they had all gone to Japan through established institutional programs, none of my millennial Japanese American interviewees lived in Japan through the "long-term resident" visa, colloquially known as the "Nikkei visa" since those who can prove they have a grandparent who was a Japanese citizen are eligible. In this way, Japanese American millennials have very different experiences from the large Japanese Brazilian population in Japan, most of whom do use the "Nikkei visa" in order to work and live in Japan (Tsuda 2003; Yamanaka 1993). Most Japanese Brazilians work in factories and perform unskilled labor, despite having been middle class and educated in Brazil.

Mixed-Ethnic Generations

Japanese American millennials include multiple ethnic generations as well as people of multiple ancestries, contrasting with earlier social generations migrating to Japan that were predominantly nisei or sansei. This diversity makes it difficult to generalize about Japanese American millennial experiences in Japan and requires discussion of the range of family-based connections to Japan.

While Japanese Americans have always varied in their knowledge of Japanese language, culture, and society, this social generation is different from earlier periods because of the ethnic generational diversity. Most of my Japanese American millennial interviewees are yonsei, a generation that did not exist fifty years ago. They are experiencing Japan alongside shin-nisei and other ethnic generations, which is different from Japanese Americans in the prewar period who were mainly nisei in Japan. Though nisei also ranged in their knowledge of Japanese language, culture, and society, the range is not as great as differences between nisei and yonsei. Moreover, nisei shared the experience of having parents who had immigrated from Japan.

Contemporary ethnic generational diversity among millennials means wide variation in terms of familial connections to Japan and exposure to

Japanese language, culture, and society, which shapes their experiences in Japan. As the children of Japanese migrants, shin-nisei typically understand and speak at least conversational Japanese. With immigrant parents, they often have uncles, aunts, and cousins in Japan, as well as grandparents, in addition to other more distant relatives. Sansei and yonsei usually have more limited exposure to Japanese language through family members, since it is their grandparents and great-grandparents, respectively, who are from Japan. The relatives that sansei and yonsei have in Japan are more distant, often siblings and descendants of grandparents or great-grandparents.

Japanese Americans are an increasingly mixed-race and mixed-ethnicity population (De La Cruz-Viesca 2011). While the Japanese American population in the United States has included mixed-race members since its inception (Nakashima, Welty, and Williams 2013; Williams 2017), in earlier periods, immigration restrictions resulted in a predominantly "monoracial" U.S.-born Japanese American population. Six of my fifteen Japanese American millennial interviewees claimed other ancestries in addition to Japanese. While my data are not a representative sample, it is worth noting that according to the U.S. Census records, about 40 percent of the Japanese American population claims multiple ancestries (U.S. Census Bureau 2013).[10] Depending on their phenotypical traits, mixed-heritage Japanese Americans may have experiences in Japan similar to Japanese Americans of only Japanese ancestry or may have experiences quite different from them. In addition, mixed-heritage Japanese Americans are of varying ethnic generations and have different knowledge of Japanese language, culture, and society.

Japanese American Millennials and Comparative Japaneseness

As a social generation who have grown up in the United States since the 1980s, Japanese American millennials have been exposed to the same kinds of constructions of Japaneseness circulating in the United States during this time period. When Japanese American millennials move to Japan, they are additionally exposed to historically specific notions of Japaneseness in their ancestral homeland. What Japanese American millennials who have lived in Japan have in common and what distinguishes them from other Japanese Americans (of all ages), then, are both the historical moments and places in which they have lived and developed their worldviews and senses of self in relation to constructions of Japaneseness.

Japaneseness in the United States

Not coming of age until the late 1990s, Japanese American millennials in the United States have grown up with a generally positive image of Japan. This contrasts with negative representations in earlier periods caused by anti-Japanese immigration sentiment in the prewar era, Japan as the enemy during and after World War II, and the U.S.-Japan trade friction in the 1980s. For various reasons, younger Japanese Americans in the United States are exposed to more contemporary Japanese culture, though complex representation in national mainstream media continues to be lacking. In Hawai'i and the U.S. continent, Japanese Americans are exposed to Japaneseness in different ways.

While in earlier periods in the United States positive exposure to Japanese culture and society was limited and ethnically focused on Japanese Americans, millennials of Japanese ancestry in the United States have learned about forms of popular Japanese culture through both mainstream and ethnic channels. Japanese food and cultural arts have become incorporated into mainstream America as people of varied ethnic backgrounds are eating sushi, sending their children to judo classes, learning *taiko* (Japanese drumming), watching anime, and reading *manga* (Japanese comics or graphic novel). At the same time, Japanese American identity and culture in the United States has become more transnational, drawing from contemporary Japanese culture and overlapping with the growth of "Cool Japan"—the global spread of Japanese popular culture (Kelts 2006; McGray 2002).[11]

Many young Japanese Americans interested in contemporary Japanese culture are finding it to be a positive source of ethnic identity in the 2000s. The majority of my millennial interviewees grew up watching anime, reading manga, or involved with Japanese cultural or martial arts such as taiko, aikido, or judo (see, for example, Tsuda 2016). Reflective of their social generation, some have become interested in Japanese culture and society as something not exclusively linked to ethnic identity or cultural heritage but because of its growing popularity in mainstream America. This differentiates millennial Japanese Americans from previous social generations who also grew up with anime and Japanese cultural or martial arts, but not as recognizable to mainstream America or positively associated with Japan as a center of contemporary popular culture.

Despite amiable U.S.-Japan relations since the 1990s, Japanese Americans are exposed to stereotypical and negative media representations of Japan (and of Asians more generally) in mainstream American society. Dominant stereotypes include people of Asian ancestry in the United States as accented foreigners, hypersexualized women and desexualized men, math and computer geeks, martial arts experts, and as the sneaky and threatening "yellow peril" (Gee 1988; Kim 2011; Lee 1999; Ono and Pham 2009). While Asian American actors and actresses are increasingly portraying more developed characters, the underrepresentation of complex Asian American individuals—partly caused by the "whitewashing" of Asian characters (Hess 2016)—in the media continues to be a problem. These stereotypical depictions reflect and contribute to a larger system of racism and inequality toward Asian Americans and other people of color in the United States. While Japanese Americans are a racial and ethnic minority on the U.S. continent, in Hawai'i they are numerically a minority but are well represented in politics, business, and the media in the islands (Okamura 2008).

When Japanese American millennials born and raised in the United States migrate to Japan as adults, they bring with them these U.S.-based constructions of Japaneseness as they interpret themselves and Japanese in Japan. In this way, the identities they construct in Japan are transnational (Basch, Schiller, and Blanc 1994), drawing from internalized cultural frameworks for interpreting the world around them that may be different from mainstream cultural frameworks where they currently are. Over time, however, through interactions with Japanese in Japan, they adapt to Japan-based "common sense" about how to categorize and understand people, including how they are perceived by most people in Japanese society.

Japaneseness in Japan

The notions of Japaneseness in Japan that millennials are exposed to when they migrate to study and work in Tokyo in the early 2000s are different from earlier constructions of Japaneseness. In the postwar era, especially since the 1970s, the myth of Japanese homogeneity and uniqueness has become the dominant discourse of Japanese national identity (Yoshino 1992). In earlier periods, however, Japanese national identity was constructed differently, including as a more multiracial identity before and during World War II.

During the period of the Japanese empire leading up to World War II, as Japan colonized nations in Asia and the Pacific, Japanese national identity was constructed to include these new "citizens" of Japan. Japanese rulers saw themselves as a "mixed nation" of hierarchically organized Japanese citizens, the newest colonial members needing much education and assimilation (Oguma 1995). Through World War II, Japanese nationalist and imperialist sentiment was strong. Japan's defeat in the Pacific War caused economic, political, and cultural restructuring in the postwar period, including giving up the colonial territories it had taken in the previous five decades.

In the postwar period, as Japan reconstructed itself as an economic superpower from the ashes of postwar devastation, a discourse of Japanese superiority and uniqueness emerged. This "myth of Japanese homogeneity," the hegemonic discourse in contemporary Japan, assumes that "Japanese" people are different from "foreign" people in terms of "blood," culture, and citizenship (Sugimoto 1997, 2010; Yoshino 1992).[12]

Images of Americans and the United States have changed with U.S.-Japan relations and global flows of culture. During the Pacific War, the United States was clearly the enemy, racialized as different (Dower 1986). But during the Allied Occupation, the United States transitioned from enemy to ally, and Japan became militarily dependent as a result of the U.S.-drafted postwar constitution—a situation that arguably continues to this day since Japan officially lacks an offensive military and U.S. Armed Forces continue to have bases and military personnel all over the Japanese archipelago (though concentrated mainly in Okinawa).[13]

As Japan has modernized and westernized in the postwar period, American influence has become noticeable from food products to fashion. During the Occupation era, the presence of U.S. military personnel and influx of American goods and popular culture in the form of films, clothing, and food products familiarized people in the greater Tokyo area with American "culture" and began to normalize an *akogare* (desire, longing) for Western, specifically American, things.[14] Now, in the 2000s, reruns of major U.S. television shows such as *Friends* play on Japanese television dubbed over in Japanese. McDonald's and Denny's can be found in large cities all over the country. In Tokyo, one can shop at the Gap or J. Crew, not to mention a host of other major American clothing brands.[15] As a result of the influx of American and other foreign goods, Japanese Americans in the 2000s do not stand out because of their American clothes in as dramatic a way as they did in earlier historical periods.

Diverse Japanese American Millennial Experiences in Japan

While they share structural experiences, there is much internal diversity among Japanese American millennials regarding their experiences in Japan.

Phenotype, Ancestry, and Visually Blending in Japanese Society

The experiences of my millennial interviewees demonstrate how one's ability to phenotypically blend in Japan shapes identification for Japanese Americans. Not surprisingly, people of only Japanese ancestry were not visually salient in Japan. In addition, people of mixed ancestries could also often blend into crowds, especially if they were of mixed Asian ethnic backgrounds. But for some Japanese Americans, their physical characteristics immediately marked them as different from most Japanese people, despite their shared Japanese ancestry. These variations in phenotype influenced whether Japanese Americans were initially categorized as "Japanese" or as "foreign," and how they learned to identify in Japan, as a result.

Japanese American millennials living in Japan who can visually blend commonly go through stages of identity formation: blending in based on physical appearance alone; then being interpreted as marginal Japanese or East Asian immigrants once their less-than-fluent Japanese language ability is taken into account by their interlocutor; then asserting place-based identities as a way to explain how they were not raised in Japan, though they are of Japanese ancestry (Yamashiro 2011; 2017, 43–63). For example, Jay reflected, "In the United States the thought of blending in never occurred to me. Psychologically it's comforting to know that if I want to I have the potential of being an average Joe [in Japan] . . . to be on the inside looking out. . . . It's superficial but. . . . It's important for me . . . because it's the first time in my life I can do that. Being unique was cool but lonely. So maybe that was the reason why I really wanted to learn how to be Japanese or to fit in when I came here. Both as an exchange student and as a JET, I felt like something inside of me was trying to make up for 20 years of not experiencing this . . . a compulsion, desire to fit in."

Some of my interviewees could phenotypically blend in Japan but claimed mixed ancestries. According to the 2013 American Community Survey, 43 percent of people in the United States who claimed Japanese ethnic backgrounds also claimed other ethnic backgrounds. By 2020, the majority of people in the United States who claim Japanese ethnic backgrounds will also claim other ethnic backgrounds. So mixed experiences and identities will soon become majority experiences for Japanese Americans.

When asked to complete a sentence about how his appearance shaped his experiences in Japan, Glen, of Japanese and Filipino ancestries, replied, "[In Japan, because I looked . . .] Japanese enough and people had no reason to believe I was a random mixed-race *gaijin* [foreigner] in the middle of the *inaka* [countryside], most people who didn't know me assumed I was full Japanese." This was an interesting experience for him, especially in contrast to his experiences in the United States, where Glen says people never assume he's just Japanese: "In a way it made me happy because I identify more with the Japanese side, [so] it was refreshing to have people think I was Japanese." I asked Glen when in Japan he was asked about his race/ethnic background, how this conversation usually went, and if people understood right away, to which he responded,

> People absolutely did not understand, even after explaining multiple times. Being Asian and specifically Japanese, but also the resident *gaijin*/American did not sit well with people. Japanese people have a very hard time separating ethnicity and nationality. It is also always so frustrating to have to explain: (1) Being ethnically Japanese has nothing to do with my Japanese language abilities. Not even my grandparents speak it; I learned it in school; and (2) Yes, I'm half Japanese, but not *hafu* in the way that you are most likely thinking about it. Most Japanese people these days are comfortable with the concept of mixed-race children when one parent is from Japan and one parent is a *gaijin*. Half Japanese American/Half Filipino American is not even in the realm of something most people I came into contact with could possibly comprehend."

Indeed the term *hafu* in Japan typically refers to the child of an international marriage between an ethnically Japanese citizen of Japan (*nihonjin*) and a foreign citizen not of Japanese ancestry (*gaijin*). Since the dominant image of gaijin is of "white" people,[16] the dominant image of *hafu* in contemporary Japan is of the child of a nihonjin and a white person. But this conflates race and nation: foreign nationals can be of Asian descent, so the children of international marriages are often not phenotypically discernable in Japanese society. For example, mixed Korean/Japanese, mixed Chinese/Japanese, and mixed Filipino/Japanese ostensibly make up the largest mixed populations in Japan since most international marriages are between Japanese and other Asians.

The conflation of people from the United States (and Europe) with whites causes confusion when Americans of color in Japan claim national identities as Americans (Yamashiro 2017). Moreover, when mixed Japanese Americans have parents who are both U.S. citizens but of differing ancestries, no term in Japanese can capture this background (see Yamashiro 2017, chap. 3).

At the same time, Japanese Americans can be interpreted as complete foreigners in Japan. Ema, who claims Italian, English, and Scottish heritage in addition to Japanese, was the only Japanese American millennial I spoke with who did not have the experience of visual blending in Japan. She explains, "In Japan, I look more foreign." She added that her Japanese dormmates at International Christian University said they have trouble telling the difference between white foreigners and people of mixed white and Japanese backgrounds. However, Ema has not always been interpreted as just looking white. She related that in the United States, people can usually tell that she is not completely white—other "halfs" can usually tell, though sometimes people think she is Latina. When she is with her mother, who is Japanese, some people can see the resemblance.

Over time, Ema has noticed how her particular phenotypical characteristics lead to certain interpretations of her. Ema described garnering unwanted attention on trains. She reflected, "At first that really bothered me. Being the one gaijin on the train sometimes I get glanced at." Over time, she learned to expect to receive those glances. "I'll turn around and catch some *obaasan* [older woman] looking at me. . . . If I looked more half, glances would register differently; there would be more curiosity. . . . There are lots of plain old gaijin in Tokyo, and I think I'm lumped in with that generalization. If I looked more half, people would wonder if I grew up in the United States or Japan."

Because of Japanese racialization of her as a foreigner, Ema feels less Japanese and more white. She recalls, "Before coming . . . in retrospect at home people ask me what I am so I guess I stick out but in Japan I stick out and have no chance of being Japanese." People are surprised when she tells them about her Japanese ancestry. She explicates, "Without explaining myself, I'm gaijin. I don't explain my ethnic background to everyone I meet so I just deal with it." She thinks that at the beginning of her stay in Japan, she did make more of a point to explain, but now says, "I'm feeling more white." As people continued to treated her like she was "just" white, Ema started feeling this way, too.

Japanese American millennial experiences in Japan are shaped by a combination of phenotype and ancestry. Those who can phenotypically blend include both people of only Japanese ancestry and people who claim mixed ancestries. Mixed Japanese Americans experience a range of racialized categorization in Japan which greatly influences how they learn to identify. While Ema, like Glenn, has one parent of Japanese ancestry, she is interpreted as white in Japan and learns to feel more white as a result. So phenotype largely shapes ethnic and racial identity formations in Japan in terms of how Japanese people interpret and reinforce certain kinds of identities as Japanese or not. While Ema's experience is an outlier for my sample of interviewees, in the future it may become less uncommon for Japanese Americans in Japan, as the larger Japanese American population becomes majority mixed ancestry.

Hawai'i Japaneseness in Hawai'i, the U.S. Continent, and Japan

The experiences of Japanese American millennials from Hawai'i living in Japan highlight the multiple constructions of Japaneseness in Hawai'i, the U.S. continent, and Japan, which I have theorized elsewhere in terms of a global ancestral group, "a population that claims shared ancestral ties [and] is dispersed across multiple societies and nation-states" (Yamashiro 2017, 5). Identity formations in Japan for Japanese American millennials from Hawai'i differ from those of their continental counterparts because of differences in both how they see themselves and how Japanese people see them (Yamashiro 2017). The distinction between Hawai'i and the U.S. continent is commonly made in both the United States and Japan: in the United States, people from Hawai'i differentiate themselves from people from the "mainland," while in Japan, Japanese people differentiate Hawai'i from "America."

Japanese American millennials from Hawai'i reacted differently to blending in in Japan as compared to their continental counterparts because of experiences in the United States. As an earlier quote from Jay, a Japanese American from California, indicates, while he was growing up it had not occurred to him that he might be able to blend in and feel like part of the (racial) majority. Representative of my Japanese American interviewees of all ages from the U.S. continent who could phenotypically blend in Japan, Jay highlighted his newfound ability to visually disappear into a crowd and conveyed his excitement at no longer being a racial and ethnic minority. In contrast, Japanese Americans from Hawai'i who could phenotypically blend were already accustomed to being part of mainstream culture and society. In Hawai'i, as compared to being on the U.S. continent, Japanese Americans tend to be less conscious of their backgrounds because the mainstream society in Hawai'i has a general understanding of their experiences. This understanding is partly a consequence of their large numbers and the proportion of their population of Hawai'i, and partly a consequence of their representational power (Okamura 2008). As Kim expressed, "In Hawai'i, being Japanese is so common."

In Japan, mainstream understandings of Hawai'i differentiated it from the United States more generally, affecting how my interviewees from Hawai'i were understood. Nancy remembers how her students thought Hawai'i was not part of the United States, "In explaining to my students about Hawai'i, which is a part of America, I also explained some background on being Japanese American/Nikkei from Hawai'i. Many of my students didn't associate Hawai'i with being a part of the United States. Instead, they considered it a separate country." One contributing factor that I noticed in the construction of Hawai'i as geographically distinct from the "United States" is the ubiquitous tourism advertising that can be found throughout major metropolitan areas. Tour packages commonly have separate information on "the United States" and "Hawai'i," the latter grouped with other Pacific Island destinations.

Moreover, my interviewees from Hawai'i were encouraged to keep identifying as being from Hawai'i since this typically elicited more interest and excitement than being from the United States. Glenn explained, "I identified myself as being from Hawai'i. Even before identifying myself as American. Japanese people are always (too?) excited when you say you're from Hawai'i; I also feel like being from Hawai'i is special—I'm 'from Hawai'i' before 'American,' even on the Mainland." Here Glenn is also pointing out that his identification with Hawai'i rather than as "American" is not limited to his residence in Japan—he also identifies as being from Hawai'i when he is on the U.S. continent. Kim, too, recalls having Japanese people identify her with Hawai'i and take an interest in her, "Japanese people . . . love Hawai'i, so I feel that was something they really were interested in and identified me with." Japanese interest in Hawai'i can be attributed to a variety of factors, including the familiarity of Hawai'i to most Japanese, either through advertising, the media, or actual visits; and a positive image in Japan of Hawai'i (Yamashiro 2017, 59). In addition, Japanese celebrities are known to visit Hawai'i over the New Year's holiday, so it is associated with famous and wealthy people.

Okinawanness in Hawai'i, the U.S. Continent, and Japan

Japanese American millennials of Okinawan descent from Hawai'i also discussed multiple constructions of Okinawanness in Hawai'i, on the U.S.

continent, and in Japan, which can be understood through the framework of Okinawans as a global ancestral group. When I asked Melody, who claims only Okinawan ancestry, how she would describe her ethnic background to someone she was meeting for the first time, she replied that on the U.S. continent (where she has visited but never lived), "I would say I'm Japanese, just because it's easier. At home [in Hawai'i], though, I say that I'm Okinawan, because people tend to understand that there is a difference." In other words, while "Okinawan" is a recognizable ethnic background in Hawai'i, it is not necessarily intelligible on the U.S. continent. In Japan, Melody asserts differences between Okinawans and Japanese, as well as differences between "Americans" and people from Hawai'i. "I always say that I'm from Hawai'i, Okinawan fourth generation. I don't think that I would identify myself as American, even though I'm from Hawai'i. Like most Japanese [in Japan], I think I tend to separate Hawai'i from the United States. I'm, I guess, "technically" Japanese, but since my ancestors came from Okinawa, and the native people in Okinawa have different racial identities from Japanese, I don't think of myself as Japanese. Plus too, if I say that I'm Japanese, then it creates that image that I was born and raised in Japan." The ways that Melody expresses her Okinawanness also differ by place: "Aside from studying the language and following traditions, I belong to the Young Okinawans (however, you don't necessarily have to be Okinawan to join), I go with my cousins and relatives to the Okinawan festival in Hawai'i, we work at our club booth, and I shop at the Okinawan goods stores around Yokohama." That is, in Hawai'i she participates in activities and community, while as a temporary resident in Japan, she shops.

Brent, who was born and raised in Hawai'i but attended college in Los Angeles, has been able to spend time in the Okinawan American community in California, allowing him to compare it with Hawai'i. He noticed how in Los Angeles, they seem interested in "the political implications of being Okinawan," while "in Hawai'i, they don't talk politics that much." Brent then added that the Hawai'i Okinawan Cultural Center received funds from the Okinawan Prefectural government, and those funds probably also came from the Tokyo central government, "so they can't talk bad about the U.S. government."[17] Brent also commented that in Hawai'i, an active member of the Okinawan community who is half German and half Okinawan doesn't have an Okinawan last name and doesn't look Okinawan, so "people don't want to listen to him," despite the fact that "he knows more about Okinawa and has spent more time there." In contrast, in Los Angeles the Okinawans Brent spent time with "don't seem to pay attention to these sorts of racial issues," implying that they are more racially inclusive, though he also believes that the latter group is "not as tight."

In terms of how he identifies, it is important to Brent that people know he is half Okinawan and half Japanese. "When people decide my identity for me, I get upset. I usually say I'm half Japanese and half Okinawan, born and raised in Hawai'i." The ways that Brent claims Okinawan and Japanese as two different ethnic categories reflect his upbringing in Hawai'i, where the boundary between Japaneseness and Okinawanness has been socially maintained. Brent's statement probably alludes to the fact that on the U.S. continent, "Okinawan" identity has been subsumed into the larger "Japanese" category, ostensibly a consequence of the small numbers of Okinawans relative to the Japanese population, as well as the small numbers of both Okinawans and Japanese relative to the larger population on the U.S. continent.

Meanwhile, the salience of Okinawan identity in Hawai'i can be explained by multiple factors in the prewar and postwar periods (Shimada 2012). Factors in the prewar period include the large number of Okinawan immigrants and Japanese discrimination against them in Hawai'i. Racial boundaries between Japanese and Okinawans and the hierarchy constructed in Japan were carried over to Hawai'i by immigrants, who had internalized these ideas. In Hawai'i, Okinawans were considered "Japanese" by non-Japanese, but "Okinawan" among Japanese: "To non-Japanese, both the Naichi [mainland Japanese] and the Uchinanchu [Okinawans] were Japanese. However, in the Japanese community, a clear distinction was made" (Hazama and Komeji 1986, 74). In the postwar period, Okinawan identity has been constructed as different from Japanese in more positive ways, including relief activities that "united them, strengthened bonds with their homeland, and bolstered ethnic pride" (Shimada 2012, 118). As a result, many residents of Hawai'i who are not of Japanese or Okinawan ancestry have learned to distinguish between these ethnic groups, which explains why Melody feels it is worthwhile to describe her background as Okinawan rather than Japanese when in Hawai'i.

Gender, Class, and Sexuality

Japanese Americans comment on gender differences as part of what they adjust to in migrating from the United States to Japan, but those at different stages in the life course compare themselves and are compared by others to differently aged Japanese, accordingly. While older women negotiate being interpreted in relation to married Japanese women who tend to be full-time housewives (Goldstein-Gidoni, 2012), younger Japanese American women are aware of Japanese "girls" and contexts outside of work and family.

Diana was a woman in her fifties who observed a significant difference between how Japanese men treated her while out shopping and running errands (ostensibly interpolated as a Japanese housewife) and their behavior, speech, and respect toward her once her higher occupational and social status as a U.S. diplomat was revealed: "I've found that *meishi* [business cards] were like a god-sent gift to me (laughs). . . . Because as soon as you pull out your *meishi* and it shows your name, title, and who you represent, it ceases to be an issue, I mean for government officials . . . or business officials. See, that's one of the reasons that when we're doing official work . . . I actually have an option." Diana's observation that she "actually [has] an option" highlights the ways in which older Japanese American (and Japanese) women without a higher social status do *not* have this option. Without this option, a Japanese American woman professional might have to more consciously negotiate the position of housewife in Japan, whereas Diana sees the benefits of not revealing her occupation and avoiding unwanted attention as a U.S. diplomat: "It's almost as good as hiding. In Japan, as a woman, you're basically kind of invisible anyway. Not as much as before, but certainly . . . you know, you're *okusan* (wife). If you're standing next to a white guy, you're probably his *okusan*." Diana's distinction between how she is treated when her status is revealed or not suggests that to her the class status and power of being a diplomat overrides the disempowerment of being a woman in Japan.

Meanwhile, Melody, a millennial, compares herself with younger peers, noting how she spends her time outside of her language classes practicing aikido. She was a full-time language student when I met her in Yokohama and had previously lived in Kobe as an exchange student in college. Melody described noticing how "Kobe girls are expensive looking [and] girls from Tokyo are a little more normal." She explained, "Kobe girls are skinnier [and] bleach their hair more. It's a richer area so maybe [they] have more money to spend on their looks. I remember looking at them and thinking 'that's not what I'm used to seeing when I look at Japanese girls [tourists and local Japanese] at home [in Hawai'i]. That was the other big shock for me. I don't think I expected them to look like local Japanese girls, but I was really surprised when they didn't." In addition to commenting on the physical appearance, aesthetics, and body shape of young Japanese women her age, Melody also makes some economic class analyses in the previous statement. She grew up as the child of pig farmers in Hawai'i, in a neighborhood where her classmates were not expected to go to college. Melody did receive a bachelor's degree from the University of Hawai'i, but, like most millennials, was still unsure of her future when I spoke with her. Outside of her language study in Japan, Melody was very involved with practicing aikido and described gender differences she noticed regarding changing clothes: "When I first went to the aikido headquarters to practice, I noticed that a lot of the women would fold their hakamas (pants worn while practicing Aikido) in the changing room, instead of on the mat. However, the men were folding their hakama on the mat—as it turns out, I can fold my hakama anywhere I like, but I remember my initial thought being, 'Why should I have to fold my hakama in the small changing room where space is really limited?'" Melody provided this anecdote as an example of how she is different from Japanese people, suggesting that her experience has made her aware of gendered differences in Japan and how she, as a woman, negotiates them.

On a slightly different note, gendered experiences in Japan can be reinterpreted by the same person later in life to reflect different views at different stages in the life course. I interviewed Erin in 2013 when she was thirty-three years old and she reflected on her experiences in Japan as an ALT in the JET Program about ten years earlier when she had been in her twenties. Erin described how living in Japan she was slightly familiar with Japanese etiquette because of what her grandmother had taught her in the United States. In contrast to her female JET colleague who became upset at the idea, "It didn't bother me at all that women pour tea [in Japan]" she explained, because in the United States her grandmother had had Erin pour tea for her father and grandfather. She added, "It's not like they're asking me to scrub the floor." Then she commented, "But if an American guy asked, that's not cool . . . because in America you don't expect people to serve you." To her it was a different cultural context depending on who she was pouring tea for, and for Japanese and Japanese Americans it seemed fine to her. She continued by describing how her grandmother would have her serve her father's rice for him. She noted that "It's not like he can't get it himself . . . and it's not like he's expecting me to do it," but that her grandmother was teaching her "etiquette." In this way, gendered customs are taken as culturally appropriate and to be culturally respectful, one must perform gendered roles. Erin reflected that she did not have expectations about her experiences in Japan so "nothing really upset me or threw me off." To her, the year was a temporary stay so she did not feel pressure to become fluent in Japanese or accept Japanese social norms as her own.

However, when asked about how she would think about it if she happened to live in Japan again now, as a working professional and perhaps more indefinitely timewise, Erin thought it might be different. She said, "I'm not sure that in the corporate world I would be willing to take a back seat. . . . I'm not sure that I would still be okay with that at work. . . . I'm a lot different now than I was when I was twenty-two. In a social setting it's okay, but in a work setting I've come to really feel that everyone needs to give each other the equal respect that we all deserve. I wouldn't mind pouring tea for someone at home or at a friend's home or something, but at work. . . ." Although Erin was unsure if the issue would even come up at work, it was hard for her to imagine what her response would be regarding pouring tea for male colleagues. She explained that in a social setting pouring tea would not be a problem because "I don't feel like I need to fight for respect in a social setting," whereas in the corporate world, women are always more embattled, so I think I might have a harder time in that setting." Her experiences as a working woman in the United States shape how she interprets what it would be like to work as a woman in Japan. Since she has experienced gender inequality in the workplace, she is more resistant to gendered work roles than gendered social roles.

Another way in which my interviewees differentiated themselves from their counterparts in Japan was in how they interpreted and discussed sexuality. For example, Ema believed that in Japan gender roles and sexuality categories are much stricter than in the United States, where she has observed more of a spectrum. She commented that in Japan she hears about gays and lesbians, "but you don't hear about bisexuals so much." As a result, Ema says, "I feel more pressure to pick a sexuality in Japan. In the United States I can think it through, and not just pick one." This pressure to pick a sexuality in Japan has been more of a daily concern to her than race or ethnicity, making her "think about it a lot."

In describing ways in which he is different from Japanese in Japan, Brent also thought about the differential social construction of sexuality in the United States and Japan. After pointing out how his patriotism toward the United States makes him different, Brent noted how he communicates directly, is open concerning sexual issues and sexual lifestyle, and gets HIV tests regularly, whether he is sexually active or not. Brent has observed that in Japan they push pornography but not safe sex. He thinks that in Japan "they think that by not talking about it, it's not gonna happen." Brent doesn't know anyone who is openly positive. When he went to the *kuyakusho* (ward office) and asked about HIV testing, he says they treated him as though he were already infected. He eventually obtained information and went to a public clinic, which was eight train stops from Yokohama. In contrast, Brent says that "in the United States, they ask questions like 'Are you having sex?' 'Are your parents HIV?' 'Do you do drugs?' But in Japan the three questions they asked were 'Are you married?' 'Are you sleeping with someone married?' 'Are you having sex right now?'" He added that in the United States, on college campuses, they often have a two-week period during which testing is free. He takes advantage of this and also has his friend go get tested, as well. Brent strongly believed in the importance of getting tested, even if one is not sexually active, pointing out that "a lot of people don't get tested, but it's important."

Conclusion

This chapter has highlighted the diversity of Japanese American millennial experiences in Japan. While Japanese American millennials have much in common because they share the same social generation and the same stage in the life course, meaning they have been exposed to the same representations of Japaneseness in the United States and Japan, they are also diverse in terms of ancestry, phenotype, geographic upbringing, gender, and sexuality.

Focusing on phenotype and ancestry is one way to see the diversity of Japanese American millennial experiences in Japan: their ability to phenotypically blend in Japan shapes how "Japanese" they are treated and feel as a result. Japanese American millennials who can visually blend in Japan include both those who claim only Japanese ancestry and those who also claim other ancestries. Thus, rather than distinguishing between those who claim mixed heritage and those who do not, in understanding Japanese American millennial experiences in Japan, it is more useful to distinguish between those who look similar to most Japanese in Japan and those who do not, while considering how claiming multiple ancestries at times further shapes Japanese American experiences in Japan.

Interviews with Japanese American millennials from Hawai'i highlight competing constructions of Japaneseness and Okinawanness in Hawai'i, the U.S. continent, and Japan. These constructions of the same ancestry that differ by society shape the understandings (and misunderstandings) that occur when people raised in one society move to another society and come into contact with people raised with different expectations of what it means to be "Japanese" or "Okinawan."

When Japanese American millennials compare themselves with people and practices in Japan, they notice differences that are shaped by constructions of gender, class, and sexual orientation. Japanese American women are compared with and compare themselves with Japanese women. Japanese Americans compare themselves with Japanese counterparts who have similar sexual orientations. So, as my interviewees, who are people of Japanese ancestry from the United States, go through the process of reconstructing identities in Japan, their racial and national identities also include sexual orientation and gender identities.

Taken together, Japanese American millennial experiences in Japan challenge the idea that identities are fixed across place and time. They demonstrate change in identification over time, as well as in moving from one society to another. Moreover, they force us to rethink essentialized assumptions that "Japanese" are the same regardless of place.

NOTES

1. Japanese Americans themselves (Kitano 1993) and researchers (Yanagisako 1985) have used ethnic generation labels to describe Japanese Americans, often assuming that these terms also refer to social generations.

2. It is important to note that historically in Japan, as well as currently to many people with ancestral roots in Okinawa, "Okinawan" and "Japanese" are different ethnicities.

3. Ryder (1965, 844) has called this group a "birth cohort," defined as "those persons born in the same time interval and aging together."

4. Wingens et al. (2011, 5) point out that there is "no unified life course theory. . . . The life course, thus, is viewed "as a theoretical orientation" (Elder et al. 2003, 4), approach, or framework, but not a "theory" since there is "no integrated and coherent system of descriptive as well as explanatory conceptions, principles, definitions, and statements which are empirically testable" (Wingens et al. 2011, 5).

5. According to the PEW Research Center, millennials are getting married later than previous social generations, with only 26 percent married by the age of 32 (Shim

2014). In addition, my Japanese American interviewees were highly educated, suggesting that they marry at an age later than the national average.

6. Two interviewees were dating people of the same sex so legally recognized marriage was not an option for them in Japan, but they did not express a desire to be in a life partner situation at the time of the interview, whether legally recognized or not.

7. Sophia University's Faculty of Comparative Culture began in 1987 and became the "first and only comprehensive university program in Japan taught solely in English." Although previously located at the Ichigaya campus, separate from the main Yotsuya campus, from 2006 it was reorganized as the Faculty of Liberal Arts and merged with the predominantly Japanese-speaking Yotsuya campus (Sophia University).

8. Before 2007, these contracts were renewable for up to three years. JET Program, accessed July 28, 2017, http://jetprogramme.org/en/history.

9. Ibid., accessed May 16, 2017, http://jetprogramusa.org/contract-benefit.

10. Census figures are based on ethnic background alone. The reported numbers documenting "Japanese Americans" in the United States technically describe people claiming Japanese ancestry who are residing in the United States, including citizens of the United States, Japan, and other nations. While they claim Japanese ethnic backgrounds, they may or may not identify as "Japanese American."

11. For example, although events at the annual Cherry Blossom Festival in San Francisco Japantown have historically focused on more traditional Japanese cultural exhibits and entertainment, since at least 2010 "cosplay (dressing up in costume as characters from anime)" has been included as an activity, with a contest and parade.

12. The economic recession in Japan from the early 1990s to the early 2000s led to resistance by the younger generations to the dominant images of salarymen and lifetime employment, resulting in a generation of "freeters" (young people engaged in temporary or part-time work, as opposed to full-time work, for various reasons) and NEET (not in education, employment or training) workers (Kosugi 2006).

13. Article 9 of Japan's postwar constitution, written by the United States, stipulates that Japan is not allowed to have an offensive military. As a result, Japan has hosted large numbers of U.S. military forces since the Occupation period, concentrated in Okinawa (Welna 2017). In line with constitutional restrictions, Japan has "Self-Defense Forces," which have become more visible in recent years. As of 2018, Japan is estimated to have "the world's fifth most-powerful military" (Lendon 2018), and Prime Minister Abe has been rallying support for revising the pacifist constitution (Asahi Shimbun 2018).

14. For an insightful analysis of the influence of U.S. military and mass media culture on the spread of American ideologies, specifically racial ones, see (Kim 2008).

15. However, Japan is not the only foreign country in which one can buy these American products; so American influence in Japan needs to be seen not only in terms of the U.S.-Japan relationship but also as part of capitalist globalization and the spread of American culture and products all over the world. At the same time, as Japanese import foreign ideas and products, they also "Japanize" or localize them (Tobin 1992).

16. I use quotes around "white" to denote that race is a social construction and humans have invented racial categories that are not based in biological difference along racial lines. For the convenience of reading, I do not use quotes throughout, though, to be clear, all racial categories were invented by humans and have become significant only because we have historically treated groups of people as if they were biologically different, thus ourselves creating social and material differences along racial lines.

17. The Japanese government depends on the U.S. government to provide U.S. military forces in Okinawa and other parts of Japan, so Brent is suggesting that a critique of the U.S. government could jeopardize that political and economic support.

REFERENCES

Asahi Shimbun. 2018. "Re-elected Abe Emboldened to Pursue Constitutional Amendment." September 21. http://www.asahi.com/ajw/articles/AJ201809210014.html.

Basch, Linda, Nina Glick Schiller, and Christina Szanton Blanc. 1994. *Nations Unbound: Transnational Projects, Postcolonial Predicaments, and Deterritorialized Nation-States*. Langhorne, PA: Gordon and Breach.

Council of Local Authorities for International Relations (CLAIR). 2015. "The Japan Exchange and Teaching (JET) Programme." Accessed May 15, 2018. http://jetprogramme.org/en/history.

De La Cruz-Viesca, Melany. 2011. *State of Japanese Americans: Decade in Review*. Los Angeles: California Japanese American Community Leadership Council and UCLA Asian American Studies Center.

Dower, John W. 1986. *War without Mercy: Race and Power in the Pacific War*. New York: Pantheon.

Gee, Deborah. 1988. *Slaying the Dragon: Asian Women in U.S. Television and Film*. San Francisco: CrossCurrent Media. Distributed by National Asian American Telecommunications Association. Video recording.

Goldstein-Gidoni, Ofra. 2012. *Housewives of Japan: An Ethnography of Real Lives and Consumerized Domesticity*. New York: Palgrave Macmillan.

Hansen, Marcus Lee. 1996. "The Problem of the Third Generation Immigrant." In *Theories of Ethnicity: A Classical Reader*, edited by W. Sollors, 202–215. New York: NYU Press. Originally published in 1938.

Hays, Sharon. 1996. *The Cultural Contradictions of Motherhood*. New Haven, CT: Yale University Press.

Hazama, Dorothy Ochiai, and Jane Okamoto Komeji. 1986. *Okage Same De: The Japanese in Hawai'i 1885–1985*. Honolulu: Bess Press.

Hess, Amanda. 2016. "Asian-American Actors Are Fighting for Visibility: They Will Not Be Ignored. *New York Times*, Accessed May 25, 2018. https://www.nytimes.com/2016/05/29/movies/asian-american-actors-are-fighting-for-visibility-they-will-not-be-ignored.html?_r=0.

Kelts, Roland. 2006. *Japanamerica: How Japanese Pop Culture Has Invaded the U.S.* New York: Palgrave Macmillan.

Kim, Elaine H. 2011. *Slaying the Dragon: Reloaded*. San Francisco: Asian Women United of California. Video recording.

Kim, Nadia Y. 2008. *Imperial Citizens: Koreans and Race from Seoul to LA*. Stanford, CA: Stanford University Press.

Kitano, Harry H. L. 1993. *Generations and Identity: The Japanese American*. Needham Heights, MA: Ginn Press.

Kosugi, Reiko. 2006. "Youth Employment in Japan's Economic Recovery: 'Freeters' and 'NEETs.'" *Asia-Pacific Journal: Japan*. Accessed May 15, 2018. http://www.japanfocus.org/-kosugi-reiko/2022/article.html.

Lauer, Sean R., and Queenie Wong. 2010. "Transnationalism over the Life Course." *Sociology Compass* 4:1054–1062. https://doi.org/10.1111/j.1751-9020.2010.00337.x.

Lee, Robert G. 1999. *Orientals: Asian Americans in Popular Culture*. Philadelphia: Temple University Press.

Lendon, Brad. 2018. "Why You're Seeing More of Japan's Military." CNN. October 16. Accessed April 11, 2019. https://www.cnn.com/2018/10/15/asia/japan-military-visi bility-intl/index.html.

Mannheim, Karl. 1952. "The Problem of Generations." In *Essays on the Sociology of Knowledge*, edited by P. Kecskemeti, 276–322. London: Routledge and Kegan Paul.

McGray, Douglas. 2002. "Japan's Gross National Cool." *Foreign Policy* 130:44–54. Accessed May 15, 2018. https://www.jstor.org/stable/3183487.

Merriam-Webster. 2019. "Generation." Accessed April 11, 2019. https://www.merriam -webster.com/dictionary/generation.

Mortimer, Jeylan T., and Michael J. Shanahan. 2007. *Handbook of the Life Course*. New York: Kluwer Academic Publishers.

Nakashima, Cythnia, Lily Anne Yumi Welty, and Duncan Williams. 2013. *Visible and Invisible: A Hapa Japanese American History*. Los Angeles: Japanese American National Museum.

Oguma, Eiji. 1995. *Tan'itsu Minzoku Shinwa no Kigen* [The myth of the homogeneous nation]. Tokyo: Shin'yousha.

Okamura, Jonathan Y. 2008. *Ethnicity and Inequality in Hawai'i*. Philadelphia: Temple University Press.

Ono, Kent A., and Vincent N. Pham. 2009. *Asian Americans and the Media*. Malden, MA: Polity.

Ryder, Norman B. 1965. "The Cohort as a Concept in the Study of Social Change." *American Sociological Review* 30(6): 843–861. http://personal.psc.isr.umich.edu/yuxie -web/files/soc543/Ryder1965.pdf.

Shim, Eileen. 2014. "The Median Age of Marriage in Every State in the U.S., in Two Maps." *News.Mic*. June 27. http://mic.com/articles/92361/the-median-age-of-marri age-in-every-state-in-the-u-s-in-two-maps.

Shimada, Noriko. 2012. "The Emergence of Okinawan Ethnic Identity in Hawai'i: Wartime and Postwar Experiences." *The Japanese Journal of American Studies* 23:117–138.

Sophia University. n.d. "Faculty of Liberal Arts." Tokyo, Japan: Sophia University. Accessed May 15, 2018. http://www.fla.sophia.ac.jp/about.

Sugimoto, Yoshio. 1997. *An Introduction to Japanese Society*. Cambridge: Cambridge University Press.

———. 2010. *An Introduction to Japanese Society*. 3rd ed. Cambridge: Cambridge University Press.

Tobin, Joseph Jay. 1992. *Re-made in Japan: Everyday Life and Consumer Taste in a Changing Society*. New Haven, CT: Yale University Press.

Tsuda, Takeyuki. 2003. *Strangers in the Ethnic Homeland: Japanese Brazilian Return Migration in Transnational Perspective*. New York: Columbia University Press.

———. 2016. *Japanese American Ethnicity: In Search of Heritage and Homeland across Generations*. New York: New York University Press.

U.S. Census Bureau. 2013. *2011–2013 American Community Survey 3-Year Estimates*. Accessed August 15, 2015. https://www.census.gov/programs-surveys/acs/technical -documentation/table-and-geography-changes/2013/3-year.html

Welna, David. 2017. "U.S. Bases on Japanese Island of Okinawa Have Long Been Contentious." National Public Radio. February 10. http://www.npr.org/2017/02/10/514458 686/u-s-bases-on-japanese-island-of-okinawa-have-long-been-contentious.

Williams, Duncan, ed. 2017. *Hapa Japan: Constructing Global Mixed Race and Mixed Roots Identities and Representations*. Los Angeles: Ito Center and Kaya Press, University of Southern California.

Wingens, Matthias, Helga de Valk, Michael Windzio, and Can Aybek. 2011. "The Sociological Life Course Approach and Research on Migration and Integration." In *A Life-Course Perspective on Migration and Integration*, edited by M. Wingens, M. Windzio, H. d. Valk, and C. Aybek, 1–26. Dordrecht: Springer.

Yamanaka, Keiko. 1993. "New Immigration Policy and Unskilled Foreign Workers in Japan." *Pacific Affairs* 66(1): 72–90.

Yamashiro, Jane H. 2011. "Racialized National Identity Construction in the Ancestral Homeland: Japanese American Migrants in Japan." *Ethnic and Racial Studies* 34(9): 1502–1521.

———. 2017. *Redefining Japaneseness: Japanese Americans in the Ancestral Homeland*. New Brunswick, NJ: Rutgers University Press.

Yanagisako, Sylvia Junko. 1985. *Transforming the Past: Tradition and Kinship among Japanese Americans*. Stanford, CA: Stanford University Press.

Yoshino, Kosaku. 1992. *Cultural Nationalism in Contemporary Japan: A Sociological Enquiry*. London: Routledge.

13

Questioning the "World"

Millennial Generation Okinawan American Identity Matters

WESLEY IWAO UEUNTEN

Suddenly the world wasn't what I thought it was, it was meant
to be broken down, analyzed, fidgeted with and put back together.
—HELEN [PSEUDONYM]

This chapter addresses the topic of millennial generation Okinawan American (hereafter MGOA) identity. Stirred by the words from the dialogue with my MGOA colleague given in the epigraph to this chapter, I realize that Okinawan American identity requires breaking down, analyzing, and fidgeting with the world and putting it back together again. This task threatens the very ground upon which comfortable notions of the world are based. This paper is part of this task as the history of Okinawa has never been comfortable; it has been burdened with the role of being on the margins of the imperial reaches of both Japan and the United States, but central to both nations' efforts to gain and maintain global economic and military dominance.

"Okinawa" was a name, or signifier, that was imposed on the Ryukyu Kingdom by Japan as it exercised its modernized military strength to annex it in 1879. Okinawans refer to the period before its annexation by Japan in that year as *Tō nu yu* (唐ぬ世), or the "Chinese world," in reference to the Ryūkyū Kingdom's tributary relation to China from the fourteenth century. The period after annexation up to 1945 is called *Yamatu nu yu* (大和ぬ世), or the "Japanese world." Survivors of the destructive Battle of Okinawa that was fought between the United States and Japan at the end of World War II and resulted in the deaths of over one hundred thousand Okinawans have called it *Ikusa yu* (戦世), or the "world of war." The time of U.S. military rule over Okinawa that followed the Battle of Okinawa is known as *Amerika nu yu* (アメリカぬ世), or the "American world." Control over Okinawa reverted to Japan in 1972, but with the continued large presence of U.S. military bases in Okinawa, it becomes evident that since 1879, "Okinawa" has been inseparable from global militarization.

Personally, the topic of MGOA identity is problematic as I am not of the millennial generation. I was born at the tail end of the baby boom. I cannot claim with a clear conscience that I speak *for* or speak *about* millennial Okinawan Americans. Consequently, for this paper I have striven to speak *with* the MGOAs on the topic of our "Okinawan identity," which is the point of contact across our diversity. It was in this conversational or dialogic process that I encountered the statement presented at the beginning of this paper. This statement about deconstructing and constructing the world represents some of the revelations that came to me in the course of both speaking with MGOAs and reflecting over our conversations.[1]

If I were to sum up those revelations, I would include among them the seeds of a "paradigm shift" in the discourse over Okinawan identity among MGOAs. In other words, the very act of entering into discourses about their Okinawan identity brings MGOAs into a position to engage in breaking down, analyzing, and fidgeting with *the world* and putting it back together again. As much as this paper is an examination of Okinawan identity matters as they relate to MGOAs, it is also an assertion that MGOA identities do *matter*. MGOA identities *matter* because they are formed in a world order in which Okinawa continues to be a militarized colony and in which differences in race, class, gender, sexuality, and other attributes continue to shape people's life chances here in the United States. MGOA identities *matter* because world order rests on the assurance that questions about self are kept from questions regarding the place of one's self in the world order.

Discourse Analysis

Important to this essay is the relationship of MGOA identity to a "World Uchinanchu"[2] discourse. As will be described in greater detail later, the World Uchinanchu discourse has been crucial in the revival of Okinawan identity throughout the Okinawan diaspora, but it also obscures the continued militarization of Okinawa and thus enables Okinawans in the diaspora to the romanticize Okinawa as an unproblematized space in the globalized military order. Simultaneously, the World Uchinanchu informs and is informed by the idea of overseas Okinawan immigrants and their descendants as having attained "success" through uncomplaining hard work—an idea that masks the racial- and class-stratified societies that have adopted them.

A theoretical perspective on discourse is valuable in framing the conversation that I had with MGOAs within the milieu of the world—or World Uchinanchu discourse. Ironically, I had once held discourse analysis as a distraction away from such "concrete" issues as the ongoing superior-inferior relationship of the Japanese mainland over Okinawa since the Satsuma invasion of 1609 and the despotic structure of white supremacy that has shaped my diasporic existence in the United States of America—both of which are responsible for the continued desecration of my ancestral homeland of Okinawa for over seventy years through its forced accommodation of over 70 percent of the U.S. military facilities in Japan. However, I posit in this essay that a major struggle over diasporic Okinawan identity takes place within World Uchinanchu discourse, which has become hegemonic because it is the most widespread and dominant ideological discourse that currently shapes diasporic Okinawan identity. This discourse is also hegemonic in the sense that it obscures the aforementioned "concrete" issues that are endemic to the dominant hierarchical political, economic, social, and cultural structures within which diasporic Okinawans exist. In obscuring these concrete issues, this discourse allows such issues to escape our consciousness. Accordingly, a critical theoretical framework is utilized in this essay as a method to understand and analyze the problematic relationship between the concrete and discourse.

Discourse analysis is useful in studying Okinawan identity formation in that it takes place in the context of externally imposed meaning systems. On this point, I draw upon the work of Stuart Hall to help me understand the problematic relationship between the concrete and discourse. His work is appealing to me because he is a diasporic scholar attuned to a marginal existence in a world of meaning systems not of one's making. Hall is informative when he says, "It's only when . . . differences have been organized within language, within discourse, within systems of meaning, that the differences can be said to acquire meaning and become a factor in human culture and regulate conduct, that is the nature of what I'm calling the discursive concept of race. Not that nothing exists of differences, but that what matters are the systems we use to make sense, to make human societies intelligible. The system we bring to those differences, how we organize those differences into systems of meaning, with which, as it were, we could find the world intelligible" (Hall 1997, 10).

Because "Okinawa" was a name forced upon the former Ryukyu Kingdom in 1879, it exists in an externally imposed system of meanings in which I assert that "Okinawa" signifies racial and cultural difference. This deeply held difference lies behind the willingness of Japan to sacrifice Okinawa as a breakwater in the Battle of Okinawa and as the U.S. "keystone in the Pacific" in the postwar years. Adding to the lexical complexity of Okinawan identity is the fact that during its occupation and rule over Okinawa from 1945 to 1972, the U.S. military used the term "Ryukyu" instead of "Okinawa." Again, however, the imposition of "Ryukyu," the name of the former kingdom, signified the archipelago's racial and cultural difference from the rest of Japan. This difference was used as a justification for the U.S. military's forced separation of Okinawa from Japan and its dictatorship over it.

The system of meanings that frames World Uchinanchu discourse does include a discursive concept of race. It is difficult to argue against the fact that race is persistent in our Okinawan diasporic existence if we consider the ambiguity that remains over our cultural citizenship in the countries even though we may have legal citizenship there. Further, despite great efforts to deny it, Japanese do not consider Okinawans as bona fide members of the ethno-nation of Japan. As recently as the fall of 2016, a video recording of a young police officer sent from the Japanese mainland to deal with Okinawans protesting the construction of U.S. military heliports showed him calling the locals *dojin*, a derogatory term that has been used to refer to racially and culturally different (and therefore inferior) indigenous peoples in Japan's imperial territories including Ainu, Pacific Islanders, and Okinawans.

However, I draw attention to the fact that I am talking about an imposed system of meanings with a discursive concept of "culture" that coexists with race, often as a surrogate. On this topic, the writing of Arjun Appadurai (1996, 12) proves useful and inspiring. In *Modernity at Large: Cultural Dimensions of Globalization*, he points out that the problem of the noun form of "culture" is that it is "some kind of object thing, or substance, whether physical or metaphysical." He adds that "This substantialization seems to bring culture back into the discursive space of race, the very idea it was originally designed to combat." As I describe in the following section, World Uchinanchu discourse is characterized by such substantialization.

World Uchinanchu Discourse

As a prelude to my observations on MGOAs, I first present my analysis of World Uchinanchu discourse as the hegemonic space in which MGOA identity formation takes place. This analysis is based on my own long interest in my Okinawan identity and culture, which led me to live, study, and work in Okinawa and Japan and to be an active participant in diasporic Okinawan communities in Hawaiʻi, Kawasaki (Japan), and the San Francisco Bay Area as a student, performer, and teacher of Okinawan music and a member of various Okinawan cultural organizations.[3] In the following section, I talk about some important components of World Uchinanchu discourse as I experience and engage with it.

The World Uchinanchu Taikai (Conference)

It would be difficult to accurately and exhaustively describe World Uchinanchu discourse because of its variations over diasporic time and space. My description is at best an exercise in generalities, but I proceed for heuristic reasons. First, World Uchinanchu discourse posits that Okinawans are different from Japanese in terms of culture, personality, and, to some extent, genetics. Further, this discourse stresses that Okinawans who have migrated overseas and their descendants persistently retained their affinity to Okinawa despite the passage of time and acculturation to their host countries. It follows that the unique culture, personality, and genetics of Okinawan immigrants and their descendants led to their economic upward mobility in their host countries. Also, World Uchinanchu discourse emphasizes that the warm, friendly, and peace-loving nature of Okinawans made it possible for them to communicate better with people from other countries and cultures (than the cold, aloof, and martial Japanese).

It is difficult to determine when World Uchinanchu discourse began in earnest, but the conditions for it to develop emerged after reversion in 1972, when Okinawa experienced both newfound affluence from being included into one of the world's most powerful economies and anxiety over losing its unique culture and identity as a result of externally and internally imposed policies to assimilate into Japan politically, economically, and culturally. Government and business leaders in Okinawa began actively rekindling ties to the large overseas Okinawan diaspora. Some of the reasons for this included the strong Okinawan identity that overseas Okinawans, especially in South America and Hawai'i, retained. Also, many overseas Okinawans retained the Okinawan language and many traditions and customs that had been discontinued in Okinawa. Further, World Uchinanchu discourse formation could also be seen in Japan's discourse of *kokusaika*, or internationalization, which had moved into the public sphere by the 1980. This discourse was shaped by anxieties over Japan and was seen by the rest of the world, particularly the United States. This anxiety led to the notion that the people of Japan had a role in working toward a better understanding between Japan and the United States. Chris Oliver (2009, 52–53) writes, "That change would entail an important and unmistakable shift in kokusaika [internationalization] discourse toward 'culture' . . . and thus toward the 'soft' realm of human subjectivity."

In any case, a discourse about World Uchinanchu would have been established by the late 1980s because the first World Uchinanchu Taikai (or "Conference") was held in Okinawa in 1990. Since 1990, thousands of overseas Okinawans have been attending the Taikai (as it is commonly referred to by its participants), which are held every five years. The Taikai is unrivaled in its role as a focal point of World Uchinanchu discourse because it draws so many overseas Okinawans to it and involves large budgets to stage cultural performances, speeches, award ceremonies, banquets, and meetings.

The most crucial feature of the World Uchinanchu discourse that it is a system of meanings that is deeply intertwined with the aforementioned substantialization of "culture." It is this feature that has enabled it to gain a hegemonic position in Okinawan diasporic identity formation and has ensured that the World Uchinanchu Taikai remains the "mecca" for diasporic Okinawans wishing to confirm their identity.

From "Okinawan Renaissance" to "Model Minority"

Importantly, an "Okinawan renaissance" discourse emerged in Hawaiʻi, preceding the development of the World Uchinanchu discourse and later interacted on the nexus of substantialized "culture." Okinawan renaissance discourse appeared around the late 1970s as nisei and sansei Okinawans in Hawaiʻi who had influence with racial and ethnic movements in the rest of the United States began to search for and assert their Okinawan identity. This renaissance discourse was further informed by the "Hawaiian renaissance" that had already been transforming Hawaiian identity and culture from signs of shame to symbols of pride. Similarly, Okinawans in Hawaiʻi found pride in the uniqueness of their identity and culture. Further, ethnic studies courses at the University of Hawaiʻi and other higher education institutions on the histories of the immigrant groups that came to Hawaiʻi to labor in the sugar and pineapple industries helped bring newfound appreciation to the working-class history of which Okinawans had been a part. Consequently, Okinawan renaissance discourse was at least initially tied to a consciousness of racial, ethnic, and, to some extent, class inequalities in the United States and Hawaiʻi.

However, by the 1980s, the resurgence of pride in being Okinawan that was stimulated by racial and ethnic movements of the 1960s and 1970s gradually melded with the variant of the "model minority" discourse in Hawaiʻi that is based on a cultural explanation for socioeconomic inequalities. That is, the notion prevailed that Okinawans achieved success because Okinawan culture was a part of Japanese culture, which emphasized hard work, delayed gratification, and had deference for rules and authority. Success was proved by the plethora of politicians, business leaders, educators, athletes, and professionals with Okinawan roots in Hawaiʻi.

The coupling of Okinawan renaissance discourse in Hawaiʻi with model minority discourse from the 1980s resulted in its development as a discourse that steered away from active questioning of structures of inequality both locally and globally. The shared emphasis on substantialized culture of both Okinawa renaissance/model minority discourse and World Uchinanchu discourse enabled them to complement each other.

Wakamono Taikai

A major link of World Uchinanchu discourse to the MGOAs was the organization of Sekai Uchinanchu Wakamono Taikai (hereafter referred to as "Wakamono Taikai"), or World Uchinanchu Youth Conferences by the World Youth Uchinanchu Association (WYUA). The WYUA was formed at the 2011 World Uchinanchu Taikai by Okinawan youth from both Okinawa and the diaspora to address the needs of younger Okinawans interested in their identity and culture. The first Wakamono Taikai was held in Brazil in 2012, the second in Los Angeles in 2013, the third in Germany in 2014, and the fourth in the Philippines in 2015. This paper examines Okinawan identity formation among millennium generation Uchinanchu (Okinawan) Americans in the context of the World Youth Uchinanchu Association's (WYUA) Wakamono Taikai held July 18 to 21, 2013, in Los Angeles.

At the Los Angeles Wakamono Taikai, young Okinawans (ages eighteen to thirty-five) clearly expressed their Okinawan identity, as they assembled from different parts of the diaspora including Argentina, Bolivia, Brazil, England, Peru, Hawai'i, and the mainland United States. Venues for expression included the opening and closing ceremonies that featured performances of traditional and contemporary Okinawan dance and music, as well as participation in workshops and discussion sessions on various aspects of Okinawan history and culture.

The imprint of World Uchinanchu discourse is evident in the stated aims of the Brazil Wakamono Taikai that was held in 2012:

To inherit an identity as Uchinanchu
To inherit and preserve Okinawan history and culture
To expand and strengthen the Global Network of Youth Uchinanchu
To train new global leaders who will lead the next generations
To produce global people who will connect Okinawa and the foreign
   countries
To share and hold global understandings and values
To provide opportunities for Youth Uchinanchus to be globalized
   persons (WYUA 2012)

The listing of the first two stated aims, "to inherit an identity as Uchinanchu" and "to inherit and preserve Okinawan history and culture," manifests a sort of resistance to such forces as assimilationism, white supremacy, racism, and ethnonationalism that Okinawans throughout the diaspora may experience. While "global" appears most frequently in the aims of the Wakamono Taikai, "Uchinanchu identity" and "Okinawan history and culture" are at the top of the list because they have more affective power.

However, this resistance has its limits and dangers because it is based on a noun form of "culture" that is susceptible to being commodified and rendered politically irrelevant. This susceptibility was illustrated by what I observed the second day of the Wakamono Taikai when the first order of business was a speech by representative of Okinawa Family Mart, part of the large Japanese convenience store chain with corporate headquarters in mainland Japan and stores throughout the rest of Asia and one of the main sponsors of the Wakamono Taikai. In the speech, the publicity manager of Okinawa Family Mart gives a good example of the larger World Uchinanchu discourse and perhaps its strong relation to commercial interests: "In Ryukyu, we have beautiful nature and a culture that heals people's hearts. This culture is not superficial, but runs deep with human love, non-violence, bravery, and wisdom and we should preserve this culture. I also keep this in mind as I strive to preserve this culture in my work. It is on this point that we have expectations of you all. Gathered here today are young people who have inherited the Ryukyuan *kokoro* (spirit or heart). It does not matter if you are from Okinawa or are Okinawan because of ancestry or race and we want you to spread this non-violent circle of friendship to your regions or schools" (Kamiya 2013).[4]

The participants of the Taikai were then instructed in a simple dance to the pop beat of "Highway Number 508" for the filming of the Okinawa Family Mart commercial. The scene of the Wakamono Taikai participants dancing for a commercial shoot for a large convenience store chain with its home office in Tokyo was disconcerting from my own perspective as it raised questions about Okinawan youth becoming a spectacle for the gaze of others to draw attention away from the hierarchical political and economic relationship between Japan and Okinawa.

Rather than imagine "culture" as temporal, situational, and subject to human creation, it is taken as determinative of Okinawan identity. Moreover, while the word "identity" (*aidentiti* in Japanese and *identidade* in Portuguese and Spanish) is used quite often in World Uchinanchu discourse, it is used interchangeably with "culture." Discussions of "identity" are thus subsumed by a discourse around recovering and preserving "culture" with as much fidelity as possible to the original. Consequently, potentially critical ontological and political questions, such as "Who am I?" "Who are we?" "How did I get here?" and "How did we get here?" are crowded out by concerns over the authenticity and legitimacy of recovered "culture." Therefore, although it has a well-used vocabulary of "culture" and "identity," World Uchinanchu discourse has retained the structure of meanings of past discourses of racial differences between Okinawans and Japanese.

"Identity" Discourse and the Wakamono Taikai in Los Angeles

Despite my concerns about the depoliticized nature of World Uchinanchu discourse as it manifested at the Wakamono Taikai, a closer look and deeper reflection and analysis revealed a discourse that was a subtle counterdiscourse. This discourse focused on "identity" itself and was represented by MGOAs. It is uncomfortable to talk about a uniquely "American" counterhegemonic discursive flow as comes across as smug American exceptionalism and cultural imperialism. However, the identity discourse that I discuss here has its roots in something that we cannot gloat over as Americans: the fact that the ideology of race is still hegemonic in the United States. It remains an insidious part of our lives and experiences.

Simultaneously, identity discourse is part of a tradition of resistance to racism. It is a link between MGOAs and the centuries-old struggle against the malevolent intentions and effects of racism. From a discursive perspective, an important moment of this tradition was the "Great Transformation" that Michael Omi and Howard Winant (1994, 96) described as a development in the 1950s and 1960s in which a rearticulation of black collective subjectivity took place. The black movement "redefined the meaning of racial identity, and consequently of race itself, in American society." The theme of the 2013 Wakamono Taikai in Los Angeles was "identity." In his opening speech, Ichiro,[5] one of the main youth organizers of the Wakamono Taikai says, "Continuing on from the first festival, the theme from the last one was spreading the global network between young Okinawans across the world. For this year's theme, we chose the theme of 'identity.' For many Okinawans across the world, especially in America—a lot of people with Okinawan blood have almost no identity to the Okinawan part sometimes" (Ichiro in Kamiya 2013). This theme significantly broke with the theme of the previous Wakamono Taikai, which focused on "inheriting identity," "preserving culture," and strengthening a "global" Uchinanchu network. While its political nature may have been muted or obscured in the intervening years since the 1950s and 1960s, as seen in the previous excerpt, identity retains its power to provoke rearticulation, reinterpretation, and redefinition of self with reference to race.

Race was an omnipresent, but often a veiled, part of MGOA identity discourse. While none of the Uchinanchu American millennium speakers or participants of the Wakamono Taikai talked explicitly about experiences of blatant racism, it was clear that a level of discomfort for being "different" was a common theme. A sushi chef who was born in Okinawa and came to the United States at a young age with his family recalled in his speech how he returned to Okinawa straight out of high school to "party." As a musician, he participated in the music scene in Okinawa to promote his music and do stage shows at clubs. However, he seems to have experienced a sense of liberation of sorts from being different. He remembers, "Also, staying there at the time, I also learned my parents' background, you know, as an Uchinanchu ... the name 'Uehara' is pretty common in Okinawa. So I said, 'Oh, hey, there's Uehara here.' 'Oh, what's your name? Oh, Kevin Uehara. Oh, I'm Uehara; you're Uehara too!' So I felt great. For the first time in my life I felt proud of my last name 'Uehara.' So I don't have a problem anymore, you know? [If] they can't pronounce it, I pronounce it for them" (Uehara in Kamiya 2013).

John (pseudonym), a yonsei organizer of the Wakamono Taikai, recalled in an interview I did with him a year later (April 11, 2015) that although he did not experience blatant racism growing up in Gardena, California, where a sizeable population of Asian Americans lived, he had "rejected his Asian

Americanism." He explained, "It wasn't like blatant racism was going on, but it was more like internalized, I guess." From his elementary school years, he reported that he had "a feeling of being different" and, despite the large number of Asian students around him, he "felt alienated." He attributed it to the influence of the media in which there was very little Asian representation.

Interestingly, it was John's involvement in the video documentation of the one hundredth anniversary of the Okinawan Association of America (OAA) in 2009 that stimulated his interest in Okinawan identity, as expressed in his personal communication of April 11, 2015:

> It was interesting because for the first time, since I was videotaping, I actually had to pay very specific attention to what was going on. It was also interesting because the OAA doesn't . . . I feel like up to then . . . every year the OAA does a lot of *matsuri* stuff and picnics and performances, a lot of *geino* [traditional performance arts], but not so much history and identity and so for the first time I was hearing all of that. Like Uchinanchu identity and also there was the symposium with all the different kenjinkai around the United States and all of that was very eye-opening. And you had given a presentation at JANM [Japanese American National Museum] . . . All that stuff was eye-opening for me.

Probably a more compelling reason why race is salient in the lives of millennial Uchinanchu Americans is because most are of "mixed race." The following excerpt from a speech by Michiko, a mixed-race Okinawan woman college student, illustrates this point:

> I always felt that my name is a reflection of my identity. Not only because it conveys the two heritages that I come from, but also because it reminds me of my struggles to understand the person that I am. . . . When I started school, I had to endure several years of people mispronouncing my first name, just being utterly confused by it. And I thought, "I don't like being named Michiko. I wish I had a more American name that's easier to pronounce." And then a few years later I was conflicted again by my last name, and I thought I wanted to change it to Michiko Nakama so that I could fit in more with my Japanese family. (Michiko in Kamiya 2013)

The major factor in the prevalence of "mixed-race" millennial Uchinanchu Americans is the long-standing presence of the U.S. military in Okinawa, which has resulted in thousands of marriages between Okinawan women and American men of different races. The U.S. military presence in Okinawa creates even more layers of complexity in the identity formation of many millennial Uchinanchu Americans. In a long-distance email interview (March 26, 2015) of Helen (pseudonym), another organizer of the Wakamono Taikai several months later, I learned of her father's complicated past. Her father was "biracial" and had been born in Okinawa. He had been put up for adoption at age three, but was returned to the orphanage for unknown reasons. He was later adopted by an African American couple and brought to the United States at around the age of seven. For understandable reasons, her father did not share his experience as an adoptee from Okinawa: "My father always told us we were half Hawaiian. He spent some of his childhood in Hawai'i and I think he felt at home there. He blended in. It was how he made sense of his roots, and it enabled him to ignore the painful complexities of being an adoptee. I also think that he thought he was making it simpler for us. Shielding us from having to tell long complicated stories about who we were to other people when they asked—and let's be real, people asked ALL THE TIME."

The complicated past of Helen's family was channeled into her leadership in the Gajumaru Family Tree Project at the Wakamono Taikai in which the participants were asked to create family trees and presented them to others. In introducing the project to the participants, she declared, "Our families are the center of our culture. That's where we get the idea of 'Uchinanchu spirit.' And yet, all of us come from different places, but our roots go back to Okinawa in one way or another" (Helen in Kamiya 2013). Interestingly, rather than invest all power to culture, she places the family at the center of culture. By doing this, she allows for the possibility of families, even those with "mixed" genealogies, to exercise agency in the interpretation of their identity.

Helen then instructed the participants to get in small groups to share their family trees with the hope that they could learn from each other about our "diaspora and global community." Through her poised leadership, she had the participants enthusiastically share their family trees with others, and in her wrap-up speech, she said,

> The purpose of this activity, and hopefully you found it, was to bond with your group mates to learn something about each other. But also to understand that, we all have very, very different histories. . . . So while we all have Uchinanchu origin, how we came to the places we are today, are very different and so sometimes that can bring challenges, but more importantly it brings a lot of wealth. And so, we are different from Uchinanchu—at least those of us in the diaspora— than people who live in Okinawa. When we go to places like Brazil, when we go to Peru—I'm from D.C.—we learn new and different things and that doesn't make us less Uchinanchu. If our parents marry someone who is not Okinawan, it doesn't mean that their children are less Uchinanchu—just different. And so I think the purpose

of this was for us to learn about what are all the different resources and talents and histories that we all bring to the table and that as we move forward, thinking what will our community look like into the future, to really utilize these things. In my group, we had a graphic designer, I had people whose grandparents experienced internment, people whose grandparents were adventurers and went to a bunch of different countries and decided to go back to Okinawa. And we even had a descendant of a princess. (Heather in Kamiya 2013)

The eloquence with which Helen expressed her ideas about the complexities of Uchinanchu identity is a reflection of the highly developed interpretation of the racial conditions in which she and others at the Wakamono Taikai lived in as racially different persons in the United States. This interpretation can also be seen as a testament of the lasting effects of people of color questioning their identity from within white supremacy, such as during the "Great Transformation," on millennial Uchinanchu Americans in that it provided a vocabulary for speaking of racial differences. That vocabulary included such words as "identity" as well as "culture," "heritage," and "diaspora," that enabled them to talk about the racial differences that were part of their existence. More importantly, however, the Great Transformation created a framework for talking about identity in terms of a "process" in which they interpreted their existence. Michiko, who spoke about her identity as a reflection of her name, talks about the process in which "it has just been growing up and being comfortable with my name has coincided with becoming more comfortable as I am as a person." Her ideas were further elaborated: "I am not just one thing. I am many things. And I am not just a collection of many things randomly glued together, because I am more than the sum of my ethnicities and my likes and dislikes and my limitations and my goals. And if this sounds contradictory, it is. While my philosophy professor would probably fail me for coming up with such a contradictory theory, my personal identity has embraced it. . . . I am one thing and many things and so are all of us, whether or not you are multiracial" (Kamiya 2013).

In the same vein, Helen later wrote to me (March 26, 2015) about her "alienating and strange" experience at George Washington University:

I didn't fit the mold but eventually found a home in women's studies. A course on the anthropology of gender my freshmen year changed me forever. Suddenly, the world wasn't what I thought it was, it was meant to be broken down, analyzed, fidgeted with and put together. Sadly, critical thinking was new to me, but this is partially what sparked my renewed interest in Okinawa and being Okinawan. I wondered about my grandmother, who she might be, how her life might have been affected by the military, about the generation of kids

like my dad who'd been systematically tossed aside . . . I began reading everything I could on Okinawa and on sex-work and gendered
relations between East Asian communities and the military bases.
My identity became more specific. I was no longer mixed or Hawaiian or "Asian." I became Okinawan and American.

Other glimpses of critical consciousness manifested themselves among the
millennials. John recalled in my interview with him that in one of the small
group sessions at the Wakamono Taikai, a discussion on "What makes an
Uchinanchu?" took place. Some of the group answered that "Uchinanchu"
should not be defined on whether or not one has "Uchinanchu blood" and that
it should be defined more on "participating in the culture." However, in the
same group, the issue of "cultural appropriation" in the context of Japan and
the U.S. oppression over Okinawa was brought up. John said he could sympa-
thize with the first argument about not defining "Uchinanchu" by blood, but
he did agree that the issue of "cultural appropriation" needed to be discussed
along with the historical and contemporary issues involving Okinawa.

Both Helen and John recalled that the discussions at the Wakamono
Taikai were civil and did not rise to the level of debate. Even in my observations, I noticed that a hegemonic notion of a shared culture of solidarity and
harmony had a profound effect on the Wakamono Taikai. For example, the
organizers of the Wakamono Taikai initially hesitated to include the topic of
the U.S. military base presence in Okinawa at the taikai as it would potentially invite controversy and heated debate among different perspectives.
After much discussion, of which I was a part, the organizers decided to include a panel on it, and I was asked to be the moderator for the panel and
discussion session. To avoid controversy, we used the title "Social Issues" for
the panel rather than explicitly refer to the U.S. military bases.

I remember that the session did involve some debate about the necessity
of U.S. military bases in Okinawa. English was the dominant language used
in the session, and this factor no doubt shaped the dialogue as the debate was
mainly between MGOAs. Over twenty people were packed in the room. A
handful of participants spoke up in the dialogue, and most were largely
critical of the presence of U.S. military bases in Okinawa, but I recall that a
younger MGOA woman expressed her strong opinion that the bases ensured
stability in Asia. I also recall that the last comment made was by a mixed-
race Okinawan American who had been born in Okinawa and moved to the
United States as a teenager. He spoke about how complicated the issue was
for him because he went through a period after coming to the United States
of despising everything about Americans because of the base presence in
Okinawa. He had since gotten over his negative feelings toward America
after living in Texas and making many friends, but he seemed to be pointing
out how the issue has deep emotional ramifications for him. Years later, as I

write this, I regret that the session ended before we could follow up on his comments, along with the comments of others in the session.

Organizing a session on the controversial topic of U.S. military presence in Okinawa involved negotiation with the World Uchinanchu discourse that emphasized a shared culture of harmony, but from my study of the MGOAs I have learned that there is a lot more going within the discourse. As seen from the personal narratives, both private and public, Okinawan identity cannot be separated from an ongoing history of militarized colonization of the homeland and racial, class, and gender hierarchies in the United States. In response to my question, "What kind of emotional ties do you have to Okinawa?" Helen wrote the following in a personal communication (March 26, 2015): "To be honest, the emotional tie is one of angst around the base issue. I feel fondness towards my family there but due to language and cultural barriers it doesn't go past that. I mostly feel angry and impotent—both the American and Okinawan sides of me feel this way."

I find hope that the discourse of identity that has formed in the United States through the questioning of the racial order in which it exists might be linked to the search for meaning that Ichiro expresses in his opening speech at the Wakamono Taikai: "It [Okinawan identity] is very, you know, vague. A lot of times [Okinawans] go through an identity crisis to try to figure out what they are. And what we wanted was for people to see what your identity was. What does it mean? Where did you really come from?" (Ichiro in Kamiya 2013). I conclude that such questions come out of an Okinawan diasporic genealogy, of which I share with MGOAs, of having externally imposed systems of meaning in which our identities are marginalized, ambiguous, and unstable. A danger exists, however, when we try to find acceptance and establish a more tangible and permanent Okinawan identity within a hegemonic World Uchinanchu identity discourse that rests on a notion of culture as a thing. In doing so, Okinawan identity itself also becomes inert matter in that it accepts those imposed systems of meaning rather than seek or create meaning. I am heartened by the fact that MGOAs have continued to ask questions related to their uncertain identities, because it is through questioning that systems of meaning and the "world" itself that Okinawan identity matters.

NOTES

1. Research for this paper relied on personal interactions and interconnections with millennial Okinawan Americans and included my participant observation at the Wakamono Taikai in 2013 as a consultant, speaker, and facilitator; follow-up phone and email conversations with organizers and participants; and content analysis of video footage of the Wakamono Taikai.

2. "Uchinanchu" is the Okinawan pronunciation of the Japanese term *Okinawa no hito*. The more accurate pronunciation is actually "Uchinaachu" (with a prolonged vowel after the *n*), but the pronunciation of Okinawans in Hawai'i seems to have become the most accepted.

3. My initial active involvement with the Okinawan cultural activities in Hawai'i started in the early 1980s when I began learning Okinawan dance from an Okinawan issei man who had come to my island of Kauai through the Crystal City Internment Camp. He was one of over two thousand Japanese Latin Americans who had been forcibly brought to the United States during World War II. This initial contact led to my joining an Okinawan cultural organization called the Young Okinawans of Hawai'i in 1982. I later went to Okinawa in 1984 on an Okinawan Prefectural scholarship for overseas Okinawans to study at the University of the Ryukyus. I stayed in Okinawa for two years, during which time I studied traditional Okinawan music and did research on Okinawan ancestor worship, while doing a self-study of the Okinawan language. It was during this time that I first met and made friends with Okinawans from Argentina, Bolivia, Brazil, Canada, and Peru. From 1989 to 1995, I lived near Tokyo, Japan, where I did research on Okinawan identity and culture in mainland Japan and later on South American Okinawans who were coming to Japan in large numbers to work as laborers. During that time, I commuted on a weekly basis to study Okinawan music in Kawasaki, where a large, mainly working-class community of Okinawans lived. From 1997 to the present, I have also been an officer of the San Francisco Okinawa Kenjin Kai and a participant in three World Uchinanchu Taikai.

4. The Japanese term that the speaker used for "culture" was *bunka*.

5. Pseudonyms are used for all informants mentioned or quoted in this paper.

REFERENCES

Appadurai, Arjun. 1996. *Modernity at Large: Cultural Dimensions of Globalization.* Minneapolis: University of Minnesota Press.

Hall, Stuart. 1997. "Race, The Floating Signifier." Northampton, MA: Media Education Foundation. Accessed March 15, 2017. https://www.mediaed.org/assets/products /407/transcript_407.pdf. Transcript.

Kamiya, Joey, videographer/editor. 2013. "World Youth Uchinanchu Festival Los Angeles California 2013." DVD for home/personal use only.

Oliver, Chris. 2009. "Kokusaika, Revisited: Reinventing 'Internationalization' in Late 1960s Japan." *Sophia Junior College Faculty Journal* 29:47–54.

Omi, Michael, and Howard Winant. 1994. *Racial Formation in the United States: From the 1960s to the 1990s.* 2nd ed. New York: Routledge.

World Youth Uchinanchu Association (WYUA). 2012. "The 1st World Youth Uchinanchu Festival in Brazil 2012." Okinawa: WYUA. Accessed March 15, 2017. http:// wyua.okinawa/wp-content/uploads/2012/06/boshu_eng.pdf.

14

Uniting Hapas

The Global Communities of Mixed-Race Nikkei on YouTube

LORI KIDO LOPEZ

A s with all racial and ethnic collectives, the community encompassed by the term "Japanese American" has undergone significant changes in recent decades and must be recognized as fluid and shifting. Given the high levels of outmarriage for Japanese Americans (Pew Research Center 2012) and the multiracial/multiethnic/multicultural children that are produced in such marriages, Japanese American millennials constitute a particularly flexible collective. Nearly eighty thousand individuals who identify as Japanese American have only one parent of Japanese descent, and their families identify in multiple ways (U.S. Census Bureau 2010). The national boundaries denoted by the term "American" within the category of "Japanese American" are also subject to questioning, as many individuals of Japanese descent identify with multiple nations, cultures, and geographic communities. For Nikkei, or members of the global Japanese diaspora, the boundaries of their ethnic and national communities may be blurry, but they still play an important role in shaping lived experiences and identities. This chapter explores the meaning of these categories and the specificities of their stories through conducting a textual analysis of YouTube channels that tell the stories of mixed-race Nikkei millennials.

Media representations of marginalized communities serve an important role in shaping how individuals see themselves and how others understand their identities and stories, particularly for communities undergoing the demographic shifts that we see in the global Japanese diaspora. In this chapter, I focus on media that are created by mixed-race Nikkei who utilize new media to portray their own stories using their own voices. YouTube's user-created channels provide a rich site for exploring the changing contours of Japanese American millennial identifications through the preponderance of "vlogs," or personal video blogs. While digital spaces such as these can host a wide variety of content (including mainstream promotional or corporate content), YouTube is often heralded for allowing everyday consumers to upload their own videos and share them with a wide audience. The genre of the vlog consists of amateur videos used to convey the user's own personal story, relying on his or her own personality and narrative to attract viewers. With 72 percent of U.S. millennials using YouTube (eMarketer 2015), examinations of Japanese American vlogs largely center around users age eighteen to thirty and can give much insight into the daily lives of these participants. Through investigating the YouTube vlogs of collectives that include many mixed-race Japanese Americans, we can better understand what it means to be Japanese American in the twenty-first century—both in terms of the multiracial, transnational, diasporic identities that are embodied by these individuals and the way that they express these identities through their personal narratives.

This investigation serves to remind us that when we study millennial Japanese Americans, we must continue to question both the ethnic and national borders of this community. The online activities of those who are active within mixed-race spaces clearly reify the salience of their identity as Japanese Americans, but that identity is simultaneously reflective of ethnic and national hybridities. Indeed, what we see in these YouTube communities are millennial Japanese Americans who are actively reaching out toward mixed-race Japanese all over the world because they believe that they share important commonalities. For today's mixed-race Japanese Americans, it is not only the commonality of Japanese American culture that connects them to one another, but experiences of hybridity and the complexity of negotiating a relationship to one's global positioning that is most salient and meaningful. From the networks and affinities we see developing in digital spaces, we can more clearly reposition mixed-race Japanese Americans within a diasporic framework of mixed-race Nikkei, rather than relying solely upon frameworks of nation as sites for belonging, identification, and the construction of ethnic community.

Examining YouTube's Mixed-Race Communities

This examination centers on the content of two different YouTube channels, HapaUnited and Max D. Capo. These channels were selected because they both focus explicitly on mixed-race Asian communities, but have a wide variety of posts specifically on mixed-race Japanese Americans/Nikkei[1] millennials and their experiences. While many YouTube videos discuss a broad array of mixed-race experiences, these two channels include over fifty videos that discuss the experiences of being mixed-race Nikkei. The content of these videos and their accompanying comments are examined in this chapter. I ask how the affordances of digital participation in YouTube communities shape the way that mixed-race Nikkei millennials are connecting to those who are similar to them and to those who are different from them, and how these online communities complicate our understanding of mixed-race Japanese American experiences. In exploring the videos posted to these channels, I argue that an apparently new form of diasporic community has come about through a deliberate performance of highlighting similarities and common experiences across communities of mixed-race Japanese and mixed-race Japanese Americans.

HapaUnited is a community whose content reflects the diversity of its many members. It was founded in 2011 by six individuals who identified as "hapa," which they define as being part Asian or half Asian. In their first video, they state that they wanted to create a space for other hapas to come together and discuss the issues that affected them. The role of "moderator" was then opened up to any interested members, and these moderators served to populate the channel with personal video blogs discussing whatever issue was of interest to them. Most of the videos from this channel elaborate very straightforwardly on the topic of the strengths and weaknesses of being hapa; causes for pride and celebration, as well as common problems, frustrations, and negative experiences. Although not all of the individuals from this community are ethnically Japanese, of the twenty-seven moderators, at least eleven identify themselves as part-Japanese (of these, eight live in the United States), and together they contributed over thirty videos to the channel. Those who state their age are all in their teens and twenties, and the tone of the conversation is decidedly youthful, focusing on the identity-development process for adolescent and college-aged hapas.

The other channel examined in this study is Max D. Capo, the personal channel for a mixed-race Japanese American millennial who was born and raised in North Carolina but moved to Tokyo during college and lived there for four years. Capo, who is in his mid-twenties, is fluent in Japanese and often works as an actor or media personality when he lives in Japan. He has posted around sixty videos since 2008 that range from humorous sketches (in the mode of Asian American YouTubers such as NigaHiga and Kevjumba) to videos that give tips about things such as acting or living in Japan. Yet he also often states that he wants his YouTube channel to serve as a hub for building community for hapas, and to that end he has a regular segment called "Hapa Hour" that currently has eight videos that are each around ten minutes long and focus specifically on hapa issues. These videos are always shot with a cohost who also identifies as hapa, and together they discuss common hapa experiences. Capo has also posted eight videos under the topic of "Other Japanese/Half Japanese Themes" that include discussions of being half Japanese within the context of life in Japan and life in the United States.

In examining the videos of HapaUnited and Max D. Capo about hapa experiences, it is important to first consider the use of the term *hapa*. This Native Hawaiian term stems from the term *hapa haole*, which referred to the mixed-race Native Hawaiians who resulted from miscegenation. In the early 2000s, there was a call to reclaim the term to be used exclusively for mixed-race Native Hawaiians, and indeed, an uncritical use of this term can inadvertently serve to erase the experiences of indigenous Hawaiians (Bernstein and De La Cruz 2008). Yet, as we can see in the naming of these YouTube channels and their content, many individuals throughout the United states continue to identify as hapa with much pride and affection (Taniguchi and Heidenreich 2005)—a troubling instance of a minority community striving for empowerment without regard for the histories of oppression and settler colonialism that may be obscured in doing so. Indeed, many videos on these two channels specifically discuss the personal significance of using this term. For instance, vloggers admit that they often did not know the term "hapa" existed until they joined a YouTube community, but that they are now happy to use this term in order to connect with other like-minded individuals. Max D. Capo tells the story of how he learned about the word "hapa" in 2011 when Asian American YouTuber David Choi used that word to describe him and that a woman told him and his half Japanese friend that they looked alike. Although they were both confused by the term at the time, this moment served to awaken him to the fact that hapas shared a common identity that was connected to common experiences such as this one. Later when he decided to make YouTube videos about his "24 years of experience as a half Japanese person," he started asking other friends about their common experiences. He used the name "Hapa Hour," but as he states, "I just borrowed this term for the sake of being able to share this video and have it easily understood as half Asian as well as half Japanese, so I hope I didn't really offend anyone" (Capo 2014). Although no discussion has taken place on either site of the contested use of this term for Native Hawaiians, it is clear that the participants see their use of "hapa" as one of empowerment and pride.

Who Are Mixed-Race Japanese Americans?

The growing population of mixed-race Japanese Americans has long been of interest to scholars within ethnic studies. In Rebecca Chiyoko King's (1997) investigation of Queen Pageants at the Cherry Blossom Festival in San Francisco's Japantown, she finds that the increasing participation of mixed-race candidates in the pageant remind us that what it means to be Japanese American is constantly changing. Pageant contestants evidence the fact that mixed-race Japanese Americans are forced to continually authenticate their ethnic identities in response to the perceptions of others that they do not fully belong. But at the same time, the Japanese American community also is in the process of changing to accommodate its shifting racial makeup and the increasing presence of mixed-race families. This process of continual change is also seen in documentary films about mixed-race Japanese Americans, such as those examined by Shima Yoshida (2013). He finds that documentary films exploring mixed-race Japanese American identity are often grounded in the impact of World War II on Japanese American families, which is often seen as the impetus for outmarriage and the creation of interracial families. Beyond the impact of the war, Yoshida also finds common ground across the documentaries in terms of narratives of assimilation into mainstream American culture, the loss of Japanese language and culture, and feelings of not physically appearing the way that they identified. These discussions of mixed-race Japanese American identifications must also be understood as continually in motion, as mixed-race Japanese Americans in particular undergo a long-term process of developing their identities in relation to their environments and communities (Collins 2000).

This research on mixed-race Japanese Americans can be contrasted with investigations of "hafu," or mixed-race Japanese individuals living in Japan. Indeed, the sociocultural context of Japan is not the same as the United States, and thus the experiences of mixed-race individuals are shaped in distinctive ways. For instance, Sara Oikawa and Tomoko Yoshida (2007) find that the expectation for homogeneity in Japan leads to considerable discrimination and shame, with many mixed-race Japanese individuals wishing they could just be treated like a "normal Japanese" (645). As with mixed-race Japanese Americans, these experiences often shift over time, with other researchers (e.g., Oshima 2014) finding that older hafu can come to feel that being of mixed race in Japan is an asset because it can garner popularity and positive attention, or can reflect a shift toward a more multicultural Japan. Shifting representations of hafu in Japanese media reflect both the marginality and celebration of cultural hybridity, particularly when considering the treatment of African American–Japanese blending, such as with the hafu star Jero, who sings Japanese traditional music called enka (Fellezs 2012). The cultural, social, and historical differences described in these studies remind us that the context of the United States and Japan are very different in shaping the way that identities are developed and experienced. Indeed, studies of Japanese American people and studies of Japanese people are quite different, and this logic follows in considering mixed-race Japanese Americans and mixed-race Japanese.

Yet in investigating the YouTube communities that form around mixed-race identities, we often see the forging of connections between these different populations—not because there are no important differences, but because these two populations have a strong desire to form a common identity and community via this digital medium. While much research on multiracial people agrees that adolescence and young adulthood are important moments for exploring and coming to terms with one's racial identity (Renn 2004), this examination of participation in online communities captures some of the ways that these explorations are manifested through the active participation of those who see a meaningful connection to one another. Mixed-race Nikkei are clearly using online communities such as those found on YouTube to work through their changing relationships to their own concept of race, ethnicity, culture, and family, because they feel that these communities offer a safe space for exploring, processing, and garnering support for these different facets of their lives. In the following sections, I first explore the affordances of YouTube for creating digital mixed-race communities and trace the affinities of those communities through analyzing the videos of mixed-race Japanese participants. I then conclude with a discussion of the idea that mixed-race Japanese American identities are fluid and ever-changing, even to the point of becoming banal, but that their diasporic configurations nonetheless help to point us in new directions for understanding the significance of forging meaningful and potentially transformative communities across racial, cultural, and national differences.

Building Virtual Communities around Mixed-Race Identities

As a site for uploading and sharing video with the motto "Broadcast Yourself," YouTube might seem like an unlikely space for building community. Yet researchers have found that despite the potential for users to merely passively consume content or to narcissistically promote their own videos, YouTube users revel in the opportunity to connect to other users (Lange 2008). Their participation in creating and sharing videos facilitates community building in terms of "the feeling of companionship, the ability to create meaningful relationships and practices, and even a sense of emotional attachment to 'their' site" (Rotman and Preece 2010, 330). In an investigation of the way that Inuit youth are using YouTube, Nancy Wachowich and Willow Scobie (2010) find that they use their fragmented videographies and visual excerpts of everyday life to create new online and offline social networks. Such outcomes are particularly meaningful for those who are geographically or socially isolated, as "storytellers might be by themselves in front of their cameras in their bedrooms at home, but on YouTube they are not alone" (100). This aspect of community creation seems to be a central motivation for those who participate in HapaUnited, particularly given that it is a group channel that is constantly inviting new participants to play a role in shepherding its continued growth. Many videos specifically discuss the fact that users enjoy meeting other hapas through the channel, such as this post: "I was curious if you guys were interested in talking on Messengers and stuff, cuz I really like making new friends, and that goes for anybody else too. I've had a few people who watch these videos comment to my profile and they talk to me and they've become my friend on Messenger and Skype and MSN and stuff. And that's cool because I like making new friends and stuff" (Hapa-United 2011). Beyond discussions within the videos themselves of the relationships that are developing, there are often dozens (sometimes hundreds) of comments following each video with new users introducing themselves and affirming a connection to the discussion at hand. The moderators often respond to the comments, particularly when the comment is related to the content of the specific video, rather than the extremely frequent posting of individuals simply stating their own racial backgrounds in the comments. While the more popular channels on YouTube fund their programming through the monetization of viewership (Kim 2012), the site remains free to use (and free from advertisements) for relatively small communities such as those on HapaUnited. This openness does not erase the general desire for participants to create desirable content and sustain meaningful connections with their viewers—on the contrary, the lack of monetary reward simply contributes to the creation of a different economy of supply and demand based on the individual's ability to communicate clearly their identity and value (Banet-Weiser 2011).

In considering the unique affordances of YouTube, we can also consider the differences between YouTube videos about mixed-race Japanese communities and documentaries or other forms of traditional broadcast media. As mentioned earlier, there have been many explorations of mixed-race Japanese families and individuals within documentary film, including *Hafu: The Mixed Race Experience in Japan* (2013), *One Big Hapa Family* (2010), *Hapa: One Step at a Time* (2001), *and Doubles: Japan and America's Intercultural Children* (1995). Yet each documentary narrative must be understood as serving to capture a moment in time and rendering it a static portrait, in order to educate viewers about the way that things were. We can particularly note the many years that it takes to shoot, edit, and distribute a traditional documentary. Furthermore, the structure of a documentary film is such that it has a beginning, a middle, and an end. Although YouTube vlogs can similarly be seen to memorialize a single moment as part of a historical record, we must also recognize that the constantly growing and shifting communities that serve to collectively produce YouTube's narrative database provide a way for stories to continually shift and be updated in real time. When users interact with a YouTube channel, they are free to watch videos in any order with little imposed direction as to the flow from one video to the next—they can watch videos that are grouped by moderator, by topic, by the date posted, or any other organizing mechanism. This flow is always changing, since there always remains the possibility that new videos can be added, or that users will add new comments to the videos that enliven new conversations and dialogues.

The Evolving Construction of Hapa on YouTube

Within these YouTube communities centered around hapa issues, we can see many specific illustrations of this potential for growth and change, rather than stasis. At the most basic level, we can see many participants on HapaUnited encountering the word "hapa" for the first time when they create their video for the site. Their lack of familiarity with this term is evidenced in their shifting pronunciation—from "happa" to "hoppa"—as they post later videos. A few of the participants include videos where they apologize for pronouncing the word wrong and thank commenters for correcting their pronunciation. Max D. Capo and his "Hapa Hour" cohosts make a similar mistake, which he explains in one video: "We got a lot of flak, you know I actually read all those YouTube comments. Like people are saying you're pronouncing 'hapa' wrong. I know, I know it's wrong . . . I was used to half, hafu, halfie, just half Japanese, it wasn't really like big enough of a thing that I thought there was a coined word for it. Hapa, I kind of learned about this word about three years ago" (Capo 2014). His explanation reveals the fact that he did not grow up identifying as hapa, but that he has just begun using the word to describe himself and connecting to other hapas through his participation on YouTube. This simple mistake in pronunciation is a reminder that many of these individuals are not already part of either mixed-race or Japanese American communities; they are learning about these communities and their role in shaping identities as they are posting these videos.

The idea of "hapa" has always been a somewhat nationalistic identity that has been taken up by those who are partially Asian, but who are primarily within the U.S. context. This Americentrism is also prevalent within discussions of mixed race on HapaUnited and Max D. Capo, particularly when we take into consideration that the language being used is English. This reliance on English serves to exclude those living in Japan who do not speak English, and thus causes us to consider whose voices are represented in these online communities. For instance, the documentary *Hafu: The Mixed Race Experience in Japan* (2013) includes the voices of those who have one parent who is Japanese and one parent who is Venezuelan, Ghanaian, or Korean, and their interviews are conducted in Japanese. This reminds us that when English is the primary language used within an online community, participation is limited to only some mixed-race individuals. Both HapaUnited and Max D. Capo center on participation by those who are American or living in an English-speaking country. Despite this Americentrism and guiding participation from mixed-race Japanese Americans, these online communities are still finding many ways to extend the borders of this community and thereby to redefine what it means to be mixed-race Nikkei.

Alone Together: Mixed-Race Japanese as Hapa

We can better understand how mixed-race Nikkei experiences are participating in these online communities by further exploring the specific content of their videos. One of the first things that we can note is that nearly all of the participants on HapaUnited (including all of the part-Japanese contributors) initiate themselves into the community with an introductory video that affirms a common set of experiences. Following is an excerpt from an introductory video that explicitly does so, particularly focusing on the way that this contributor came to understand her own racial identity as different from those around her, which was uncomfortable and even distressing:

> I think for the most part, growing up as a hapa is pretty much the same for everyone. Just, maybe at different times and whatnot. I'm pretty sure that's what really makes people be able to be closer to other hapas is that they're the same. But I'll still give you a bit of a story anyway. When I was little, I would grow up around Japanese people. As a child I didn't notice it, I didn't notice race, as I got older I would start to feel uncomfortable or like I didn't fit in. I always felt too big or too small. If I was at my Japanese friend's house, I would feel like a foreign friend, a white foreign friend. If I was at my non-Asian friend's house, I would feel like the foreign friend! No matter where I would go, I was always the foreign friend. So I couldn't really escape that and I started to feel not accepted anywhere. (HapaUnited 2012b)

This video serves to affirm and reify a set of shared experiences around feelings of being the racial "other" that are familiar for many hapas. Although she references her specific experiences as a mixed-race Japanese American in her story, she clearly indicates that she doesn't feel that this ethnic or national identity is significant—on the contrary, her feelings of foreignness are meant to be understood as universal for all hapas, regardless of ethnic specificities.

The universality of these narratives across national contexts is also indicated through the absence of familiar Japanese American generational terms such as issei, nisei, sansei, or yonsei. The failure to identify with this generational tradition is in line with James Fuji Collins's (2012) finding that bicultural Japanese Americans feel more comfortable identifying with the term "Nikkei" because it connotes a sense of multiple identities that are less fixed within a single context. Although none of the hapas on YouTube use the term

"Nikkei" to identify themselves (as mentioned throughout, the term "hapa" and identification with a Japanese parent are the only ascribed identities), it is useful, nevertheless, to orient this discussion around a term that is flexible yet can apply to mixed-race Japanese across the globe.

We can see a similar inclination toward creating a unifying narrative across hapa experiences in Max D. Capo's early videos as well. His first "Hapa Hour" video, partnered with his half-Japanese friend Shizuka, is called "12 Things Half Japanese (half Asian) People Get All the Time." The name alone indicates that there is a focus on their specific experiences as mixed-race Japanese Americans, but that the video has a broader aim of widening its relevance to all half Asian people. Their list includes questions such as "What are you?" and "Which half are you more of?" as well as accusations about not looking Japanese or white "enough," about being exotic, and assumptions that the mother is Japanese and the father is white. While these descriptions are clearly ethnically specific—and even can be connected to specific sociohistorical constructs, such as the prevalence of marriage between white soldiers and Japanese women (Murphy-Shigematsu 2001)—the two hosts want to frame their experiences as universal across all hapas.

The predominance of these homogenizing discourses helps us to better understand the meaning of mixed-race Japanese American participation in these YouTube communities. The online testimony of mixed-race people serves to construct a common identity through reinforcing pride in their mixed-race experiences, as well as through marking the singularity of these experiences as a unique identity. This kind of storytelling is a common practice for those seeking to build identity-based affinities; for instance, members of South Asian student clubs have also been seen to downplay differences despite observable in-group differences (Shrikant 2015). In these YouTube videos, mixed-race participants affirm the common experiences of feeling like an outsider, being uncomfortable with the questions that others so often ask about their appearance and background, and struggling to develop a cohesive identity. We can clearly see that mixed-race individuals feel a strong desire to assert their existence within a world that is indefatigably biased toward assumptions of monoraciality, and where their identities are constantly being questioned and undermined. Yet we can also consider the fact that it is important for hapas to collectively articulate the commonalities of this identity in the face of extreme heterogeneity—after all, the collective of mixed-race peoples, even if narrowed to only those who are part-Asian, is a vastly diverse community. It includes individuals whose identities comprise an infinite array of ethnic, racial, cultural, generational, linguistic, class, religious, and other identifications. If scholars of race and ethnicity must continually point to the diversity contained within a single racial category such as Asian American or African American, this acknowledgment is doubly true for mixed-race communities. In the face of such clear heterogeneity, it makes sense then that many mixed-race individuals can feel isolated and alienated amid the process of racial identity development and seek to reach out to others who share even the barest similarity of experience.

Boundary-Crossing in the Nikkei Diaspora

For mixed-race Nikkei in these videos, we can also see the significance and salience of connecting to the Japanese diaspora, rather than restricting their community within the borders of the United States or North America. As mentioned earlier, the use of English language in both of these communities certainly privileges the participation of Americans and those whose heritage includes an American parent. Yet we also see a vibrant contingent of participants from all over the globe. Of those who are part-Japanese, we can see participants who are half Japanese and half English (princesspinkypeach), half Japanese and half New Zealander (ItsLisaDoll), as well as half Japanese and half Greek (Pinkribbonsxo). These three participants identified speak English with the accents of their native British, New Zealander, and Greek homelands, which serves to position them globally amid the other American-accented speakers. ItsLisaDoll, from New Zealand, discusses how hapas fit into various social groups. She described her own happiness at being accepted by Japanese students in New Zealand: "At my school, the Japanese people invite me along to stuff, which is really cool. Even though I'm half I'm still included. They actually gave me a nickname, 'Champon,' which is like a noodle mixture dish, a mixture of things, and I think that's sort of making reference to my nationality, I'm a mixture of things, half Japanese, half New Zealander." This brief anecdote reminds us that there are many national and ethnic identities at play in the lives of mixed-race Nikkei, even as such stories speak to common experiences. Beyond including these diasporic participants among their ranks, we can also note that many of the mixed-race Japanese Americans who participate in HapaUnited and Max D. Capo's "Hapa Hour" have spent time living in or visiting Japan. Capo himself frames his entire channel around his experiences as a mixed-race Japanese American coming to live in Japan and adapting to life there. Through his "Hapa Hour" videos, we are then introduced to many of the mixed-race Japanese American friends he meets while living in Japan, and together they discuss their humorous encounters and experiences.

Although Japan has had a long history of its populations flowing outward to all parts of the world, the concept of "diaspora" is not commonly used to describe these formations. Japanese Americans in particular have not tended to maintain the sense of connection to an idealized homeland or identification with members of the global diaspora that distinguish other migrant members of a diaspora (Butler 2001). The idea of a diaspora is sometimes used within the Latin American context, and the term "Nikkei" itself indicates a population of Japanese outside of Japan (White 2003). I argue that a diasporic perspective can help us to better understand the connection that the part-Japanese members of HapaUnited and Max D. Capo's "Hapa Hour" feel to one another. A diasporic perspective can help to more accurately describe the many different participants—who, as described earlier, represent a complicated and heterogeneous population of those who live all over the world and are constantly moving to new locations, including Japan. But it also helps us to make sense of the emotional connection that participants feel toward this global community of hapas and to their own identification as part Japanese.

This becomes particularly evident when looking at the videos posted by mixed-race Nikkei individuals on their own personal YouTube channels, which are always included as a link from the HapaUnited or Max D. Capo YouTube channels. On their own individual channels, when they are freed from the constraints of needing to talk exclusively about being hapa, many of the mixed-race Nikkei post videos of themselves singing covers of Japanese pop music, doing tourist activities in Japan, practicing their Japanese language skills, or doing "beauty hauls" where they describe purchasing Japanese beauty products. Although examining the videos of these personal YouTube sites in detail is beyond the scope of this chapter, they nonetheless provide evidence of the connection that mixed-race Nikkei from all over the world feel to Japan as a site for cultural and personal engagement. This identification with Japan and its culture reinforces the relevance of a diasporic identity within these mixed-race Nikkei millennials, as opposed to a distinctly national identity such as "Japanese American" or "Japanese Australian." In fact, the term "Japanese American" is not used on any of the YouTube communities studied in this chapter, and the term "Japanese" is only used to describe ethnic identity, rather than national affiliation.

The failure of hapas to identify as Japanese American is also reflected in the way that Capo labels his videos; he is always very careful to make the distinction that he is hapa, mixed race, or half Japanese. This distinction is most apparent in his "Hapa Hour" series that focuses on the topic of mixed-race Japanese experiences where he clearly foregrounds his mixed heritage, but we can also see this distinction in his other videos, which include a wide range of material including skits and humorous sketches, playing video games, doing silly challenges, giving tips for actors, and otherwise creating records of his life. In these other videos, we might expect to see some discussion of being a Japanese American living in Japan, or meeting other Japanese Americans who live in Japan, or otherwise identifying with the larger category of Japanese Americans. Yet this is not the case—he avoids using the term "Japanese American" to describe himself or the incongruity of his experiences living in Japan, despite the fact that so many of his videos focus specifically on what makes living in Japan strange or uncomfortable. More-over, we can also see that he does not describe himself as Japanese either. For instance, one of his videos is titled "Two and a Half Japanese Guys Punching Each Other," as it features himself and two friends. Similarly, in a video featuring a diverse ensemble cast, he includes in the description, "Fun Fact: There are a total of 3 1/4 Japanese people in this video!" It is clear that he does not identify as fully Japanese or fully Japanese American and allows for no slippage between himself and those who are 100 percent Japanese. It seems as though he does not see any common ground between himself as a mixed-race Japanese American and a full-blooded Japanese American or Japanese.

Such a framing can be seen to challenge the standard definitions of Jap-anese American identities as rooted in national citizenship and, moreover, may be implicitly critiquing the assumption that Japanese American com-munities are necessarily inclusive of mixed-race families. This stance does not deny that mixed-race individuals actually do identify as Japanese Amer-ican, but that they seem to avoid doing so within these mediated spaces for hapa community formations. As with all forms of self-branding, such iden-tifications must always be understood as a performance of only one version of themselves that takes specific audiences into consideration. In this case, the lack of identification with Japanese American communities may signal the perception that Japanese Americans are not the targeted audience or that a significant collective of Japanese Americans who could be interpellated by such videos is lacking. Yet it also clearly indicates that this specific identity is not central to their characterization of their own heritage, background, or sense of affiliation.

The absence of national identifications is even more striking in compari-son to the wide range of mixed-race identities subsumed under the category of "hapa," which is the central mode of identification. We can see this inatten-tion to nationality in the Capo's videos—he seems quite rigid in how he de-fines "Japanese" (in that he is not Japanese), but he is flexible and fluid in the way that he defines the term "hapa." His cohosts on the "Hapa Hour" segment come from many different backgrounds, including individuals who are half white and half Burmese, three-quarters black and one-quarter Japanese, half Taiwanese and half white, and half white and half Japanese like himself. He invites each of these individuals to share the screen with him in discussing topics such as "More White or Asian? Parent, National Pride, Identity" and "Do All Half Japanese / Half Asians (of the Same Mix) Look Alike?" By invit-ing those who are of different racial and ethnic backgrounds from himself to join in his discussion of mixed-race experiences, we can see how as a mixed-race Japanese American, he seems to feel he has more in common with other hapas from around the world than other Japanese Americans.

The identification of slippage within the boundaries enclosed by categories such as "nation," "ethnicity," "culture," and "citizenship" reflects a common way of viewing mixed-race communities. As literal embodiments of hybridity, mixed-race people are often theorized as occupying "third spaces" that transgress or disrupt many different kinds of fixed categories (Bolatagici 2004). Beverly Yuen Thompson (2000) writes about how her experiences of racial complexity as a biracial woman overlap with and complement her experiences of sexual fluidity as a bisexual woman, while Rafael Perez-Torres (2006, 4) reminds us that the body of the mixed-race Chicanos, or *mestizaje*, have always undertaken projects of decentralization and forging new relational identities wherein the body is a "site of tenuous, complex, and conflicted change." Given that mixed-race coupling and marriages are often the result of immigration and other forms of shifting racial geographies (Wright et al. 2003), this potential for hybridity in terms of national identification is clearly relevant and is evident in the mixed-race Japanese Americans analyzed in this chapter. The hybridity embodied by these mixed-race Nikkei is what helps to more firmly constitute a diasporic sensibility, as diasporas too are sites that are always in motion and adjusting to accommodate global identifications within local contexts.

The Banality of Being Mixed-Race Japanese American

While we have seen some of the ways that mixed-race Nikkei discuss the meaningful aspects of their identities that draw them together with other hapas, these are not the only ways that identity is discussed on these YouTube channels. Another common theme within the videos is a discussion about struggling to come up with new content. This theme may seem counter to the reality, which is that over 120 videos are posted on the site and it was clearly quite lively with new content until it began to wane in 2013, yet many videos focus on this problem. One woman discusses the experience of identifying mixed-race people on the street and then states, "That's all I really have to talk about. It's kind of hard sometimes to think of hapa-related topics . . . Sorry, this was probably a little lame." Another one of the site's moderators says in a video, "I feel bad because everyone really knows what they're going to talk about, but I have no idea. . . . Are you guys maybe interested in learning Japanese? I could do that. What type of stuff do you guys want me to talk to you about?" Many individuals profess that they are not sure what they should be talking about and ask their audience to be sure to submit topics they want to hear more about. This struggle could possibly be attributed to the somewhat strict schedule that the moderators often impose, given that at the site's height its schedule called for a new video every two days.

But it also may be the case that a resistive potential of mixed-race Japanese Americans is being made visible within these struggles. Indeed, discussions of how difficult it is to find new ways to mine the depths of one's identity may point to the fact that one's identity can often become banal and that not all who participate within the HapaUnited community find their own mixed-race identity to be a generative source for discussion and commentary. One video that depicts the nuances of this struggle features two high school mixed-race Japanese Americans. They are having a conversation where a male participant is trying to get the female participant to stay on target in discussing hapa issues. Yet she resists, refusing to answer his questions with any depth, eventually making a flippant joke and brushing off the entire conversation.

> A: You being half Asian, what do you think of all of the cookings your mom makes?
> B: It's awesome, Japanese food rocks! I like Italian food, too, though.
> A: No, you have to talk about, like, how being half Asian influences what your mom makes.
> A: Um, she's Japanese, that influences what she makes.
> B: Does she still cook like American food?
> A: No. My mom doesn't. . . . She cooks Japanese food, because she Japanese! Oh, I need to go to CVS later. (HapaUnited 2012a)

We can see in this exchange that the male asking questions feels some responsibility to keep the conversation focused on how being half Asian becomes meaningful or important. Yet we must also consider that this evaluation is perhaps not the case—perhaps she truly feels that the reflection of her ethnic identity in her food choices is not meaningful or significant. Later in the video, we witness the following exchange, with the male participant again asking questions of the female participant:

> A: If you were to be born in Japan instead of America to your same parents, and were to live in Japan, would you be different?
> B: Probably, because the culture is different there.
> A: If you were full Japanese and were born and raised in America, do you think you would be any different [from who] you are right now?
> B: No.

Again, we see the refusal to consider that her identity as a hapa or a mixed-race Japanese American has made a significant impact on her life. Although she briefly considers that life in Japan would be different than life in the United States because of external differences such as culture, she does not even consider the fact that changing her own racial or ethnic identity would make her life in the United States any different. Such a statement seems to directly contradict the arguments that other participants make about how significant their identities are or that being hapa has had a profound effect on their ability to find community and feelings of belonging. The woman interviewed in this video does not seem to want to consider or discuss her identity in this way, and yet she remains an active participant within the HapaUnited community. She posts a total of six videos, including discussions of cooking and eating, dating, beauty, and responding to common questions. Within these videos are many references to the common experiences of hapas, such as her video complaining about the repetitive questions that hapas are always asked. Given that she continues to post these videos, we can see that she clearly values the community aspect of participating in HapasUnited—that participating in this community is what is meaningful and worthwhile, perhaps more so than actually hashing out what her own identity means to her.

Videos such as these remind us that participating in identity-based communities requires labor in order to construct a proper performance. The relentless repeating of mantras and affirmations of common experiences across the different videos together produce the ideal hapa subject position. These videos work to discipline the variety of hapa experiences into a cohesive whole, as if there can possibly be unity within this constructed identity. Yet within the videos narrated in this section, we can see resistance to this dominant positioning. Rather than continuing to rehearse the acceptable narratives, this woman refuses to participate and begins to expose her disinterest or perhaps even frustration with these questions about her hapa identity. Although no videos are posted within these communities that actively work to deconstruct narratives of a collective hapa identity, the enthusiastic participation of even those who are weary of discussing their identity further foregrounds the struggle inherent to building diasporic communities.

Conclusion

The videos analyzed in this chapter help to reveal some of the different ways that mixed-race Nikkei are using online tools to reify the construction of a global hapa community that is deeply connected to a diasporic sense of Japanese identity. These videos make up only a small sample of mixed-race Nikkei perspectives, and the cultural norms of these specific YouTube communities profoundly shape the discourse that is shared through these individual vlogs. Yet, even these limitations clearly help to point to the existence of a meaningful discourse about mixed-race Nikkei experiences: within a digital community that is premised on mixed-race belonging, we can ask why it is that so many participants feel obligated to repeat the same narratives over and over, and what is gained in doing so. This study particularly helps to shed light on the ever-growing population of mixed-race Japanese Americans, who we can see must be distinguished from monoracial Japanese

Americans in many ways. Through their active participation in online communities that center both hapa and diasporic Japanese identifications, we are reminded that the fluidity and hybridity of shifting identifications for mixed-race Japanese Americans can work toward deconstructing the fixity of categories such as "race" and "nation," even as they work toward collectively building something new.

NOTE

1. Throughout this chapter, I attempt to differentiate between mixed-race Japanese Americans and mixed-race Japanese, who together make up mixed-race Nikkei (along with other part-Japanese individuals all over the world). Yet it is often extremely difficult to distinguish between these categories, as the identities of mixed-race individuals reflect complex relationships to race/ethnicity, nation, culture, citizenship, community, and family background.

REFERENCES

Banet-Weiser, Sarah. 2011. "Branding the Post-Feminist Self: Girls' Video Production and YouTube." In *Mediated Girlhoods: New Explorations of Girls' Media Culture*, edited by Mary Celeste Kearney, 277–294. New York: Peter Lang.

Bernstein, Mary, and Marcie De La Cruz. 2008. "'What are You?' Explaining Identity as a Goal of the Multiracial Hapa Movement." *Social Problems* 56(4): 722–745.

Bolatagici, Torika. 2004. "Claiming the (N)either/(N)or of 'Third Space': (Re)presenting Hybrid Identity and the Embodiment of Mixed Race." *Journal of Intercultural Studies* 25(1): 75–85.

Butler, Kim. 2001. "Defining Diaspora, Refining a Discourse." *Diaspora* 10(2): 189–219.

Capo, Max D. 2014. "1000 Subs?! | Half Japanese-ness, "Hapa", and Announcements." YouTube. December 14. Accessed April 4, 2019. https://youtu.be/VaYewuvwuoM.

Collins, J. Fuji. 2000. "Biracial Japanese American Identity: An Evolving Process." *Cultural Diversity and Ethnic Minority Psychology* 6(2): 115–133.

———. 2012. "Growing Up Bicultural in the United States: The Case of Japanese-Americans." In *Navigating Multiple Identities: Race, Gender, Culture, Nationality, and Roles*, edited by Ruthellen Josselson and Michele Harway, 75–90. Oxford: Oxford University Press.

eMarketer. 2015. "Netflix, Cable Battle for Millennials' Attention." eMarketer. March 5. Accessed April 4, 2019. http://www.emarketer.com/Article.aspx?R=1012167.

Fellezs, Kevin. 2012. "'This Is Who I Am': Jero, Young, Gifted, Polycultural." *Journal of Popular Music Studies* 24(3): 333–356.

HapaUnited. 2011. *Friends & Relationships*. August 6. Accessed February 21, 2017. https://youtu.be/QqjWjHX0s3A.

———. 2012a. *Being Hapa (Hoshi Vlog 1)*. March 14. Accessed February 21, 2017. https://youtu.be/oFMQ_ngRDv0.

———. 2012b. *Rinko Introduction*. August 12. Accessed February 21, 2017. https://www.youtube.com/watch?v=MwOIu1lKFfg.

Kim, Jin. 2012. "The Institutionalization of YouTube: From User-generated Content to Professionally Generated Content." *Media, Culture and Society* 34(1): 53–67.

King, Rebecca Chiyoko. 1997. "Multiraciality Reigns Supreme? Mixed-Race Japanese Americans and the Cherry Blossom Queen Pageant." *Amerasia* 23(1): 113–128.

Lange, Patricia. 2008. "Publicly Private and Privately Public: Social Networking on YouTube." *Journal of Computer-Mediated Communication* 13(1): 361–380.

Murphy-Shigematsu, Stephen. 2001. "Multiethnic Lives and Monoethnic Myths: American-Japanese Amerasians in Japan." In *The Sum of our Parts: Mixed Heritage Asian Americans*, edited by Teresa Williams-Leon and Cynthia Nakashima, 207–216. Philadelphia: Temple University.

Oikawa, Sara, and Tomoko Yoshida. 2007. "An Identity Based on Being Different: A Focus on Biethnic Individuals in Japan." *International Journal of Intercultural Relations* 31:633–653.

Oshima, Kimie. 2014. "Perception of Hafu or Mixed-Race People in Japan: Group-Session Studies among Hafu students at a Japanese University." *Intercultural Communication Studies* 23(3): 22–34.

Perez-Torres, Rafael. 2006. *Mestizaje: Critical Uses of Race in Chicano Culture*. Minneapolis: University of Minnesota.

Pew Research Center. 2012. *The Rise of Asian Americans*. Pew Social and Demographic Trends. Washington, DC: Pew Research Center. Accessed April 4, 2019. https://www.pewsocialtrends.org/2012/06/19/the-rise-of-asian-americans/.

Renn, Kristen. 2004. *Mixed Race Students in College: The Ecology of Race, Identity, and Community on Campus*. Albany: State University of New York Press.

Rotman, Dana, and Jennifer Preece. 2010. "The 'WeTube' in YouTube: Creating an Online Community through Video Sharing." *International Journal of Web Based Communities* 6(3): 317–333.

Shrikant, Natasha. 2015. "'Yo, It's IST Yo': The Discursive Construction of an Indian American Youth Identity in a South Asian Student Club." *Discourse and Society* 26(4): 480–501. doi:10.1177/0957926515576634.

Taniguchi, Angela S., and Linda Heidenreich. 2005. "Re-Mix: Rethinking the Use of 'Hapa' in Mixed Race Asian/Pacific Islander American Community Organizing." *Washington State University McNair Journal* (Fall 2005): 135–146.

Thompson, Beverly Yuen. 2000. "Fence Sitters, Switch Hitters, and Bi-Bi Girls: An Exploration of 'Hapa' and Bisexual Identities." *Frontiers: A Journal of Women Studies* 21(1/2): 171–180.

U.S. Census Bureau. 2010. "Asian Population by Number of Detailed Groups: 2010." Accessed April 4, 2019. https://www.census.gov/prod/cen2010/briefs/c2010br-11.pdf.

Wachowich, Nancy, and Willow Scobie. 2010. "Uploading Selves: Inuit Digital Storytelling on YouTube." *Études/Inuit/Studies* 34(2): 81–105.

White, Paul. 2003. "The Japanese in Latin America: On the Uses of Diaspora." *International Journal of Population Geography* 9:309–322.

Wright, Richard, Serin Houstin, Mark Ellis, Steven Holloway, and Margaret Hudson. 2003. "Crossing Racial Lines: Geographies of Mixed-Race Partnering and Multiraciality in the United States." *Progress in Human Geography* 27(4): 457–474.

Yoshida, Shima. 2013. "Examining Cultural Identity through Documentary Film: The Case of Mixed-Heritage Japanese Descendants in the U.S. and Canada." *Japan Studies Association Journal* 11:65–85.

Contributors

Dean Ryuta Adachi is currently a Ph.D. candidate in U.S. History at Claremont Graduate University. His research focuses on the early transnational history of Japanese American Christianity.

Christina B. Chin is Assistant Professor of Sociology at California State University, Fullerton, and coeditor of the anthology Asian American Sporting Cultures (New York University Press, 2016). Her research has been published in *Ethnic and Racial Studies*, *Amerasia Journal*, and *Social Justice*.

Brett J. Esaki is Assistant Professor of Religious Studies at Georgia State University, with a specialization on the religions and arts of Asian Americans and African Americans. He is the author of *Enfolding Silence: The Transformation of Japanese American Religion and Art under Oppression* (Oxford University Press, 2016).

Kyung Hee Ha earned her Ph.D. in Ethnic Studies at the University of California, San Diego, and is currently a lecturer at Meiji University in Tokyo, Japan. Her research examines Korean schools in Japan at the imperial nexus of North and South Koreas, Japan, and the United States with an interdisciplinary approach.

Chenxing Han is an independent scholar and writer whose work has appeared in the *Journal of Global Buddhism; Religions*; Pacific World; *Buddhadharma*; the *International Journal of Communication*, and elsewhere. She holds a B.A. from Stanford University and an M.A. from the Graduate Theological Union and the Institute of Buddhist Studies in Berkeley, California.

Lisa Hirai Tsuchitani is a lecturer in the Asian American and Asian Diaspora Studies Program of the Department of Ethnic Studies at the University of California, Berkeley.

A graduate of UC Berkeley's School of Education in Social and Cultural Studies, she has been involved with Suzume no Gakko for over twenty years as a student, a parent, and a board member.

Rebecca Chiyoko King-O'Riain is Senior Lecturer in Sociology at Maynooth University in the Republic of Ireland. She is the author of *Pure Beauty: Judging Race in Japanese American Beauty Pageants* (University of Minnesota Press, 2006) and the lead editor of *Global Mixed Race* (New York University Press, 2014).

Lori Kido Lopez is Associate Professor of Media and Cultural Studies in the Communication Arts Department at the University of Wisconsin, Madison. She is the author of *Asian American Media Activism: Fighting for Cultural Citizenship* (New York University Press, 2016) and coeditor of the *Routledge Companion to Asian American Media*.

Dana Y. Nakano is Associate Professor of Sociology at California State University, Stanislaus. His research has been published in *Contexts, Sociological Inquiry, Sociological Perspective*, and *Asian American Policy Review*.

Michael Omi is Associate Professor of Ethnic Studies at the University of California, Berkeley, and the coauthor of *Racial Formation in the United States*, 3rd ed. (Routledge, 2015).

Amy Sueyoshi is Associate Professor and Associate Dean of the College of Ethnic Studies at San Francisco State University. She is the author of *Queer Compulsions: Race, Nation, and Sexuality in the Intimate Life of Yone Noguchi* (University of Hawaii Press, 2012) and *Discriminating Sex: White Leisure and the Making of the American "Oriental"* (University of Illinois Press, 2018).

Takeyuki Tsuda is Professor of Anthropology at Arizona State University. He is the author of *Strangers in the Ethnic Homeland: Japanese Brazilian Return Migration in Transnational Perspective* (Columbia University Press, 2003) and *Japanese American Ethnicity: In Search of Heritage and Homeland across Generations* (New York University Press, 2016).

Wesley Iwao Ueunten is currently Associate Professor in the Asian American Studies Department at San Francisco State University. An Okinawan sansei from Hawaii, he has been active in Okinawan cultural and community activities in Hawaii, Okinawa, Kawasaki (Japan), and Northern California. His research has been published in peer-reviewed journals in the United States, Japan, and Okinawa.

Aki Yamada is Assistant Professor at Tamagawa University, College of Arts and Sciences. Her research interests include globalization, contemporary Asian immigration, transnational identity, and internationalization of higher education.

Jane H. Yamashiro is currently a Research Justice at the Intersections Fellow at Mills College, Oakland, California. She is the author of *Redefining Japaneseness: Japanese Americans in the Ancestral Homeland* (Rutgers University Press, 2017).

Jeffrey T. Yamashita is a Ph.D. candidate in Ethnic Studies at the University of California, Berkeley. His research focuses on gendered racial formations of the war hero in postwar Hawaii and the construction of local identity.

Index

Also in the series *Asian American History and Culture*